Christo and Jeanne-Claude

Burt Chernow

With an Epilogue by Wolfgang Volz

Christo and Jeanne-Claude

A Biography

St. Martin's Press ❧ New York

www.stmartins.com

Designed by Fritz Metsch

Library of Congress Cataloging-in-Publication Data

Chernow, Burt.
    Christo and Jeanne-Claude : a biography / Burt Chernow ; epilogue by Wolfgang Volz.
    —1st U.S. ed.
        p. cm.
    Simultaneously published in German.
    Includes bibliographical references and index.
    ISBN 0-312-28074-2
        1. Christo, 1935– 2. Jeanne-Claude, 1935– 3. Artists—Biography.   I. Title.
N7193.C5 C468 2002
709'.2'2—dc21
    [B]   2001048736

First published in Germany by Verlag Kiepenheuer & Witsch under the title *XTO + J-C: Christo und Jeanne-Claude: Eine Biografie*

First U.S. Edition: February 2002

10   9   8   7   6   5   4   3   2   1

To my family:

David, Katherine, Melissa and Elizabeth Chenok, Perrin, Ted, Elena, Natalie, and Benno Stein, Paul and Karina Chernow, Daniel, Jill, Hannah and Eva Chenok and Paige Chernow, Mark and Maya Rose Konings.

With love.

Contents

Christo and Jeanne-Claude

1

Behind the Iron Curtain

It was the coldest winter in Christo Javacheff's memory. On January 10, 1957, he and fifteen other hushed defectors stood shivering in an unheated freight car somewhere in Czechoslovakia, concealed with a shipment of medical supplies. A knifelike wind howled outside. Carrying minimal baggage, they had climbed into a battered freight car, half-filled with cardboard cartons piled six feet high. No one spoke as the door locked behind them. There would be no turning back. There was nothing to do but wait as their inhospitable transport crept forward with painful slowness, stopping repeatedly along the final eighteen miles before reaching the Austrian frontier.

Up to this point, Christo Javacheff's life had been a string of small adventures, but this nerve-shattering episode, his first grand gesture, would prove unforgettable. Concealed in a boxcar, surrounded by walls of cardboard boxes, he was involved in a collective effort to escape the Communist world. The many things he experienced at this time would later reverberate through his and Jeanne-Claude's work. It would not be the last time that Christo faced possible catastrophe. In the future, he repeatedly gambled everything on risky ventures. But never were the stakes higher or the events as dangerously unpredictable as on this first journey. In the years ahead, the young artist was to become an expert at redefining territory, challenging authorities, and living with fear; he was also to fashion some of the most dramatic moments of twentieth-century art. Whether this flight to freedom came from an irresistible impulse to defy imposed limitations or from what his older brother Anani later called his "destiny," Christo knew that this journey marked the turning point in his life.

At the same time, almost a thousand miles away in Tunisia, Jeanne-Claude Marie de Guillebon was enjoying the fruits of privilege. She had been adopted by a highly respected French war hero, who had married her mother.

Jeanne-Claude's and Christo's lifestyles and aspirations could not have been more dissimilar. Yet they were destined to come together in one of the most astonishing collaborations in art history. Whether coincidentally or through some celestial guidance, both had been born on the evening of June 13, 1935. Their complex story is every bit as extraordinary as the unsettled times in which they have lived. Shaped in large measure by their respective childhood experiences during World War II, each was to bring to the other and to their art indispensable elements that have fused together in a manner that can only be described as serendipitous.

Christo Vladimirov Javacheff* was born and raised in Gabrovo, Bulgaria. There lie his roots and some of the keys to his enigmatic art. Christo benefited from a rich heritage. His first twenty-one years in Bulgaria shaped his unique vision and prepared him to engage constructively in the capricious nature of everyday life. As a child, he witnessed the unsettling events on the fringe of a catastrophic war, and then he weathered Bulgaria's convulsive transformation from a capitalist monarchy to a Communist state. Living on the edge of disaster in a country where intrigue is part of the landscape, Christo became a connoisseur of appearances.

The nation's tumultuous history is written on the faces of its people and across the varied landscape. Located at a crossroads where countless military ventures have taken place, Bulgaria is the victim of its own topography. Even the most superficial history reveals a dizzying succession of antagonists. The displaced people of Macedonia in particular have seen their state repeatedly carved up and its fragmented populace absorbed by Yugoslavia, Bulgaria, and Greece. Christo's maternal grandfather, Christo Dimitrov, for whom he is named, and his grandmother Anna were both fierce Macedonian nationalists. During the Balkan Wars of 1912–1913, Christo Dimitrov was arrested and executed by the Turks for his "revolutionary activities." Fearing for their lives, Anna, her daughter, Tzveta (Christo's mother), and son, Bojidar, fled north of Sofia, taking only a sewing machine.

In Sofia, their home became a favored meeting place for left-wing activists, Bolshevik agitators, and, particularly, Macedonian separatists. Anna's irrepressible spirit and the atmosphere of revolutionary fervor in large measure shaped Tzveta's character, and, in so doing, prescribed Christo's future, as well.

Christo speaks with obvious pride of his Macedonian heritage. Smiling, he once said, "You know, they were professional revolutionaries, very imaginative, flamboyant, romantic, and a bit anarchist. I think everything I am comes from there." Certainly, his Macedonian heritage looms larger in his development than is generally understood.

In 1925, an exciting world of art opened to Christo's mother when an

---

*Christo uses this spelling of his family name. The other members of his family, however, use "Yavachev." Both spellings appear throughout the text.

Razgrad, Bulgaria, 1879: Christo's grandfather Anani Yavachev and his great-grandfather Ivan Yavachev (sitting). (Photo: Archive XTO+J-C)

uncle helped her secure a choice job as administrative secretary to the director of the Sofia Academy of Fine Arts. Christo's paternal grandparents were also deeply involved in artistic and intellectual pursuits. His Czech grandmother, Anna Turnicheck, was an accomplished concert pianist, and his grandfather, Anani Yavachev, was a celebrated Bulgarian scientist. He became a member of the Academy of Sciences, a founder of the Archaeology Institute in Sofia, and was the author of *Botanical Dictionary*, a standard reference work. A street and an archaeological museum in Razgrad bear his name. The couple had seven children, three girls and four boys, the last of whom was Christo's father, Vladimir.

Born in 1901 in Varna, Vladimir chose to pursue a career in science. After studying chemistry and physics at a university in Vienna, he returned to Bulgaria in 1923. At his first job, which was with a Gabrovo textile manufacturer, he devised special chemical solutions used to prepare virgin fabric for various stages of processing. Soon he had his own chemical factory and began patenting formulas used to treat textiles of every description.

Vladimir's future became even more promising when twenty-three-year-old Tzveta Dimitrov decided to visit a girlfriend in Gabrovo. When she and Vladimir were introduced at a dance, it was love at first sight. Within a year, Tzveta left her rewarding life at the academy and began a new one in Gabrovo. The following year, they married.

The couple settled in Gabrovo and had three sons: Anani, Christo, and Stefan. Anani, born on October 18, 1932, was high-spirited and restive, in part because his family was less authoritarian than most Bulgarian families. Tzveta's second son, Christo Vladimirov Javacheff, was born on June 13, 1935, an event whose consequences Bulgaria would be decades in acknowledging.

Far from Sofia's hotbed of discontent, Tzveta found herself part of a prosperous, prominent family. During her six years at the academy, she had made many friends, who now formed a steady stream of visiting artists, architects, writers, and performers. At age six, Christo began to receive drawing and painting lessons. He was curious and quick to learn. Everyone in the family knew that art would be his domain. From the outset, he displayed the incredible level of energy, which was to mark his later efforts. Some relatives attributed his facility for drawing to the art-oriented family of his Czech grandmother, Anna, whose brother and cousin were both painters. More likely, it resulted from his special home environment. While his father fluctuated between being tolerant and supportive, his mother's influence proved decisive. She personified art for her children.

Like many others, the Javacheffs were helpless witnesses to the dawn of an apocalyptic war. Bulgaria, long ruled by a German king, once again sided with Germany in World War II, as it had in World War I; in each case, reclaiming Macedonia and other lands became the burning issue.

The chafing effects of the war were remote from Gabrovo, but six-year-old Christo saw German troops in flag-decked tanks pass through his peaceful town. Neighbors talked of battles happening elsewhere. Windows were taped and blackened, and during air raids, the family took refuge in their basement. Occasionally, the boys were wakened and, still clad in pajamas, taken to a huge Piranesi-like community shelter carved into nearby rock formations.

Seeking safety and a comfortable distance from the pro-Nazi central gov-

Gabrovo, 1929: Christo's parents, Tzveta Dimitrova and Vladimir Yavachev, one year before their wedding. (Photo: Archive XTO+J-C)

ernment, a number of Tzveta's friends gravitated to Gabrovo. Anani recalled, "Many of the painters who came to the house were poor, and Mother arranged for them to do portraits of wealthy people."[1] Tzveta also hired struggling artists and architects to give Christo private lessons. Their instruction proved far more stimulating than any offered at school.

A part of Christo's education fostered an early awareness of the ephemeral nature of borders. The fluid periphery of Bulgaria and the vanished extremities of Macedonia were discussed at school; maps illustrated shifting frontiers but gave no clue as to the causes and effects of these changes. What

Gabrovo, 1939: Tzveta Yavacheva with Anani and Christo (Photo: Vladimir Yavachev)

could a youngster deduce from these tangled circumstances but that frontiers, borders, and lines of demarcation are man-made and can easily be unmade? Christo learned to see physical reality as ephemeral, not fixed.

A number of wartime episodes left an indelible impression on Christo. He never forgot a winter afternoon in 1942 when German units set up roadblocks in and around Gabrovo. Residents were ordered to remain at home while soldiers searched for partisans. Christo's parents debated whether or not to destroy Tzveta's collection of handsomely illustrated books of modern Russian literature, which might be seen as Communist propaganda. After timidly

Gabrovo, 1939: Vladimir Yavachev with his sons Anani and Christo. (Photo: Archive XTO+J-C)

protesting, Christo watched his mother burn the books. He would always regret their loss, and he periodically recalled specific images created by Tatlin, Gontcharova, and other avant-garde artists.

Throughout the war, the Yavachevs lived in a modest apartment in the heart of Gabrovo. At daybreak one morning in 1943, the quiet gave way to loud clanking sounds on the cobblestone street. From his second-story window, Christo saw men chained together, wearing striped prison garments. He watched in disbelief as hundreds of German troops herded a seemingly endless procession through town. Another frightening incident occurred in late 1943 or early 1944. Anani and Christo observed a group of partisans being

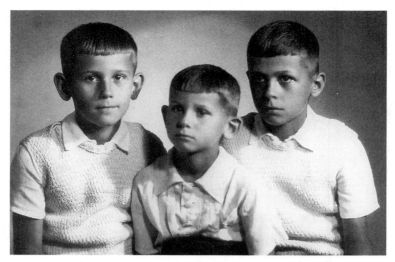

Gabrovo, 1942: The three brothers: Christo, Stefan, and Anani. (Photo: Vladimir Yavachev)

Varna, 1941: Tzveta Yavacheva with Christo and Anani during a vacation by the Black Sea. (Photo: Vladimir Yavachev)

pushed and dragged by soldiers into a square located diagonally across the street from their home. Tzveta pleaded futilely with her sons not to watch as a firing squad executed the men. The bodies were left as a warning to those inclined to resist. Shortly after the killings, a friend staggered to the door, crying hysterically because her home had been burned to the ground; she had harbored partisans.

Tzveta and Vladimir became increasingly concerned for the safety of their sons. During periodic evacuations and school closings, the boys stayed with a family that lived in the sparsely populated hills overlooking Gabrovo. Vladimir had discovered their small, near-forgotten hamlet during a hiking excursion. The Yavachevs call this secluded place "Katchori." It became Christo's magic domain, drawing him back repeatedly until his last brief stay in 1956. The plowed fields and carved slopes seemed to contain a life force that flowed from the remote past. Here, in a wellspring of antiquity, Christo and his brothers ground wheat, cared for cows and sheep, and invented their own recreation.

Christo savored nature's grandeur and the old ways that governed life in their small community. He sensed something apart from the twentieth century, something inexplicable that fostered respect for working by hand, utilizing natural, vulnerable materials, as people had for centuries. He would remember Katchori as "a very special, very beautiful place" that provided a tenuous connection to a mythical past. It was perhaps the central experience of his formative years.

Christo felt completely secure in the quiet isolation of the village, but even Katchori did not remain untouched by the war. Near Christmas 1943, the Yavachevs saw Bulgarian and German troops searching the snowbound landscape for British agents said to have parachuted into the mountains. In addition to seeing Allied bombers on their way to Romanian oil fields, the boys had recently watched low-flying aircraft dropping supplies for the Resistance. Bulgaria's cities became targets for American and British bombers. Family and friends died in air attacks.

In early 1944, Gabrovo bristled with anxious anticipation. Christo heard veiled accusations of widespread German atrocities, which were made more plausible by the photographs he saw of slaughtered Russian peasants in the German magazine *Signal*. His parents listened clandestinely to BBC news reports of grim battles on the Eastern Front. By mid-1944, the war's outcome was no longer in doubt. When the Russian army entered Bulgaria unopposed on September 5, 1944, the Yavachevs and much of the population celebrated. The next day, the formerly underground leftist coalition Father Front declared war on Germany, began organizing a new government, and, on October 28, agreed to return most of the land Bulgaria had annexed. Once more, boundaries were reshaped.

The odious monarchy gave way to an equally repressive Communist state, which bore little resemblance to any vision entertained by the architects of the Bolshevik Revolution. Utopian goals for an independent Bulgaria again fell prey to intrigue and violence. During the next two years, elections established a servile People's Republic of Bulgaria, school programs were overhauled to reflect Marxist-Leninist doctrine, and the government began nationalizing private property. Tzveta and Vladimir's hopes gradually turned

In the garden of their home outside Gabrovo, 1945: Anani and Christo with their dog Sharo (Photo: Vladimir Yavachev)

into heartbreaking despair. The war years had been troubling; the postwar era was to prove far worse.

In 1947, the Yavachev family lived two and a half miles outside of Gabrovo. Their modest quarters adjoined the small factory and laboratory that Vladimir had built. Early one morning, just before Christmas, Revolutionary Guards matter-of-factly occupied the complex. Christo watched his parents huddle, searching desperately for a way to avoid disaster. This indignity was just the first in a tragic series of events that would dramatically alter the Yavachevs' lives.

The menacing group demanded that the family pack and leave without delay. They left no room for discussion. Nationalization had come, and suddenly the Yavachevs found themselves on the street. Stunned, carrying only a few possessions—including a bolt of fine wool fabric Vladimir had hurriedly wrapped around his waist—the Yavachevs were given temporary lodging at a friend's house. Vladimir had ignored his wife's warnings, believing government assurances to owners of private property. He and Tzveta would always regret not having seized the opportunity to emigrate, or at least to transfer some of their assets prior to the upheaval.

In the village Katschori outside Gabrovo, 1945: (l-r) Christo, his older brother Anani, "Aunty" Penia's daughter-in-law, Christo's younger brother Stefan, and Penia with a grandchild. (Photo: Archive XTO+J-C)

Ironically, Vladimir was assigned to work at his former plant as a state employee. One day in 1948, he failed to return home. Tzveta heard that her husband had been arrested, but the circumstances were as unclear as the charges. Had he been accused of a crime or been condemned for having been a capitalist? Shortly after Vladimir disappeared, the family saw HERE LIVE ENEMIES OF THE PEOPLE painted on the wall of their apartment house. Christo vividly remembers being mocked by a group of young Communists who barred his way to school. Many of the family's affluent friends were indiscriminately accused of collaborating, arrested, and either executed or sent to camps for Marxist indoctrination. During this dark period, Christo, unaware of his father's status, periodically heard machine guns in the distance carrying out the tribunals' sentences.

The details of Vladimir's arrest emerged one week after his apprehension. A Communist party member who worked at the factory had accused him of sabotage after excessive bleaching destroyed a large vat of fabric. Vladimir protested that his coworker had been drinking and had failed to follow established procedures. Using all of her resources, Tzveta worked to secure her husband's release. She heard that the Gabrovo's National Theater needed plush "capitalist" furnishings for a production. She succeeded in getting hold of the furniture they had left behind, sold it, and thus was finally able to secure Vladimir's release.

This unhappy succession of events had a lasting emotional impact on the boys. Long before these disturbing incidents, Christo had been painfully shy. At age seven, he was an excellent student, but so withdrawn that his father tried to create social situations in the hope of drawing him out. But despite his shyness, he possessed a cheerful disposition and a talent for concentrated listening. His brown eyes shone with impish humor as he carefully observed his surroundings. Christo may have appeared bashful, but he had a boyish courage that often bordered on recklessness.

Few activities appealed to him more than exploring unknown terrain. In 1943, he became captivated by adventure stories by Karl May about the American frontier and other distant places. Christo was inspired to create his own Wild West novel. The meticulously written 160-page volume measured six and a half by eight inches, illustrated with black-and-white and color pencil drawings of cowboys and Indians. His grandfather also gave him two maps of the United States. To Christo's surprise, they contained no reference to war, and he became absorbed in studying them.

The Norwegian explorer Roald Amundsen became another of Christo's role models. After a heavy snowfall, the nine-year-old adventurer demonstrated his natural aptitude for flirting with danger. While reenacting Amundsen's discovery of the South Pole, he fell through the ice covering a river. Anani and Tzveta barely saved him from drowning. This collision of reality and Christo's imagination left his mother frenzied and Anani with a vision of his brother as Don Quixote.

Christo's predilection for drama emerged in 1948 when he offered his first project for public consumption. He read and adapted several of Shakespeare's plays for presentation to an invited audience of friends, family, and visiting artists, some of whom were associated with Gabrovo's National Theater. Twelve-year-old Christo directed three or four teenage readers. A gold picture frame the width of a doorway had been commandeered from one of Tzveta's artist friends, then masked with burgundy curtains, which also concealed the cast. Lighting focused attention on a revolving circular stage, divided into several sections to facilitate rapid scene changes. Christo employed his considerable drawing skills to create more than four hundred realistically rendered small puppetlike figures, as well as a variety of backdrops and scenic elements. These stationary cutouts were then carefully painted and attached to sticks that Christo deftly manipulated. He also made playbills and tickets. Even then, Christo solicited a response from his public; paper and pencils were distributed following each performance so that viewers could submit their critical comments. Not to be outdone, Christo triumphantly wrote glowing reviews, as accurate as they were self-serving.

Coerced by his younger brother, Anani reluctantly made his theatrical debut as the narrator of *Romeo and Juliet*. At one point, Anani became so embarrassed by what seemed to be childish activity that he climbed out of a window to avoid participating. Christo pursued, caught, chastised, and finally convinced him to return. "Christo was a general then," Anani later recalled,

Gabrovo, 1949: Christo, on the left, during a drawing lesson. (Photo: Archive XTO+J-C)

"and he never really changed."[2] However tentative, the parallels between these carefully orchestrated youthful stagings and Christo's subsequent efforts are inescapable.

Tzveta's significant role in shaping Christo's bent toward modernism cannot be overestimated. As early as age six, he listened attentively to the heated arguments of visiting artists. During these discussions, his mother invariably defended every form of innovation. She often stood alone in support of non-conformist options. Christo gradually adopted her staunch opposition to the status quo. He found it hard to believe that the notion of modern art could generate such scorn among otherwise-convivial artists. He prized invention and dreamed of the time when he might make a singular contribution to art.

Christo's public school experience under the monarch and his subsequent proletarian education afforded him the worst of both worlds. His artistic prowess was no secret, so his teachers expected him to produce a variety of propaganda materials, including posters to celebrate the October Revolution and large roadside banners announcing May Day festivities. At a movie theater in Gabrovo, he dutifully collaborated in creating massive portraits of Marx, Engels, and Lenin. Using a projector to enlarge an approved image, Christo and his fellow students painted one section after another on material from atop a high stage. Praise for his Stalinized art left him indifferent. He attended required classes in Marxist-Leninist principles, dialectical materialism, and the history of the Bulgarian and Russian Communist parties, but no ideology

Gabrovo, 1949: Christo's drawing of his mother. (Photo: Eeva-Inkeri)

would give direction to his innermost longing. His only desire was to become an artist.

What little knowledge Christo had of the Russian avant-garde came almost exclusively from his mother. In Bulgaria's restrictive environment, art textbooks were either obsolete or, with the imposition of Stalinist rule, censored. In effect, the history of art ended abruptly with the early works of Edouard Manet. Worse, most of the painters at the academy had not even reached the level of nineteenth-century mediocrity they most admired. The faculty consisted of uninspired offspring of the Munich school, tedious academicians, and, later, social realists; what they shared was an aversion to Postimpressionism, Cubism, Surrealism, or any other viable form of twentieth-century expression.

Christo's involuntary remove from modern Western art had a positive side: The forced isolation left him ample time to develop his talent by engaging in traditional modes of drawing and painting. Between 1947 and 1956, he became increasingly preoccupied with making realistic portraits. Few failed to be impressed by the ease with which he worked. His rapidly drawn, matter-of-fact portrayals were the result of an enjoyable physical act, as natural to Christo as talking. Farmers, factory workers, peasants, friends, and acquaintances became the subjects of tireless visual interrogation. Particularly fascinating is a 1950s series of probing self-portraits, along with repeated studies of Anani, Tzveta, and Vladimir. Each convincing depiction reveals a sure touch, an active line, and fidelity to the model. While many of the works have been lost, given away, or destroyed, several suitcases containing his drawings have survived. Cumulatively, these autobiographical drawings are a visual chronicle of Christo Javacheff's last decade in Bulgaria and represent one of his least-known accomplishments.

With a growing sense of urgency, Christo recognized that his future as an artist hinged on achieving success at the Sofia Academy of Fine Arts. It was the center of Bulgaria's art world, such as it was. However, he knew that the academy selected few applicants, and the children and relatives of working-class parents, antifascist heroes, and Communist party members were given preference. His father's clouded past might present an insurmountable barrier, though Anani had gotten into the Higher Institute of Dramatic Arts in Sofia.

Despite this, Christo had complete confidence in his abilities and looked hopefully to Tzveta's friends, who had promised to help. In particular, Detchko Uzunov, an illustrious painter and teacher at the academy, had stated unequivocally that he would treat Christo like a son, helping him in every possible way. Uzunov was a robust, well-established artist, and he remained in good standing because of his chameleonlike nature, gracefully changing styles with each new government or trend. But he cast only one vote on an admission jury that included Party hacks who could, without explanation, veto any applicant.

Filled with apprehension, Christo arrived in Sofia in the late spring of 1953, armed with high grades from a comprehensive high school test, a certificate of outstanding accomplishment in evening art classes, and a recommendation from Detchko Uzunov. His arduous trial began as he and hundreds of other applicants endured a grueling battery of tests in literature, philosophy, science, and Marxist-Leninist ideology. Then, at the Academy of Fine Arts, Christo completed compositions drawn from nature, plaster casts, and live models. The jury accepted him into the fine arts program without qualification; he and his family were overjoyed. However, the aspiring young artist was soon to discover the truth Oscar Wilde had observed: The two greatest tragedies in life are not getting your heart's desire and getting it.

With a growing sense of exhilaration, Christo prepared to begin this new

Plovdiv, 1949: Christo's drawing of his father resting. (Photo: Eeva-Inkeri)

phase of his life. He overflowed with optimism, anxious to prove himself. He would live with a friend of his parents, Professor Raina Katzarova. Anani lived next door in the home of an Eastern Orthodox priest, whose daughter, Maria, he would later marry. Lively, attractive, and very likeable, Anani could often be found in the company of young women. With his expressive face and resonant voice, he lightheartedly portrayed himself as an enfant terrible.[3]

After being separated for nearly two years, Anani and Christo were now always together. With gleeful irreverence, they darted about the stagnant campus area. Christo's interest in theater was stimulated by his brother's total immersion in the discipline. Filled with admiration for Anani, Christo registered for several theater classes. Theater, stage and costume design, drama students, and faculty all engaged Christo's attention. Once a month, using pencils and

Plovdiv, 1951: *Anani Reading* by Christo. (Photo: Eeva-Inkeri)

oil paint, Christo designed costumes and decor for Anani's assigned play productions. He also painted portraits of his brother, in and out of costume, and sketched anyone who would pose.

"We often spoke about art," Anani mused. "We talked and argued, and our friends knew one another. All day, every day, he had pencils growing out of his pockets. I can't say that I knew he was going to be great, but I can say that I knew he was special."[4]

Unfortunately, Christo never realized his naïve expectation of a challenging adventure at the art academy. Instead, he endured a distorted, unremittingly dull education. Drawing from plaster casts and copying mediocre paintings hardly proved inspirational. Christo soon realized that to survive required suppressing individuality and imagination. This was not the same art academy where his mother had once worked. Although the program appeared hopelessly antiquated, Christo did learn something about failed ideology, unrealized ideals, and human nature.

Bulgarian premier Vulko Chervenkov was patterning his harsh one-man rule after Stalin. Arrests, police-state terrorism, corrupt bureaucracy, and a government campaign to purge all Western influences continued unabated. No dissident movement took shape. The stifling atmosphere made it imperative to be guarded in one's conversation. There seemed to be opportunistic watchdogs everywhere, and even one's friends could cause unintended harm. Anani was taken in for questioning after his girlfriend repeated a joke he had made about the incompetence of a Party boss; he gave a convincing performance while explaining the unfortunate misunderstanding.

Plovdiv, 1953: Christo's self-portrait. (Photo: Eeva-Inkeri)

An ubiquitous political presence extended its heavy hand into the production of art. All forms of communication had designated roles in building a new society and were therefore under the direct control of the Central Committee. In the visual arts, subject matter and style were dictated by a rigid interpretation of the only authorized form of expression—socialist realism. Artists were expected to depict agricultural and factory scenes, idealized landscapes, and heroic images of the proletariat and its leaders. The uninspired results had little to do with art. Christo tried to devise a pragmatic response to a bankrupt system, but this proved impossible.

Few prominent artists working in the second half of the twentieth century have been as isolated from modern art in their formative years as Christo.

But he was intensely curious about a tantalizing world that was closed to him. Friends covertly introduced him to the unauthorized Skira art books. Accustomed to a limited selection of censored publications with black-and-white illustrations, he found the quality color reproductions and content of this Swiss-produced series astonishing. All at once, a modern alternative that he had only heard about became visible.

The appearance of several visiting Russian art professors at the academy also proved stimulating. They were forgotten men in their sixties, currently working in a socialist realist mode, but they had been active participants in the postrevolutionary Soviet avant-garde, an era later discredited. Occasionally, these artists invited Christo and others for a drink. The more they drank, the more their conversation focused on the goals and shattered hopes of Russian modernism. Enticed by these transient lectures, Christo became familiar with Vladimir Mayakovski's poetry, Vsevolod Meyerhold's pioneering theater, and the graphic work of many Soviet artists. Mayakovski's now-famous statement, "Let us make the streets our brushes, the squares our palette," proved to be an intriguing abstraction for Christo.[5] In the future, it might be read as his battle cry. Meyerhold created a new realism using the dynamism of actual objects and active sites for his performances. In time, Christo, too, would utilize the potent energy of real objects and public spaces. The Russian Constructivists, like the Berlin Dada group before them, employed collage and photomontage to create striking compositions; so, too, would Christo.

One driving force behind Russian modernism was a firmly held belief that art and life had to be brought into a closer, more harmonious relationship. To that end, artists, writers, composers, and performers enthusiastically took to the streets. They appeared at factories, farms, train stations, and any other place where they might educate the populace and, through the practical application of their arts, construct a classless society. Impromptu performances, large temporary constructions, and street pageants sprouted up in unlikely places. The ensuing dialogue embodies the artist's socially active role.

Growing listlessly out of a once-passionate initiative, socially useful work projects were assigned to academy students on weekends throughout the academic year. Christo participated unhappily, wondering what these imposed jobs had to do with either art or the realities of life. On a typical weekend morning, Christo and other student workers contributed to a brave new socialist state by painting quotations from or images of notable Communist personalities on walls and billboards.

The most memorable of Christo's assigned work experiences was the face-lifting job done along a vast stretch of track used by the Orient Express. With Bulgaria virtually sealed off from the West, this periodic intrusion gave foreign passengers a fleeting glimpse of the nation's proclaimed economic productivity. But the illusion of an advanced socialist state extended no further than the panorama visible along the train's normal itinerary. Bands of students advised the farmers on how to arrange farm machines against the horizon for optimal visibility. Unsightly accumulations were covered or cleaned up. Bales of hay and equipment were displayed on either side of the railroad tracks. Sometimes the items were wrapped in tarpaulin and tied up for protection or concealment.

Still somewhat shy, Christo nevertheless found ways of approaching and gently persuading laborers to cooperate. His manner was warm and unpretentious. The process of convincing an indifferent public would in time prove to be a commonplace activity for him and Jeanne-Claude. Christo also developed a visceral sense of landscape as he trudged through ancient foothills and fertile valleys. These designated work projects with real materials in real spaces instilled a keen understanding of human scale. With his interest in theater, he likely saw each site as a sort of stage whose decor needed revamping. As much as any traditional art material, real space was subject to manipulation; it contained inherent theatrical, sculptural, and architectural possibilities. Equally important, Christo discovered the potential energy of group efforts in recomposing objective reality on an environmental canvas. An awareness evolved, perhaps unconsciously, that if state edicts could transform the environment, so, too, could art.

Between 1954 and 1956, Christo managed to earn some money by working for brief periods as a location scout for the state-owned cinema. Feature films were shot on location, and artists were routinely hired to find the best-possible place for each scene. Usually accompanied by a member of the film crew, the young artist roamed the city or suburbs, selecting alternate locations and making sketches relative to a script's action. These assignments underscored the potential for employing actual places to convey artistic intent. Like his weekend propaganda activities, this employment began and ended with the malleable components of physical reality.

After his first year at the academy, Christo managed to secure his own apartment. Like all men enrolled at the university, he was required to perform his military service during summer breaks. In 1954, Christo endured the first of three disquieting tours of duty. A sadistic captain made the recruits' lives miserable. A forced march, knee-deep in a river at 3:00 A.M., typified the training exercises designed to harden these young men. Gratuitous insults and harsh discipline were a way of life. In what little free time he had, Christo sketched army companions, while carefully concealing his contempt for the system.

After completing his unrewarding freshman year with the highest grades, Christo registered for the studio class of Detchko Uzunov. Uzunov's imposing figure and flamboyant manner left little doubt that he was indeed a great artist. He punctuated each statement with emphatic gestures, his finely honed voice flawed only by occasional unrestrained volume. It soon became clear that his lavish presentations were designed primarily for the benefit of female students. The overbearing skirt-chaser that Christo saw in the classroom bore little resemblance to the familiar visitor he had known in Gabrovo. Though Uzunov took personal pride in Christo's abundant gifts, he offered only rare critiques, and those were distressingly shallow. Alas, his was the best art instruction Bulgaria had to offer. The young artist felt bitterly disappointed. The depressing reality of his second year of study gave way to another grim summer in the armed forces.

Christo began the fall semester of 1955 with no illusions about the limited educational opportunities ahead. However, he never suspected that his third year at the academy would also be his last. He directed all of his energy toward art, producing drawings, paintings, and stage designs. What little social life he had revolved around art. Christo shared a mutual attraction with a young woman writer, who also had an interest in art. A brief encounter marked the first occasion on which the still-shy twenty-year-old artist kissed and became physically intimate with anyone. The relationship proved short-lived, since her politics were adamantly pro-Communist.

Christo knew exactly what the faculty expected from studio classes, and with each assignment, he gently tested the imposed limitations. Invariably, he encountered unbending resistance. In one course, he painted two large, almost identical compositions of four farmers at rest in a field. One variation had restrained natural hues, the other, heightened, more imaginative color. His teacher became incensed by the more experimental color. "The workers look tired and oppressed," he complained. "Why aren't they resting happily?" Christo accepted the criticism silently.

At a student exhibition, there seemed little doubt that Christo's impeccably rendered drawings and paintings were in a class of their own. By chance, a French diplomat named Bonavita saw the show. Impressed by the work, Bonavita asked Christo to visit the consulate to see a display of books. Christo accepted the invitation and went to see other Western publications at the envoy's house. Christo also accepted an invitation to lunch and a subsequent commission to do a series of portraits of Bonavita's family. He suddenly realized that his ability to portray a likeness might provide a means of support. In fact, portraiture was to be the key to Christo's economic survival in the years ahead. Open, stimulating conversation with Bonavita piqued Christo's curiosity about the world outside Bulgaria. At two critical junctures in the not-too-distant future, this elegant Frenchman and his political connections would prove invaluable.

In 1956, Christo completed his third laborious year at the academy and readied himself for another pointless summer in the army. Anani graduated from the Institute of Dramatic Arts, secured a position with Gabrovo's Na-

In the countryside outside Sofia, 1956: Portrait of a farmer. (Photo: Eeva-Inkeri)

tional Theater, and began looking for living quarters for himself and his fiancée, Maria. Late that summer, prior to Anani's wedding, Anani and Christo
made their last trip together to Gabrovo and Katchori. With Anani resettled in
Gabrovo, the academy's depressing atmosphere became even more unbearable
for Christo. He knew that he had to get away for a while. With Bonavita's help,
he finally obtained permission that fall to visit relatives in Prague. The trip was
allowed only because he had an uncle, aunt, and cousins who lived there. He
had very little money and gratefully accepted a loan for the airfare from one of

Uzunov's assistants. He was soon to discover a quickening tempo and freedom unknown in Bulgaria.

Christo arrived in Czechoslovakia from Bulgaria with no intention of defecting. As he kissed his mother good-bye at Sofia's airport, she burst out crying. Christo had no way of knowing then that he would not see her again for more than twenty years.

Unlike Sofia, Prague reflected an image of old European opulence, seemingly untouched by the war. Though Communist, it remained an exciting, freer, distinctly Western city. There, Christo spent as much time as possible at the avant-garde Emile Burian Theater. Burian, the impresario of Prague's avant-garde theater, embodied hope for him. Burian had a way of making everything seem possible. In an eight-page letter to Anani written on December 24, 1956, Christo wrote, "I feel reborn. . . . For the last two weeks I have been unusually happy and going through so many things in order to draw. I am enchanted by the director, E. F. Burian. Unbelievable things have happened. I have never talked so openly with a celebrated person in the art world. He is made of gold."[6]

Christo's cousin had arranged the introduction. A long conversation and several of Christo's recent painting impressed Burian. The director introduced him to artists, galleries, private collections, and arranged a visit to the National Gallery's storage facilities to see modern art. Christo wrote:

This evening I had a stimulating talk with Burian. He has been to France and is a friend of Picasso and a number of French artists, actors, and musicians. For him, art is discovery, innovation, a profound mission to find the most contemporary, novel expression. . . . He says that art, more than anything else in life, is beauty. Art creates what no one has seen before. . . . Anani, you understand that I have never encountered such warmth from a person in the arts. . . . Burian is usually democratic. He is a People's artist, very influential in the government and party. He says, "Method is the social realism." But what is the method?[7]

Christo bitterly described his training in Bulgaria. "Back home it is a real catastrophe. Is there anything in the academy? Nothing. I will no longer take classes with people who don't understand me, who are egotists. For four years—suppression, brainwashing, and art made as they dictate. Those four years do not compare with the last month here." Perhaps sensing his next move, Christo said, "I cannot be where there is an insincere attitude toward art. . . . To be a discoverer requires more than reading books—one has to feel the pulse of the time. . . . Write dear brother, I can never forget you."[8]

With Russian tanks on the move in the autumn of 1956, fears of a third world war were very real throughout Europe. The news of mass arrests and heartless suppression in Hungary confirmed Christo's worst fears. Prague was abuzz with reports of large numbers of Hungarians and even Czechs fleeing to Vienna. Christo sensed that he had little left to lose by joining the exodus. For him, art and freedom were as inseparable as they were in short supply.

Seventeen days after writing his letter to Anani, Christo bolted to freedom.

After many hours, the frigid cargo train came to a screeching halt at the border. Looking through horizontal slats, the young artist saw a barren landscape. Trees had been removed, and light towers illuminated the area, leaving no place to hide. The passengers heard security guards and their barking dogs. They held their breath.

After what seemed an eternity, the train finally lurched forward into neutral Austria. After forging ahead a safe distance, it stopped. All the stowaways began pounding on the walls and shouting until railroad workers opened the door. The new immigrants were ordered to wait at a nearby station for service to Vienna.

Christo's adventure was hardly over. On the ride to Vienna, his euphoria mingled with undiminished anxiety. He had very little money left after paying the equivalent of three hundred dollars for his share of the customs inspector's bribe. Further complicating the situation was the fact that he spoke only Bulgarian and a few words of Czech and Russian. In addition, he had not only defected but deserted, having not yet fulfilled his military service in Bulgaria. His greatest fear was of being confined indefinitely at one of the refugee camps.

Christo's hopes rested on a scrap of paper with the name Sabev—an old friend of his father—and an address that had been current thirty years earlier. Rather than chance being interned with the swelling number of Eastern Europeans arriving daily, Christo left his baggage behind and, when the train stopped, hustled into the congested terminal. He hurried onto the street and into a taxi, whereupon he presented his tattered paper to the driver without a word and hoped for the best as they drove through the wintry city. He reasoned that, at worst, he would be arrested for not paying the fare; that seemed no worse than detention.

The cab pulled up on front of 8 Spiegelgasse sometime around 7:00 P.M. Christo gestured at the confused driver to wait as he ran to the front door. Miraculously, he saw a doorbell marked SABEV. He rang; a loud buzz answered! Christo raced to the fourth floor, and there stood his father's old friend.

Sabev was a short, chubby businessman in his mid-sixties. He and his wife had been entertaining guests and were obviously irritated by the interruption. A reddening round face glared up at Christo. Grasping for words, Christo tried to explain himself. Fortunately, Mrs. Sabev was a Bulgarian. Christo explained who he was and pleaded for help. Captivated, then convinced, the Sabevs not only paid the taxi fare but also offered Christo a place to sleep.

In the days ahead, the young artist's good fortune continued. He recovered his baggage at the train station's lost and found, obtained work loading produce trucks, washing dishes, and cleaning cars, and, with the help of the Sabevs, registered at the Vienna Fine Arts Academy. Christo still faced an uncertain future, however, as he turned in his Bulgarian passport, renounced his citizenship, and asked for political asylum. Abruptly, he became a stateless person.

Through all the traumas of exile and survival, Christo clung to a deep-seated, childlike part of his character, which allowed him to remain joyously irrational. He would live and work with uncommon integrity and extraordinary determination in the face of opposing political, social, and economic systems. As a product of an education and life experiences that differed radically from those of his Western contemporaries, Christo was fated to become a singular artist. With byzantine cunning, this mild-mannered troublemaker began taking sly pleasure in playing a different game, one with different rules and unmistakably different results. Transplanted, Christo Javacheff simply reinvented himself.

2

The General's Daughter

Unsurprisingly, Jeanne-Claude recalls almost nothing of the lacerating experiences of her childhood. She remembers loud explosions in Casablanca's harbor, an infant boy who had not yet learned to be hostile toward her, and an impression that trees were her friends. Everything else was just hearsay. Born out of wedlock, frequently separated from her mother, she spent most of World War II in a degrading, inhospitable environment. Like France itself, Jeanne-Claude was torn by the powerful forces that fractured Europe. Her resolute parents were the embodiment of a struggle that left Jeanne-Claude and countless others victims.

Her mother, Précilda, was the first female officer to enter liberated Paris with Free French forces on August 25, 1944. Serving as General Berges's chief of staff, she could barely move through the jubilant crowds that surged forward to greet the troops. The next day, her photograph appeared on the front pages of newspapers as banner headlines proclaimed a resurrected Paris. Précilda's long, fierce resistance to fascism and the Vichy government was one of the many untold heroic efforts that collectively determined the outcome of the war. Her story reveals an indomitable character, a woman as tough-willed as any of the illustrious men in her life.

And yet, much will never be known about Précilda. Jeanne-Claude observed, "My mother is the most marvelous mystery in the world." Unknowable by design, majestically feminine, Précilda's shrouded origins are terra incognita, even to her family. According to some, Précilda's standard description of her early childhood was pure invention. As she told it, her Russian mother, Princess Orlov, who was seven and a half months pregnant, sailed to Brazil in the wake of the 1918 Bolshevik Revolution. En route, the story goes, she received the news that most of her remaining relatives in Russia had died, and this caused premature labor pains. As a result, the boat docked in Casablanca, where the princess died while giving birth to Précilda.

A woman, whom Précilda describes only vaguely, is said to have nursed her as an infant. Then, months later, she took the child to Brazil, where Précilda's father, Frenchman Charles Laporte, lived. According to Précilda, this Jewish Moroccan lady materialized fortuitously and taught her Arabic. Some relatives maintain that this Good Samaritan was part fact, part fiction. Over the years, variations of Précilda's tale persisted.

Précilda insists that in 1918, at six months of age, she arrived in Brazil, where her father owned one of the major rubber plantations, a huge factory, boats, and several residences. "It was heaven for me," Précilda recalled, adding, "In my memory I don't know whether it was a Tarzan movie or my imagination."[1] In 1925, she said, she and a new governess, named Gertrude, moved to Switzerland.

The cold Swiss weather proved as unpleasant as the Brazilian heat, and so her father bought her a luxurious estate on the outskirts of Casablanca. Lovely gardens and pink sands shielded from the sea by two breakwaters made a dramatic setting for intense sunrises and sunsets. Whatever the facts of Précilda's childhood, Casablanca is where her headstrong character took shape.

Late in 1934, at age sixteen, Précilda met Major Léon Denat at the annual Admiralty Ball, where she wore her first designer dress from Paris. The handsome major was from a good family, elegantly attired, tall, fair, and evidently irresistible. The physical attraction was mutual. Précilda said, "He loved me immediately."

Denat commanded a garrison in the Atlas Mountains region. Brushing aside their twenty-two-year age difference, he soon proposed marriage. The law required parental consent for anyone under the age of twenty-one to marry, but they were married illegally by the chaplain at the army base. She became pregnant shortly thereafter and gradually recognized that their romance had been only a passing infatuation. Léon was too stern with the native population and far too demanding domestically. One morning, Précilda announced that she had a doctor's appointment in Casablanca. Later in the day, she telephoned Léon and vowed not to return. Nothing he said mattered; it was over.

Legally, no marriage had taken place, and she never assumed Denat's name. During that trying period, her father continued to provide more money than she needed, but the separation left her feeling alone and unloved. Précilda desperately wanted the child she carried, "as something of my own," as she put it. On the evening of June 13, 1935, a Swiss Army doctor delivered Jeanne-Claude. The seventeen-year-old mother's hospital room overflowed with flowers sent by a friend, Montie Alazrachi. After leaving the hospital, she and Jeanne-Claude moved in with him.

Précilda remembered meeting Montie for the first time in 1933 at a swimming club. Montie dated their initial meeting two years earlier, in 1931. She was fifteen at the time, and he was twice her age. Whether they were lovers

Casablanca, 1935: Jeanne-Claude with her mother, Précilda. (Photo: Archive XTO+J-C)

before she met Léon Denat is a matter of dispute. Montie and Précilda married in 1937, after living together for two years. They resided at his home, while she maintained the seaside estate her father had purchased. That summer, the newlyweds left Jeanne-Claude with relatives and took a two-month honeymoon in Scotland. When they returned, Jeanne-Claude seemed extremely overwrought. It had been the child's first prolonged separation from her mother. Afraid of being abandoned again, she clung to Précilda every day and insisted on sleeping with her each night.

The Alazrachi marriage lasted less than four years. They had one child, Joyce-May, born on May 14, 1939. Her birth marked the beginning of an irreparable cleavage for the couple. Précilda observed a total shift in Montie's affection from Jeanne-Claude to Joyce, although he denied it. Never prone to moderation, Précilda had all the rationale she needed to begin planning an end to their relationship. Montie began working longer hours than ever to support his growing family. Mounting frustration in the household must have been aggravated by the alarming sweep of world events.

On June 14, 1940, the Nazis marched into Paris. Like most of the world, Casablanca felt the shock waves. The majority of the French population chose the path of least resistance, supporting the new Vichy government, headed by Marshal Henri Philippe Pétain. Précilda Alazrachi, however, frantically sought

Jeanne-Claude in Taroudant, Morocco, 1939. (Photo: Archive XTO+J-C)

out the Free French and offered to help the Resistance in any way possible. In July, Pétain broke off relations with Great Britain and ordered British diplomats to leave French territories at once; that edict applied to the Alazrachis.

During her last days in Casablanca, Précilda forged papers for twenty-eight Frenchmen. Twenty-six of them arrived safely in London; two were captured. As a result of their confessions and her subsequent activities, Précilda

Casablance, 1939: Jeanne-Claude holding her baby sister Joyce-May Alazrachi.
(Photo: Archive XTO+J-C)

Alazrachi became notorious in Vichy circles. Reportedly, even Marshal Pétain demanded to know why she had not been arrested.

Shortly after arriving in Tangiers, Précilda volunteered to work for the Free French military command. There, she met Charles Luizet, a Vichy intelligence officer who also directed covert Gaullist operations in French Morocco. In December 1940, he asked her to return to Casablanca to help enlist Arab support in the struggle against fascism.

At that point, Précilda's marriage was under considerable strain. Their situation became further complicated by a religious disagreement. Précilda claimed, "Montie never told me he was a Jew until one day he said, 'I am going to the synagogue.'" It seems incredible that this revelation took nine years to surface. Whatever the story, clearly a rupture occurred between her and the Alazrachi family in December 1940.

Apparently, Précilda had a penchant for impulsive action. She gathered her belongings and left with Jeanne-Claude. Joyce remained with her father. Four-and-half-year-old Jeanne-Claude left behind the only father she had known. Abrupt relocations, a war she knew nothing about, and the family's dissolution were incomprehensible adult doings. A succession of traumatic events was about to heighten Jeanne-Claude's already deep insecurities.

In March 1941, Vichy police arrested Précilda. A bewildered Jeanne-Claude saw her mother taken from their home; Jeanne-Claude was placed at Saint-Marie, a local religious boarding school. After several days in a Casablanca prison cell, the obstinate Précilda was transferred to the detention camp at Settat, forty miles from Casablanca.

That summer, Précilda was forced to relinquish legal custody of Jeanne-Claude to Denat. News of Nazi military victories reached Settat with disheartening regularity. One morning in March 1942, Précilda saw a familiar face among the new prisoners en route to the Settat police station: Lord Roy Anderson. They had met previously at the British Club in Casablanca. The handsome, tall blond Englishman in his thirties emanated as much charm as his aristocratic background and discretion allowed. To most people, he appeared to be no more than a rich, carefree tourist, living and traveling with his mother. Précilda sensed something more. (Indeed, as she was to learn much later, he had been the covert head of British Intelligence in North Africa.) The couple became inseparable. After a brief courtship, he proposed marriage; she accepted without hesitation. Their attorney negotiated a quick divorce agreement with Montie's lawyer. In mid-1942, Précilda and Lord Roy Anderson were married by the solicitous mayor of Settat.

Précilda's newfound happiness was tempered by nagging worries about the welfare of her daughters, especially Jeanne-Claude. Indeed, Jeanne-Claude was being underfed and tormented. The Denat family treated her with a mixture of abuse and neglect. She remembered hearing her mother repeatedly characterized as a "Gaullist witch." Her aloof father remained occupied with duties elsewhere. His quiet but menacing wife, Charlotte, and her sisters, Françoise and Jacqueline Duhez, made no effort to conceal their resentment of her. Among Jeanne-Claude's few pleasant memories that predate the end of the war are those of rare, forbidden moments with Charlotte's blond, blue-eyed baby, Charlie; he was good-natured and too young to share his mother's hostility.

On the morning of November 8, 1942, thick smoke billowed over Casablanca's port area. Rumors of a possible Allied invasion had seemed far-fetched, but not anymore. That day, 400,000 American troops made simultaneous landings in and around Casablanca, Oran, and Algiers. The startling news of an American assault electrified the prisoners at Settat. After the announced surrender of all Vichy forces on the morning of November 11, retrieving Jeanne-Claude became Précilda's highest priority. Stunned by the lightning American victory and eager to please, Denat's family quickly released the unwanted child. Précilda, now several months pregnant, a disoriented seven-year-old Jeanne-Claude, and Lord Roy Anderson moved into a house next door to his mother, Lady Anderson.

Yolande Karsenti, a cousin, remembers Jeanne-Claude as more of a sister.

"She was different from the other children in the family. She was very slim, with blue eyes, blond hair, and so pretty."[2] When Roy, Précilda, and Jeanne-Claude visited Yolande in late December 1942, Jeanne-Claude brought along an expensive Christmas present she had been given by her mother. It was a Louis Vuitton doll's traveling case, complete with drawers, hangers, doll, and the doll's wardrobe. Yolande said, "My mother gave me only a small doll. When I saw it and Jeanne-Claude's gift, I didn't want to play with the doll. Jeanne-Claude was only seven, but she saw my face and immediately understood how unhappy I was. She said, 'Let's exchange.'"[3] Yolande never forgot her cousin's generosity.

Soon after this visit, Roy Anderson received orders to leave for England. In her present condition. Précilda had no choice but to remain in Morocco. She gave birth to Allistair Anderson on June 18, 1943. As the head nurse, an ardent Vichyist, carried the newborn from the room, Précilda heard her mutter, "Here is one more English in this tumult." A few nights later, the nurse entered her room and announced, "Your British boy is dead!" Précilda grabbed a clock and threw it at her. The nurse staggered out of the room, pressing a hand to her bloodied forehead. When a doctor arrived, Précilda demanded that he call the police. Even General de Gaulle heard of this alleged Vichy crime.

Shattered by the loss of her son, Précilda and Lady Anderson used their considerable influence to secure passage on a convoy bound for England in late 1943. Because of wartime travel restrictions, the fear of a dangerous voyage, or for some other reason, Précilda concluded that it would be impossible to take Jeanne-Claude with her. Given that predicament, she inexplicably took her daughter back to the Denat family and convinced them to look after her again. Perhaps she feared that the military or political situation might change. Whatever her reasons, her anxiety led to the youngster's unhappy placement. Yolande Karsenti said, "Précilda didn't want any problems, and Denat's Vichyist family probably seemed a safer haven than our home."[4] Précilda promised her confused eight-year-old that when the war ended, she would return immediately. "I was very frightened," Jeanne-Claude recalled. "I knew that my father's family didn't love me at all." She would suffer two long years of abuse and neglect before she and her mother were reunited.

Précilda and her mother-in-law left on a Greek freighter, expecting a voyage of three or four days; it took three harrowing weeks in rough, submarine-infested waters. Précilda and Lady Anderson became so ill during a brutal winter storm that each expected to die.

In London, Roy suggested that she telephone a friend of his, Foreign Secretary Anthony Eden. Eden arranged for Précilda to go to work for General de

Gaulle, even though she was a British citizen. De Gaulle said that he wanted her to serve as his chief of information, propaganda, and press. Précilda was overwhelmed, but de Gaulle said, "Luizet has told me what you can do and I believe him." Précilda Anderson accepted a key job and the general's trust.

Précilda focused on her work until a clash pitted her against a resolute thirty-four-year-old French career officer. She telephoned his office, demanding confirmation of what proved to be an unfounded report of the sinking of a ship transporting Free French troops to England. Seconds later, Précilda barged into Maj. Jacques de Guillebon's reception area just as his orderly was announcing that a Lady Anderson insisted on speaking to him. She stormed into Guillebon's office as he, without looking up from stacks of paperwork, shouted, "If this old dame shows up, kick her in the ass." Précilda swirled around, bent over, and trumpeted over her shoulder, "Don't stand on ceremony; do it yourself." They exchanged uncomfortable glances. That scene would be remembered as one of the few adversarial moments in a loving relationship that was to endure for more than forty years.

Jacques de Guillebon wore about him the noble look of a modern-day knight. De Gaulle once called him "the most faithful of the faithful ones."[5] Jacques had served as Gen. Philippe Leclerc's chief of staff since early 1941, when they led Free French forces to their first military victory in Africa. By mid-1944, sixteen thousand men of the French Second Armored Division were assembled in England. When, on August 1, Leclerc's divisions left to join the battle in Europe, Précilda confidently promised Jacques that she would be in Paris on the day he arrived. He laughed and said, "I hope so."

Précilda's brash pledge went beyond wishful thinking. Several days earlier, after she had presented her daily file to de Gaulle, he put it aside and said, "You have been very precious to me, Lady Anderson. What will you do when we soldiers return to France?"

She answered, "General, the one thing that I want with all my heart is to be in Paris on the day that you arrive." Surprised, he told her to return the next morning. The next day, de Gaulle asked her to deliver a letter to her new commander, Gen. Georges Berges, head of air, land, and sea transport. Berges asked her to serve as his chief of staff.

Précilda ordered two stylish uniforms. The afternoon they were completed, Berges revealed they would be leaving for France the next morning at 5:00 A.M. sharp. Précilda left the house a few minutes early; the general's car awaited her. As they drove through the cold darkness toward Southampton, a V-1 bomb overhead went silent and then exploded behind them. Berges looked back and said, "That was not far from your place." Later that day, she received a cable stating that the housekeeper and the woman's son had been killed and the house destroyed at exactly 5:00 A.M.

Paris, 1946: Lady Précilda Anderson (wearing the tartan of her former husband Lord Anderson) with her fiancé, Lieutenant Colonel Jacques de Guillebon. (Photo: Jeanne-Claude)

Still dazed by the news, they boarded a ship carrying a contingent of American troops. Landing craft brought them ashore on a windswept Normandy beach near Sainte-Mère Eglise. Précilda and General Berges drove along badly damaged roads toward Paris. Drenched by driving rains and exhausted, they finally reached the American front lines. It was several days before she and Berges caught up with Leclerc's stalled division.

On Monday, August 21, with his division held back by the Allied command and supply problems, a frustrated General Leclerc wrote to de Gaulle,

"Guillebon has been sent with a light detachment—tanks, machine guns and infantry towards Versailles with orders to make contact, and enter Paris if the enemy falls back."[6] On Friday, August 25, slowed only by delirious crowds and some scattered German resistance, Guillebon led the first column of returning French soldiers into Paris. Luizet and Guillebon stood solemnly at Leclerc's side as Gen. Dietrich von Choltitz signed the surrender paper that had been prepared by Guillebon.

On Saturday, Précilda at last caught up with Guillebon at Leclerc's temporary headquarters. Guillebon's unshakable reserve dissolved when he saw a radiant Lieutenant Anderson emerge from the crowd and rush toward him. He swept her up in his arms and kissed her with uninhibited delight.

On May 5, 1945, three days before V-E day, Précilda received a telephone call from Berchtesgaden, where Jacques's unit had just captured Hitler's mountain retreat. He called to say that it was almost time to keep her promise to Jeanne-Claude. General Berges arranged for a plane, and Précilda left for the airport just before Paris exploded in a final victory fête.

On Tuesday, May 8, 1945, the guns fell silent. Précilda landed in Casablanca late that afternoon and hurried to the Denat residence. She was unprepared for the shock that awaited her. When the door opened, a frightened Jeanne-Claude recoiled, shrieking. Précilda had to look again to make sure it was her daughter. She recognized her child's outgrown, tattered clothing, which had been new when she had last seen it. Worse than the unexpected hysteria was Jeanne-Claude's physical condition. She trembled, her hair knotted with dirt and infested with lice, her stomach swollen from malnutrition. Précilda felt repelled by her own child. Léon Denat had apparently been absent since the American invasion of Morocco. His family gladly released Jeanne-Claude. Précilda took her daughter's unwilling hand and left in a silent rage.

Précilda rented a small villa overlooking the sea. She scrubbed her child with chlorine and fed, clothed, and pampered her. The lice and dirt were removed, but not the scars of a traumatic childhood. Almost ten years old, Jeanne-Claude was ill-educated, insecure, and altogether disoriented. Her fears, particularly the dread of being abandoned, gradually receded. In time, she came to view her mother's reappearance as a miracle that provided for every material need. They spent a carefree week together before they boarded an army plane for Marseilles. It was Jeanne-Claude's first flight and her first trip out of Africa. They were about to begin a new life in postwar Paris.

Shortly after arriving in Marseilles, Précilda accepted an invitation from a government official and his wife to dine at an elegant restaurant. During the first course, everyone looked aghast at Jeanne-Claude grabbing her food and slipping beneath the table to eat. Précilda tried to conceal her embarrassment

Garden of the Palais de Chaillot, Paris, 1948: Jeanne-Claude's mother, Précilda de Guillebon. (Photo: Jacques de Guillebon)

by explaining the abuse her daughter had suffered while in Casablanca. From then on, the loving mother was also a stern disciplinarian; Jeanne-Claude quickly learned flawless table manners.

Précilda purchased a new wardrobe for Jeanne-Claude and found a desirable apartment on the Right Bank. She enrolled her daughter in a religious boarding school from which the child returned home each weekend. At first, Jeanne-Claude could barely read or write, but she made impressive strides. Meanwhile, Précilda obtained an uncontested divorce from Roy Anderson.

Jacques had proposed marriage to Précilda in mid-1944 in London; her

Paris, 1946: Jeanne-Claude receiving her first camera from her mother. (Photo: Jacques de Guillebon)

response had been noncommittal. She made it clear that no man would be acceptable unless he pleased her daughter. As a result, Jacques had devised a plan to write to Jeanne-Claude secretly in Morocco and win her affection. He reported regularly on her mother's activities, signing each letter "Your friend, Jacques." In November 1946, when Précilda announced that her good friend Jacques would be taking them to dinner, Jeanne-Claude's face lighted up, and she asked, "How do you know him?" Her usual cranky aloofness toward male visitors vanished when Guillebon arrived. He swept her off her feet in a warm embrace; she hugged and kissed him. When Précilda saw her child's head come to rest on his shoulder, she smiled from across the room and nodded yes. She and Jacques were married on January 10, 1947. Jeanne-Claude carried the train of her mother's black wedding dress.

From early 1948 to late 1951, Jacques was assigned to be the military attaché to the French embassy in Bern. He then served for almost a year as commander of the Chartres region. During this period, Jeanne-Claude attended several Catholic schools. She studied for two and a half years at a French Dominican school in Fribourg, followed by a brief stay at a school administered by English sisters. While she excelled academically, her disruptive actions as class clown overshadowed this accomplishment. Her friends, among them the granddaughter of Swiss-born painter Félix Vallotton, were mostly from wealthy families. They found the rigid discipline intimidating. Not Jeanne-Claude. She reveled in what for her was a less restrictive environment than the one her

Paris, 1946: Jacques de Guillebon and Jeanne-Claude with her first camera. (Photo: Précilda de Guillebon)

mother created at home. Her unrestrained behavior led to tearful dismissals from several schools.

Jeanne-Claude was the only Guillebon child until 1948. That year, Norbert de Guillebon was born in Bern on August 25, the fourth anniversary of Paris's liberation. Then Alexandra de Guillebon was born on August 25, 1952, in Amiens. The remarkable coincidence prompted de Gaulle to remark, "Guillebon delivers everybody on the same day." Précilda spent over a week in the hospital after giving birth to Alexandra. When she returned home, the servants complained that Jeanne-Claude, home from Sacred Heart School in Amiens for the summer, had proved an even more difficult taskmistress than her mother. The fussy seventeen-year-old never tired of inspecting routine jobs and sending back food that had not been prepared precisely as she instructed. Précilda shrugged off the complaints and took pride in her daughter's high standards. High standards or high-and-mighty manner, Jeanne-Claude simply mirrored her mother's style, which would continue to shape her values in the years ahead.

Like Précilda, Jeanne-Claude wanted to enjoy the advantages of social status. Adopted into the ranks of the upper class, educated in the protocols of the affluent, the savvy teenager learned ways of wielding power. She became a sophisticated hostess and relished a sense of belonging that had long eluded her. Jeanne-Claude appeared relaxed, but her place in society and the privileges that status embraced did little to give direction to her life.

In the late summer of 1952, Jacques de Guillebon was appointed military commander of Gabès and the embattled southern territories of Tunisia. The Guillebons arrived during the first week of October, with an ongoing struggle for independence manifesting itself in riots, strikes, and terrorism. Reestablishing order in an impoverished region plagued by acute unrest became Guillebon's primary task.

Jacques's command post also served as the family residence. The large mansion looked out on spacious grounds, featuring a tennis court, sizable gardens, and an enclosure for a small herd of gazelles. A quarter mile from the house, a long, inviting beach on the Gulf of Gabès cast its spell. Over a mile of the coastline was reserved for the Guillebons. Army guards manned the front gate and patrolled the stone walls surrounding the complex. Their number increased in direct proportion to the prevailing tension in the area near their home. The servants seemed legion. Curving symmetrical staircases ascended from each side of a fountain in the entry foyer to the family quarters on the upper floor, where Précilda and Jacques, Jeanne-Claude, Norbert, six-week-old Alexandra, and her nurse each had a room. Jeanne-Claude quickly developed a penchant for using a maze of bells and buzzers in the dining room, living room, guest room, and bedrooms that, with a touch, brought

Lallah Meryam, South Tunisia, 1955: Jeanne-Claude in her boat *The Picardie*. (Photo: Archive XTO+J-C)

forth an array of services. During the next four and a half years, for better of worse, she became accustomed to a lifestyle befitting royalty.

Jeanne-Claude's happy life revolved around swimming, sailing, dancing, playing tennis, and horseback riding. Correspondence school occasionally intruded on her leisure time. At eighteen, after one year in Tunisia, Jeanne-Claude obtained her baccalaureate degree, completing her formal education. A second, longer commitment grew out of her concern for poverty-stricken Arab children. It began in 1952 when she met Dr. Jean-Claude Poirot, who was about to initiate a UNESCO health-care project in the territory. Stirred by his dedication, Jeanne-Claude agreed to distribute medicine to children who suffered from an eye affliction that led to blindness if not treated.

Almost every day, Jeanne-Claude rode off on her horse, her pockets bulging with a supply of candy and small tubes of Aureomycin. Her destinations were various oases, scattered among endless sand dunes that fanned out from Gabès into the arid countryside. As she went, Jeanne-Claude quickly identified those children in need of the ointment.

In 1954, after twenty years of prolonged service as a colonel, Jacques de Guillebon finally achieved the rank of two-star general. Jeanne-Claude possessed enviable social advantages long before her stepfather's promotion, however. Every officer under Guillebon's command tried to win her favor. Some men were physically attracted to her, some tried to impress a potentially powerful ally, and others were simply polite. Whatever their motivations, Jeanne-Claude made the most of them. "Everyone offered to play tennis or invited me

Essertaux, Picardie, France, 1958: Jeanne-Claude's parents with four of their African greyhounds, or "saloukis." (Photo: Wjera Fechheimer)

to dance," she recalled. "They had to be nice." It is a matter of conjecture whether an intimate link to authority enhanced or blurred her self-image.

Jeanne-Claude had few female friends, and certainly none with her status, other than the resident general's daughter, Isabelle de Hauteclocque. In a curious way, both young women were trapped by privilege. The fact that they were always expected to adhere to proper decorum and that they were in the public spotlight conspired to make their comfortably insulated world somewhat less than perfect. At Jeanne-Claude's first military ball, a group of officers flocked around her, each vying for her attention. She blithely violated the rules of good behavior by dancing with one man most of the night, and, to make matters worse, she left with him for an hour in the midst of the festivities. The next day, Jacques summoned her to his office and lectured her on the importance of appearances.

Jeanne-Claude snapped, "I don't care."

"You must care!" Jacques insisted.

Jeanne-Claude soon discovered an acceptable way to share her time unequally with men. She became engaged three times in Tunisia. Each engagement followed a ritual pattern. After a boyfriend proposed and Jeanne-Claude consented, her suitor would ask to talk to her father. Before the young man presented himself, Jeanne-Claude would inform Jacques, "He is going to request an appointment, and guess what?" Her father would reply with resignation, "I think I know what."

Jeanne-Claude's first fiancé came from one of the richest European families in the south. Their stormy engagement ended abruptly when her mother discovered them half-naked in bed. Enraged, Précilda chased the young man from the house. Jeanne-Claude halfheartedly attempted suicide, swallowing some iodine. The tempestuous eighteen-year-old then rushed to her mother, shouting, "Take me to the hospital. My stomach is burning."

Précilda responded coolly, "That will teach you to do something stupid. Call the hospital yourself." Jeanne-Claude burst into tears. Her mother said, "If you want to die, you can."

Choking back her sobs, Jeanne-Claude whispered, "I don't want to die."

Without a trace of sympathy, Précilda asked, "Are you sure?"

Jeanne-Claude answered faintly, "Yes."

A car finally rushed the ashen teenager to the hospital, where her stomach was pumped.

Before long, another of Jeanne-Claude's admirers arrived at Guillebon's office seeking the commander's blessing. Wearing a spotless uniform and white gloves, Lt. Michel Montagné stood at attention, answering the customary questions regarding his family, finances, and intentions. He was noticeably older than Jeanne-Claude, wrote poetry, grew roses in the desert, and was inclined to flights of imagination. Montagné had a less-than-distinguished background and hardly conformed to the spit-and-polish military type her stepfather preferred. Précilda was equally unimpressed by the lieutenant. Montagné's unit operated in the southernmost Sahara. His thoughtful letters arrived regularly, but the physical gulf separating the couple, aggravated by her parents' persistent opposition, led Jeanne-Claude to terminate the relationship.

A fastidious captain, François de Villèle, erect and smartly attired, sporting a small red mustache, waited in the background. With the chilly formality of a partner in an arranged marriage, the captain asked for and received permission to become engaged to the commander's daughter. François's blend of charm and aristocratic good form barely concealed the fact that he had a drinking problem. He outdid his predecessors by offering Jeanne-Claude the choice of an emerald, ruby, or diamond ring to mark the happy event. She asked for an MG convertible instead; he smiled meekly and agreed. Jeanne-Claude drove the sleek sports car with gleeful abandon, injuring no one, fortunately. Other than this lavish gift, it is difficult to imagine what possessed her to enter the arrangement. She did not drink, nor did she feel physically attracted to him. "He respected me thoroughly," she later said—so thoroughly that they never even kissed. When the two separated in 1957, Jeanne-Claude cried because her mother insisted that she return the automobile.

The frantic commotion of transient encounters, self-indulgence, and spirited naïveté revealed a mercurial and vulnerable young woman. At twenty-one, Jeanne-Claude had not yet come of age. The pursuit of love and happiness consumed her; soul-searching was not to come until later. Each romantic romp, despite elements of fantasy and rebellion, can also be seen as part of a youthful search for a life of substance, a life worthy of her illustrious parents. Jeanne-Claude had everything but a sense of purpose. However, events were soon to change her carefree lifestyle irrevocably.

General de Guillebon's North African assignment concluded when Tunisia achieved independence in March 1956. His next assignment was to serve as director of the prestigious Ecole Polytechnique in Paris. Jacques's good fortune and the prospect of hundreds of eligible young men waiting to court her delighted Jeanne-Claude.

While the general's daughter may have appeared to be a sophisticate in the sandy environs of Gabès, Parisian standards were another matter. The transition from a barren outpost to a vibrant urban setting would not only polish Jeanne-Claude's rough edges but test her values. The family moved to Paris in July 1957. For the next two years, she lived a fantasy life, pursued by an endless number of suitors, which culminated in a perfect marriage—or so it seemed.

3

In Transit: Vienna and Geneva

In January 1957, a quarter of a million refugees strained Vienna's already-overtaxed resources. Earlier that cold gray winter, Soviet troops had brutally crushed the Hungarian uprising. Christo recalled, "Many residents had plane tickets to Salzburg or Munich because they were expecting the Russians to walk over the border and take Vienna." This atmosphere and an immigrant's anxiety over sudden displacement tempered the exhilarating sense of freedom that had accompanied his escape to Austria.

Christo had turned in his passport and requested political asylum; now he prepared to face the unrelenting demands of daily survival in self-imposed exile. His itinerary would be that of a worker, not a tourist. Wherever Christo went, patterns of day-to-day activity, streets, and even shabby neighborhoods evoked historical and cultural associations. He saw the still-visible patina of a great past beneath darkened layers of slush and snow. The previously illustrious city of Klimt, Freud, and Mahler astride the once-blue Danube no longer stood at the center of an empire. With few exceptions, the Viennese preferred to think of their city as a fin de siècle hub of music and gaiety, rather than as the breeding ground for fascism it had been in the 1930s and 1940s.

Christo's brief stay with the family of his father's college friend had been cordial but uneasy. Mr. Sabev missed no opportunity to point out the financial burden imposed by his unexpected tenant. Christo observed his reluctant host's involvement in a variety of capitalist enterprises: He was a connoisseur of and dealer in rare stamps, as well as an almost feudal landlord, who leased tracts to farmers and subsequently bought and sold their produce. To defray expenses, Christo seized an opportunity to work for Sabev. His landlord also helped him find other jobs, such as cleaning cars and washing dishes, until he could save money to secure separate living quarters. Within a few weeks, Christo managed to rent a room in an apartment owned by one of Sabev's friends.

Christo enrolled at the Vienna Fine Arts Academy and received a student identification card. This scant bit of paper proved indispensable; in the absence of a passport, it represented bureaucratic evidence of his legitimacy. For over a year and a half, this unimpressive document, together with a small government refugee card, tenuously provided his only shield against the authorities.

Conflicting feelings of delight and despair, self-confidence and doubt, optimism and loneliness must have filled Christo Javacheff in late January 1957. At twenty-one, he looked rail-thin and boyish; a fierce determination and a resolute will to succeed lay behind his youthful modesty and gentle manner. At this critical juncture, Christo needed all of his energy just to set his life in order and begin functioning as an artist. He remained poor, stateless, and vulnerable, although unwavering in purpose.

Most of his art supplies and recent work had been left behind in Prague. As a result, Christo took jobs at all hours to survive and to pay for essential art materials. An elderly Robin Andersen[1] served as his professor at the academy, which seemed tediously academic. As in Bulgaria, Christo found his inspiration outside the classroom. The school's very small but lovely museum provided an important source of stimulation, introducing Christo to the work of the Impressionists, Cubists, and Cézanne. Another happy discovery in the heart of the city was the small Galerie Nachst Saint Stephens, adjoining the famous Gothic cathedral of the same name. On his first visit, he saw a Sophie Taüber-Arp exhibition. The show had been mounted by Monsignor Otto Maurer, who had founded the innovative gallery in 1955. Christo and the Roman Catholic priest immediately developed a warm relationship. He was also impressed, if not inspired, when introduced to Arnulf Rainer at a one-man show of large cross-shaped paintings by the twenty-seven-year-old Austrian artist at the Wiener Secession Gallery. In Vienna's complacent, intellectually arid atmosphere, many saw Rainer's gestural monochromatic work as subversive or even perverse. The public display of art aimed at confronting the establishment fascinated Christo.

Christo remained intensely curious about uncensored Western plays and movies, and, by working long hours at menial jobs, he scraped together enough money to attend some productions. Life in the capitalist world was wrenching, but Christo's interest in its culture had little to do with escapism. In his first letter to Anani from Vienna, dated March 23, 1957, he praised his older brother for a performance that had been reviewed favorably in *National Culture*, an important Bulgarian weekly newspaper. Since his last letter from Prague had addressed the world of theater, Christo chose to focus this time on cinema. He compared the appeal of American and French directors with German-language films that generally left him cold. He wrote, "*Moby Dick* was the most exquisite film in colors [sic] that I have ever seen . . . and what an artist Gregory Peck is . . . extraordinary in his mask and diction. There were scenes in his cabin on the boat where he can't sleep and walks on his wooden leg—thud, thud, without music for three minutes of continuous horror." He also reacted to *Gone With the Wind*, "After I saw it I couldn't sleep until two in the morning. I kept thinking about the Americans and their giganticism."[2]

About himself he wrote, "My eyes are directed toward Italy and Paris. After establishing myself financially, I am going. Otherwise, I'm still alone and slowly adapting." Christo mentioned writing to their mother and requesting some clothes, a trench coat, cheese, halvah, and a Greek drink called *mastik*. He confided, "I live a bearable, modest life. With God's help and the wings of invaluable friends, I'm personally getting rid of suffering and worries. And, I'm painting. I paint and I believe." Christo concluded, "I wouldn't want you to think a lot about me after reading this."

Christo realized that being alone and far from home, one often had to rely on strangers. In the same letter, he reported that Sabev's oldest son, age twenty-two, had become "a good friend who helps a lot." He mentioned doing two portraits of Hariklis Baxevanos, a twenty-one-year-old Greek actress currently performing in Vienna. Her boyfriend purchased one of the paintings, and, more important, she helped secure other commissions, "three before Easter, and five after."

In the early spring of 1957, Christo's fortunes improved dramatically as a result of two new acquaintances. An Austrian relative of his mother helped arrange meetings with several well-to-do Bulgarians living in Vienna. One expatriate, Slavtscho Zagoroff, a professor and dean of economics at the University of Vienna, had served as Bulgarian ambassador to Berlin during the war. After the Russians occupied Bulgaria in 1944, he chose not to return. Zagoroff and his family moved to Switzerland, then, in 1951, the United States. In 1955, he returned to Vienna. His son, Dimiter (Mitko), remained in the States and years later became one of Christo's trusted friends, playing a key role in several major projects. Professor Zagoroff took a paternal interest in Christo and purchased two city-landscape paintings for his office. He also provided a string of referrals that helped ease the financial pressure on the young artist.

An equally important contact in Vienna was a Mr. Kalenjieff, a distinguished businessman living in an opulent apartment near Saint Stephen's Cathedral. When Christo visited him, bringing a group of portraits, still lifes, and landscapes, Kalenjieff quickly commissioned portraits of his wife and daughter. A number of Kalenjieff's affluent friends who saw the paintings took advantage of the bargain-priced service. Soon Christo had a waiting list of new clients. He knew that these commissions were only exercises in survival, unrelated to his aspirations as an artist.

Christo rejected lucrative overtures from right-wing Bulgarians claiming to be financed by the CIA. They offered money and other inducements for him to join them in Munich. Christo refused to get involved in the Cold War, finding the notion of anything political or Bulgarian to be distasteful. His only interest was art.

In late April 1957, Christo went on a ten-day trip to Italy sponsored by the Vienna Fine Arts Academy. In May, he wrote enthusiastically to Anani, "As our train crossed the border there was a breeze of fabulous air. I was smitten. I fell in love, completely went mad in this paradise with its marvelously temperamental people."[3] He reported, "I had plenty of orange juice to make up for what I couldn't have in Bulgaria. . . . We work in the villa of the academy. Florence is a wonderful city with a huge Renaissance park, baths, and fantastic comforts. I was hypnotized all morning at the Medici Chapel, then the Uffizi and Pitti galleries." At every turn, the past came alive. Christo marveled at Uccello's battle scenes and described Botticelli's *Birth of Venus:* "There are no illusionistic similarities for sea and grass, each element is unique. If you like abstraction which synthesizes everything, it is more than reality. There is no eternal, classical beauty, only the fact that it is great art."

Florence heightened Christo's awareness of how physical space could be manipulated. He wrote:

> I am in reverence before the beautiful modern buildings, roads, and other creations of the most ordinary Italian bricklayers and workers. Here the modern is not boring. It is a different direction as in America. We live in the twentieth century and the genius of modern architecture demonstrates a great new tradition. That inspiration must be saved instead of letting it become like the routine of an old clerk. The continuity in the arts is not in imitation, but the flame.[4]

Christo resumed his nonstop work routine after returning to Vienna. Only the occasional luxury of an exhibition, film, or play interrupted odd jobs, portrait commissions, and classes. In the spring of 1957, he attended a performance of *Titus Andronicus* starring Vivien Leigh and Laurence Olivier. Leigh's portrayal of Titus's mute daughter remained etched in his memory. Christo no doubt identified with her painful struggle to communicate.

The necessity of learning an unfamiliar language while adjusting to an uncertain future required, whether consciously or not, the creation of an adaptable new identity—part would-be Orpheus, part Macedonian revolutionary. Cut off from family and friends, he remained linked to his homeland through intermittent letters and by an umbilical cord that no circumstance would fully sever. Years later, Saul Steinberg, himself an immigrant artist, commented, "Christo and I are our own grandfathers in the sense that we made the transition from Eastern and Western men abruptly, in a period that otherwise might have taken generations. I admire Christo as a artist who invented himself. He not only invented himself; he invented his art, and, even more amazing, he invented his public."[5] The metamorphosis of Christo Javacheff into Christo the artist/conjurer had begun.

By October 1957, Christo had saved enough money to venture a step closer to Paris. The twenty-two-year-old artist had grand dreams and a one-way third-class ticket to Geneva. He carried a thirty-day visa and a suitcase containing personal belongings and art supplies. Christo left behind any illusion of completing his formal education. His one semester at the Vienna Fine Arts Academy had been tediously unrewarding. He had not risked so much to endure another rigidly conservative program.

Christo's expectations soared as his train entered the neatly manicured Swiss countryside. Nineteen-year-old Alexandre Todorov, affectionately known as "Sacho," awaited his arrival at Geneva's railroad station. They had been close friends at college in Sofia before Sacho left for Budapest to study medicine. After only fifteen days of classes, in the midst of the Hungarian rebellion, Sacho and his host family had simply walked to Austria. He continued on to Switzerland and, with his father's help, enrolled as a medical student at the University of Geneva.

Christo had learned of Sacho's whereabouts from a Viennese friend. Sacho pleaded with him to come to Geneva, offering to arrange for a sponsor who would guarantee the lodging required for a temporary visa. Agreeing to join his friend, Christo promised to contribute whatever he could to meet expenses. Each would help the other cope with the hardships of displacement. Communication presented a significant obstacle, since the Cyrillic alphabet and Bulgarian have no counterparts in Western Europe. Gradually, they came to learn French.

Christo and Sacho spent most of their joint residency in Geneva at an inexpensive old town house, where they lived in small adjoining rooms under a dormer off a common entryway. "It was a tough time," Sacho recalled. "Our place looked very shabby."[6] His litany of problems included stringent academic requirements and having barely enough money for necessities. But both young men were prepared to endure almost anything except failure in their chosen endeavors.

Christo continued to feel drawn to Paris. The closer he came to that center of cultural activity, the greater its pull. He found Geneva's art world no less provincial than Vienna's. The artistic energy in each city originated elsewhere: German precedents in Vienna, French influences in Geneva. Christo took a variety of low-paying jobs while trying to find Swiss clients for portraits. Zagoroff and Kalenjieff had supplied leads in Vienna, but opportunities developed slowly in reclusive Geneva, even with written introductions. The uneasy task of converting names and addresses into paying work was complicated by the fact that Christo's visa specifically forbade employment. To succeed, he would have to demonstrate technical proficiency, personal charm, and discretion.

Christo had been referred to Assen Ivanoff, a Bulgarian expatriate in his mid-twenties. Ivanoff offered advice and had close contacts at the United Nations and among aristocratic French families. With his guidance, Christo began to make headway, as one portrait led to another. He produced flattering images in the styles of various modern masters, such as Renoir and Matisse. Even without the spark of originality, they were impressive.

Christo happily discovered the kindhearted Bretton family in Geneva. Jean Bretton owned a precision-instruments factory. Christo repeatedly visited their large mansion just outside of Geneva and painted their thirteen children. He began to save money and develop new connections.

In December 1957, during the university's Christmas holiday, Sacho and Christo set out for Basel, where they toured the Kunstmuseum. "That was the biggest revelation," Christo recalled, "one of the most fabulous collections of modern art." The scope and quality of the collection surpassed anything he had encountered in Geneva, Vienna, or Prague. In the days ahead, they continued on a haphazard jaunt, sight-seeing and visiting museums in Lucerne, Zurich, Locarno, Lausanne, and other stops along the way. Christo drew at every opportunity.

Up to this point, Christo's avant-garde attitude had not been reflected in his art. There was always a clear distinction in his mind between the portraits and his other work. The commissions were generally a time-consuming chore; any enjoyable social interaction derived from this labor was incidental to the necessity of raising money. By the end of 1957, each commercial portrait, even the studies of intimate friends, bore the signature "Javacheff." He reserved the "Christo" signature for everything he considered serious. The latter consisted of simultaneous experimental ventures, ranging from occasional landscapes or still lifes to an assortment of recent textural near abstractions. In the weeks ahead, he returned alone to the Kunstmuseum in Basel and the Zurich Kunsthaus. These visits sparked a decisive change in his work. The artworks that most stimulated Christo had one common quality: a rich, tactile surface. He had discovered a small Joan Miró collage in the storage bins at the National Gallery in Prague; then, in Switzerland, he saw Cubist oils, Dada collages, thickly painted canvases by Nicolas de Staël, and, perhaps most significant at this point, Jean Dubuffet's early work. These memorable pieces were prime motivators during the artistically pivotal winter of 1957–1958.

Christo met a medical student named Chokofé shortly after returning to Geneva. She had a striking, strangely exotic face. "It had an aura," Sacho said, "with those big dark eyes, olive skin, and long, flowing, curly black hair."[7] The daughter of a wealthy Iranian-American couple, she was petite and intelligent, totally conscious of her sex appeal. She spoke French fluently, while Christo struggled with it; yet despite this, an immediate friendship developed, as did Christo's infatuation with her. Painting her portrait gave him another means of communicating, of overcoming his shyness. Despite her protective family, the new friends soon became lovers. Throughout their relationship, he frequently drew and painted her, working realistically or in the manner of various well-known artists.

In the cold gray of early January, with Sacho and Chokofé busy at school and portrait work at a standstill, Christo found himself contemplating his recently completed group of encrusted envelopes. They were little more than meditations, indecipherable wall reliefs, yet somehow they were important to him. He had been searching for a visual means of expressing his as-yet-unintelligible inner voice. Several dozen of these strange pieces with weathered, volcanic patinas were scattered about his room. Each paper surface had been crumpled, then coated with layers of glue and resin. Other sheets of paper were pressed against tacky areas and lifted to create various textures. Finally, varnish, sand, earth tones of pigment, and, in a few cases, string or pieces of torn newspaper became part of each envelope's hard outer skin. These unlikely crinkled surfaces, along with a handful of textual canvases, provided the impetus for Christo to define his private world.

Not even Christo can say precisely what prompted him to begin encasing things. It started in January 1958, with a small empty paint can. He wrapped the ungainly object with resin-soaked canvas, tied it in twine, and coated it with the same glue, varnish, sand, and shades of brown and black automobile paint that he had used on the envelopes. That instinctive gesture at once transformed the mundane into something mysterious. Not only had the can been relieved of its intended function but, to his delight, something significant remained equivocal, untold. The shrouded vessel no longer belonged to the realm of real things; it had been converted into a disenfranchised semblance of reality. The initial gesture might have been a matter of improvisation, a hunch, or an accidental transformation, but it was nothing less than a revelation.

Sacho observed Christo's production with the curious detachment of a scientist who knows nothing about art. He saw a split artistic personality and what appeared to be a natural progression from, first, literal transcriptions of reality, to translations of other artists' work, and, finally, to personal, more radical statements. He listened carefully to Christo's reasoning, and in retrospect, he insists that he felt like an objective witness to a coherent evolutionary process.[8] Whether he or Christo could grasp a new language in which elusive, irrational elements play a large part, the first wrapped can and the revised commonplace objects that followed reflected Christo's instinctual vision. For the next two years, he continued to amass paint cans, bottles of powdered pigment, and other containers, some encased or partially veiled, some unmodified. The ensemble was part of what was later known as *Inventory.* This modest beginning accurately foretold adventures to come.

In some way, every work of art is a self-portrait. Christo's earliest wrappings reveal a containment that paralleled his own circumscribed existence at the time. The images evoke the repressive atmosphere of his youth under the Communists, as well as his sense of cultural isolation. An unobtrusive group of enclosed and exposed cans and bottles stood as drab emblems of exile, suspended in time, in limbo between their original purpose and ultimate destruction. Like its maker, each obscured parcel projected a plaintive intimacy. Feelings of displacement, loneliness, and loss may have provided the autobiographical content of these wrappings. Christo has always been reticent to analyze his art, but he later admitted, "The work had a lot to do with that sad dimension. There was a kind of 'miserablism.' *Misérable* also means 'poverty' in French." Christo's privation contributed to, perhaps even dictated, his choice of materials. He liked the notion that his work was nontraditional, nonprecious, three-dimensional, and portable. He later speculated that the process of creating transient, manipulable sculpture related to "unconsciously moving in a much broader sense."

In February 1958, Christo's residency in Geneva became precarious. His thirty-day visa had already expired several times. One each occasion, Assen Ivanoff assisted in arranging an extension. Christo had disregarded renewal deadlines, hoping a low profile would help him evade detection. "I was thinking that they would forget me, but every Swiss is a spy," he quipped. One day as Christo worked in his room, a uniformed immigration official appeared at the door. The stern functionary examined his invalid passport and asked how he managed to support himself. Christo, who could barely speak French, was at a loss for words and, he said, "very embarrassed, very frightened." Once again, Ivanoff came to the rescue, convincing the authorities to grant a final extension. To complicate matters, a Bulgarian friend of Sacho's father paid an unexpected visit. He reported back that Sacho had been depriving himself by subsidizing a struggling artist; Sacho's father became outraged and told his son to part ways with Christo. His advice turned out to be unnecessary. By then, Christo had saved enough money for a third-class train ticket to Paris and to cover his living expenses for several months. He had also collected letters of reference and portrait referrals from several wealthy French families. However, even the well-connected Ivanoff could not help him obtain the prerequisite French visa. Officials told Christo that he would have to return to Vienna to apply for authorization. Somehow, he managed to reestablish contact with Bonavita, the French diplomat who had befriended him in Sofia. A series of telephone calls from Bonavita finally convinced the French consulate in Geneva to provide a temporary French visa stamp on Christo's Austrian refugee card.

In late February 1958, Christo said good-bye to Sacho and Chokofé. He packed his possessions, including a small group of *Inventory* pieces. In the weeks preceding his departure, a rash of household items inexplicably disappeared; Sacho's only concern was for a missing bronze candleholder. It was several years before Christo confessed to having appropriated it in the name of art. In time, he devised other, more startling aesthetic strategies, but for now, fabric had become his magician's trick mirror and cord his cloud of blue smoke.

4

Paris: Like Brother and Sister

On March 1, 1958, Christo boarded a third-class carriage for the last portion of his long pilgrimage. On January 31, the United States had launched its first space satellite, *Explorer,* in response to an earlier Russian success with *Sputnik;* on March 27, Nikita Khrushchev would be installed as the Soviet premier. The speed of changing events that most Western Europeans took for granted only heightened Christo's sense of adventure. A year and two months after leaving Bulgaria, he still saw miracles everywhere: in ordinary objects, roads, buildings, and routine activities.

In Paris, individual destinies crisscross and, on occasion, cohere, but before the fateful joining of Jeanne-Claude de Guillebon and Christo Javacheff in late 1958, the trajectories of their lives seemed random. They were strangers, with nothing in common but a birthday and an uncertain future. Jeanne-Claude, with her parents' reluctant consent, worked as a *hôtesse de Paris,* assisting travelers at one of the city's railroad stations. Christo needed no help as his train eased into the Gare de Lyon. He hurried to a taxi, which sped him to 8 rue Quentin-Bauchart on the Right Bank. The elegant building, located between the Champs Elysée and avenue Marceau, exceeded his expectations. Accommodations and nominal rent had been arranged by the Cabarusse family, French aristocrats Christo had met in Geneva. He occupied a maid's room on the top floor during a servant's leave of absence. The seven-floor walk-up had been accurately described: a small bedroom tucked under a sloping roof, with no built-in water supply or toilet facility. The space did provide privacy, however. Christo unpacked his few belongings and set up a corner work space.

The days were too short. There were galleries and museums to see, leads for portrait commissions to pursue, artwork to produce, and, most urgent, an extension of his visa to procure. Feeling very much a foreigner and dogged by an intense fear of being expelled, Christo again contacted Bonavita, who accompanied him to the Prefecture of Police. Bonavita coaxed an expressionless committee into begrudgingly issuing a *carte de séjour.* Valid for one year, the coveted refugee card could be renewed annually. With this credential, Christo could travel outside France simply by securing a routine *billet de voyage,* along with the appropriate visa. The relieved young artist thanked Bonavita warmly.

Christo quickly learned to navigate the narrow streets and teeming boulevards of Paris. In this diverse, frantic city, he enjoyed his anonymity. He became enthralled by the surface appearance of things. Elegant shop windows, cars, smoke-filled cafés, lavish presentations of a vast array of products, and particularly a multitude of art and antique establishments fascinated him. Christo could see and breathe the fruits of freedom. He devoured every image.

The sheer number of cultural events was staggering. Each outing to a theater, gallery, or museum provided an invigorating break from his daily struggles in the studio. More important, witnessing the breadth of modern art in Paris gave Christo an essential criterion against which to measure his own work. Before long, his makeshift work space overflowed with wrappings and various experimental paintings. He clearly needed a separate studio space.

In Geneva, Christo had met René Bourgeois, a fashionable hairdresser with a flourishing trade on the second floor of Paris's posh Grand Hôtel at place de l'Opéra. When the young artist arrived in Paris, Bourgeois introduced him to his colleague Jacques Dessanges. Christo's touching mixture of charm, vulnerability, and absolute commitment to art prompted Dessanges to offer an unused maid's room just above his apartment as studio space. It was small but suitable. Christo had saved enough money to pay for several months' rent at both locations, and he hoped to cover future expenses by resuming his portrait commissions.

Christo increasingly referred to these portraits as a form of prostitution. They paid the rent. The mass of work that began to fill his studio did not remotely suggest salability, but his materials—discarded items, bargain-priced merchandise, paper, canvas, paint, lacquer, sand, glue, and fabric—were, by necessity, either inexpensive or free. Christo seemed to be guided by a will to alter or destroy everyday appearances. Rather than adhering to the uninspiring nature of an object, he overcame its predictability. The simple gesture of wrapping brought the identity of an object into question. The ongoing *Inventory* series revealed that a revisited state of the ordinary could disrupt perceptions and arouse latent feelings, that the act of concealment elevated the banal to the mysterious. The exposure of an object's innate poverty contrasted with its more tragic state of bondage. A matter-of-fact juxtaposition of unaltered cans, bottles, and other objects to their wrapped counterparts generated unease. Were these depictions of freedom and entrapment or reassertions of his earlier agitprop activities? Autobiographical or unconscious, symbols of repression or a proclamation of newly won freedom, *Inventory* sparkled with irony as it defied explanation.

While the proliferating *Inventory* ensemble awaited the attention of an audience, Christo remained in an acute state of social isolation. It had been barely six months since he began battle with the French language in Geneva. By the time he reached Paris, his reading ability had advanced far beyond his halting, heavily accented attempts at conversation. Language was only part of the problem. As he later said, "I will be a displaced person all of my life," adding, "to be a displaced person can be disorienting, but it can also be inspiring."

Christo still carried with him from Bulgaria the names and addresses of two close family friends. One was a Mr. Rosenkranz, who manufactured textiles in Germany. Christo's letter to him included an invitation to visit his studio. Surprisingly, Rosenkranz's son responded shortly afterward. Thirty-two-year-old Dieter Rosenkranz and his glamorous twenty-two-year-old wife, Edith, reacted positively to the artist and his work. They lived in totally different social and economic spheres, but Christo and the couple quickly became friends. The Rosenkranzes purchased several small wrapped objects and invited Christo to spend some time with them in Germany that summer. Initially, Dieter might have just been helping the near-destitute son of his father's friend, but in time, he became one of the most knowledgeable collectors of Christo's work.

Christo also called his mother's old friend Anna Staritsky, a fifty-five-year-old Paris School painter. Like many White Russians, she had fled in the aftermath of the civil war; her friendship with Tzveta Yavachev had developed while Staritsky completed her art education at the Sofia Academy of Fine Arts. In March 1958, Christo introduced himself to her and visited her Montparnasse studio.

Lourdes Castro and her husband, René Bertholo, became Christo's first real artist friends in Paris. The attractive Portuguese couple met Christo through Dominique Lacarriére, a struggling actress and mutual acquaintance. Lourdes, René, and Christo were poor, about the same age, and shared the unspoiled optimism of youth. The trio was intent on defying the status quo and breaking new artistic ground; most important, they were practiced outsiders observing a comfortably entrenched art scene. They established an immediate rapport and alliance. Lourdes and René, like Christo, were determined to exploit the bewildering possibilities of their newly adopted city, despite an intimidating art establishment, chauvinistic social barriers, a new language, and the stifling effects of poverty. Did Christo worry about earning a living from untested enterprises like *Inventory*? He insisted, "I never, never thought about it."

Christo instinctively gravitated toward the most adventurous new art. His recent experiments revealed his preference for Jean Fautrier's painterly surfaces, Antoni Tàpies's "scorched earth" compositions, and, above all, the uninterrupted abstract expanses of Jean Dubuffet's 1958 *Texturologies* series.

In the spring of 1958, the state of contemporary French art might be described as somewhere between sedate and comatose. Where were Picasso's, Matisse's, and Duchamp's heirs? Bernard Buffet, Antoni Clavé, and other equally tame artists held the spotlight. At center stage were the ever-so-elegant Paris School paintings and the latest fashion: geometric abstraction, associated with Galerie Denise René. That situation changed on April 28. That Monday evening, Christo attended a bizarre opening. Between 9:00 p.m. and midnight, several thousand curious onlookers milled about the tiny Galerie Iris Clert. Numerous celebrities, artists, and writers were enticed by an enigmatic invitation that arrived in a blue envelope bearing a blue stamp. The brief text printed in blue script had been written by Pierre Restany, a young critic soon to play a significant role in Christo's life. The exhibition, titled "The Void," was a quasi-theatrical event staged by Yves Klein. Klein had painted the large street-level window a deep ultramarine blue, known as "International Klein Blue," or I.K.B. Swept along with the crowd, Christo elbowed his way into the building under a newly installed blue canopy, beneath which were stationed two deadpan Republican Guardsmen in full regalia. The walls of the gallery were bare. Visitors sipped blue cocktails in a jammed corridor leading to the gallery as groups of ten were organized to enter the small space for a brief time.

The opening of "The Void" resounded with heated arguments, nervous laughter, and sarcastic comments about the merit of Klein's work. Much of the hostile reaction found expression in the gallery guest book. More restrained critics accused Klein of simply rehashing Dada. Some saw the event as a manifestation of the existential predicament. Detractors viewed it as a nihilistic hoax. Christo felt that the carefully planned theatrical pageantry surrounding the show distracted from the audacious concept of bare walls on exhibit.

With the art world still buzzing about Klein's irreverent antics, Anna Staritsky visited Christo's rue Saint-Senoch studio in early May 1958. She arrived with no idea of what kind of work her friend's son produced, and she grew increasingly annoyed as she climbed the six flights of stairs leading to the former maid's room. Even more upsetting were Christo's thickly encrusted paintings and equally depressing wrapped objects. Everything in the studio violated the conventions of traditional easel painting. She implored Christo to learn more about art and avoid the frivolous doings in the Parisian art world. He listened quietly to a diatribe on Klein's "so-called art" and everything wrong with the contemporary art scene, until finally, mercifully, she stopped, knowing her reprimands were pointless. The only constructive suggestion she could muster was to tell him to contact a less hostile person. She grimaced, pointed disdainfully at a wrapped object, and said, "Try Pierre Restany; he thinks like that." She provided him with the critic's address, offering the one glimmer of light in an otherwise-dismal meeting, the last between the two artists. It was four months before Christo could lure Restany to his studio.

Lourdes Castro and René Bertholo were more sympathetic than Staritsky, although probably no less confused by much of what they saw. Lourdes recalled that Christo "used cans to mix colors—gray, brown, and much black, including thick ink mixed with sand."[1] She and René soon acclimated to the strange objects wrapped in canvas and encased beneath a textural glue and varnish patina.

During the last week of May 1958, Christo watched in amazement as armed troops took positions along the Champs Elysées. Like painted toy soldiers, they also stood in silence at other key intersections throughout Paris. "There was an incredible excitement in the city," he recalled. The unsettling maneuvers were the latest manifestations of a crisis that had begun in Algiers on May 13 when a coalition of right-wing settlers and disgruntled French army officers launched an insurrection. For Christo, the uneasy events of mid-1958 overshadowed other concerns. "It was very frightening," he recalled. The unfolding action offered a chilling reminder of the totalitarian atmosphere he had left behind. Abruptly, all of Paris seemed gripped by fear of a coup d'état; most conversation focused on a person Jean-Paul Sartre disparagingly called "the interminable man": Gen. Charles de Gaulle.[2] His towering figure had reemerged after years of seclusion. A succession of chronically weak governments paralyzed by factional politics had brought France to the brink of civil war and anarchy. Inflationary pressures and the forty-two-month-old Algerian war were bleeding the divided, near-bankrupt nation at a rate of 1 billion francs a day.

Christo kept abreast of the fast-changing developments while still trying to concentrate on his work. Christo moved out of his Rue Quentin Bauchart maid's room. His new residence was another maid's room on Place des Etats Unis. His explorations intensified, and the gesture of wrapping became a central obsession. Christo had an astonishing capacity for sustained work, a seamless activity sustained and energized by internal and external forces. On the surface, the results of his labor seemed to evolve from a Dada or Surrealist framework. On the contrary, however, his proliferating *Inventory* offered a new formulation, one rich in dark, haunting, starkly familiar images. For the moment, classification seemed unnecessary. With its roots nourished in Bulgarian soil and pollinated in the West, each wrapped object appeared strangely impenetrable.

With the onset of summer and the traditional exodus from Paris, Christo's only way of earning a living required bringing his craft to the country homes of wealthy clients. In late June and early July, he painted portraits for friends and relatives of his first French landlord, Countess Jeanne de Cabarusse. His friend René Bertholo observed, "He managed to live by making very realistic portraits, but with an indefinable something that made them interesting."

Christo gratefully accepted the Rosenkranzes' invitation to spend a few weeks in Wuppertal, Germany. He took two small wrapped *Inventory* pieces as gifts. Edith and Dieter introduced him to a lively art milieu. Dieter recalled, "It was a very important time for him and a great time in Cologne."[3]

Edith and Dieter had many artist friends, one of whom was Mary Bauermeister. She was to become known for her rhythmic assemblages of smooth pebbles and her enigmatic boxes containing various lenses. The latter appeared to descend from Marcel Duchamp's *To Be Looked at with One Eye, Close to, for Almost an Hour.*[4] Her compulsive enclosures often incorporated drawing, words, and images that shifted as the viewer moved or changed focus. Edith and Dieter took Christo to Bauermeister's Cologne studio, where she frequently organized avant-garde events. Most, if not all, of Bauermeister's guests were committed to prodding or overturning the status quo in music, theater, or the visual arts. Christo developed an immediate rapport with Karlheinz Stockhausen, who, at thirty, already approached legendary status in vanguard music circles for his modernist compositions and theories. Christo met the soft-spoken American pioneer composer and provocateur John Cage. His innovations utilizing chance procedures and new techniques inspired a variety of artists. Bauermeister credited Cage with reviving Duchamp's spirit in the late 1950s and early 1960s in Europe.[5] In the United States, Cage had already influenced the early work of Jasper Johns and Robert Rauschenberg; and, after being motivated by Cage's teaching in New York, Allan Kaprow was at that time introducing the genre he called Happenings. Christo also met pianist David Tudor, Cage's associate since 1952, as well as Nam June Paik, a young Korean artist working at a Cologne electronic-music studio and attending Darmstadt summer courses.

On this trip, Christo developed a lasting friendship with Joseph Beuys. Fourteen years Christo's senior, destined to become a cult figure in contemporary art, this then-unknown artist offered kindness and support. Christo also met three emerging artists: Heinz Mack and Otto Piene, founders of Group Zero in Düsseldorf, and Günther Uecker, who later joined the group. The Rosenkranzes' brisk itinerary included Georges Mathieu's exhibition mounted by Alfred Schmela, a relatively new yet important dealer in avant-garde art. Christo's whirlwind days brought him to studios, galleries, museums, private collections, and, invited by Stockhausen, a lively few days at the Darmstadt Music Festival. By 1958, Darmstadt's summer events had become the preeminent international forum for the most advanced forms of contemporary music. Experimentation and radical concepts engaged Christo at every turn. He saw Lucio Fontana's work for the first time. The controlled destruction in Fontana's austere punctured or slashed canvases impressed him. The work also enticed John Cage. In 1958, he composed *Fontana Mix,* "a) a score for the production of 1 or more tape track(s) or for any kind and number of instruments(s), or b) prerecorded tape material to be performed in any way."[6] Clearly, provocations aimed at a tired system were not confined to Paris.

In mid-August, Christo decided to return to Paris by way of Belgium. A brief stopover in Brussels allowed him to see the much-heralded Expo '58, the world's fair that had opened in April. He became one of over 40 million visitors to the carnivalesque extravaganza, an event unlike any he had ever seen. The dramatic centerpiece of activity was the glittering Atomium, an iron crystal re-created as a silvery metallic structure 200,000 times actual size. The pavilions of fifty-one nations branched out from it in a sprawling orgy of capitalist diversity. Only two exhibits provided lasting memories. One, an impressive Belgian display, featured a selection of central African sculpture and artifacts; previously, Christo had seen only reproductions of tribal art.

The other memorable experience occurred at the United States Pavilion. There, he encountered *The Americans,* an imposing mural by another East European immigrant, Saul Steinberg. This immense work, drawn, painted, and collaged on a series of ten-foot-high panels was over 240 feet wide. It presented a vast panorama of American life in eight separate thematic sections. He captured a uniquely American quality in lighthearted, boldly graphic subject matter, including trailer camps, shopping center, billboards, motels, hillbillies, comic-strip culture, brash ponytailed young women in blue jeans, long-legged farmers and railway workers, small-town main streets and drugstores, big-city cocktail parties, and more. His use of collage elements such as a Harry Truman shirt, cigarette packaging, and cut or torn pages of comic strips provided a foretaste of Pop Art. Most of Steinberg's zany figures were constructed from ordinary brown wrapping paper, a material that Christo would use years later. Steinberg's whimsical labyrinth of playfully exaggerated stereotypes included a work called *Good and Bad Cowboys,* which appealed to Christo's long-standing fascination with the Wild West. Steinberg's portrayal revealed a gigantic land of leisure. Seeing this imaginative depiction of a quirky, distant civilization, along with several recent Hollywood films, intensified Christo's interest in America.

Christo returned to an uneasy Paris. On August 28, a citywide police dragnet rounded up almost three thousand Algerians. It seemed nothing could stop the divisive Algerian war from dragging on. One month after Christo returned to France, 80 percent of the population voted to approve de Gaulle's model for the Fifth Republic.

Christo studied the changing times like a sailor watching the winds in his sails. Still a displaced person coming to terms with Western society and its uncertain crosscurrents, he found his vulnerability demanded alertness. The stimulating antiestablishment concepts of Klein, Cage, Stockhausen, and other radical artists gave impetus to Christo's continuing process of self-creation.

The time had come to give shape to his own private mythology, to begin disturbing the peace. Christo resumed work with renewed intensity. He knew that labor alone would not be enough; to have any impact, he desperately needed a dealer or critic to present his art and articulate his position as an artist. That September, a long-awaited potential supporter arrived at the studio.

Christo remembered the silhouette of twenty-eight-year-old Pierre Restany in the doorway of his small studio. Thin, clean-shaven, and poker-faced, Restany looked more like the quintessential bureaucrat than a fervent missionary. But he had recently separated from his wife and left a secure government job because writing part-time about art no longer satisfied him; it had become a total obsession. Restany was determined to champion an art that few others were willing or able to recognize as the most relevant expression of the time. He had already written a book about the Paris School, *Lyrical Abstraction*. Timely connections with Klein, Jean Tinguely, Arman, and others soon placed Restany in the powerful position of spokesman for a generation of postwar artists. Within a few years, Restany and his new companion, Jeanine de Goldschmidt, were to open a gallery devoted to avant-garde art.

Anna Staritsky's recommendation had aroused Restany's curiosity. He recalled visiting Christo's studio: "I saw some high reliefs, a little like Dubuffet, and the first heavily pasted, wrapped objects."[7] Restany became intrigued by *Inventory* and the gesture of wrapping. The work resisted simple explanation. Could this strange imagery be deciphered, and could it fit into some grand design? Restany later reflected, "I was very much attracted to the man, not only because of what he was doing, but by his exact vision." With a mixture of poor French and richly expressive gestures, Christo implored Restany to help arrange an exhibition and perhaps write about his work. His pleas seemed refreshingly direct. The young artist's intense visual statement more than compensated for his difficulty at expressing himself with words. Restany responded with cautious encouragement. A friendship developed that was to bring Christo both hope and bitter disappointment. The incredibly competitive, often Machiavellian Parisian art world was rife with severed relationships, and Restany had his own agenda. Eventually, Christo found that the best way of avoiding the intrigue and distasteful politics associated with the gallery system would be to create his own set of rules.

Chance or perhaps fate guided Christo to the Latin Quarter on a sunny afternoon in early October 1958. He had come to meet an affluent new client, Précilda de Guillebon. On her last visit to René Bourgeois's salon, she had seen portraits by a young man described as "a penniless Bulgarian with great talent."[8] Précilda eagerly arranged an appointment.

A uniformed cadet at the Ecole Polytechnique escorted Christo to the main entrance of Pavillion Boncourt, the Guillebon family residence, a lavishly appointed three-story Louis XVI building. An impeccably attired army officer led Christo to the second floor and ushered him into an enormous living room, where he saw three seated women. Attractive, thirty-nine-year-old Madame de Guillebon rose to greet him. Précilda later described Christo as cultivated, quick to smile, and effortlessly ingratiating in manner. "When he extended his hand to me he looked so noble."[9] His brown eyes sparkled with a smile of their own. She introduced the unusual visitor to Jeanne-Claude and Isabelle de Hauteclocque. The two young women smiled politely, said hello, then withdrew to Jeanne-Claude's bedroom, giggling.

First impressions are forceful and fickle. Christo could not miss Jeanne-Claude's blue eyes and commanding presence. "She was very French and very beautiful in a blue dress," Christo said later. Her fleeting, aloof glance had revealed the social gulf between them. He said, "It was very strange because I felt so nonexistent." In the future, Jeanne-Claude would say, "My life began when I met Christo," but her initial reaction hardly reflected that assessment. In the privacy of her bedroom, she quipped to Isabelle, "That man is obviously homosexual. He has long, thin hands and is so skinny, and he is an artist." Hardly love at first sight. That afternoon, while Précilda posed for Christo, Jeanne-Claude approached Jacques and wisecracked, "Look, Papa, Mama brought home a dog without a leash."[10] That evening, she repeated her unfounded explication of Christo's sexual preference. The gratuitous cruelty ignited Précilda's anger. She reprimanded Jeanne-Claude and told her how little she knew about men. Précilda announced that Christo would be returning regularly to do other family portraits, and she demanded that her daughter display greater respect in the future.

Several months before Christo arrived in her life, Jeanne-Claude had attended the debutante's ball at Versailles. She had been escorted there not by one dashing officer but by a troupe of five, among whom was Patrick Peugeot, "the curly-haired, bespectacled, aristocratic heir to the automobile fortune."An August 1958 magazine photograph shows her happily dancing a bebop or cha-cha, reaching out for the anonymous hand of one of her companions. Jeanne-Claude is seen smiling, wearing white flowers in her hair and a ruffled white lace Christian Dior dress. She had a date or party almost every evening. Handsome young officers anxious to please and well-heeled men from business and society were part of an ongoing parade of eligible bachelors seeking her favor. Jeanne-Claude's life of pleasure unfolded with secure predictability. No wonder she viewed Christo as a deviant.

The ongoing parade of friends and dignitaries visiting the Guillebon family would have impressed anyone. Christo remembered the beautiful Madame de Guillebon and her debonair husband presiding at gatherings of their guests. "The general was very dignified, very important. There were always officers

Ecole Polytechnique, Paris, 1958: Jeanne-Claude spending an evening with some cadets. (Photo: Archive XTO+J-C)

saluting, clicking heels, and all those politicians and ministers coming and going." The illustrious procession included cabinet members, ambassadors, high-ranking military personnel, scientists, writers, show-business celebrities, and industrialists—in short, no one ordinary.

Précilda kept the young artist busy. She knew that commissions were his only source of desperately needed income. After he completed a second painting of Précilda, Jeanne-Claude became his next subject. She posed for a formal portrait in the garden behind the family residence. This time, they talked and gently studied each other. She had never met an artist. Her initial naïve aversion to Christo's fragility, heavily accented speech, and vocation underwent rapid transformation. The reversal in attitude had little to do with her mother's stern counsel and everything to do with Christo. The strained atmosphere that had separated them dissolved. His unpretentious tenor struck her as genuinely charming and refreshingly honest. To her delight, Jeanne-Claude discovered that they shared the same birth date. Best of all, she had found a trusted friend. Christo later recalled her beaming face: "I remember she smiled and laughed all the time." Her unreserved good humor was exactly what he needed.

In the course of painting their portraits, Christo endeared himself to the Guillebon family. His frequent visits quickly became anticipated events. He soon found himself treated as a member of the family. Précilda recalled, "He was very proud. At first he refused my invitation to lunch. I said, 'Christo, I'm not asking to please you; it is for my pleasure.' Finally, he smiled and consented. A few days later, he was like a son."[11] If Précilda had found a son, Jeanne-Claude had found a brother, and Christo a surrogate family. Before long, he began sharing daily meals with them. Coaxed by his wife, the general provided Christo with a large light-filled studio room on the top floor.

Précilda decided to help Christo financially by arranging for steady work. In the months ahead, he completed three portraits of Précilda painted in successively, classic, Impressionistic, and Cubist styles, two of Jacques—one in uniform and another in a beige velvet jacket—and studies of the children and several family friends. His artistic ability, sensitivity, and intellect impressed everyone. Previously, the family had not given much thought to art. They lived in an architectural landmark, but aesthetic considerations were of little consequence to them. Christo offered to introduce Jeanne-Claude to an unfamiliar world. She cautiously accepted. He began a systematic educational program, starting by guiding her through the Louvre. For several days, as if following a curriculum, he discussed ancient, Renaissance, and modern masters. Before they approached recent twentieth-century painting and sculpture, Christo traced relationships between works of art to show an evolutionary process. Jeanne-Claude asked to see his studio. "Not yet," he said.

Their friendship grew stronger. Each deliberate step in Jeanne-Claude's art education proceeded at the intervals permitted by her fast-paced social life and Christo's busy work schedule. She enjoyed teaching him French, sometimes mocking his thick Bulgarian accent. He, in turn, introduced her to serious theater.

In the winter of 1958, Christo moved out of his room on Place des Etats Unis and rented a one-room bachelor's apartment on the Ile Saint Louis that belonged to Robert Cointreau, the son of owner of the Cointreau liquor distilleries. Situated on the Seine, connected by bridges to the Right and Left banks and the Ile de la Cité, the picturesque Ile Saint Louis was only a short walk from the Ecole Polytechnique. Two massive old wood doors led into an inner courtyard at Christo's new residence, a rectangular furnished room one floor above the narrow street. A single window on the wall adjacent to the entry door provided a view of the courtyard. It seemed luxurious, with both a toilet inside the room and, unbelievably, a telephone. He said, "To have a telephone in Paris in the late 1950s was a miracle. You needed to wait ten years or be a prime minister to get a telephone." A signed Picasso etching hung incongruously alongside examples of his own work. Christo had purchased the exquisite *Vollard Suite* print several months earlier at Berggruen Gallery for the equivalent of a few hundred dollars, paying for it in installments. It was an incredible extravagance.

On November 21, Christo wrote to Anani. He confessed to having no "big love" in his life. He mentioned a letter from Ida, an attractive Italian blonde with green eyes, but he characterized his relationships with women during the past two years as friendly, not passionate. "I always have girlfriends who are very warm and sensible, not only in France, but in Switzerland and

Italy. They are also intriguing and extremely pretty. Tomorrow I will be at Jeanne-Claude's. . . . She is like an ancient, beautiful Persian, a fantastic, true Scheherazade."[12]

January 1959 marked the second anniversary of Christo's defection. Periods of moody introspection alternated with exhilaration as Western notions became increasingly familiar. After two years of Bulgarian self-denial, he felt a compulsion to immerse himself in artistic events and to assimilate the urgent realities of contemporary existence. Christo's letters to Anani continued to record his cultural calendar in Paris. He wrote, "The days are full, then mad dashing to exhibitions and in the evenings theater, ballet, opera, and concerts." His goal remained "to realize a rich, dynamic work" of his own, "to demolish any traditionalism. . . . [My work] must come through as avant-garde, expressing the new thought and feeling."[13] Even before arriving in Paris, Christo had acquired an addiction for the latest news. Decades later, his studio would resound with the repetitive patter of New York's round-the-clock radio-news stations.[14]

On January 8, 1959, the French media focused on Charles de Gaulle's installation as president of the Fifth Republic. At the exact moment of his investiture, a twenty-one-cannon salute bellowed into the cool, sunny sky over the Seine. De Gaulle was granted more authority than any French head of state since Napoleon III. Civil war and anarchy had been averted, but the overriding question of Algeria's fate remained unanswered.

The art world turned its attention to a midwinter exhibition of Maurice Utrillo's work at Galerie Charpentier. The retrospective consisted of Utrillo's various depictions of Sacré-Coeur and the streets of Montmartre. The familiar imagery attracted public and critical acclaim. However, it was not this saccharine display that captured Christo's imagination, but two shows at the Musée National d'Art Moderne: "The New American Painting" and "Jackson Pollock," linked in spirit and by a joint catalog, opened simultaneously on January 16.

"The New American Painting," organized by the International Council of the Museum of Modern Art in New York, had premiered nine months earlier in Basel. It offered Christo an introduction to works by Willem de Kooning, Robert Motherwell, Mark Rothko, and other emerging Abstract Expressionists. The second show served as a memorial to Pollock, who had died in 1956. Over fifty of his canvases were testimony to dramatic change. The sheer size of the work impressed Christo. He said, "I remember the Pollocks very well. I even remember the room where *Blue Poles* hung. It was not so much the painting, an extremely relaxed painting, but the physicality of the canvas. I loved it. The most attractive part of this American art was an airy dimension that came from the space, the emptiness, and probably some kind of nonchalance. It looked very beautiful, very exciting, very strange, and unique." In a letter to Anani, Christo raved about both shows, quoting many of the artists. Their work and words exemplified freedom. Few European observers suspected that the exhibitions marked the beginning of a gradual yet decisive shift of the art world's capital to New York. Within five years, the image of Paris as the dynamic center of international art would be shattered.

Also in January 1959, Christo went to the opening of Jasper Johns's first one-man show in Paris, an unheralded event at Galerie Rive Droite. Johns, who had made a big splash in New York the previous year, represented a new generation. His work marked a conscious break from Abstract Expressionism and offered further evidence of the emergence of a distinctly American art. "I liked it very much," Christo recalled. Pierre Restany had written a brief text for the catalog. The enigmatic, concentrated work—a coat hanger, flags, numbers, each on a flattened picture plane—fascinated Christo.

Christo studied each new exhibition zealously. In becoming conversant with modern masters, he learned to distinguish between innovative and derivative work. The intoxicating process of self-education peaked when an audacious presentation arrived on the scene: Jean Tinguely's 1959 show at Galerie Iris Clert. The thirty-four-year-old Swiss-born kinetic artist exhibited a group of coin-operated machines that created gestural paintings. His lighthearted devices not only utilized motion but embraced the element of chance. Tinguely observed, "The only stable thing is movement. Life is movement, life is perpetual change. . . . The moment life becomes fixed it stops being real."[15]

Christo found the "Eighth International Exhibition of Surrealism" equally stimulating, calling it "the last Surrealist show." Seventy-five artists were represented by work related to the theme of eroticism. Another memorable 1959 show was "The Sources of Twentieth-Century Art," organized by Minister of Culture André Malraux. Christo said, "It was one of the most exciting exhibitions in Paris: a huge exhibit, very beautifully mounted, of not only art but industrial design and architecture. It was incredible . . . something I had never been confronted with."

Paris continued to provide an ideal setting for Jeanne-Claude's parties, receptions, card games, and tennis matches—for dancing and sleeping late. Her carousel of pleasure ceased only on Sunday, when the family routinely went to church. Years later, she was to reflect, "I was a society girl doing nothing, absolutely nothing. I was totally useless." Despite her seemingly enviable lifestyle, Jeanne-Claude felt restless and unfulfilled. She had wanted a job for some time. After almost a year of protracted arguments, Jeanne-Claude finally received begrudging consent to pursue a respectable salaried position. She had her heart set on becoming an airline stewardess. Even though Précilda shuddered at the demeaning thought of any Guillebon serving as "a maid in the sky," Jeanne-Claude began working for Air France in April 1959.

At twenty-three, she entered a new phase of her life. She gladly shed her privileged standing as the general's daughter for the role of working woman. "I loved it," she recalled. "While I was earning pocket money the other people were earning their bread and butter. That taught me a lot." She had little time to ponder the glamour and excitement of her job. New stewardesses were usually assigned various African itineraries. Jeanne-Claude's route included stops in Dakar, Lagos, and Brazzaville. These tortuous flights took more than twenty hours on a narrow, crowded propeller aircraft and required her to provide meal service between each city. Jeanne-Claude's Air France job represented a small step toward independence. During the remainder of 1959, she continued to undergo radical change. Her years of partying would soon end.

Joyce May Alazrachi's life in Casablanca seemed full of promise. By 1959, Précilda's second child, Jeanne-Claude's half sister, had blossomed into an attractive nineteen-year-old; she was five feet three and had dark brown hair and lively hazel eyes. Montie Alazrachi had remained a loving, perhaps overly protective father since Précilda and he had divorced. He saw to it that Joyce received a private education; she became fluent in English, French, and Spanish and excelled in music. She began playing the piano at seven, studied voice at sixteen, and attended the conservatory of music in Casablanca.

Joyce saw Précilda for only a few days every two or three years. Joyce recalled, "My father always got angry when my aunt brought letters and photos from my mother. He feared losing me and said he was terrified that Mama would have me kidnapped. I was happy to have the photos. My father knew that I had this enormous pull toward her."[16] One day, Montie saw Joyce moping about with a distant look in her eyes, and he asked, "Are you thinking about your mother?" She nodded yes. He said, "Do you want to see her?" She replied, "I'd like to." A recent letter from Précilda had suggested that Joyce live with her for a year, continuing her music studies in Paris. Montie loved his daughter enough to let her go.

In early May 1959, Joyce Alazrachi arrived in Paris full of dreams. With Jeanne-Claude preoccupied by an entourage of suitors and often absent because of her job, Joyce quickly became an important part of the household and the family lavished attention on her. The sudden transition from Casablanca's protective environment to the breathtaking social swirl engulfing the Guillebon family could not have been more dramatic.

Joyce quickly felt at home with the family. Précilda introduced Christo as a sort of adopted son, and Jeanne-Claude referred to him in a brotherly manner. "At first, I couldn't figure out a word he said," Joyce recalled. "But he was so charming. I was impressed by his manners, education, and warmth." Joyce and Christo soon became friends. She admired his intelligence and commitment to art. "He would talk about everything from opera to politics, always on top of things and extremely erudite. I was also impressed by how firm he could be when he wanted to work. If there was a social event and Mother insisted that he come, Christo would say, 'No, no, I must do my work.'"

Joyce adjusted to scurrying military servants, adhered to unfamiliar protocols, and survived the scrutiny of keen observers. Comparisons with Jeanne-Claude were inevitable. Reserved, introspective, plainspoken, Joyce appeared less flighty, less pretentious, far less spoiled, and much more independent than her estranged half sister. At first, they were strangers, having only a mother in common. Gradually, they discovered common responses and shared quirks. Before long, the strangers became friends. "We were giggling all night," Jeanne-Claude recalled.

High-spirited and feisty, with a host of young men in pursuit, Jeanne-Claude had much to be giddy about. Her latest devotee was Philippe Planchon, a handsome thirty-four-year-old engineer who had met her at a *soirée littéraire* hosted by a mutual friend. Philippe joined Jeanne-Claude's entourage of captivated sweethearts. Their slow-developing relationship might best be described as unadventurous. He played tennis with her and participated in the Guillebon's after-dinner bridge games. Philippe excelled in both endeavors, yet Précilda and Jacques were lukewarm about their daughter's latest lovesick companion. He had only modest means, was lackluster, and lacked impressive accomplishments or significant potential. The best they could say about Planchon was, "He is a solid citizen." Even gregarious, brotherly Christo found it difficult to relate to Jeanne-Claude's new boyfriend. "She was going out with many handsome men before Philippe Planchon," Christo said, "but he was much older. He was very serious, very proper, very handsome." But for the moment, he remained one of many admirers.

On May 14, 1959, barely settled into Paris, Joyce celebrated her twentieth birthday. Précilda commissioned Christo to paint a portrait to mark the occasion. The Renoiresque painting depicted Joyce in a green dress against a pastel background. Précilda liked it so much that she decided to keep it, telling Joyce that she could have it on her twenty-first birthday. Christo immediately offered to do another portrait as *his* birthday gift. Joyce was overwhelmed.

Joyce found that Christo's observations were consistently honest and insightful. She recalled, "He thought that Jeanne-Claude had the most wonderful asymmetric face. Every face is, but he saw hers as particularly asymmetric and fascinating." Christo and Joyce became close friends. They talked and went for walks. Both were guileless, dedicated to their respective artistic careers, and far from home.

Christo told her about his latest venture. Lourdes Castro and René Bertholo had introduced him to printmaking. Working in their home, he created a five-by-nine-inch print, which appeared in the May 1959 issue of Castro and Bertholo's *KWY*. Produced on a shoestring budget, the publication featured graphics, occasional essays, and poems. The fourth issue of the quarterly contained Christo's first contribution, mistakenly credited on the title page to "Christo Gavacheff," as well as a lithograph and silk screen by Jan Voss, a twenty-two-year-old German artist who was to become one of Christo's closest friends. In addition, there were original serigraphs by Castro, Bertholo, and two other Portuguese artists, Costa Pinheiro and Viera da Silva.

Christo's spattered small black-and-white abstract image left Joyce at a loss for words. His assertion that painting portraits amounted to little more than prostitution only added to her confusion. She had little experience with the visual arts and was unprepared for what she encountered during a subsequent visit to his studio. After climbing six flights of stairs, Joyce saw, she said, "canvases with spots and drips of paint," wrapped cans, and bottles. Joyce recalled Christo's absorption with the *Inventory* pieces: "He really looked at them. I was confused. I tried to understand, but I didn't know what questions to ask. If I had seen that work without seeing his enthusiasm and the intensity on his face, I might not have been convinced he was doing something worthwhile."

Jeanne-Claude had visited Christo's studio several months earlier. He introduced her to Castro, Bertholo, and Voss. At first, this unglamorous milieu of impoverished artists who lived in small rooms puzzled her. "Christo took me to his little maid's room studio at the other end of Paris," she later recalled. "I reluctantly went in and said, 'My God, what is that?' He showed me his art. I said, 'I don't think you can explain it, but go ahead and try.' After seeing some avant-garde galleries with him, I felt more comfortable. I knew he wasn't the only insane person on this planet. I laughed and said, 'You're crazy, but so what. You're a nice guy and paint beautiful portraits.' He told me that painting portraits paid the rent and kept him alive. Even then he talked about *revealing an object by concealing it,* about using fabric, fragility, and the temporary nature of things in a civilization where packaging means so much. Slowly, I understood."

By late May 1959, Jeanne-Claude was becoming aware that there was more to life than having a good time. She had exuberance but no direction. Unlike Jeanne-Claude, Joyce had clearly defined goals. Recalling the frantic rush of fascinating people at Pavillion Boncourt, she said, "It was beautifully social, but I really wanted to get into music, to attend opera, ballet, concerts, and plays." Joyce's transparent, familiar longings prompted Christo to invite her to the opera. She happily accepted. At considerable expense, he purchased excellent orchestra seats for *Rigoletto*. The gesture touched her. After that evening, they went out occasionally. Joyce was flattered by Christo's attention. He also took her to see a performance by Marcel Marceau. It proved to be an enchanting, memorable experience. "That night it was absolutely pouring, Christo held the umbrella and held me close to keep me dry. He was so sweet. That's when I started getting very interested in him," Joyce remarked years later.

June 1959 proved fateful for both Joyce and Jeanne-Claude. Philippe Planchon paid a formal visit to Jacques de Guillebon's office at the Ecole Polytechnique. In an all-too-familiar scene, he revealed his intentions toward Jeanne-Claude and asked for the general's blessing. Jacques reluctantly consented. She said, "I thought he was perfect. At twenty-four, I felt like an old maid. I had to be serious now because if I didn't marry, I would probably be too old for any man to ever want me again." Précilda begrudgingly approved the planned union. That did not stop her from grumbling about it, however.

Joyce's independent behavior also irritated Précilda; it seemed more like disrespect than an expression of a free spirit. The friction came to a head one June weekend. Joyce's paternal grandmother happened to be visiting Joyce's father's oldest sister in Paris. For several days, Joyce left early and returned late, without joining the Guillebons for meals or Sunday church services. She had appointments with friends, a dinner date, a concert, a luncheon with her grandmother, and other preoccupations—all without her mother's permission. Over breakfast on Monday, Joyce tried to explain her busy weekend. Précilda listened with icy disdain. Then she lashed out, saying, "I hope you are enjoying our hotel-restaurant." Joyce felt humiliated and believed that she had to choose between unquestioning obedience and the bitter consequences of independence. She left. The falling-out proved devastating. It would be more than a year before they spoke again.

Christo knew that his intervention would be futile. He continued to visit the Guillebons regularly, but he also stayed in touch with Joyce. She needed his friendship more than ever now. "Christo felt sorry for me," Joyce said. "I had been a sort of fifth wheel in my mother's family. He became protective toward me, and even more so after the split-up." Friendship, compassion, and also physical attraction and a shared sense of dislocation led Christo to spend more time with her. "I thought he was wonderful," Joyce commented. In the privacy of his small room, their warm relationship blossomed into passion. During the next few weeks, 24 rue Saint-Louis-en-l'Ile became the site of their secluded rendezvous. At the time, Jeanne-Claude had no idea that they were lovers; she had left her Air France job and was busy with marriage preparations. Joyce told her just part of the story; "I mentioned going out now and then with Christo but didn't see any point in telling her more. I knew she would repeat things to mother." Years later, Jeanne-Claude joked about the liaison, saying, "They didn't go out; they only went in."

Joyce posed for a number of drawings. At various times Christo gave her several sketches, copies of *KWY*, a scarf, a necklace, and a tiny handmade booklet filled with his drip and spatter paintings. Each small page contained a signed abstract composition with a dedication. "They were really an offering, a piece of himself," she said. These miniature works reflected his continuing fascination with textural surfaces, Dubuffet, Pollock, and the American Color Field painters. He had also seen Sam Francis's splashy paintings and Arman's work, which at the time had an abstract overall flow akin to field painting. Christo spoke enthusiastically about his friends Bertholo, Castro, and Voss, but Joyce never met them. Immersed in studying music, she had neither the time nor the inclination to come to grips with the unfathomable complexities of modern art.

Their brief romance ended abruptly. Joyce recalled the scene at his studio: "He used to tease me about a beautiful woman who posed for him. That day, I was in a rotten mood and got very upset, very undignified. He had given me a pretty silk scarf. I ripped it and threw it at him. I got very upset and just stomped out."

In Joyce's mind, the affair had ended. At the same time, whatever glowing possibilities Paris promised faded in a chill of unfulfilled expectations. That July, she flew back to the physical and emotional warmth of life in North Africa. Then she learned that Montie had recently been operated on for cancer, a disease that had killed his father at the same age. He and Joyce were told that the operation had been a complete success. In fact, Montie had another operation to endure and just over a year to live.

Throughout the summer of 1959, Christo sent Joyce affectionate letters and postcards. She never answered. During their separation, his routine remained unchanged: long hours working in the studio, searching for a dealer, writer, or collector who would help him arrange an exhibition, attending art events, and painting portraits to pay the bills. He continued to feel close to the Guillebon family, all the while hoping that one of their influential friends might assist him in finding a gallery. One friend, Henri Rustin, commissioned Christo to paint his portrait, then asked to visit the studio. Putting aside his misgivings about modern art, he later purchased several pieces. Rustin's generosity led everyone to call him "Santa Claus." Christo said of him, "He was a typical Russian soul, with all these problems, and I really loved him."

The family spent most of their summers at Essertaux, the family's château in Picardy. During the vacation, friends were invited for less formal visits. Précilda arranged several portrait jobs for Christo and also hired him to paint a portrait of the castle. In the summer of 1959, Essertaux looked its well-

Paris, 1959: Jeanne-Claude with General Charles de Gaulle in her parents' home.
(Photo: Ecole Polytechnique)

groomed best. The lawns, trees, and gardens were resplendent. However, the pastoral setting scarcely distracted Jacques from the smoldering situation in France and North Africa. The general received a steady flow of reports about the unfolding Algerian tragedy. Jacques made no secret of his opposition to the savage war. He favored reconciliation, as he had with respect to Tunisia. His moderate stance pitted him against a hard-line military power structure.

Several times during the summer of 1959, de Gaulle summoned Jacques to his office, knowing that Jacques could be counted on to speak honestly. No officer spoke more candidly about the questionable tactics and unclear goals of the military. Jacques argued for independence, counseling that unless Algeria gained its freedom, as had neighboring Tunisia and Morocco, the undeclared war might last for generations.

During one of their talks, de Gaulle asked Guillebon to assume command of the Constantine sector of Algeria. Jacques refused. He, too, was a proud man, unwilling to take an ill-defined job with less responsibility and initiative than he had previously enjoyed in Tunisia. Jacques told de Gaulle that the only way he could accept the Constantine assignment would be with specific written instructions regarding the ultimate objective. According to Joyce, he said, "If you want to keep Algeria French, I know how to fight. If you want an independent state, I know how to do that, too, but I won't go without written orders." De Gaulle was not yet ready to clarify his intentions, however.

Jacques had not anticipated the painful outcome that rejecting de Gaulle's request would necessitate. In one of the most difficult moments in a long career, he composed a letter of resignation. Several days later, de Gaulle returned it. It was sent back and forth for over a month, leaving the matter unresolved. While de Gaulle pondered his next move, Jacques's pride and principles were on the line.

In July 1959, with her wedding less than a month away, Jeanne-Claude occupied herself with domestic chores at Essertaux. Christo continued making portraits, which began to fill the château's walls. Among them were paintings of Précilda, Jacques, the children, a Fauvist-like depiction of Jeanne-Claude with long, wavy hair, and a brooding Cubist self-portrait. One Sunday, Jeanne-Claude went to pick up some fresh bread in the next village. Christo joined her for the drive. This errand marked a turning point in their lives. They were in high spirits that pleasantly warm morning. As they drove, Christo impulsively made advances, fondling her. Unable both to hold him off and continue driving, she pulled off the road. Then their repressed physical attraction exploded. Their exuberant first kiss broke one of Christo's teeth. Undeterred, the youthful lovers ecstatically embraced each other, and their fate. Jeanne-Claude thought of this amorous jaunt as a last fling. She later admitted, "I wasn't thinking, This is the man of my life. He had no money, a funny accent, and everything was wrong with him." And yet, everything felt right. As they drove back to Essertaux, Jeanne-Claude and Christo were unsure whether their passionate liaison would ever resume. It did. In fact, they continued meeting secretly until the time of her marriage.

Arrangements for Jeanne-Claude's August 11 wedding to Philippe Planchon proceeded on schedule. However, beneath her composed facade, the young woman who wanted luxuries and power felt unarticulated stirrings. She tried to sort out contradictory sensations. The potency of her illicit relationship with Christo raised troubling questions. Ironically, in contrast to her steamy relationship with Christo, her relationship with Philippe during the period of their engagement was marked by sexual abstinence. She and Christo knew that Précilda and Jacques accepted Christo as a son; however, the thought of him being intimate with their daughter would have been intolerable. Besides, Jeanne-Claude saw his work as a dominating, greedy mistress. In addition to these complications, Christo was due to leave for Corsica and Italy to paint some portraits that he had been commissioned to do. In late July, when he said good-bye to the household, everyone insisted that he return in time for the wedding.

Christo embarked on the long train and boat journey with no clue that his illicit relationship with Jeanne-Claude would ever represent more than a joyous interlude in his life. His goals were fixed; she had a very different agenda. If fate meant to unite them, its blueprint remained well disguised. He wrote to Joyce in Casablanca, asking her to join him in Corsica. She never answered.

After doing several portraits, Christo set out for Rome. Still uncertain about exactly what had caused their sudden breakup, Christo wrote to Joyce for the last time. His three sentences were written on a large "singing postcard" containing a 78-rpm recording of "Arrivederci Roma" impressed over a photograph of the Colosseum and the Arch of Constantine. Joyce saved the card, but their romance was beyond salvation. Christo had gone to Rome to meet Felician Brys, a former client and Belgian-born Swiss citizen who worked for the United Nations in Geneva. Brys had arranged a series of portrait commissions at his summer home in Sorrento. Christo returned to France several days before Jeanne-Claude's wedding, feeling, as he put it, "very, very disturbed."

Jeanne-Claude had grown accustomed to getting what she wanted, and she wanted Christo. Their compelling physical attraction had become almost irresistible. Just days before marriage vows and conventional expectations were to alter her carefree behavior, Jeanne-Claude and Christo resumed their secret liaison. "He was only for fun," she recalled. "Any rich woman, young or old, wants to treat herself to an artist. Then, after you've had your artist, you go back to real life. He was my artist. But he was a superb lover. That doomed me."

Jeanne-Claude's disregard for social taboos soon shocked even her best friend, Carole Weisweiller. Jeanne-Claude's plan to wed Philippe Planchon had surprised Carole. She later confessed, "My impression of him was zero. She halfheartedly tried to persuade me and herself that he was wonderful. I was not convinced." Carole suggested another reason for the marriage. "I think Jeanne-Claude wanted to escape her mother's influence. She wanted to be free. I remember at twenty she still could not choose a dress without asking, 'Mommy, what do you think?' Unfortunately, at that time she wanted to imitate her mother, to talk like her mother, to be as brilliant as her mother."[17]

On August 11, 1959, the Guillebon family prepared to attend the small civil ceremony customarily held the day before a French church wedding. Jeanne-Claude wore a matching white jacket and skirt. Précilda exploded at the last minute, imploring Jeanne-Claude not to go through with the marriage.

With an air of impending doom, she prophesied, "I know it won't last a year. If you want to do this stupid thing, go ahead and do it." Agitated and impetuous, she suddenly slapped Jeanne-Claude's face. The worst damage, caused by her mother's ring, was a bruised area beneath one of her eyes. By the time they arrived at city hall, Jeanne-Claude's cheek had become swollen and red. Précilda marched into the building and barked, "Goddamn it, where are we supposed to go in this damn mess?" As everyone arrived, Jeanne-Claude burst into tears. Philippe looked bewildered. Even though the formalities went smoothly, the Planchons were off to a bumpy start. The newlyweds returned to their respective homes until the next day when church services would formally unite them in wedlock.

On Wednesday, August 12, tensions eased in the Guillebon household. Précilda assumed the role of loving mother; her heartfelt affection replaced the cutting words and actions of the previous day. Jeanne-Claude emerged in apparent high spirits, wearing a white Christian Dior wedding gown, a single string of white pearls, white gloves, and white satin shoes. The family walked from the Ecole Polytechnique to a nearby church. En route, Jeanne-Claude's gown swirled, while her veil kept blowing skyward in gusts of wind. A young Jesuit priest conducted the ceremony as the couple knelt between two tall candles. A photograph shows Jeanne-Claude Marie Denat de Guillebon Planchon leaving the church, carrying flowers and looking somewhat confused.

Jeanne-Claude and Philippe honeymooned at Lallah Meryam, the Guillebon family's seaside home in southern Tunisia. It offered privacy and the luxury of several servants. They had a little more than two weeks and a lot to discover about each other. They landed in Tunis during a mid-August heat wave. The first night passed without lovemaking. The next evening's long-awaited sexual union failed to produce conjugal bliss. They were absolutely mismatched. Jeanne-Claude recalled the honeymoon fiasco: "I made love with Planchon twice in Tunisia. I knew right away I didn't love him. On that, I can be categoric. He was not for me, and I knew he didn't like it. Did I ask myself, What am I doing here when I could be in Christo's bed? I don't remember. But I'm sure that instinctively my entire body called out to Christo."

Two weeks in a Mediterranean paradise became an interminable time for the blandly unemotional husband and his spoiled, vivacious spouse. The marriage would be of shorter duration than their celibate three-month courtship. Philippe's subsequent divorce papers charged that she demonstrated "a totally inexplicable coldness" on the honeymoon. Also cited were her "unreasonable behavior," the fact that she had provoked "eccentric nervous scenes," and her demands for "total submission to the slightest whims."[18] Philippe had no idea how insurmountable his wife's expectations were. However attentive, there was no way he could supplant a lively throng of past admirers or her thoughts of Christo. Philippe projected the kind of solid, reliable image that might appeal to any security-conscious woman. But not Jeanne-Claude. She had a zest for living and an ill-defined dream. However unreasonable, she yearned for a soaring, heroic life, one worthy of her parents. The Planchons returned to Paris on the last weekend in August, suffering from a sobering overdose of each other.

Jeanne-Claude and Philippe moved into her tidy living quarters, which Précilda had arranged for them. The moment for Jeanne-Claude to attempt domestic life had finally arrived. It would be sincere and short-lived. She later recalled this time: "I was shopping and cooking. The first day, he came back from the office, opened the door, and said, 'Your hands smell from onion.' Later he told me that I couldn't have my own bank account. That was it! I exploded inside, I didn't say anything, but the next day when he left for work, I called a locksmith and changed the lock." Then she called Christo. Her precipitous actions were sufficiently headstrong to beg comparison with Précilda's. Philippe went back to live with his parents. His divorce papers offer a different account of the breakup. The document states that several days after returning from their honeymoon, Jeanne-Claude announced "her intention to travel alone to Corsica in a month. When he refused, the apartment was taken back by his mother-in-law and henceforth they stopped living communally."[19] He also sought reimbursement for his airfare to Tunisia. Adding an ironic twist to the already bizarre situation, Philippe telephoned Christo and asked him to reason with Jeanne-Claude. Christo was astonished by the request, but, as her close friend and "brother," he agreed to try, even if halfheartedly.

Bending to pressure on all sides, Jeanne-Claude agreed to try "a new, trial engagement." If Philippe wanted to see her, he would have to make an appointment. Jeanne-Claude remembered, "One evening we went to a restaurant and then to the theater. Later, he tried to make love to me. I was wearing a belt with lots of metal pieces on it, which I took off and used to defend myself. The next day, I called my family and said, 'Please leave me alone. I don't like this type of engagement.' I was finished with him." Précilda recalled the moment: "It was eight days after she came back from Tunisia. She said, 'Mama, please don't ever leave me alone with him.' Poor darling."[20]

Jeanne-Claude had never given much thought to breaking free from Précilda. But if Carole Weisweiller had been correct in sensing Jeanne-Claude's repressed need for independence, even a failed marriage represented an important first step in slipping out of the Guillebon family's golden shackles. Although Carole saw little to admire in Philippe, she had counseled Jeanne-Claude to reconsider her impulsive decision to leave him. Carole could not believe what she heard when they met to talk about the crisis. She said, "I remember Jeanne-Claude's words precisely. She said, 'First, I'm pregnant. Second, I'm going to divorce. Third, I'm in love.'"

Carole sputtered, "You're in love with whom?"

Jeanne-Claude replied, "You'll never guess. Try." After an expectant pause, Jeanne-Claude named Christo as the father of her unborn child.

Looking back, Carole said, "It was like a novel. I immediately saw trouble ahead and asked, 'Were you in love with Philippe?' Jeanne-Claude answered, 'Not really. I haven't been able to admit to myself until now that I'm absolutely in love with Christo.'"[21]

5

Turning Point

Joyce returned to Paris in the fall of 1959, still intent on pursuing a career in music. In September, she obtained Jeanne-Claude's new address and visited her for the first time since leaving for North Africa. They talked about many things, yet Joyce remembered only one jarring bit of trivial conversation about some mostly unused wedding presents. Joyce reflected, "Jeanne-Claude had been such a snob. While she sat with me looking at her wedding presents, I was shocked to hear her say, 'Oh, that's mockery. This one is nice. They haven't made fun of me; it's a decent present.' She could be a prize bitch."[1] Joyce was right. Even Jeanne-Claude later said, "Calling me a snob was minimizing it. I was a supersnob."

A changed world was about to temper Jeanne-Claude's pretensions. The dream of a blissful marriage had gone awry, and, worse, before long, everyone would learn of her pregnancy. Given the tangled web of circumstance, Jeanne-Claude and Christo could not conceive of marrying, living together, or even revealing their feelings for each other. Telling the truth would only have made things worse. Besides, Jeanne-Claude was not willing to reveal her infidelity. For his part, Christo remained supportive and caring as he tried to adjust to the unexpected news and the prospect of raising a child. A logical strategy evolved. Jeanne-Claude and Christo decided simply to go along with the general presumption that Philippe was the father. Doing so would deflect further scandal and promise a degree of legitimacy for their offspring. Six months later, however, Planchon's divorce papers stated that the child that bore his name "had not been an issue of this marriage."[2]

After her superficial stab at reconciliation, Jeanne-Claude resumed an approximation of her previous lifestyle. "I was crushed," she said. "I went out almost every night with the same people I had dated before, all my old friends. They didn't know Christo. I was seeing him as a lover, but my official life consisted of going out with everybody else." There were also frequent visits to her parents. However, circumstances had changed. Jacques's resignation had finally been accepted. In his last days at the Ecole Polytechnique, the general helped choose his successor, while Précilda located new living quarters. Précilda and Jacques now lived in an elegant apartment near Jeanne-Claude. But no apartment could rival the grandeur of Pavillion Boncourt, with its numerous cadets in waiting. As hard as Jeanne-Claude tried to convince herself otherwise, it soon became apparent that there could be no return to those carefree days.

Jeanne-Claude spent most days at her parents' home, then met Christo secretly at her apartment every night. As surrogate son, Christo remained part of the Guillebon household. He periodically joined the family to paint portraits of the children, sketch Jeanne-Claude, and dine with them. Sometimes at meals, Précilda thought it amusing to say, "When Alexandra grows up, Christo will be a famous artist and make a perfect husband for her."[3] She was partially right. According to her high-society standards, until fame arrived, he would be miscast in any role but that of the struggling artist and oddball family friend. Jeanne-Claude said, "Mother loved Christo and wanted him as a son, not as a son-in-law. He was too poor, not suitably polished, a delightful brother, but definitely not what I needed. How could he buy me dresses at Christian Dior and all the other things I was used to?"

Jacques had been deeply concerned about Jeanne-Claude's welfare, but that September and early October, her personal problems were overshadowed by the growing crisis in Algeria. Although Guillebon had returned to civilian life, President de Gaulle continued to summon him for consultations. Their increasingly frequent meetings coincided with the quickening tempo of events. On September 16, 1959, de Gaulle finally clarified his intentions regarding Algeria. His previous ambivalent pronouncements were superseded by a dramatic offer of self-determination, a conditional variation of the position Guillebon had long advocated.

De Gaulle's remodeled Algerian policy did not stem the nation's economic woes or end the nationalist insurgency. His new formula may have softened some internal and international opposition, but it also intensified resistance from the right, adding dangerous elements of political and military instability to an already-complex equation. The uneasy realignment of forces boiled over on October 8, when nine cabinet ministers resigned. De Gaulle immediately moved to find replacements and asked Guillebon to serve as head of the War Ministry.

Jacques relayed the news to Précilda. She minced no words, telling him, "If you take that job I won't live with you anymore." Her response was part instinct, part shrewd analysis. He replied. "Don't worry. I'm going to set conditions nobody could accept."[4] He presented his terms to de Gaulle: a five-year appointment, complete control of the army, and the power to reorganize it as he saw fit. Predictably, his conditions were unacceptable. De Gaulle told Jacques that he needed him, and he asked him to be realistic about his conditions. Guillebon remained firm and proposed another man for the post. He said, "Consider my friend Pierre Messmer. He is a good bureaucrat and will not set any conditions."[5] Indeed, Messmer made no demands and became the minister. Meanwhile, the war raged on.

To one degree or another, the Algerian tragedy affected everyone in France. Christo Javacheff was no exception. His choice of materials and the manner in which he employed them reflected the turmoil, repression, and uncertainty of the times. In late 1959, he explored the act of wrapping as no artist ever had. As a result, his work underwent a pivotal transition.

Christo's ability to devote himself to his work remained astonishing. In a letter to Anani, he wrote about the need for courage and persistence in making art: "Everything requires time, talent, and endless work."[6] Although he visited the Guillebon family regularly and saw Jeanne-Claude secretly each night, he frequented art events and devoted every remaining minute to working in the studio. Poverty and a cramped work space did not hamper Christo's desire to create large-scale compositions. Throughout 1959, altered and unaltered bottles, cans, and other modest domestic objects in the ongoing *Inventory* series gave way to larger, more architectural elements. He impulsively purchased a group of wooden boxes at the Marché aux Puces (flea market). Shortly afterward, he began acquiring more oil barrels. The recent discovery of oil in Algeria had become another national issue. Yet aside from any possible symbolic connotation, the choice of steel oil drums as a basic raw material in Christo's widening palette had more to do with their size, shape, durability, surface, and potential as building blocks. The barrels were also readily available as discards or low-cost salvage. In the future, he was unable to recall exactly what had motivated him to begin using barrels, or where the first one even came from. Whatever the origin, Christo felt drawn to the barrel, its form, and its expressive possibilities.

Like their predecessors, these larger pieces were either tightly wrapped or just cleaned and varnished. By late 1959, Christo's studio overflowed with a variably treated assembly of tied, encrusted containers. The transient clutter of objects and random-looking totemic stacks resembled a warehouse more than an artist's studio.

A significant change occurred that winter. Christo's packages took on a vulnerable appearance. In a small but decisive conceptual step, snugly fit, hard-surfaced wrappings gave way to bulkier, softer, more varied packages. For almost two years, he had furnished each wrapped object with a skin hardened by coats of lacquer. Treated with sand, washed in acetone, provided with stiff textural finish by the application of a final coat of lacquer, *Inventory* and related works had included rigidified fabric, without any natural resiliency. Blurring the distinction between rigidity and suppleness were pieces like *Package* in 1958. Akin to the later wrappings, it is a compact work of lumpy fabric harnessed in a web of ropes and seemingly petrified beneath layers of automobile lacquer.

By the end of 1959, however, Christo was allowing the fabric to breathe. He sacrificed the appealing volcanic surface and accepted materials at their face value. Like the wrappings, his newer packages had the power to disquiet; some were partially veiled, some fully concealed. Found materials and objects of humble origin were rescued from oblivion, covered with paper, plastic, or fabric, then secured with rope, cord, or twine. Though lacking their lacquer cocoons, the more vulnerable offspring were no less shrouded and were potentially more ambiguous than their predecessors. The new genre of packages may have been less tidy, perhaps even clumsy, but they were uniquely Christo's.

If Christo had one central formative influence, it grew out of the tradition of Tatlin and the Russian Constructivists' use of "real materials in real space."[7] Using the simplest of materials, his packages achieved what art critic David Bourdon later described as "revelation through concealment." Bourdon wrote, "No other artist so fully illuminated the twentieth century preoccupation with packaging."[8] Christo said, "All these objects are related to territory organization, territory limits. It's something like clothing on a woman. The cloth on a woman is much more revealing than the naked woman."[9]

It is unclear precisely how and when packaging took hold as a theme in Christo's work, but evidence suggests that by late 1959 the packages had become the artist's major concern. Whatever their meaning, they clearly revealed that something crucial was at stake in their formation. Airtight or loosely bundled, hardened or pliant they remained at the heart of Christo's work. Each secretive package contained a stillness at its core. Tightly drawn knots canceled an object's normal function. Art historian Stephen Prokopoff would later call the impoverished contents "repositories of insignificant history."[10] Each cloaked element posed questions. What is it and what does it mean? Why is it covered? Where did the now-camouflaged interior come from and where is it ultimately going? Each enigmatic piece hinted at or masked its contents, evoking ill-defined, contradictory feelings. Christo focused on the intersection of art, absurdity, and gritty reality.

Christo's draped objects took on many guises. Some resembled landscapes or the topography of a person. Others suggested meager gifts, mummified corpses, household belongings awaiting transport, veiled phantom presences, tragic apparitions, bound and gagged objects, or tantalizing, unknown entities. While the outer coverings protected the submerged contents, they also created intimidating separations. For the moment, all cloaked elements were placed in a state of suspended animation and made functionally impotent. Had Christo chosen to cast his packages in bronze, nothing ambiguous would remain. A permanently fixed image has nothing to hide, nothing gasping for breath beneath the cloth, nothing mysterious teasing or disorienting the senses. The riddle maker left few clues. Common objects—tables, chairs—were deprived of individual characteristics. Only modified contours or the occasional exposed piece signaled what was inside.

With *Inventory* nearly complete, Christo enlarged his visual vocabulary, intensifying the work's inherent sense of disquiet. Old and new pieces shared a subversive tone. Throughout this transition period, the Western notion of packaging continued to fascinate Christo. He rejected slick, chic commercial packaging designed to promote sales in favor of a consciously impoverished image, endowing his scruffy-looking bundles with a proletarian signature and primitive look. They were knowingly makeshift. Any unsuspecting person stumbling into Christo's studio might think that the artist was about to move an array of castoffs into storage. The closer one looked, the more irrational his ensemble seemed. Only years later would his leap of illogic be acknowledged as art. As much as any contemporary work, these expressionist packages, with their cloudy pasts, obscure presents, and unknown futures, demonstrated a fresh and compelling vision. The unexplored territory that Christo staked out and sought to master would provide him with fertile ground for decades to come.

Jeanne-Claude and Christo had every reason to be more discreet than ever in seeing each other. Jeanne-Claude's pregnancy and the contested divorce with Philippe dictated extraordinary caution. A court appearance for the Planchon "nonreconciliation ordinance" had been scheduled for February 12, 1960. The hearing represented the first official step in a process that each party hoped would speedily end their unhappy union.

An unexpected guest further complicated the situation. Précilda invited a friend, Blanche Ackerman, to stay with Jeanne-Claude for a while. The small ground-level apartment had only a living room, bedroom, and large bathroom, part of which had been converted into a small kitchen. Even though they risked exposing their carefully guarded secret, Jeanne-Claude and Christo continued their late-night rendezvous. While Ackerman slept in the living room, they repeatedly cautioned each other, "Shhh."

Along with the apartment came a substantial space in the basement, where Christo stored some of his ever-proliferating work. Jeanne-Claude might have been relating a modern version of the myth of Sisyphus when she recalled, "Christo would buy old, dirty barrels, some covered with oil, and bring them to avenue Raymond Poincaré. Then, one by one, he would take a barrel on the subway, take it to his studio at rue Saint-Senoch, carry it up seven floors, clean it, polish it, sometimes varnish it, and sometimes wrap it. He then took it back to avenue Raymond Poincaré for storage and picked up another one. Each barrel went back and forth. The female concierge once told someone, 'He is such a nice young man, but there is something wrong with him. He spends his day going up and down the stairs carrying the same barrel.'"

The herculean effort went beyond the arduous transport and modification of barrels. Christo labored over other types of common containers and continued to fashion ungainly packages. By 1960, a growing number of American and European artists were employing collage and assemblage techniques. Christo's use of fabric and the innocuous residue of everyday life coincided with this trend, yet his work had no parallel. Having long since mastered trompe l'oeil, he now used real materials to generate an air of unreality. Wrapped and partially wrapped objects were not simply covered but brought into question, as well.

The act of shrouding can set routine perception askew. In 1928, René Magritte painted several versions of *The Lovers*. The subject of one is a couple kissing. The man is wearing a suit and tie and is slightly taller; the woman leans up as their heads come together—everything is normal except that they have cloth draped around their heads. The result is profoundly disquieting. Like Magritte's lovers, Christo's seemingly impromptu, anonymous parcels await, even insist on, emotional transactions. Fragile, imbued with hidden meaning and worth, they evoke incongruous feelings and expectations. Packages are meant to be opened. Making one presumes its eventual coming apart. Each has a life span and an uncertain afterlife. Ironically, an innate sense of a package's transitory state contradicts the traditional, conditional view of an art object as a permanent entity. Christo has always rejected the notion of permanence as illusory. He later said, "In a way, we are surrounded by ruin and debris in our museums, and we try to pretend that they are art."[11] In a world where artists dream of immortality, his works brashly assert their mortality.

An urge to redefine and reinvigorate art united Christo and other avant-garde artists. Christo, his young artist friends, and those contemporary painters and sculptors he most respected shared a resolve to challenge the establishment's stodgy premises. He found encouraging signs of change. Four months earlier, in October 1959, he had attended a much-heralded exhibition at the Palais de Tokyo in Paris. The first "Biennale des Jeunes" offered a measure of government support for vanguard artists. André Malraux organized the show to focus attention on a diverse group of emerging artists from forty countries. None of the artists was older than thirty-five. France had become aware of its eroding status as the epicenter of advanced cultural development, and Malraux hoped that this biennale would demonstrate that Paris had not only a rich past but also a promising future in the visual arts. The jury, which included Henry Moore, Ossip Zadkine, and Edouard Pignon, never considered

Christo's work for inclusion, but it did select work by Klein, Tinguely, Friedensreich Hundertwasser, Rauschenberg, Johns, and other artists.

Tinguely became the star of the show, exhibiting his meta-matic machines inside and on the promenade outside the museum. Several of the pieces were familiar to Christo, who delighted in the lively machines. "I loved them very, very much," he said. The most recent construction, Tinguely's tall, thin, noisy, hyperactive *Meta-matic No. 17,* was a machine that produced an estimated forty thousand abstract drawings. No two were the same. The sculptor might have been speaking for Christo and a new generation of artists when he said, "Forget hours, minutes, seconds. Live in the present: Live in harmony with the times and live for a marvelous and absolute reality!"[12]

In the early months of 1960, Tinguely and Klein both made advances that were profoundly in sync with Christo's inclination toward commonplace material. Beginning in the summer of 1959, Klein had intensified his assault on the conventional values of the art establishment. Pierre Restany shared the urge to do battle with the system he later portrayed as "Fortress Paris" or the "Big Paris Mafia."[13] In late February 1960, Klein, Restany, and Count Maurice d'Arquian, the director of the Gallery of International Contemporary Art, worked out a format and the details of Klein's newest work, which Restany had named *Anthropométries de l'Epoque Bleue.*

Klein's *coup de théâtre* took place at exactly 10:00 P.M. on March 9, 1960. A handpicked group of one hundred elite guests had to present numbered personal invitations to enter the black-tie gala. The piece began with a chamber orchestra playing one continuous chord for twenty minutes, followed by twenty minutes of silence. Throughout, three nude women, who were following Klein's cue, smeared themselves from breasts to knees in blue paint, rubbed, slid, and pulled one another across sheets of canvas on the floor, and climbed on platforms to press their bodies against sheets tacked to the wall. After forty minutes, the music, silence, and art concluded. Overnight, this odd, irreverent episode, documented by photos, film, press reports, and word of mouth, became the talk of Paris.

Tinguely, one of Klein's most ardent supporters, did not attend the extravaganza at d'Arquian's gallery, since he was working feverishly at New York's Museum of Modern Art, assembling a demented machine designed to destroy itself. Tinguely might not have been working at all had he not seen Klein's "Void" exhibition in 1958, which had affected him profoundly. He had not made sculpture for two years at the time he encountered the empty, repainted, and "purified" space. Daily visits to the "Void" show revitalized him.

The following year, Tinguely accepted George Staempfli's offer to exhibit at his New York gallery in January 1960. During his voyage to the United States, he became obsessed with a vision of an eccentric contraption that would come to life and quickly go down in a burst of glory. He concluded that the work must be born and had to die in the Museum of Modern Art's Sculpture Garden. The impossible odds against securing that location never troubled him, even though he couldn't speak the language and his work was barely known in the States.[14] In the process, Tinguely was foreshadowing Christo and Jeanne-Claude's later modus operandi.

After a museum official rejected Tinguely's offer, he enlisted the help of *New York Times* art critic Dore Ashton. She presented the idea to Peter Selz, curator of painting and sculpture exhibitions, who had seen and been impressed by Tinguely's machines at the recent "Biennale des Jeunes." He brought the concept to director René d'Harnoncourt. Whatever resistance Selz and a small band of Tinguely supporters encountered dissolved with the complete success of Tinguely's show at the Staempfli Gallery.[15]

On March 17, 1960, the completed sculpture, *Homage to New York,* included eighty bicycle and carriage wheels, dozens of motors, smoke canisters, a rusty oil barrel, steel tubing, a large electrical fan, a huge meteorological balloon, a drum from a washing machine, a battered American flag, a baby bassinet, a radio nailed to an upright piano, a noisy Addressograph machine, typewriters, an enamel bathtub, and much more.[16]

That evening, a formally dressed crowd of invited guests stood in the slush-filled Sculpture Garden in a cold rain, awaiting the destruction. Most observers did not realize that Tinguely's machines relied on chance. Erratic behavior and malfunctions were typical. Engines convulsed, smoke spewed, sponges made drawings, typewriters clicked, a radio chirped in, a bell rang, and a piano played its last tune. Other objects joined in a deafening chorus. Robert Rauschenberg had added a device that sprayed silver dollars on the audience. A small burning wagon dashed toward a *Paris-Match* reporter; he redirected it toward some television equipment. After pounding, burning, and sawing itself, Tinguely's wounded machine still refused to die. Finally, New York Fire Department axes and fire extinguishers laid the creation to rest.[17]

In a later interview, Tinguely said, "Maybe it is possible to make things that are so close to life that they exist as simply and changeably and permanently as a cat jumping, or a child playing, or a truck going by outside, and if so I would very much like to make them. Life is play, movement, continual change. Only the fear of death makes us want to stop life, to 'fix' it impossibly forever. The moment life is fixed, it is no longer true; it is dead, and therefore uninteresting."[18]

Klein and Tinguely felt that traditional means of artistic expression were obsolete. In a stagnant aesthetic climate, any defiance of the established order was a breath of fresh air. It demonstrated once again that aloof Paris no longer had a monopoly on innovation. Klein and Tinguely may have been publicized upstarts, but they were clearly part of something larger. A new generation of artists, impatient with the status quo in America as well as in Germany and France, added its weight to a gathering transatlantic storm that would soon change the face of the art world.

Twenty-four-year-old Christo had a role to play in that breakthrough. He understood the spirit of the times. Like many of his contemporaries, he had already made a commitment to commonplace materials and had begun to find ways of transcending their banal nature. He would consistently maintain that there is a mortality to all art. Past artistic achievements revealed stunning sparks of imagination, not lasting certainties. He would insist that art communicated best in its own time, that a piece removed from its time and place, hermetically sealed within a museum's confines, speaks with an altered, muffled voice, if at all. Christo insisted that the "prime time of the art" mattered most. In the years ahead, his major works were to live and die in prime time. If his projects, fleeting grand gestures, were to address posterity, they would have to do so as memory and myth. Books, photographs, films, drawings, and eyewitness accounts would only hint at the breadth of his unrepeatable fantasies; preliminary studies and reproductions offered only glimpses of how his provocative, short-lived extravaganzas reveal the ceaseless transformations, beauty, and fragility of life.

Jan Voss had by this time become one of Christo's best friends. Voss painted on paper out of economic necessity, and his linear, fanciful works hovered between cave painting and cryptic cartoons. He remembered being introduced to Christo by Lourdes Castro and René Bertholo. "Christo was so animated that even if you didn't know what he was saying, you understood his gestures and body language. It was as if you had taken the lid off a pot. He was open to ideas, lively, anxious to meet people, and very curious about this new world." Christo's energy amazed Voss more than anything else. "Christo was always very busy, moving from one portrait to another, carrying barrels from one place to another, always moving, never taking his coffee on boulevard Saint-Germain. Never."

Voss lived and worked in a large Gentilly stockroom in a quiet industrial neighborhood. Christo asked if he could store some barrels there. Voss agreed. "I remember moving oil drums to different places. A few times he had to rent a truck and hire people to help. He was really struggling. Sometimes Christo had no portrait work and felt really depressed by money problems. He wanted things to move quickly. He was restrained by a lack of supplies, he couldn't always pay his phone bill, things like that. I tried to encourage him, but all of us were in the same situation." Lourdes Castro and René Bertholo had a modest scholarship from the Gulbenkian Foundation, which kept food on the table. "They fed us," Voss recalled.[19] Lourdes also portrayed Christo as always in a

Paris, 1960: Jeanne-Claude in "La Cave," 4 avenue Raymond Poincaré, in the middle of *Inventory*. (Photo: René Bertholo)

hurry, running off with his paint box and canvas to work on a portrait. However, there were dry spells. To make ends meet, Christo made barter arrangements. "He found a dentist on Faubourg Saint-Honoré who traded dental services for a portrait of his wife. One day I even had my hair done gratis at a place de l'Opéra salon because of a portrait he did."[20]

Up to this point, Jeanne-Claude had never worried about financial matters. On March 1, 1960, the "non-reconciliation ordinance" between her and Philippe was adjudicated. The judgment awarded her monthly payments of six hundred francs—a tidy sum, though not yet a divorce settlement. Another outcome of the proceedings came in the form of advice from Jeanne-Claude's lawyer. He cautioned her about the French law, according to which a man is allowed to visit a woman's premises at night; however, if he is found there after sunrise the next day, her final divorce claims could be jeopardized. Christo continued his nocturnal visits, but he habitually took the first subway at 5:00 A.M. back to his apartment.

Voss's first impression of Jeanne-Claude was less than enthusiastic. He said, "At first I didn't think of her as very profound. Jeanne-Claude came from a different, well-situated society. She seemed flighty and didn't know anything about art." Soon Voss discovered another side of her character. He observed an openness, a curiosity, and, most important, a contagious optimism. "She believed in all of us, especially Christo," he said.[21] Jeanne-Claude's crash course in art and subsequent tutoring by Christo began to show results. With his guidance, she developed insights into contemporary art. Her enthusiasm, cheerfulness, and support for the artists associated with *KWY* helped Bertholo, Castro, and Voss put aside their initial aversions to her high-society pretensions. From the outset, she and Pierre Restany had a noticeable rapport. Both had been born in Morocco and immediately felt an affinity for each other. She applied all of her charm, knowing that Christo hoped to find a champion in Restany.

Restany's first Nouveau Réalisme manifesto appeared on April 16, 1960, coinciding with the opening of "Les Nouveaux Réalistes" at Galleria Apollinaire in Milan. Restany and Guido Le Noci, the gallery's owner, organized the exhibition, which included work by Arman, François Dufrêne, Raymond Hains, Yves Klein, Jean Tinguely, and Jacques de la Villeglé. Restany wrote about the exhaustion of traditional means of art expression and the inevitable "progress toward a Nouveau Réalisme of pure sensitivity." "Easel painting" he announced, "like any other classical means of painting or sculpture, has served its term. Still sublime at times, it is approaching the end of a long monopoly." Restany had thrown down a gauntlet, but it took another six months before his vague "new expressivity," or a roster of sanctioned exponents, emerged with any clarity. Like other artists, Christo hoped for a chance to participate in this latest challenge to the establishment, but was not invited by Restany.

Restany and his growing band of malcontents were orchestrating an insurrection against values dear to the existing power structure. Voss observed, "That movement was really the first interesting art development in Paris after the war. It fascinated me. Restany was an extremely intelligent man. He appeared at the center of this new group, not as a pope. He acted more like an attentive friend than a dictator."[22] Not everyone shared that judgment. Some saw Restany as a tyrannical leader of loud, untalented pretenders—nihilists trying to exhume Dada's corpse. Christo and other young artists grappled without success to find a place in this polarized climate.

Restany advocated the use of real materials—the stuff of contemporary, industrial, urban society—and minimal artistic intervention, and Christo heeded him. Their occasional meetings at openings and elsewhere were always cordial, and Restany followed the evolution of the young artist's work closely. However, Restany expressed a preference for works like Duchamp's readymades, where the hand of the artist remained virtually unseen. Jan Voss remembered one unexpected accommodation by Christo: "He accepted Restany's suggestion to stop painting the wrappings—immediately. That amazed me." Indeed,

Christo had no trouble in complying; he was going in that direction anyway. In 1960, he finished *Inventory*. In that and other works, he stopped applying a mixture of sand and lacquer to the fabric's surface. Given his recent obsession with packages, the addition of color probably began to seem superfluous and distracting. Even when he did paint a surface, the muted result looked less applied than discovered, as if in a natural state of decay.

Like Restany, Voss had studied Christo's enigmatic *Inventory*. He found the tightly wrapped and contrasting nonwrapped objects fascinating but saw no way to develop the concept further. When Christo began creating packages, Voss responded enthusiastically. The new strategy seemed rich in possibilities. "I liked the packages very much," Voss recalled. "The first ones were rectangular shapes, like paintings. They included everything he could find and pack, including objects from the street and his own refuse. He had a small studio and disposed of most waste by making packages. I know because we made a trade. Some packages were very heavy. He told me they contained bottles. I chose a light one so that I could carry it easily."[23] Tied in rope, two-thirds of the work had been enclosed in a white cloth and the remaining third in a tan fabric. Cardboard at the core accounted for its modest weight.

Between February and May 1960, when her pregnancy could no longer be disguised, Jeanne-Claude stopped dating and spent most of her time with her parents. On Sunday, May 8, she felt quickening contractions, and Précilda rushed her to Bégin Military Hospital. Jeanne-Claude had practiced breathing exercises in preparation for a natural childbirth. Painkillers were not administered. The examining physician found no dilation. For three days, three doctors alternately employed massage techniques to facilitate the delivery. It did not help. Her doctors wanted to perform a cesarean. Précilda stopped them; she had experienced the same problem while giving birth to Jeanne-Claude. "Finally, on May eleventh," Jeanne-Claude recalled, "the child was good enough to come out. He was so long, he never ended."

Jeanne-Claude's only male visitors were her father and Christo. Unable to tell anyone but Carole Weisweiller the truth about Christo, Jeanne-Claude designated him godfather. That role helped explain his constant presence and fatherly concern. Carole agreed to be the child's godmother. Christo and Jeanne-Claude named their son Cyril, after the ninth-century saint said to have invented the Bulgarian Cyrillic alphabet. Although Philippe Planchon denied being the father, Cyril bore his surname officially.

Jeanne-Claude spent two months after her discharge from the hospital with Cyril at Essertaux, losing unwanted pounds. A month after their twenty-fifth birthday, Jeanne-Claude and Christo cautiously settled into a new rou-

Paris, Avenue Henri-Martin, May 1, 1960: Sketch by Christo. Eleven days before Cyril was born. (Photo: Archive XTO+J-C)

tine; she returned to her small avenue Raymond Poincaré apartment with Cyril, and Christo covertly resumed his nightly stays. Their physical attraction remained intense, as did the sense of danger that permeated their veiled relationship. The general's haut monde daughter and her penniless immigrant lover had grown accustomed to living with risk. She said, "I thought Christo and I were having a perfect time in my apartment with our baby. We assumed it would remain our secret forever." Love overcame the disquieting contradictions of their daily lives. Christo experienced the reawakened joys of family life: the emotional warmth, the intimacy, the sense of belonging. For the moment, their masquerade went undetected.

Planchon did not make things easy. His court-ordered payments to Jeanne-Claude were so tardy that her lawyer wrote a letter threatening to garnish his salary. Jeanne-Claude could have turned to her parents for money, but Christo felt obliged to find additional portrait commissions. Referrals in and around Paris and periodic jobs in Switzerland allowed him to meet his own expenses while contributing in a small way to the household. Whenever he found a new client, he treated Jeanne-Claude to a dozen red roses.

Throughout 1960, Christo met many artists. Bertholo and Castro took him to Maria Elena Viera da Silva's studio. She seemed somehow distant and intimidating to him. A mutual friend introduced him to Tériade, an important publisher of Picasso prints. Tériade invited Christo to a brunch at Galerie

Essertaux, July 1960: Jeanne-Claude holding Cyril. (Photo: Wjera Fechheimer)

Louise Leiris to meet the celebrated artist. Christo declined. He recalled, "I was trying to be very radical." Two years earlier, he had gone into debt to purchase a Picasso etching, but now this artist represented an institutionalized past that Christo sought to revolt against. Tériade shrugged in disbelief and said, "You're out of your mind, you arrogant son of a bitch." Several days later, Christo quietly went to see the exhibition.

In the fall of 1960, Niki de Saint-Phalle visited Christo's studio with her lover and mentor, Jean Tinguely. At thirty-five, the short, dark, powerfully built Tinguely remained the subject of considerable notoriety as the result of his kinetic contraptions. Saint-Phalle, a petite, attractive, bicultural woman, recalled the rue Saint-Senoch work space, "It was a small place with all these wrapped things that I thought looked great. I felt really enthusiastic about what I had seen and talked to Jean about Christo's work. He came to see the work and liked it, too. I remember Christo having great charm. I also remember Jeanne-Claude. When I admired one of his pieces, she said, 'Why don't you buy it?' I said, 'I'd love to, but I don't have enough money to buy my own plaster.' I was surprised that she asked. It was a different art scene. Nobody had any money. We were excited about art and what we were doing. The money didn't come into it. I found her a little bit frightening, but I admired his work."[24] Jeanne-Claude could not recall the incident. In fact, she dated her first conversation with Tinguely a year later, insisting that she was never present when he visited Christo's studio. For one reason or another, Tinguely developed an antipathy toward her.

One chronically poor artist did buy a Christo package in 1961. Arman recalled his purchase: "Christo showed me his earliest packages. I bought a small, very mysterious piece for the ridiculous amount of two hundred francs." He and Christo had been introduced to each other in 1959 by Pierre Restany. They met again at gallery openings and later became friends.

On October 27, 1960, Restany unfurled his own grandiose conception. He gathered his band of upstart artists to announce the creation of Nouveau Réalisme to the world. The opening salvos had been the publication of Restany's first manifesto on April 16 and the "Les Nouveaux Réalistes" exhibition in Milan. Throughout the spring and summer, Restany met with Yves Klein, Raymond Hains, and Jean Tinguely to determine guidelines and select participants for the new movement. Friendships and powerful egos came into play. Finally, ten artists were formally invited to establish Nouveau Réalisme: Yves Klein, Martial Raysse, Jean Tinguely, Daniel Spoerri, Raymond Hains, Jacques de la Villeglé, François Dufrêne, César, Mimmo Rotella, and Arman.

Doggedly, Restany managed to cajole the divergent personalities into subscribing to what he later described euphemistically as a "Statement of Principles . . . drawn up under my supervision." Each of the parties begrudgingly accepted Restany's few all-encompassing but vacuous words. Their unifying banner read, "On Thursday, October 27, 1960, the Nouveaux Réalistes took note of their collective singularity. Nouveau Réalisme = new perceptive approaches to reality." Born of anger, confusion, and compromise, the first potentially serious new wave since Abstract Expressionism in America leapt headlong into a sleepy Paris art scene. Restany later described his coalition: "Unlike other groups it has no leader and no hierarchy but presents a united front . . . and . . . clearly defined objectives." Restany glossed over the New Re-

Paris, winter 1960: Christo in his studio, formerly a maid's room, on rue Saint-Senoch.
(Photo: Jean-Jacques Lévèque)

alists' disparate impulses and tried to focus on common denominators. He pointed to a new "sociological reality" that absorbed artists and to their view of contemporary nature as "industrial, urban, and aggressive."[25]

Restany ruled out Christo's participation in the movement. Christo never asked to join the group, for he cared little about its ideology, and even less about the fierce behind-the-scenes politics that seemed to go hand in hand with inclusion. In retrospect, the exclusion proved to be a blessing in disguise. Nonetheless, at the time, he felt the pain of a marvelous opportunity lost. Christo said, "I was hurt. Like all young artists, I wanted to exhibit my work." Restany rationalized his rejection of Christo by saying that the packages were not pure enough and involved too much artistic intervention. In contrast, he cited Arman, whose work appeared to be a textbook example of Restany's evolving definition of Nouveau Réalisme: Arman presented an object *as is;* Christo did not. The latter's wrapping, the obsessively tied knots, the aesthetic decisions, imbued an expressivity that Restany compared negatively to the pureness of Klein's monochromatic blue paintings, the clarity of a readymade, and the inherent poetry of unaltered objects. Christo recalled, "He was also very critical of Rauschenberg and Johns because they transformed the object too much. He said my work lacked indifference and told me, 'Be cool, cool.'"

Missed opportunities were becoming an all-too-familiar state of affairs for the young outsider. In time, Restany found reasons to validate and even claim credit for Christo. But collaboration had never been Christo's purpose, and being shut out of the movement actually reinforced his independent nature. Exclusion assured the freedom and impetus to work without the distraction of either constricting guidelines or a manifesto with an implied pledge of allegiance. Restany's doctrinaire analysis proved increasingly irrelevant to Christo. Interpretations of his art and that of his contemporaries would change; Christo's singular vision would not.

Christo's problems were not limited to art. One day in November 1960, Jeanne-Claude told her parents that she and the baby were ill; it seemed like a good way to ensure an evening's privacy. She disconnected the telephone. It never occurred to her that her mother would persist in calling throughout the night. Fearing that her daughter and grandson might be in trouble, Précilda prodded Jacques into action. In the middle of the night, Jeanne-Claude and Christo were awakened by a knock at the door. Christo bolted out of bed, naked, and leapt out of a window. Jeanne-Claude called out, "Who is it?"

"Your father" came the reply. She slipped into a robe, hastily checked for anything Christo might have left behind, then opened the door. After being reassured that everything was fine, Jacques left. Embarrassed and chilled to the bone, Christo slipped back into the apartment.

Jeanne-Claude began spending nights at Christo's apartment. There were no unexpected callers. Précilda began to complain, saying, "I call you and you're never home. Do you leave the baby alone?"

"Of course not," Jeanne-Claude replied. "The baby was with me."

"Well," Précilda demanded, "where were you? Tell me what's going on."

Under ceaseless interrogation, Jeanne-Claude finally confessed. "I have a steady lover," she told her mother, who seemed relieved. Jeanne-Claude said later, "She assumed he was a rich man. Mother assured me that it was normal for a healthy young woman with physical needs to have a lover. But she told me to remember that men were put on this planet to spoil women; therefore, I should be rewarded with a mink coat, a diamond, or my own apartment."

After the confession, Précilda missed no opportunity to inquire about what gifts Jeanne-Claude had managed to coax from her boyfriend. The answer each time was, "Nothing." At one point, Précilda erupted: "What do you mean nothing? This has been going on for weeks, and you still haven't gotten a present?" Jeanne-Claude recklessly blurted out, "He can't buy me things. For God's sake, Mother, the man I love is Christo."

After a moment of openmouthed silence, Précilda exploded. "You whore," she shrieked, "you can't control your ass. You should be taking care of your child, but instead you dishonor your family. I forbid you to see him again." When Jeanne-Claude refused, Madame de Guillebon roared, "Then you are no longer my daughter. And since I pay the rent for your apartment, you can get out."

Précilda felt that Jeanne-Claude and Christo had callously betrayed the family's trust. After all the love and support she and Jacques had given Christo, how could he repay them with such disrespect and deceit? she wondered. He may have been an ideal surrogate son, but the thought of him as a son-in-law was intolerable. When Jeanne-Claude left her mother's home, her days of plenty and years of privilege, as well as her life of dependence and real or simulated obedience, were over.

The news stunned Christo. They went to Jeanne-Claude's apartment, gathered her clothing, the baby's things, and a few possessions, then loaded them in a taxi and went to 24 rue Saint-Louis-en-l'Ile. That night, as Jeanne-Claude and Christo discussed their dire reversal of fortune, the phone rang; he answered. A familiar voice said sternly, "Mr. Javacheff, I would like to talk to you." Christo listened nervously as Précilda issued an ultimatum: "Let my daughter go or I will see to it that you are expelled from France within twenty-four hours." Suddenly, the situation was frighteningly ominous. Certainly Précilda had the connections to have Christo expelled. Panicked, he called several of his influential portrait clients, pleading for help. In the following days, Jacques, Madame Leclerc, Carole Weisweiller, and others urged Jeanne-Claude to consider what she and her child were giving up. A steady stream of callers also counseled Christo to face the facts. He said, "People told me to be sensible, to leave that lady alone. 'She's from a different class. She's not for you,' they said." It would be hard to invent a scenario that would better test a couple's character and love. The emotional stress only strengthened their mutual resolve.

In retrospect, it is unclear whether Précilda's threat had been a bluff or a vindictive action that was subsequently countered by one or more of Christo's elite clients. Whatever the case, a stalemate developed. One telephone exchange may have been the decisive one. Jeanne-Claude recalled, "Mother stopped threatening when I said, 'I don't mind going to Bulgaria with Christo. You just won't see your grandson anymore.'"

The Guillebon family resumed their lives as if Christo, Jeanne-Claude, and Cyril did not exist. Their names were never brought up in conversation, and there was no mention of what had happened. Despite being shut out, Jeanne-Claude and Christo, with their infant son and large dog, were determined to stay together. Friends later applauded their bravery under fire. In fact, from their perspective, no other alternative existed. No matter how bleak the circumstances, Jeanne-Claude and Christo were tied together by passion, loyalty, and a growing realization that their fates were inseparably bound. His strength and gentleness gave her courage.

On December 9, 1960, Christo left Jeanne-Claude and France, not forever, as the Guillebon family might have preferred, but to attend the opening of a *KWY* group exhibition at the Calouste Gulbenkian Foundation in Portugal. The *KWY* group consisted of Christo, Jan Voss, and six Portuguese artists: René Bertholo, Lourdes Castro, Goncalo Duarte, José Escada, Costa Pinheiro, and Joao Vieira.

Christo showed a variety of *Inventory* items and some related drawings. The modest catalog did little to illuminate his work. Guy Weelan wrote about each of the artists. One page featured a photograph of Christo smiling in his studio. Alongside the picture, five rambling paragraphs addressed, among other things, the reinvention of Dada and the use of "rejected materials." Weelan stated that the art was "not easy to look at . . . even less easy to accept." Christo later called this first critical commentary about his work "double-talk."

Like any aspiring artist, Christo had hoped to engage an audience and achieve a degree of recognition. Instead, *KWY*'s premiere and his long-anticipated first exhibition generated scant public reaction. Jan Voss observed philosophically, "We were a diverse group, some good, some not so good. There were a few press reviews, but the critics couldn't be very kind because the exhibition was not very good. The show disappointed Christo. That astonished me. He really anticipated far more public reaction."[26]

Christo returned to Paris just before Christmas. Having witnessed the political repression in Portugal, whose dictatorship reminded Christo of the Communist system he had escaped, he was even more determined to maintain his tenuous hold on freedom while keeping his besieged family together. With youthful optimism, he and Jeanne-Claude adapted to a threadbare existence that was fraught with worries. What else would Jacques and Précilda do to punish them? they wondered. Would the now-common knowledge of their illicit relationship complicate the pending divorce settlement with Planchon? And without her parents' help, how could Jeanne-Claude continue to pay for legal services? Christo had already learned to survive hard times, so even with depleted cash and only an occasional portrait commission, he remained optimistic.

Jeanne-Claude had never sought independence; it arrived with the realization that freedom and potential do not provide personal comfort. She later remarked, "Spending money never added excitement to my life, but being impoverished with Christo was exciting. I didn't mind starving with him. We were never poor; we were just without money." Despite their depleted funds, Jeanne-Claude and Christo did manage to keep abreast of the current art scene, even going out for dinners with groups of artists. Jeanne-Claude remembered, "While everyone else ate, we sat at the end of the table, sharing a cup of coffee."

Carole Weisweiller witnessed Jeanne-Claude's sudden transition from prosperity to privation that winter. Looking back, she recalled, "Jeanne-Claude grew up very quickly. It took courage to stay with Christo, but their love was very strong. Standing up to her mother took enormous strength, but her father's role really devastated Jeanne-Claude. She truly admired him. He always treated her exactly like his own daughter. Then everything became very ugly. Jacques was driven by Précilda. I don't think he wanted to create problems, but she was like a tiger."

Carole continued: "I remember they were starving. Christo was not earning any money and was under great pressure, yet he never said a bad word about Précilda. Jeanne-Claude completely devoted herself to him and the baby. They seemed so much in love. I went to see her several times in that cramped room. Cyril was seven or eight months old. The heating wasn't very good, and sometimes I dared ask, 'Do you have enough food?' She would respond firmly, 'Of course—what do you think?' Jeanne-Claude was very proud. She was still well dressed and didn't want to admit that they were broke. When I asked about food again just before Christmas, she turned away without answering."[27]

Their grim financial picture did not change in early 1961. Unlike portrait commissions, the bills for rent, telephone, food, and other necessities arrived with sobering regularity. Jeanne-Claude concocted a potpourri that became the family's regular menu. A benevolent butcher provided free marrow bones. A woman at a vegetable stall gladly negotiated for blemished produce. "I would put the bones in a big pot of water," Jeanne-Claude explained, "with salt, parsley, potatoes, carrots, onions, and every other vegetable I could find. They were not very good-looking, not very fresh, but once you peeled them, the center was fine. After three hours of boiling, we had a fantastic, very healthy soup." She laughed. "It was crazy."

Any sale of Christo's work seemed miraculous. In early 1961, an American named Mrs. Barman purchased a small vertical bundle for the equivalent of seventy dollars. That amounted to less than a third of his standard portrait fee, but it covered a month's rent. "I saw how happy that made him," said Jeanne-Claude. "It wasn't a matter of money. When he did a portrait, we were suddenly 'rich.' So there was always hope. Each commission allowed us to pay the back rent and fill a small space-saving refrigerator that hung over Cyril's crib. We also stocked up on canned food. The rest of the money went toward supplies—not shoes or diapers, but all for art."

Paris, 1961: Christo and Cyril in the garden of Nôtre-Dame. (Photo: Jeanne-Claude)

Several developments increased Christo's need for art materials. A *KWY* exhibition had been scheduled for April in Paris. Christo hoped that perhaps this time people would take notice and, more important, react. Another promising opportunity came when Haro Lauhus, a fledgling private dealer Christo had met in Germany, paid a visit to his studio. Lauhus liked the work. He spoke about plans to open a public gallery in Cologne and, unexpectedly, proposed a one-man show in June.

Filled with excitement and confidence, Christo began working feverishly. He devised various packages, wrapped and transformed objects, and continued assembling sculpture using wrapped and nonwrapped oil barrels. He bought, borrowed, and found materials wherever and however he could. Household items began disappearing; first a chair, then a pair of Jeanne-Claude's shoes became grist for his artistic mill. Christo worked so obsessively in early 1961 that even a lucrative portrait commission became an unwanted distraction.

On January 6, 1961, two days before the French electorate went to the polls, Charles de Gaulle delivered an impassioned address, calling upon voters to support his vision of the Fifth Republic and his plan for Algerian self-rule. The referendum allowed only a yes or no vote on his reform policies. Frustrated citizens with no viable alternative found varied reasons to give him a 75 percent vote of confidence. Except for occasional terrorist attacks, the six-year-old rebellion abated as a provisional government began haltingly to take shape.

De Gaulle once again summoned Jacques de Guillebon to the Elysée Palace. The two men had not spoken for over a year. De Gaulle had recently relieved the hard-line general Raoul Salan of his command. More than ever, de Gaulle needed trustworthy men in key army positions. Jacques had been one of the earliest supporters of self-determination and remained principled, respected, and, above all, loyal. De Gaulle appealed to Jacques's patriotism, saying, "I ask for six months, no more."[28] Jacques could not refuse. The key element of his appointment entailed reorienting many of the half a million military personnel soon to return from North Africa. A deep malaise existed in the army. De Gaulle insisted that Jacques was the only man respected and reliable enough to prevent disgruntled officers from committing "misguided acts." A cheerless General de Guillebon left the presidential office as the new commander of the fifth military region in Toulouse.

That afternoon, coincidentally, several government officials and their wives called unexpectedly on Précilda. When Jacques returned home, he greeted the visitors but curiously avoided eye contact with Précilda. "You've accepted some assignment, haven't you?" she asked. He finally looked at her and confessed. Précilda snapped angrily, "If you want to do that, I'm going back to England."[29] Suddenly, each guest began defending Jacques's decision, explaining its importance to France. Précilda ran from the room crying. Jacques followed her, offering reassurances until, at last, she relented. They would have to leave Paris soon. Jacques telephoned Jeanne-Claude. He pleaded with her to be sensible and rejoin the family in Toulouse. She refused.

It would take more than poverty to sidetrack Christo's ambition. He later wrote to Anani about his frenzied work schedule. There was no mention of Jeanne-Claude, Cyril, or financial difficulties. "Since my return from Lisbon a lot of work has piled up. I've spent the last months nonstop in the studio—then running here and there. The days pass with such speed that you have to run after them."[30]

In addition to his intensive work regimen, Christo continued his routine gallery, studio, and museum visits. A major retrospective exhibition of four hundred Jean Dubuffet paintings, drawings, and sculptures highlighted the Paris art scene from mid-December 1960 through February 1961. Dubuffet could have been describing Christo's work when he said, "Art should not announce itself. It should emerge unexpectedly, by surprise." And speaking of nourishment, he stated, "The need for art is as basic as the need for bread, perhaps even more so. Without bread one dies of hunger. But without art, one dies of boredom."[31]

Christo looked forward to the *KWY* group show in April, but events threatened to overshadow or even cancel his introduction to the Paris art scene. On April 22, 1961, six days before the *KWY* opening, four retired French generals seized power in Algeria, vowing to keep it French. The next day, de Gaulle denounced the generals' action and called upon the armed forces to crush the coup. On April 24, airfields around Paris were closed, tanks and machine-gun posts were set up near government buildings, and access to most Seine bridges was blocked. That afternoon, 10 million French workers took to the streets and joined a general strike; Communist, Catholic, and socialist trade unions were determined to prevent the rebellion from spreading to France. On April 25, French troops in Algeria regained control of Oran and Constantine. The next day, loyal army units began retaking key locations in Algiers. The generals' revolt collapsed.

Christo and his *KWY* colleagues breathed a collective sigh of relief. However insignificant in the scheme of things, their long-anticipated show opened quietly on Friday, April 28 at Galerie Le Soleil dans la Tête. Christo, Bertholo, Castro, Duarte, Escada, Pinheiro, Vieira, and their friends filled the small, corridorlike space. Although the opening had none of the notoriety associated with the Nouveaux Réalistes, it provided a welcome diversion from the nightmare of recent events. Christo displayed a shelving unit filled with wrapped and nonwrapped cans, along with other works and related drawings. As in Lisbon, the event went practically unnoticed. Later, an expanded version of the show traveled to Saarbrücken University, in Germany, where it again received a large dose of benign neglect.

Undeterred by the lackluster response to the *KWY* show, Christo prepared for his first one-man exhibition at Galerie Haro Lauhus in Cologne.

Through Christo Jeanne-Claude acquired a taste for modern theater. She said, "It was a new world to me." For years, a troupe of performers at the intimate Théâtre de la Huchette had been staging Eugéne Ionesco's *The Bald Soprano* and *The Lesson*. She said, "I laughed so loud and nonstop that the cast began laughing and had to stop performing." He still had work to do. Many of the thirty or so pieces for the show were finished before the opening, but other, larger works needed to be done on-site. These latter were to provide the first clue to the artist's grandiose vision. This group included *Dockside Packages*— the most ambitious work. Christo had noticed barrels and rolls of paper stacked along the Rhine waterfront near the gallery. With the permission of the bemused director of the port authority, Christo paid mechanical-hoist operators to assist him in rearranging the stockpiles. They also let him borrow some tarpaulins. The dockworkers were no doubt mystified by his curious reaccumulations and repackaging, which bore no resemblance to any art they were familiar with. One critic said of *Dockside Packages,* "Though scarcely distinguishable from longshoremen's work, they had the large scale and formal purity of Egyptian mastabas or Mycenaean stonework. Christo demonstrated that an artist can elicit mystery and astonishing beauty from the most ungainly materials and by the simplest statement."[32]

Mary Bauermeister, one of the exhibit's organizers, recalled the excitement generated by the show. "It was an incredible thing in Cologne. For us, the art scene divided into two camps: those who did figurative art and those of us who wanted to change society. We immediately recognized Christo as one of us. Our group felt like a secret society defending new values. Duchamp, not Picasso, was our hero, because we didn't want new objects; we wanted a new consciousness."[33]

Galerie Haro Lauhus consisted of two big rooms. Inside, Christo displayed large oil-barrel structures and various-sized packages. *Wrapped Car* may have been the most subversive bundle. He had purchased a damaged, motorless Renault for a pittance, draped it, then fastened the package with tightly knotted ropes. Christo had had to convince Lauhus to remove a large plate-glass window in order to get the vehicle inside. Two Nam June Paik pianos that Lauhus had confiscated, because of a dispute with the artist over a bill, presented a problem.[34] To make the pianos less of a distraction, Christo shrouded them in fabric and rope. He then placed one so close to the entry door that visitors were forced to squeeze their way in. Asked if he hadn't worried this would prove discouraging, he smiled and replied, "I liked the difficulty in entering. It looked like a place where a mover had come. You had to make an effort, an adjustment." Imprisoning a piano in fabric qualified as a gentle provocation, but using it to obstruct the gallery entrance introduced an element of mischief.

In addition to a car, two pianos, and the materials found stacked by the river, other wrapped objects included cans, soup spoons, a teakettle, a car rack, a coffee grinder, a typewriter, a stove, and bottles.

Most observers seemed to find the show more amusing and theatrical than profound. One newspaper photographed five people contemplating the exhibition. The headline read BETWEEN ART AND NONSENSE, with the subtitle "The Most Talked-About Exhibition Cologne Has Ever Seen." Readers were warned, "You will think you are in a warehouse or a junk shop." Art critic Siegfried Bonk observed, "Unlike the old master, Duchamp, who also removed function from everyday objects, Christo employs no wit or irony. What he leaves us with is a kind of naïve astonishment about the sculptural qualities of everydayness. . . . Neither surreal illusion nor abstract effects are intended by Christo; he preaches the mortality of all earthly things." Bonk also took note of another calculated obstruction by Christo: "We go through a small, dark passage which is left between piles of oil drums. It is a narrow space that barely allows us to get into the back room. There our walk is stopped when we are confronted by a wall of stacked barrels. . . . When compared to this, Arman's garbage cans seem like miniatures. The mummified packages reveal a special attitude. It is with these objects that Christo goes beyond the New Realist fetishism."[35]

The slim Lauhus catalog contained eight photographs of Christo's art and three paragraphs by Pierre Restany, who never saw the exhibition. He acknowledged "special monumentality" in Christo's barrel accumulations but cited Arman as "the pioneer in objective appropriation" and credited Daniel Spoerri as another artistic predecessor. In fact, Christo had begun wrapping and assembling *Inventory* in early 1958, a year before Arman's first accumulations and almost two years before Spoerri's found-object assemblages.

Christo left Cologne almost penniless. He had spent what little money remained from his last portrait commission on the exhibition. When he called Lauhus to make arrangements for returning the work, the dealer declared the art "worthless" and claimed to have destroyed everything. Christo recalls listening in disbelief. He never recovered any of his work or received compensation. Lauhus said nothing about having sold any pieces, yet Lucio Fontana maintained that he bought two wrapped cans; on his way back to Italy, border guards questioned Fontana at length about the suspicious-looking objects that he insisted were works of art. Jeanne-Claude and Christo believe that whatever Lauhus didn't sell or trash, he simply kept. "I think he probably destroyed half the pieces," lamented Christo. "Lauhus was very brutal."

During his work in Germany, Christo traveled to Frankfurt to see his father for the first time in five years. Vladimir Javacheff had managed to arrange a business trip that coincided with his son's stay in Cologne. The Lauhus experience had its brighter side: creating and installing the exhibition helped Christo to focus his ideas, a large number of people saw the show, and Pierre Restany began seriously considering inviting Christo to join the Nouveaux Réalistes. In mid-1961, Christo gladly accepted an offer from Restany to participate in a group show at Galerie J that fall.

During 1961, a number of young American artists, most notably Jasper Johns, Robert Rauschenberg, and Larry Rivers, spent considerable time in Paris, where they established bonds with their French contemporaries. A widespread receptivity to new ideas fostered interaction, cross-fertilization, and occasional collaborative efforts. On June 13, Jeanne-Claude's and Christo's twenty-sixth birthday, Christo met Jasper Johns at the opening of a show of his at Galerie Rive Droite. A painted bronze sculpture depicting a Savarin coffee can filled with brushes impressed Christo and baffled Jeanne-Claude. She said, "I remember Christo showing me what looked like a bunch of brushes stuck in a can and saying that Johns was a great American artist."

On another evening, Johns, Rauschenberg, Saint-Phalle, and Tinguely created works of art at an event honoring pianist David Tudor. Later that June, Jeanne-Claude and Christo attended Niki de Saint-Phalle's first solo show. They found time to frequent Galerie Daniel Cordier and Galerie Rive Droite, both of which often showed the work of non-French artists. It was during this time that Christo began preparing for the Galerie J group show. He felt that it would be just a matter of time before he earned a one-man exhibition and a wider audience in Paris. In the summer of 1961, Jan Voss let him use his Gentilly garage studio and an adjoining spacious yard, where Christo wrapped a motorcycle and assembled barrels into various sculptural arrangements.

Jeanne-Claude recalled that one day a woman called and said she wanted a portrait of her child. When she told Christo this after he had returned from his studio, he immediately rejected the idea, "No! I've just started something and I'm not going to do it." His fee would have been the equivalent of more than four months' rent, and they were completely broke.

Frustrated, Jeanne-Claude complained, "You spend the whole day doing those stupid packages, and you won't make a portrait."

"If my packages are so stupid, there's the door," Christo replied.

"From that day on, I adored his packages," Jeanne-Claude recalled with a laugh.

Jeanne-Claude did not realize that Christo, though absorbed by his work, had already begun to set up a series of portrait commissions in Switzerland for August, scheduled to coincide with the marriage of his old friend Sacho Todorov. Until their financial situation improved, Jeanne-Claude would find ways to make ends meet.

Having spent what little money he had on art materials, Christo scavenged for discarded objects and covertly appropriated family property. Jeanne-Claude said, "One day, I came home and took off my shoes to put on my comfortable old ones. I looked everywhere, but I couldn't find them. When Christo returned, I said, 'Sweetheart, where are my shoes?' He blushed and said, 'I don't know.' Later, I saw them wrapped in his studio. Then a dress vanished." In 1961, Christo entirely covered their night table with one of Jeanne-Claude's old cotton bedsheets, then tied it in rope. He also confiscated the landlord's table and chairs. His partially covered *Wrapped Table* contained a group of cans shrouded with linen and canvas. "I wrapped everything that was available," Christo later admitted.

6

Borders and Barriers

That summer, Précilda phoned for the first time since Jacques had assumed his command in Toulouse. "How is your bastard?" she asked nonchalantly.

"Fine, thank you," Jeanne-Claude responded.

"Does he walk?" Précilda asked.

"Oh, yes, he walks."

"Well, bring him here, you idiot."

Jeanne-Claude accepted the invitation, arranging to visit her parents while Christo went to Geneva to attend Sacho Todorov's wedding and paint the portraits he had been commissioned to do. True to her mercurial nature, Précilda shed her acrimony and began the transformation from menacing antagonist to loving mother and adoring grandmother. Accommodation with Christo would come more gradually. The worst was over, however.

In Geneva, Christo and nine other guests attended the Todorov wedding ceremony at Saint François Catholic Church. Christo gave them a wedding present of magazines wrapped in clear plastic, tied with cord. Two days later, he began to work on the first of the portraits. In mid-August, the Berlin Wall began to rise. A week later, Christo returned to Paris. He fixed his attention on an idea that was both to take his work in a new direction and clarify a preexistent impulse. Triggered by the ominous barrier to freedom taking shape in Berlin, he began to contemplate borders, separation, and passage.

In September and October 1961, Christo visualized a series of audacious projects using words and images. These projects would be monumental in scale and would demand far greater public involvement than his earlier work. He had already produced sizable barrel constructions in Gentilly and Cologne, but these works blended with their surroundings and could easily be mistaken for routine commercial stockpiles. Christo now envisioned works that, directly or indirectly, would address the despair of oppression and the joy of freedom, themes related to what was occurring in Berlin.

In September, Christo made his first study for what would become known as *Iron Curtain—Wall of Oil Barrels, Rue Visconti, Paris*. In a photomontage, he depicted an "Iron Curtain" of oil barrels. The plan was to blockade a narrow street on the Left Bank with several hundred barrels. He discussed the concept with Restany, who agreed to help negotiate with the city of Paris. "Pierre had political connections with someone at the Saint-Germain police station," Christo recalled. "We walked into the prefecture, got an application, and talked to the person in charge. It was my first real negotiation with a government agency." By the time they requested permission, Christo had convinced Restany and Jeanine de Goldschmidt to hold a one-man show in conjunction with the event.

Christo adopted the word *project* for the first time in spelling out his artistic intentions:

PROJECT FOR A TEMPORARY WALL OF METAL DRUMS

Between the Rue Bonaparte and the Rue de Seine is the Rue Visconti, a one-way street 592 ft. long, with an average width of 12 ft. The street ends at number 25 on the left side and 26 on the right. There are few shops: a bookstore, a modern art gallery, an antique shop, an electrical supply shop, a grocery store.

The wall will stand between number 1 and 2, completely closing the street to traffic, and will cut all communication between the Rue Bonaparte and the Rue de Seine. . . .

This "iron curtain" can be used as a barrier during a period of public work in the street, or to transform the street into a dead end. Finally, its principle can be extended to a whole quarter, eventually to an entire city.

CHRISTO
Paris, October 1961

Christo envisioned two other projects in September and October 1961 that confirmed his growing inclination toward monumental scale. Again he combined words and pictures. A photographic collage and accompanying text outlined his *Project for the Wrapping of the Ecole Militaire*. Attached to the center of the composition was a tiny cutout photo by Harry Shunk and Janos Kender of *Package*, which had been exhibited in the Cologne show.[1] Christo had pasted it over a photographic image of the Ecole Militaire. The revised structure could be seen through the base of the Eiffel Tower, with cars and people in the foreground. Christo claimed to have selected the location for his colossal package not because of its connection to the armed forces or to Jeanne-Claude's father, but simply because it was famous. His typed comments appeared on the same sheet as the collage and detailed the site, discussed the method of wrapping, and listed ways that the proposed project might function.

A second, larger Shunk print of *Package* was attached to another photograph to create *Project for a Wrapped Public Building,* conceived in October 1961. This time, Christo reversed the top and bottom of *Package.*

If the restraint to freedom inherent in a package had been too subtly presented in his Cologne exhibition, his proposals for wrapping buildings clearly dramatized confinement. In a later interview, Christo stated, "The building does not exist, it is anonymous. . . . I suggested using it as: parliament, sports stadium, museum, concert hall, or prison. In *Project for a Wrapped Public Building* the tone of my text is very serious, as if it would really happen. With *Project for the Wrapping of the Ecole Militaire,* I stated, 'It is to be wrapped.' However, in truth, I never seriously had any hope to wrap this building."[2]

The lure of monumental scale and the appeal of disrupting or denying everyday function continued to seduce him. The three small project studies for rue Visconti, the Ecole Militaire, and a hypothetical public building brought Christo to a decisive juncture. His growing mastery of the process revealed that the gesture of wrapping had the potential elements of a new visual language. "Christo was completely different than other artists," Shunk mused. "He was like the concept artists of a later generation."

As the dynamic art world continued to change, hierarchies shifted. Pierre Restany received a telephone call from Arman, who reported that a trial had just concluded at Yves Klein's apartment. Restany had been the defendant in absentia. Restany's portrayal of Nouveau Réalisme and his constant references to Duchamp had enraged Klein. Klein summoned artists and four art critics: John Ashbery, Pierre Descargues, Otto Hahn, and Alain Jouffroy. They listened in amusement as Klein presented the charges. Arman recalled, "The writers didn't like Restany, but they didn't rush to help Klein, either. They found it odd and funny that Klein wanted to depose Restany as pope of Nouveau Réalisme."[3]

On October 8, 1961, Klein, Raysse, and Hains announced the dissolution of Nouveau Réalisme. They blamed Restany's unilateral second manifesto for its demise. The unexpectedly vehement revolt tarnished Restany's reputation and challenged his role as spokesman for vanguard art. "Pierre seemed very nervous," recalled Harry Shunk.[5] Restany tried to concentrate on Galerie J's new exhibition that fall, "The Adventure of the Object." The participants included Christo, several sculptors, and DuChateau, a group that collectively produced works of art. Christo showed a wrapped table, wrapped chairs, other wrapped objects, and a motorcycle wrapped in opaque fabric, transparent plastic, and ropes.

Preoccupied with the apparent collapse of the movement he had established, Restany was obviously distracted. He and Jeanine de Goldschmidt routinely availed themselves of a bar set up in the back of the gallery, where they were joined by a stream of friends and acquaintances. Christo lamented, "I was hurt that Pierre and Jeanine were not more interested in my work. The gallery became a bar, and people were going there just to drink."

In November, Philippe Planchon unexpectedly showed up at 24 rue Saint-Louis-en-l'Ile. Jeanne-Claude described the encounter: "I remember that innocent look of his. He had no idea we were lovers. After seeing our room, he said, 'I thought you were close friends, living together like brother and sister.' He accused us of abusing his confidence. Philippe was not the kind of guy to start screaming, but he was shocked." After Planchon left, Jeanne-Claude worried that his child-support payments, which were already "as slow as he could get away with without going to jail," would stop altogether. The winter arrived with no art sales, no portrait commissions, and no sign of Planchon's check.

Jeanne-Claude and Christo had met Yves Klein many times during the last few years, but he had barely acknowledged their presence. That changed abruptly one December evening in 1961. Jeanne-Claude described the incident: "Rotraut, Klein's fiancée, was pregnant and they were planning a big wedding. I heard she was looking for a wedding dress. She and I were about the same size, so I naïvely said, 'I can save you some money. I have a Christian Dior wedding dress you can have.' Klein paused and for the first time really looked at me. He said, 'You got married in a Christian Dior!' I said, 'Yes.' Then someone told him about my family. The Guillebon name really impressed Klein. From that moment on, we became quite friendly, and suddenly he began treating Christo like a valid artist." Klein also suggested a collaboration, a wedding portrait of himself and Rotraut. Klein painted the left portion of the composition blue, and he planned eventually to affix one of his gold sponges to that area.* The portrait required several sittings in their apartment before and after the ceremony. Christo described the large canvas as "very academic, à la Manet." He considered it a wedding present. Christo later traded a large package for one of Klein's blue paintings.

Yves Klein's marriage physically reunited the Nouveaux Réalistes and at least momentarily restored their tenuous bonds. Klein put aside his grievances and ordained Restany patriarch at both the wedding and subsequent group affairs. With the infighting suspended, the exasperating effort to embrace a disparate flock under Restany's philosophic umbrella resumed. For his part, Klein envisioned a more concrete coalescence.

In the first months of 1962, Klein proposed collaborative works of art with each of the Nouveaux Réalistes. Collaboration with Klein left Christo

---

*The sponge was never added, because Klein died before he could do so.

with a bitter taste in his mouth. He found no challenge and little satisfaction in coproducing the wedding portrait of Yves and Rotraut. Christo later lamented, "I didn't collaborate; I cooperated. It was flattering to be asked. I would have preferred exchanging works or collaborating on equal terms. I didn't want to make a portrait, but he insisted. Christo did not collaborate; Javacheff did."

On April 10, Larry Rivers's first solo show in Paris opened at Galerie Rive Droite. His drawing over loosely painted canvases revealed a technical virtuosity that impressed Christo, and the two men developed a warm rapport. That spring, Tinguely also proposed a collaboration. Once again, Christo was flattered, but this time he politely declined. Preparations for *Iron Curtain* and his simultaneous one-man show at Galerie J in June demanded immediate attention.

In early May, Yves Klein flew to the south of France to attend the premiere of Gualtiero Jacopetti's *Mondo Cane* at the Cannes Film Festival. A segment featuring Klein directing nude women as paintbrushes had been filmed the previous summer at Galerie Rive Droite. He expected it to provide the exciting finale to the film, not to appear as a kinky oddity. "His explosion of impotent rage brought on a first heart attack," Pierre Restany recalled.[4] A few days later in Paris, Klein engaged in several angry exchanges during a panel discussion at the Musée des Arts Décoratifs. He then attended the opening of "Donner à Voir" at Galerie Creuze, where he suffered another heart attack. Three weeks later, on June 6, with Rotraut seven months pregnant, Yves Klein died of heart failure in his rue Campagne-Première apartment.

At first, many refused to believe the news, suspecting another bizarre hoax. Larry Rivers recalled, "Yves asked if he could cast me, face and body, cock and all, in blue plaster. On the day friendship and solidarity forced me to come by his studio and be cast, he died. He was thirty-four years old. In his own apartment, in a room full of his work, he was laid out on his sculpture *Blue Table,* dressed in the uniform of the Ancient Order of Saint Sebastian, a dark blue cape draped over one arm, like a Napoleonic naval hero. Immobilized on his own sculpture, he looked like another Yves Klein work."[5] Jeanne-Claude also had a vivid recollection of this: "He looked blue lying there on the platform in their living room. The man who came to make a cast of his face didn't even bother to remove the bits of plaster from his eyebrows or inside his ears. It looked terrible. I didn't want Rotraut to be upset, so I cleaned his face."

Because of an unresponsive bureaucracy, the fate of *Iron Curtain* remained uncertain. Despite this fact, Christo had found a new role: disturber of the peace, an improviser in the face of obstacles. Large, prominently placed posters on boulevard Saint-Germain and elsewhere trumped Christo's first one-man show in Paris. The exhibition dates at Galerie J were June 27 to July

3, 1962. The bottom half of the poster announced a "unique presentation," *Le Rideau de Fer* (*Iron Curtain*), scheduled to occur June 27 between 9:00 and 10:00 P.M. on rue Visconti. It had been eight months since Christo had applied for permission to blockade the narrow street. There had been no approval, no denial, no comment. With family relations now considerably warmer, Jeanne-Claude turned to her father for help in obtaining a permit. Gen. Jacques de Guillebon, commander of the Toulouse Region, wrote to the official authorized to rule on Christo's request, Maurice Papon, the Prefect of Paris. Papon could not agree to close a public thoroughfare, even when requested to do so by a war hero and friend. In his letter to Jacques dated June 25 but mailed late enough to arrive after the proposed "cultural manifestation," Papon stated, "Not wishing to place the discussion in the realm of art where it appears all opinions are valuable, I will stand on the firmer ground of jurisprudence. A public way by definition must be free to all traffic. The authority that I represent cannot allow it to be closed, even for a few hours. . . . Believe my regret and please my general and dear friend, accept my best regards."[6]

The Guillebon family set out for Paris. Précilda had agreed to look after Cyril; Jacques intended to see Christo's uncommon art activity. Everything had been arranged—except for the police consent. Tantalizing invitations were mailed. The text announced a gallery party at 8:00 P.M., followed an hour later by the erection of a temporary monument on rue Visconti. A black-and-white aerial photograph of the area included a red line marking the route between Galerie J and rue Visconti. On the reverse of the flyer, Pierre Restany's text referred to the imminent obstruction as "not a barricade improvised in the excitement of a riot [but] a coherent entity and a monumental image of our time." Restany concluded by saying, "The language of Nouveau Réalisme is also that of Christo." His belated embrace meant less to Christo than overcoming the final obstacles to the project.

Christo wanted to show a large and varied group of works, as he had in Cologne. That was impossible. Galerie J measured approximately twenty feet by twenty feet; windows and doors further reduced the space. A small photomontage study for *Iron Curtain* and photo enlargements of tiny sketches of various barrel configurations, *Project for the Wrapping of the Ecole Militaire*, and *Project for a Wrapped Public Building* were exhibited for the first time in Paris. However, one work dominated the show: One hundred and twenty multicolor oil barrels, stacked horizontally against the back wall from floor to ceiling, loomed over the gallery. Each barrel had been found or purchased during the last year, taken to Christo's studio in Gentilly, and then reassembled. The piece echoed both the imposing wall of barrels Christo had installed at Galerie Haro Lauhus a year earlier and the *Iron Curtain* he envisioned for rue Visconti. Responses to the installation were varied. Some viewers saw a menacing presence, others a rhythmic field of beautiful coloration.

The wall may have represented many things, but a salable commodity was not among them. Jeanine de Goldschmidt displayed little enthusiasm for Christo's work or for a show with no price tags. "She was against it," Jeanne-Claude said, "but Pierre interceded." Restany still dreamed of a momentous future for Nouveau Réalisme, and in his mind, Christo typified the continued vitality of the movement.

Restany and Christo shared a growing anxiety in the hours prior to the opening. The invitation and poster called for the construction of a temporary monument, but as of Wednesday afternoon, June 27, no permit had been issued. The official silence intensified their sense of foreboding. On the previous night, Jeanne-Claude and Christo had taken to the streets near the gallery, armed with posters, a wallpaper brush, and a pail of glue; under cover of darkness they violated the *Défense d'afficher* laws.

"Jeanne-Claude's determination helped a lot," Restany recalled. "She kept saying, 'We'll do the project no matter what.'"[7] Everyone agreed to go ahead. Christo knew that he might be arrested and could go to jail. The barrels for the project had been rented, and Christo had carefully selected the number, color, and texture of barrels needed, negotiating a very reasonable rate for one day's use. The fee included a truck, a driver, and another helper to deliver and return the cargo. With the Galerie J show installed, the driver, the helper, and Christo loaded the truck and drove it to the congested Sixth Arrondissement.

At 6:30 P.M. they arrived at rue Visconti. A warm summer light lingered. The large rig stopped near the rue de Seine, where Jeanne-Claude and several friends stood waiting. The workers immediately began handing barrels down to Christo from the truck's rear platform. He quickly constructed the base of a barricade by laying ten drums side by side across the road. Disruption was immediate. Traffic ground to a halt, people gathered, and horns blared. Nonetheless, the unloading continued. Christo looked like a beleaguered high-wire performer balanced atop the growing structure. A series of pictures taken by a *France-Soir* photographer show a rail-thin Christo looking intensely serious and exhausted. "I kept watching Christo," Jeanne-Claude recalled. "He seemed so tired and harassed. I was mesmerized by that wall and by him. I don't remember being afraid, except for Christo. He was very frail. The barrels looked so much heavier and sturdier than he did. He unloaded them as if they were dynamite ready to explode." He said, "The truck platform was like a ladder. Near the end, standing on the barrels made me higher than the truck. The work went very fast. We were finished in less than thirty minutes." The first policeman arrived while Christo and his helpers were still unloading the barrels. Jeanne-Claude intercepted him. The dumbstruck gendarme studied the frenzied scene and asked, "What is this?"

She smiled and nonchalantly explained, "It's a work of art."

"It is forbidden to do that. Tell him to stop!" he protested.

Jeanne-Claude never flinched. "I can't interfere. He isn't even finished yet." She called the activity legal and temporary. When he commanded that the work stop, Jeanne-Claude insisted on speaking to someone with higher authority. By the time he returned with several officers, the truck had left; a festive, good-natured crowd was milling about, the press was having a field day, and a new French barricade had become history.

"We could hardly see anything until the truck left," explained Jeanne-Claude. "Then, suddenly, Christo's *Iron Curtain* became visible. A rhythmic expanse of ninety red, white, yellow, blue, black, gray, brown, and rust-colored circles—enhanced by spigots, logos, lettering, embossing, and a variety of weathered surfaces—rose almost fourteen feet high, pressing against both sides of the street.[8]

Jeanne-Claude looked glamorous in her dark green Christian Dior evening dress, a holdover from her earlier, more affluent life. Christo wisely let her do the talking. She fumbled through her purse and flashed as many papers as possible at the policeman. None were relevant. Trying to buy time, Jeanne-Claude urged him to visit the nearby Galerie J and look through the windows. She contended that the wall of barrels at the gallery proved *Iron Curtain* was a legitimate artistic expression. The deadpan police chief listened patiently, then demanded a permit. Restany witnessed the scene. "At the last moment, she used the only card she had left, her name. That gave us enough time," Restany later explained.[9]

Jeanne-Claude asked that the wall be left intact until midnight. The officer's parting words were, "If this thing is still here at one A.M., you will all go to jail." A policeman stayed behind, while others fanned out in an attempt to reroute traffic. Gen. Jacques de Guillebon stood amid the commotion. "I didn't ask him to come," Jeanne-Claude said, "but we were extremely happy to see him."

René Bertholo and Lourdes Castro lived only a few blocks away. They arrived in time to see Jeanne-Claude hold off the police, and at nightfall they watched Christo's bright assembly of colored barrels come to life under a battery of spotlights. René recalled, "People in the quarter were shocked that someone would barricade their street. They thought it must be a scene from a film."[10] Jan Voss relished the chaos. "People were mostly amused," he said. "It was an artists' district, so everybody supported Christo. Even then he wanted a social reaction. When you close a street and separate things that were never separated, it presents problems. Christo forced people to react. The wall was beautiful and left a lasting impression."[11] The American artist Richard Tuttle also found the evening of June 27, 1962, memorable. *Time* magazine quoted him as saying, "I think you could call this work 'leftover existentialism.' There is so much despair about it, yet it is so beautiful to me."[12]

René Drouin owned an art gallery on rue Visconti, and Christo was al-

Paris, June 27, 1962: Christo in front of *Iron Curtain—Wall of Oil Barrels, Rue Visconti, Paris.* (Photo: Journal France Soir)

lowed to store materials there and draw electricity from the gallery to light the project. The American art dealer Leo Castelli had once been Drouin's partner. In 1957, Castelli opened a New York gallery, which by 1962 represented Johns, Rauschenberg, Stella, and other emerging stars. On June 27, 1962, he arrived in Paris from the Venice Biennale and visited his former partner. "René had already introduced me to Christo and arranged a studio visit," Castelli said. "His *Iron Curtain* was a great event. It was totally understandable because my artists had the same conceptual approach. The idea of blocking that street was pure Duchamp."[13]

Paris, June 1962: Jeanne-Claude in front of the wall of oil barrels inside Galerie J. (Photo: Raymond de Seynes)

Not everyone shared Castelli's enthusiasm. Drivers caught in the near gridlock that paralyzed traffic were among the disenchanted. Some rue Visconti residents were angered by the carnival-like atmosphere of the event. They expressed their displeasure by shouting verbal abuse and hurling various liquids from window perches. About 11:00 P.M., one tenant, exasperated by the noise, emptied his chamber pot on the street below. Several bystanders were doused. Pierre Restany's clothing sustained the worst damage. "I was absolutely soaked," Restany said. "Something like twenty-five liters of very dubious substance ruined an expensive suit I had bought that day in Milan."[14]

Carole Weisweiller was among those who did not succumb to the charms of *Iron Curtain.* "I liked Christo's drawings, but I was not impressed by his packages or that wall. I didn't take it very seriously," she said.[15]

Arman had mixed feelings about the work, since he felt Christo's colorful array of barrels too closely resembled his own accumulations. He recalled, "A few months before that I was in Nice harbor with Pierre Restany and signed an enormous [found] accumulation of barrels. They were stacked and ready to be shipped. I did things like that many times."[16]

Christo's event had become a party and a provocation. Restany complained, "Some people were laughing because they thought it was a joke. It quickly became a kind of village gathering, with the same type of strange, anonymous crowd that you have at fires or accidents. The wall was a really mysterious thing that people didn't understand."[17]

The wall evaporated between midnight and 1:00 A.M. The truck returned, barrels were whisked back to Gentilly, and normal traffic in the neighborhood resumed. Cafés in the area buzzed with postmortems. Did Christo's flamboyant architectural gesture reflect the Berlin Wall, the divisions in France, the disintegration of modern life, the shortcomings of Western consumer society, or the beauty of commonplace industrial trappings? Whatever its message, Christo's barricade had broken the law. On Thursday, June 28, the art world's latest celebrity and Jeanne-Claude were summoned to the Saint-Germain police station. Christo was reprimanded and warned. He smiled and pledged in his erratic French never to do it again.

With its strange mix of order and chaos, *Iron Curtain* aroused many interpretations, but Christo confined his comments to material facts, not decipherment. He would later declare, "I don't define art; I make it." The ephemeral *Iron Curtain* had an inherent social context, one that engaged even the most passive viewers. The provocative act represented a defining moment during Christo's early years in Paris. His exhibition remained on view for one week following the removal of the barricade. Anyone visiting Galerie J could not have guessed how accurately the interior wall of encrusted barrels and small diagrammatic studies for large-scale projects forecast adventures to come.

Christo's preferred theater of operations would continue to lie outside the traditional museum or gallery setting. While he and Galerie J had expended considerable time, energy, and money on *Iron Curtain,* sales were never a consideration. And although Restany had become Christo's friend and advocate of his work, he also continued to exclude him from all exhibitions of the work of the Nouveaux Réalistes. "It was very protected territory," Christo recalled.

Christo remembered the gulf between his thinking and Restany's seemingly artificial orthodoxy. "There was a great amount of appropriation in the air. Artists everywhere were using the found object, the readymade object. Incorporating the object into works of art did not suddenly become a hot idea. There was the 'Art of the Assemblage' show at the Museum of Modern Art. Everyone was doing collage and assemblage. It was not something the Nouveaux Réalistes discovered."

Jeanne-Claude shared Christo's disappointment in Restany. "I remember we thought this man would make a big difference in our lives." Painful evidence of Restany's rejection emerged in the summer of 1962, when Christo received an invitation from New York art dealer Sidney Janis to submit two Packages for a fall exhibition. Christo discovered that Restany had tried to exclude him from the show. When Janis showed an interest in Christo's work and asked for the artist's address, Restany had grown silent. He later explained, "The participants were supposed to have been New Realists and the American 'Neo-Dada' artists, not other people. That was the concept."[18]

During the summer of 1962, Jeanne-Claude and Christo met three young American men visiting Paris: Dimiter (Mitko) Zagoroff and Albert and David Maysles. Each of them was eventually to play a significant collaborative role in their art. Mitko's father, Slavtscho Zagoroff, had helped Christo in Vienna by purchasing several paintings and providing referrals for portrait commissions. Mitko was twenty-seven, the same age as Jeanne-Claude and Christo. He had arrived in Paris after attending an international conference on documentary films in Lyons. He had been developing a movie camera small and light enough to be toted on a person's shoulder, and he had become acquainted with some of the movie pioneers who were producing quirky improvisational films.

Mitko had met the Maysles brothers at an experimental film studio in New York. They had been invited to Lyon to screen *Showman,* a fifty-three-minute documentary film they had just completed about movie impresario Joseph E. Levine. They believed that everyday speech was more compelling than any script. Rather than utilizing the traditional techniques of running narration and face-to-face interviews, the Maysles tried to capture the spontaneity of real life. Their films reflect stark, imperfect reality.

Mitko introduced the Maysles brothers to Jeanne-Claude and Christo after a midnight screening of *Showman* at the Paris Cinemathèque. Albert recalled, "They were enthusiastic about *Showman.* Like all of our films, it was made the way Christo projects are made. Even then there was a similarity in the way that we worked."[19]

·　　·　　·

In late 1962, a lethargic Paris barely noticed the ongoing shift of the art world's center of gravity toward New York. Within two years, the American ascendancy would be complete. The October 31 opening of New Realists at the Sidney Janis Gallery signaled a historic moment in this realignment.

Janis rented additional space to accommodate this ambitious undertaking. The show consisted of fifty-four works by twenty-nine artists from five countries. It revealed some fresh approaches that were about to alter irrevocably the face of contemporary art. Few surveys of recent art by young artists would attract more attention, arouse more controversy, and offer more surprises.

Janis had taken upon himself to include Christo—who sent two 1961 *Packages*. Restany's handpicked French contingent, three Englishmen, five Italians, two Swedes, and twelve Americans were the other artists exhibiting their work. The lively troupe included Peter Agostini, Jim Dine, Robert Indiana, Roy Lichtenstein, Robert Moskowitz, Claes Oldenburg, James Rosenquist, George Segal, Harold Stevenson, Wayne Thiebaud, Andy Warhol, and Tom Wesselmann. Janis rationalized increasing the number of participants as a means of ensuring diversity. "The spirit of the common object becomes the common subject for these artists," he wrote in the catalog.[20]

The confusing title of the show, "New Realists,"* provoked some critics. They argued over how to better define the new tendencies evident in the show. Sidney Janis's wife, Harriet, proposed "Factual Artists," which, like "Neo-Dadaists" and "Popular Realists" won little acceptance. Max Kozloff suggested "New Vulgarians." In his foreword to the exhibition catalog, John Ashbery wrote that New Realism is "another kind of realism," where objects "are common ground." He stated, "New Realism is not new. Even before Duchamp produced his first readymade, Apollinaire had written that the true poetry of our age is to be found in the window of a barber shop."[21]

American writers seemed to enjoy comparing the abstract, cerebral inclinations of the French artists to their more literal and figurative American counterparts. Of course, the Europeans were found wanting. Sidney Tillim remarked that Americans "give you the thing itself—pow."[22] Lucy Lippard wrote:

[T]he European contributions looked pale, overworked, and strongly Surrealizing compared with the new Pop Art. . . . [The] Americans take their daily reality straight. . . . Stylistically and formally, the European artist is not as aggressive as the American, but he is given to manifestoes and demonstrations

---

*There is a significant difference between Nouveaux Réalisme, the French movement, and New Realism, the American movement, which also included Pop Art, assemblage, et cetera.

that are ferocious, emotional, and *engagé* in contrast to the "cool" Anglo-American viewpoint, which spurns group identification. The Parisian attitude . . . is far more literary.[23]

Jan van der Marck, an authority on vanguard art, observed:

In the shuffle for international attention, "Frenchness" became a liability; to young American artists the tradition was bankrupt. Original ideas, gestures and inventions by Klein, Arman, Spoerri, and Christo were prejudicially compared by American critics to the more familiar ideas, gestures and inventions of American artists. . . . [They] anticipated—they did not imitate, as is sometimes claimed—similar approaches by Americans.[24]

"It was unfortunate timing for Parisian artists who saw their role in the avant-garde associated with a Paris of the past. Arman, Klein, Tinguely, Spoerri, and Christo were viewed by American critics as poor alternatives to the developing young pop artists in New York," Van der Marck noted some years after the show.[25]

Restany strongly suspected that he and his group were victims of a conspiratorial ambush in New York. He arrived home to find another problem. A new outpost for recent American art and a rival to his leadership of the avant-garde had been established in Paris. Galerie Ileana Sonnabend opened November 15, 1962, directed by Leo Castelli's former wife, Ileana, and her husband, Michael Sonnabend.

Restany kept a watchful eye on the newcomers. He stated, "Ideally, Ileana would have preferred a desert in Paris where she could have landed with all that Pop Art. I think she considered me a potential enemy because I had a permanent laboratory, a living workshop at Galerie J. The fact that we were so active irritated her. I could show the quality of Nouveau Réalisme spirit while she promoted Pop Art."[26] For their part, the Sonnabends felt Restany displayed chauvinistic French hostility. Michael characterized Restany as "a nice bohemian, very articulate, but, like so many French people, when it comes to art, he is all words, no real substance. He put together a team of artists. If you were there and doing something that didn't sell, you were his meat."

"Pierre and Jeanine thought we were interlopers and threatened to keep French collectors out of our gallery," Ileana Sonnabend recalled. "He fought us on the grounds that he was defending European humanism. We were American barbarians."[27]

Nineteen sixty-two had seen enormous familial upheavals, as well. That summer, Jacques and Précilda de Guillebon unexpectedly added a son to their family. One night at a formal dinner in Toulouse, an army social-service aide mentioned an orphaned boy who had been found several years earlier by soldiers in the Algerian mountains. He reported that thereafter the youngster had lived with French troops but that now they needed to relocate him.

"I'll take him," Précilda suddenly responded.

Flabbergasted, Jacques said, "What?"

Précilda declared, "That's it! You're not going to complain, Jacques." He acceded to her wishes.

Jeanne-Claude recalled, "The boy was so handsome and adorable that everyone loved him immediately." Jean-Marie's adoptive parents gave him the surname Essertaux and designated his birthday as August 25, the same birthday that Norbert and Alexandra de Guillebon shared.

September 1962 marked a pivotal juncture in the lives of Précilda's two oldest daughters. First, Joyce Alazrachi left Paris for Vienna. Second, a vexing issue arose between Jeanne-Claude and Christo: marriage. Every time Jeanne-Claude brought up the subject, Christo demurred. "I very much wanted to be married," she explained. "He kept saying that an artist must be committed to his art and nothing else. But his art competed with our lives, like another woman, only more so. Mother and Father had been pressing me to get married. They said, 'Stop living in sin. If he doesn't marry you, it means he doesn't love you.' Of course I would never admit to anyone that Christo wouldn't marry me. I'd say, 'We're happy the way we are. This is the sixties; living together is modern, so why get married and spoil everything?' But I really wanted that commitment."

In mid-September, Jeanne-Claude risked everything on an age-old ultimatum. "Either you marry me or I'll have to go," she told him, pointing out that he could travel more easily were he married to a Frenchwoman and wouldn't need to rely on his refugee card. And furthermore, as man and wife, they could save money. "In those days every hotel in Italy, except bordellos, required you to pay for two rooms if you had different names on your passports," she explained later. "We could hardly pay for one room. Late that day, he finally acquiesced—'Okay, we'll get married.' In the future, I would tell people that we got married to save money on hotel rooms, but that's not the truth. I wanted to get married."

Once he agreed, Jeanne-Claude employed a new strategy: She played hard to get. Before long, Christo started pressing, "We should get married." The more certain he became, the more Jeanne-Claude feigned hesitation. There was still the matter of a pending divorce with Philippe Planchon. Once her divorce finally became official, Jeanne-Claude telephoned her parents to report that she would no longer be living in sin. Précilda and Jacques were gratified, but they chose not to make the trip from Toulouse, since there would be no church wedding, only a small civil ceremony.

On Wednesday, November 28, 1962, Jeanne-Claude Marie de Guillebon and Christo Vladimirov Javacheff finally finessed each other into wedlock. "There were only four of us," he recalled. "We walked to the city hall on a gloomy, cold, gray, rainy day." Pierre Restany and Jeanine de Goldschmidt were the witnesses. "I wore one of the world's first fake-fur coats," Jeanne-Claude said. "It had short, curly gray hair. My hair was rolled up in a bun. We went to a huge room at city hall in the Fourth Arrondissement, where a lady mayor married us. She was in her forties and had a lovely laugh. When Christo made a boo-boo, we all burst out laughing and had to start the ceremony over again. I had been training him to speak politely in French, not to say 'Yes' or 'No,' but "Yes, sir' and 'No, sir.' He tried to be well mannered when the time came to answer the mayor's question, 'Do you take this woman to be your wife?' Instead of saying, '*Oui,*' as I had told him to, he said, '*Oui, madame.*' Everyone became hysterical, because that's not the proper legal answer. Christo became irritated and asked, 'Why is everyone laughing?' He turned accusingly to me and said, 'That's what you taught me!' "

Restany said, "I still remember Jeanne-Claude's face when she said 'Yes' to the mayor. She had the same resolute look later at the wedding dinner. It was something like an inner revelation, a moment of truth when she linked her life with Christo's. She was very happy. Now, people say she is ambitious or immodest. They don't know her as I do. I knew her when she was a loving woman with an absolutely true and perfect love. I offer testimony to the pure feeling, to the truth, of their love."[28]

Mr. and Mrs. Javacheff wore no wedding rings. Jeanine de Goldschmidt's mother, Marie-Louise Lafont, paid for the wedding reception. "We didn't invite any friends or relatives," said Christo. Jeanne-Claude added, "We wouldn't have dreamed of asking anyone; we couldn't even pay our rent in those days." The modest affair took place at a small Left Bank restaurant a few blocks from Saint-Germain-des-Prés Church. Most of the guests were Jeanine's friends and relatives. After the meal, Madame Lafont presented the newlyweds with a key. It afforded them a luxurious one-night honeymoon at her avenue Foch duplex apartment. A large four-poster canopy bed adorned with satin sheets awaited them. Jeanne-Claude said, "It was great. There was champagne, a fantastic bedroom, all the things we didn't have at home."

On January 4, 1963, Jeanne-Claude and Christo boarded a train to Nice. Cyril stayed with his grandparents while his parents began a working vacation. In Venice they met Giovanni and Sabina Camuffo and Attilio Codognato, who had recently opened a tiny gallery near Piazza San Marco. Camuffo had seen Christo's art initially "in a small magazine." He remembered, "There was an illustration of a package, and I loved the work. I wrote a letter offering him a one-man show in Venice."

By early 1963, Pierre Restany's puritanical definition of Nouveau Réalisme had become more accommodating. He finally invited Christo to show with the group. The "Nouveaux Réalistes" exhibition and related activities highlighted the Second Nouveau Réalisme Festival, which opened February 8 at Munich's Neue Galerie Künstlerhaus. Minor adjustments in Restany's doctrine were evident. Added to his original roster were Christo, Gérard Deschamps, and Niki de Saint-Phalle. Heretofore, Christo had never shared the public spotlight with the Nouveaux Réalistes, but this time he would capitalize on the opportunity to do so.

Restany reflected, "I thought it was natural for him to join the group. He and all the artists were perfectly aware consumers, incorporating industrial, urban objects into their work. By clear choices Christo entered into the pure orthodoxy of the movement."[29] Christo, however, had never considered himself a member of the group. In his mind, his loose affiliation with the group and his belated participation in their ventures provided a welcome opportunity to exhibit, not a loss of independence or an affirmation of Restany's rhetoric. In the future, Christo would contend that he had never really been a Nouveau Réaliste, pointing out that no group manifesto bore his signature. "Maybe I would have signed," he said, "but no one ever asked."

The Munich participants were trying to create their own visual language. To that task, Christo brought a sense of adventure. He showed several pieces in a long, corridorlike gallery space leading to an interior courtyard. One work, *Package on a Luggage Rack,* consisted of a mattress and a child's stroller, wheels upward, covered by clear plastic and tied to an automobile luggage rack by rope and rubberized cord. For the building's inner courtyard, Christo rounded up numerous barrels and stacked them horizontally in a series of connected archways that viewers could approach from the open courtyard or a surrounding covered arcade walkway. The structure echoed his walls of oil barrels at Galerie Haro Lauhus and Galerie J. Pierre Restany proclaimed Christo's "temporary monument, a monumental accumulation" and "a beautiful performance."[30]

In Paris, Christo resumed work with impatient exuberance. As he and other artists sharpened their imagery, Restany took aim at rivals to his presumed leadership of the avant-garde. "Pierre Restany writes of a gap between Paris and New York, and defends his flock with pathos," one journalist observed. "American Pop Artists, whom he called Neodadaists, seem to him less well armed to face the complexity of tomorrow. He seems very sure of himself, as always."[31] The dealers and promoters of new American art, Sidney Janis, Leo Castelli, and, most visibly, Ileana and Michael Sonnabend, were at the forefront of those challenging both the establishment and Restany's exalted vision of a vanguard revolution.

Christo witnessed the escalating confrontation with discomfort. "Pierre created an evangelistic, partisan attitude. He made it unnecessarily complicated for French artists by highlighting differences. It was completely ridiculous. He said that the Nouveaux Réalistes would take over America. I found the polemic infuriating. It was wrong to start a political, aesthetic war between New York and Paris." Yet hostilities did develop. Motivated by conviction or self-interest, artists, critics, and dealers consciously or unwittingly contributed to the strife. Restany's unyielding sociological focus on the raw objects of a technological, urban, consumer society would prove no match for clearly legible words, symbols, and figurative images of American everyday life and culture. Restany reflected, "At that time, even though we didn't know it, the art-market war was already over. Paris had lost. There is nothing you can do to stop global events."[32]

As the battle for artistic dominance unfolded, Christo returned to Germany in February 1963 to prepare for a one-man exhibition at Galerie Schmela. Because Schmela refused to pay shipping costs, Christo arrived several weeks prior to the opening, intent on creating all the work in Düsseldorf. Before joining him, Jeanne-Claude took Cyril to Toulouse, where he would stay with her parents. She was no longer blond. She recalls that in June 1962 she had gone to a cheap hairdresser. "He flocked my hair completely, and suddenly I had blue hair like the old ladies do. He refused to change it unless I paid again. I left, furious." Jeanne-Claude arrived at the Guillebons' wearing a black leather skirt and black fishnet stockings. "I looked very hip," she recalled. "All our friends dressed like that. When my mother saw me, she screamed, 'What's that?' I looked behind me, pretending not to understand, and said, 'What's what?' She shrieked, 'Your hair! It's blue!' I asked, 'Do you like it?' She said, 'It's horrible. Does Christo like it?' I lied. 'He loves it!'" A few weeks later Jeanne-Claude transformed her old-lady blue into blond.

She and Christo relished the idea of traveling together, meeting new people, seeing new places, and discovering art. Jeanne-Claude had blossomed from an upper-class neophyte into a visually literate woman who drew energy from a network of European and American artists. For Christo, the prospect of creating a body of work in an unfamiliar place promised excitement. In Düsseldorf, the Christos stayed in the unoccupied, unheated studio rented by Günther Uecker, Rotraut Klein's brother. Jeanne-Claude remembered that "it was a very old concrete loft that Uecker couldn't use in the winter because there was no heat." "Schmela was so stingy," Christo added. "We had to sleep on a freezing floor."

Alfred Schmela had opened his tiny Düsseldorf gallery with an exhibit of Yves Klein's blue paintings in 1957. He introduced Klein, Tinguely, and

Fontana to Germany. "In those days," said Jeanne-Claude, "an exhibition with Schmela amounted to consecration. He had the biggest little gallery in Europe: biggest in name, biggest because of the fantastic quality, and biggest in its reputation for supporting advanced art. Schmela had seen Christo's 1961 Haro Lauhus show in Cologne. The next year, he visited us in Paris. He spoke only German and kept pointing at the work, saying, 'Prima! Prima!' and other words that, even with our language problem, we knew meant 'Great, great, you art, me money.' He seemed eager to show the work. We smiled and agreed. That was our contract."

During two weeks of tireless work in Düsseldorf, Christo and Jeanne-Claude also managed to visit Edith and Dieter Rosenkranz, artists' studios, and exhibitions. Much of the time was spent scrounging for discarded or inexpensive materials that could be transformed into an ensemble of packages. "We worked in that cold place and in what looked like a bombed-out house next door," Jeanne-Claude recalled. "It was a wonderful location because there were nails, wood planks, and all kinds of debris that I rescued and took to Christo as fast as I could. He would stuff things into fabric-covered packages to give them bulk, then tie ropes around the whole thing."

Hans Möller, a printer, and his wife, Gisela, owned two floors in the building. "They had two little boys," Jeanne-Claude said. "We met one of them while we were working there. One day, on television, the child saw Christo wrapping a Volkswagen. Later, he brought a toy car to Christo and asked him to wrap it. Christo was so touched that the boy would sacrifice his toy that he not only wrapped it but glued it to a wood backing and signed it. It was lovely. On our next trip, we met the other son. He wouldn't say hello. We discovered that it was his car that his brother had sacrificed for art."

On February 11, 1963, nine days prior to his opening, Christo and Jeanne-Claude joined Pierre Restany at Zum Uerigen, a Düsseldorf tavern frequented by artists. Christo recalled, "Pierre got drunk. He wrote about me on a beer coaster." Restany jotted down a few cryptic sentences about Christo hanging on a cross and about the veil with which he covered and thereby revealed the poetry and truth of objects. Restany initialed, dated, and inscribed the name of the establishment on his enigmatic pronouncement. When Christo designed the announcement for his Schmela show, he included a reproduction of Restany's beer-coaster essay and photographs of three earlier works: *Package, Wrapped Bicycle on a Luggage Rack,* and *Project for a Wrapped Public Building.*

Joseph Beuys attended Christo's opening, wearing his familiar gray hat. "He was a very kind and extremely humble person," remembered Christo. "Beuys was also quiet, thoughtful, and complex, not at all arrogant. He did everything Alfred Schmela asked him to, even baby-sitting."

Earlier that month, Beuys had organized a major Fluxus concert. The two-day event, called "Festum-Fluxorum-Fluxus," had been designed as a colloquium for students at the Düsseldorf Art Academy. Among the sixty names listed on the poster were George Maciunas, John Cage, Daniel Spoerri, Emmet Williams, Dick Higgins, Yoko Ono, Robert Filliou, Nam June Paik, and Wolf Vostell. Thanks to Edith and Dieter Rosenkranz, Christo had already become acquainted with many of those now joined under the Fluxus banner, a Neo-Dada group that presented street performances, Happenings, provocative publications, and subversive actions of every stripe.

Although Christo never considered himself a Nouveau Réaliste or a member of Fluxus, he contributed significantly to the revolutionary atmosphere both groups thrived on. His Schmela opening attracted a restless mix of intellectuals, collectors, and subterranean artists, who filled the gallery and overflowed into the street. The show consisted of wrapped objects, one large package, and about a dozen smaller ones, including a diptych composed of equal-size black-and-white bundles. Also on view were *Wrapped Adding Machine, Wrapped Printing Machine,* and salvaged and repaired *Wrapped Supermarket Cart.* "The prices for packages ranged from thirty to eighty dollars," Jeanne-Claude recalled. "In the middle of the opening I went to Alfred and asked why he had red dots next to most of the work. He said, 'They are sold.' I asked who had bought them. He pointed to a lady and gentleman. So I approached them and introduced myself. I asked the woman, 'What made you buy that one?' She said, 'It's very simple. Two years ago, Alfred had a Fontana show and told me to buy. I didn't. Today it's four times the price. Now I buy.' Then I went to the man and said, 'Sir, Alfred told me that you bought this piece. I'm very pleased, but may I ask why you bought it?' He said, 'A year ago, Alfred grabbed me by the tie and threatened, "If you don't buy something, you can never set foot in my gallery again." Now I buy at every exhibition.' I didn't ask anyone else because I feared what they might say." The sales astonished Christo. He said, "I couldn't believe it, but almost everything sold."

In the crowd was one of Christo's newest friends and supporters, Charles Wilp, a Düsseldorf photographer and collector. Schmela had introduced them two weeks earlier. Encouraged by Schmela and Wilp to do some additional pieces, Christo decided to wrap a nude woman. "Wilp provided the model," Christo said. "I did the work in his studio because there was no room at the gallery. I tried but couldn't convince Schmela to exhibit the wrapped nude on a pedestal for a short while. The idea was to show an organic object on a sculpture base." The shrouding took place a few days before the opening, attended by about thirty journalists and friends. One magazine described the model embedded in layers of plastic and rope as "a well-rounded nude blonde with a demure pageboy hairstyle. In a well-rehearsed 'striptease in reverse,' he swathed her in dozens of feet of transparent polyethylene." After tying the last knot, the artist offered some comments and answered questions. "Wasn't

Cologne, 1963: Christo with his wrapped Volkswagen. (Photo: Charles Wilp)

wrapping a naked blonde really a Happening?" someone asked. Christo responded, "Not at all! The package was a real piece of sculpture even if it lasted only a few hours."[33]

Years later, Christo observed that "the idea of obscuring a person's sex by wrapping may have come after I saw a photograph of Giacometti's studio.[34] It was a spectacular picture because all of his working sculptures were covered to prevent drying. The cloth made the figures anonymous, ambiguous. That fascinated me. I was impressed that the forms were no longer male or female. They became unknown."

Heartened by the results of Christo's temporary package and his own striking series of photographs documenting the process, Wilp helped the artist borrow a Volkswagen for the same purpose. Christo approached the task enthusiastically, seeing an opportunity to replace, at least temporarily, the wrapped car that had been shown and later destroyed at Galerie Haro Lauhus in 1961. Wilp's series of pictures show the slender figures of Jeanne-Claude and Christo, dressed in black, wearing high rubber boots as they work in a snow-filled courtyard near his house. She passes him rope as he obsessively harnesses an opaque fabric about the vehicle. Christo reminisced, "I have the impression that we tried to take the car to the gallery, to park it outside for a short time. I'm not sure if we did it." To thank Wilp for the use of his space, Christo wrapped his host's tripod-mounted Rolleiflex—the same camera Wilp had used to photograph Klein's exhibition "The Void."

Christo and Jeanne-Claude returned to Paris on March 3, 1963. Shortly afterward, she went to see her parents to pick up Cyril. During Cyril's absence, Christo had pirated his son's toy horse. The child returned to find *Wrapped Horse;* Cyril's prized sixteen-inch-high stallion on wheels had been wrapped in canvas and tightly bound in rope. Only a tattered strawlike tail had escaped confinement. Fortunately, Cyril also had a rocking horse given to him by Carole Weisweiller. Though Christo rarely worked at home, Cyril's childhood would be spent in close proximity to fabric and rope, witnessing a procession of transformed objects that had fallen victim to his father's hand.

For almost a year Christo had been devoting every free minute in Paris to organizing the spring 1963 issue of *KWY.* It would prove to be *KWY*'s most ambitious and most successful production. Christo invited Pierre Restany and the New Realists to submit material, but he also selected other artists outside the group. For the cover, Christo selected an oval Shunk/Kender photograph of Jeanne-Claude to be silk-screened in black over violet. Floating above her image are *KWY* letters "exploded" by Raymond Hains.

In the spring of 1963, while Christo had been frantically compiling his *KWY* issue, Jeanne-Claude unhappily found herself pregnant. At that moment, the uncertainty of life at the poverty level and a certain loss of freedom were tormenting to contemplate. In 1961, shortly after Cyril's birth, Jeanne-Claude had managed to pay for an abortion. However, it would be impossible to raise that kind of money again. "Doctors who did abortions wanted cash. It was extremely expensive, like twenty times our rent. In France, we thought that taking a high dose of quinine provoked a miscarriage. So I swallowed a large portion. I began vomiting, but it didn't work. The next day I took even more. I was very stupid." That same afternoon, with Christo away at his studio, she impulsively decided to self-abort. Jeanne-Claude had seen how her doctor did it years earlier; she began using a knitting needle. She only provoked bleeding. Christo returned to find an ashen Jeanne-Claude in bed, running a high temperature. The next morning, he rushed her to an emergency room. Jeanne-Claude recalled, "I almost died. . . . Christo took me home the same day. There was no charge." Soon after, perhaps in response to her brush with death, Jeanne-Claude recalled, "I got dead drunk for the first time."

In May 1963 Christo and Jeanne-Claude set out for London, where the rare luxury of a bath awaited them. "We spent a few weekends that spring at

Charles Wilp's place in Roland Gardens," Christo recalled. "We loved it." Jeanne-Claude added, "Charles had given us the keys to his London apartment. Before leaving Paris, we called him in Germany. Charles mentioned that he would be in London, too. I said, 'Oh, then we can't stay there.' He said, 'Sure you can. Let's get Christo to wrap another woman so that I can document it in a film.'"

Wilp's film begins with a shapely nude model standing alone, back to the camera. Her right arm points upward, while the left arm curves over her head, grasping the right elbow. Then the strange ritual begins. Christo springs into action, swathing the model in layer after layer of clear plastic, until she is completely covered except for a small opening around the mouth. He ties the first knot at the top of her vertically extended right hand and then, circling his catch, continues entwining downward. The sound track consists of nothing more than rustling sounds of plastic and rope as the artist tightens his stranglehold. The figure is finally turned toward the camera. Ropes crisscross protruding breasts, and the feet appear fused in a tree trunk–like form, widest at the floor. Christo lays his package down and rolls it over. The final footage is a close-up of the entrapped model's partially open, unmoving mouth.

Like the other wrapped nudes, the London one lasted less than an hour. Christo recalled, "I used many layers of clear plastic. It made some forms visible, some less visible. You would look and think, Is it a man or a woman? Where is the mouth? Fabric makes everything invisible, but plastic makes you want to see what is inside."

That May, "American Pop Art" at Galerie Ileana Sonnabend overshadowed a host of shows in Paris of European contemporary art. Despite his loose association with the Nouveaux Réalistes, Christo felt removed from the deepening argument over French versus American artists. "There were many artists in America and Europe appropriating the object and using it in their work. Pierre's unnecessary arguments and partisan polemic damaged French artists," Christo remarked. One month earlier, Arman had moved to New York. Canal Street would become his new flea market. An exodus had begun. That summer, Mary Bauermeister left Germany for the emerging capital of the art world, and Larry Rivers returned to New York.

In early June 1963, Jeanne-Claude and Christo prepared to leave for Milan. They had purchased a battered fifteen-year-old Renault, which cost the equivalent of a month's rent. Jeanne-Claude estimated that the vehicle would save them as much as 90 percent of their shipping costs, train fare, hotel bills, and so on.

Christo had never driven a car and refused to learn. The artworks for Galleria Apollinaire filled the back of the vehicle and the luggage rack, on

On the side of the road, 1961: Jeanne-Claude and the *Juva 4 Renault 1948*. (Photo: Christo)

which a group of packages were wrapped and tied in a large bundle. At the Italian border, customs inspectors had doubts about accepting the ensemble of packages as art, but after an animated discussion and an anxious wait, a confused-looking official shrugged and allowed the ungainly vehicle and its jittery occupants to continue. When they finally chugged into downtown Milan and stopped to ask directions at a busy intersection, a well-dressed traffic policeman glared down at them and grimaced. He ordered their embarrassing relic out of the central city. Despite this, they eventually found a hotel.

The Apollinaire invitation incorporated photographs of *Wrapped Motorcycle, Wrapped Car—VW,* a group of packages, and even a Shunk and Kender picture of Jeanne-Claude curled up on her bed wearing high heels, with scattered text from *Fortune* magazine advertisements. One page had illustrations of three artworks separated by lettering which read "We're deep in packaging" and "Packaging often ranks next to product in influence upon a buyer." On another page, beneath the photomontage of *Project for a Wrapped Public Building,* it read "Why not let our packaging people help you?" There was also a short essay by Pierre Restany.

On June 18, 1963, five days after Jeanne-Claude's and Christo's twenty-eighth birthday, the exhibition opened at Guido Le Noci's Galleria Apollinaire. A crowd filled the small space, spilling into via Brera in the heart of the city. Among the art-world celebrities present were Lucio Fontana and Marcel Duchamp. Both men encouraged Christo and became supporters of his work.

Once again, pieces sold. Fontana bought a large parcel nestled on the gallery floor. He referred to his mannequin wrapped in plastic as "Floating Angel" and hung it horizontally on his wall. Christo said, "Fontana had bought two wrapped cans in Germany long before we met. In Milan, we became very close."

In October 1963, Galerie Ileana Sonnabend in Paris launched its fall season with George Segal's first European exhibition. One sculpture, *Gottlieb's Wishing Well*, was a life-size tableau of a white plaster male figure stooped over an actual pinball machine. This was Segal's only major piece made in Europe, and it asserted a jarringly un-French, deliberately lowbrow presence. Jan van der Marck observed, "Creating this work in Paris would seem as manifest a rejection of European culture and life style as ordering a hamburger in a gourmet restaurant."[35]

Segal and Christo were introduced by Ileana and Michael Sonnabend. "We became good friends," remarked Segal. "We were aroused by the ideas of Duchamp and Cage. I found excitement in making environmental sculpture into which you would walk. It had to do with people, putting plaster on people, and using all the objects with which they are involved in daily life. Each of us followed the road dictated by our temperaments. Christo's work commanded great respect from his contemporaries. I think he is an excellent sculptor, making a very personal and original statement. Christo takes a found object that exists in the real world, wraps it with material, and totally transforms the shape of the object and its recognizability. His intervention diverts our attention from all the normal associations we have with that object. It is the process of the sculptor."[36]

Christo, Segal, and many of their colleagues converted scavenged commercial goods into a reformulated reality. Presented straight or altered, mass-media iconography and ordinary consumer products were manipulated to produce novel visual statements. Some in the avant-garde fashioned complex coded works, some used subtle deadpan imagery, and others aimed at highly charged provocation. Out of this ferment, a handful of artists succeeded in challenging traditional perceptions of what constituted a work of art. Not everyone was prepared to acknowledge that Arman's accumulations, Christo's packages, Oldenburg's painted plasters, or Warhol's silk-screened images were actually art, let alone a fountainhead of visionary ideas.

When the Christos drove to Venice in October 1963, few could have recognized their overflowing cargo as art. A jumble of packages, tools, and art materials filled the rear of the car, and *Package on a Luggage Rack*, a collection of metal pots and pans wrapped in frosted plastic, occupied the roof.

Giovanni Camuffo and Attilio Codognato operated the only avant-garde art gallery in Venice. Located on Ponte dei Dai (Bridge of Dice) near Piazza

San Marco, Galleria del Leone was very small. Both partners were surprised when Christo arrived with only a few finished pieces and a bag of tools. Camuffo recalled, "I was very confused. His bag contained a chisel, hammer, nails, all the things a workman uses—no art materials. He and I went to buy books, canvas, furniture, and other items. He tied magazines in clear plastic, then he wrapped a metal wall sconce and put it into a large black oval frame we found. Christo did all the work on our gallery floor."[37] His largest piece consisted of a wrapped chair and a wrapped fake seventeenth-century table; frosted plastic covered a broken Murano chandelier on the tabletop, creating an ambiguous form. Christo also wrapped an old washbasin, suspended waist-high on its curvilinear metal stand; it stood dysfunctionally in the middle of the gallery, awaiting the October 11, 1963, opening. *Package on a Luggage Rack, Wrapped Magazines,* and other small bundles of humble origin were hung and dramatically illuminated with spotlights. *Wrapped Table and Wrapped Chair* had been placed against a wall and, like every other work, rendered nonfunctional.

Camuffo and Codognato liked the work. Before the opening, they negotiated a modest price for the entire exhibition. Christo and Jeanne-Claude were delighted. Christo accepted an invitation to show again the next year during the Venice Biennale. "Because they were so kind and bought everything," he said, "I made them a few more pieces." Camuffo, who liked *Package on a Wheelbarrow,* placed it in the gallery's street window. "We found an old wooden wheelbarrow in my courtyard," he recalled. "Christo wrapped a mattress with opaque fabric and tied it to the wheelbarrow. There was something tragic about that piece." Beneath the mysterious package, timeworn handles, carriage, and wheel remained visible, weathered by decades of hard labor.

The prominent display of *Package on a Wheelbarrow* ended abruptly. After several complaints from the bishop of Venice, a law-enforcement officer arrived with an order demanding the work's removal and the closure of the show. Camuffo said, "The local prefect of police told me it was dishonest to sell *Package on a Wheelbarrow* as a work of art, and he called me a thief." Camuffo and Codognato reluctantly complied, but they pleaded with the authorities to allow them to resume business. They and Christo were baffled by the talk of "blasphemy" and "obscenity." In their fashionable section near Piazza San Marco, where shop windows displayed precious jewels, gold, and antiques, obviously someone took exception to the display of "junk." In retrospect, Christo said, "It was not only that it was junk—putting it in the window and calling it art seemed preposterous to people; it offended a beautiful city, rich in culture and elegance. The closing was a big story. I didn't understand the uproar." After three days, Camuffo and Codognato won permission to reopen the exhibition, but only by promising never again to show *Package on a Wheelbarrow* in the window. The maligned art object eventually found its way into the collection of New York's Museum of Modern Art.

Beginning in 1963, Christo and Jeanne-Claude's visits to Venice began to include pilgrimages to Padua, twenty miles west. The fourteenth-century Giotto murals adorning the walls of the Cappella degli Scrovegni—the Arena Chapel—became an enduring attraction for them. Thirty-eight scenes, including *The Last Judgment* on the west wall, are linked by a pervasive blue. Christo spoke reverently of Padua, the quiet small chapel, and Giotto's greatest achievement. "All the frescoes were done by him, no assistants. Every panel is small, composed with huge, incredibly charged empty spaces. It's very rare that painting can balance so much emptiness with something happening at the bottom. Giotto created large expanses where there is little indication of a landscape or figure, just enigmatic, relaxed areas where nothing happens. I feel an enormous freedom in those empty spaces." Perhaps even more important to Christo is the rendering of robes and other draped garments. "All of the figures are simple, sculptural, and wrapped in fabric. Giotto reveals each person's form by the way he paints fabric."

After a brief return to Paris, Christo, Jeanne-Claude, and Cyril left for Rome, where another exhibition was scheduled to open on October 29 at G. T. Liverani's Galleria la Salita. Christo took along several pieces from Paris, but most of the work had already been created in Rome the previous summer. An installation photograph shows two barely recognizable overlapping blurred images of Christo in the midst of six pieces. In the upper right of the snapshot, *Wrapped Candelabra* is seen suspended from the ceiling. Beneath the wrapped fixture, set on a low platform, is the 1962 *Package on a Baby Carriage,* a pink plastic bundle tied to the seat of Cyril's stroller. Mounted on a wall is a large orange package fastened to a car luggage rack. Next to it, on a pedestal, is a vertical monolith, *Wrapped Postcard Rack.* He had bought the revolving unit, along with a group of picture postcards, from a Roman shopkeeper and then veiled the display in frosted plastic that allowed only a hint of each image to peek through. Rounding out Christo's strange brood were two packages, five magazine bundles, two wrapped portrait paintings, *Wrapped Toilet Washstand, Wrapped Shoes, Wrapped Chair, Wrapped Statue on a Pedestal,* a second *Package on a Luggage Rack,* and *Wrapped Vespa.*

Liverani seemed more aloof than Schmela, Le Noci, and Camuffo and Codognato. If there were sales, he never mentioned them. He also showed no immediate inclination to buy any of the eighteen pieces on view. Christo appreciated the opportunity to exhibit, but from late 1963 through most of 1964, Christo and Jeanne-Claude were again to suffer indignities and financial loss at the hands of art dealers. Events that Jeanne-Claude later called "part of a painful education" gradually elevated her from business novice to sophisticate. "We were so dumb," she said. "In those days we didn't know that works should be measured and photographed, or that you should make a consignment list and ask the dealers to sign a receipt. We would rather have died than show we didn't trust them."

Three days after the la Salita opening, Christo decided to wrap a large carved sculpture situated in the Villa Borghese garden. He proceeded without permission from the authorities. A handful of journalists and photographers watched him cover the classical Venus with layers of plastic and some ropes. The Venus remained wrapped for more than four months, while most passersby seemed to assume that conservation work was in progress.

No one who saw Christo's second Apollinaire exhibition in 1963 could have accused him or Guido Le Noci of commercial motives. The November 15 opening featured only two works of art: an enormous package that occupied the entire gallery and a small unframed oil painting on canvas. Neither was for sale. It served as the artist's response to Marco Valsecchi, who in June had said that Christo couldn't draw and was dishonest. With an impish smile, Christo reconstructed the scene: "I decided to make a huge package, so big that it was almost impossible to get into the gallery and walk around. I used metal scaffolding for an armature and built the structure around it with thick, beautiful fabric and rope. There was a narrow space of about three feet between the package and the walls. When you went around the package, you were confronted by a very realistic portrait of Mr. Le Noci."

An unexpected development greeted Jeanne-Claude and Christo on their return to Paris. In mid-November 1963, their landlord informed them that if they did not buy their space at 24 rue Saint-Louis-en-l'Ile, he would market it elsewhere. His price was the staggering equivalent of eight thousand dollars. "That kind of money was out of reach," Jeanne-Claude recalled. "It would be like asking me to raise five billion dollars today." The thought of giving up their pleasant neighborhood, the luxury of a telephone, and convenient credit arrangements with local merchants was tempered by the fact that they had for some time been considering a move. For over a year they had often discussed the possibility of living in the United States. Jeanne-Claude said, "It had a kind of magic aura, like the promised land. We had become friendly with Ileana and Michael Sonnabend. They always talked about New York's art world. And, Leo Castelli had told us that Christo's art would fit right into the New York scene." Castelli recalled, "By 1963, Christo and I had become very close, and I wanted to help him. I not only encouraged Christo but offered him a show in May 1964."[38]

Christo and Jeanne-Claude were approaching a turning point in their lives. What they had seen in films and heard about New York from Allan Kaprow, Larry Rivers, George Segal, Albert and David Maysles, Mitko Zagoroff, and others suggested exciting opportunities.

During this unsettled time, Christo began exploring a radically new direction in his work: a series of drawings and low-relief constructions, studies that would culminate in life-size facsimile *Store Fronts*. Their origins can be traced to a group of showcases done in the spring of 1963. These vitrines had a humble, anonymous look. They were ordinary rectangular units purchased new or secondhand or built by the artist. Most were banal display or medicine cabinets with brown wrapping paper or fabric attached to the inside of a glass window. Occasionally, Christo installed an electric or neon light, directing attention to the obscured inner space. Just as his packages denied normal function to their contents, inoperative showcase doors, veiled windows, and illuminated interiors enticed a viewer while denying visual access. In their own way, his inaccessible packages and uneventful showcases were no less extreme visual statements than Klein's "Le Vide" ("The Void") or Arman's "Le Plein," ("The Fullness").

Why did the showcase format fascinate the artist? Typically, Christo avoided speculating about meaning. He matter-of-factly cited his fascination with "the glass and facade structure" and his desire "to block the view of the interior space." Unlike his packages, with their unknown or partially exposed objects, these works often packaged nothing more than a void. In each case, the act of concealment or a hint of unspecified contents could evoke mystery, suspense, feelings of alienation, separation, emptiness, or territorial consciousness. Christo later called the Showcases "pedestal-size" pieces, which he did not find entirely satisfying. By late 1963, he formulated plans to construct large replica *Store Fronts*. Each would have the frontal quality of a stage set—handmade, life-size, and without utilitarian function. The storefronts would allow him to incorporate sizable real elements into the work, projecting an architectural, environmental scale.

The couple still counted every centime. Christo arranged a final round of portrait commissions in Switzerland to help pay for a five-month exploratory stay in New York. Christo and Jeanne-Claude reached out to collectors and dealers in a frantic attempt to sell his work. Among those who responded was Jean-Marie Rossi, a well-known antique dealer with a taste for contemporary art; he bought a storefront study. Jeanne-Claude calculated that by February they would need at least thirteen hundred dollars: six hundred for travel and seven hundred for expenses. What they had squirreled away, plus additional portrait fees and a few art sales, added up to about one thousand dollars.

Jeanne-Claude offered one of Christo's most important works to collectors Philippe and Denyse Durand-Ruel. Philippe, grandson of a prominent nineteenth-century dealer, had seen *Wrapped Motorcycle* at "Salon Comparaisons," a survey of current art. Christo said, "He was really very wealthy and had already bought a long vertical package and some small wrapped things." Jeanne-Claude priced *Wrapped Motorcycle* at three hundred dollars *or* a round-trip ticket to New York. "Either way, the piece is yours," she told him. Philippe responded, "Three hundred for that thing! No way. It's much too much." Seven years later, he purchased *Wrapped Motorcycle* for ten thousand dollars.

Another potential buyer was Raoul Levy, an affluent movie producer. Christo and Jeanne-Claude brought him to *La Cave,* a basement storage area at Précilda's apartment. Christo had been using the space as storeroom for several years. He recalled, "I showed him some packages and drawings. We desperately hoped he would buy something." Levy stood erect, looking at the work dispassionately. A large wrapped canvas facing the wall caught his eye. "What's that?" he asked. Christo showed him *Wrapped Portrait of Brigitte Bardot.* Levy had just broken his contact with the famous French star, whose films he had produced. He immediately bought it.

In February 1964, Christo created *Wrapped Statue,* an unauthorized temporary work of art that took shape on the bustling Place du Trocadéro, facing the Palais de Chaillot. The event was filmed for Belgian TV. Shunk and Kender also documented the action. Their series of black-and-white photos show a slender young man wearing a dark sweater and black-frame glasses gracefully scaling a tall sculpture base as he covers a six-foot-high gilded bronze woman in layers of frosted plastic, then binds her with rope. The TV coverage tied in with his exhibition at Antwerp's Galerie Ad Libitum. That show consisted of packages and wrapped objects, including *Wrapped Road Sign, Wrapped Road Lamp, Wrapped Shoes, Wrapped Mirror, Wrapped Table, Wrapped Bicycle on a Luggage Rack,* some pure packages, and several wrapped paintings. *Wrapped Bicycle on a Luggage Rack* and a few other pieces sold at the February 15 opening. Reminiscing, Jeanne-Claude said, "It was a miracle that we already had two round-trip tickets to New York. John Trouillard, the gallery owner, gave us some money, and suddenly our lives seemed to be improving. For a long time, we had dreamed of living in America, but before committing ourselves, we wanted to make sure our wish was not a foolish thing."

In February 1964, Jeanne-Claude and Christo brought Cyril and Guelbi, their African greyhound, to Précilda and Jacques in Toulouse. They boarded the *SS France,* bound for New York.

7

In Transit Again

On February 12, 1964, ecstatic crowds greeted the Beatles on their premiere visit to New York. Two weeks later, Christo and Jeanne-Claude arrived, unnoticed. They felt exhilarated seeing the city for the first time from the ship's deck. Christo could not wait to explore this new frontier, though he spoke only Bulgarian, broken French, and a handful of German and Italian words. Jeanne-Claude had learned English in school and as a teenager during two summer stays with British families outside of London.

The cab ride to the Chelsea Hotel quickly shattered Jeanne-Claude's confidence: "I thought I was fluent in English. But I had the shock of my life. Between the harbor and the Chelsea Hotel, our driver asked me three questions. I broke out crying and told Christo I couldn't understand a word the cabbie said. I have always had difficulty hearing and saying some words that sound the same, like *ship, sheep, cheap.* When we arrived at the Chelsea and saw an unmade bed, I called downstairs and said, 'Can we please have some shit?' They said, 'What? You want shit, ma'am?' I said, 'Yes, for the beds.'"

All of their friends had recommended the Chelsea. Built in 1884, the twelve-story, four-hundred-room landmark, with its pink brick facade laced with baroque wrought-iron balconies, has housed Sarah Bernhardt, Mark Twain, O. Henry, Tennessee Williams, Hilton Kramer, John Sloan, Jackson Pollock, Yves Klein, and numerous other art, music, and literary figures.

Clarissa and Larry Rivers lived on the third floor and his studio was on the ninth floor. He recalled the scene in February 1964:

[It was the] home of rock-and-roll bands and Leonard Cohen and Bob Dylan; Dylan Thomas and Thomas Wolfe; Brendan Behan, the Irish bard, George Kleinsinger, the composer and animal lover who lived with snakes, lizards, beautiful women, and wackily plumed birds; a floor below the terrarium, in burnt-umber rooms, the noble Virgil Thomson, composer, deaf as the snakes above him, surrounded by picture-crowded walls; Arthur Miller typing away on his play in progress, *After the Fall;* another Arthur, Clarke, writing the novel *2001* . . . superstar painters de Kooning, Alechinsky, Dine, and Arman in his black leather jacket, pushers and users of heroin, cocaine, opium, Quaaludes, speed, mescaline, LSD, angel dust . . . and transient hookers, male and female, indistinguishable from most of the permanent residents, plying a lively trade.[1]

If there was rampant prostitution and widespread drug use, Christo and Jeanne-Claude never noticed. Jeanne-Claude said, "We were completely unconscious. For us it was paradise. I felt a great freedom that I didn't feel in France. In Paris, even though I was an artist's wife and dressed in black leather skirts and black fishnet stockings, it was like a disguise. In New York, it seemed normal. Everybody was crazy. I wasn't trying to shock anybody. I dressed like everybody else."

Christo recalled his first impression: "New York was like the movies I had seen. There were many funny things. I vividly remember on our first or second day going for breakfast at a Horn and Hardart Automat next door to the Chelsea. There were little glass doors with food behind them. You put nickels in a slot. It was lovely and old-fashioned, like an old movie. That was the first time I encountered a city with so much 1930s architecture and accessories. It looked very strange and beautiful."

They began to phone everyone they knew in New York. Their first dinner guest was Ray Johnson, the patriarch of mail art. He and Christo had corresponded but never met. Johnson recalled, "I first saw Christo's work at the 1962 Sidney Janis show, 'New Realists.' I saw a burlap package on the floor that I wanted to buy. It cost twenty-nine dollars. I felt it and there were bottles inside. Later, I got Christo's Paris address from Arman or Daniel Spoerri and wrote."[2] Johnson's letter stated that he had little money but would like to have a piece. Eventually, a package arrived in the mail. Johnson opened it, only to find a Harry Shunk photograph of the unopened package, along with a letter from Christo saying that since the artwork had been destroyed, he could keep the picture as a souvenir. It also said that he and Jeanne-Claude were coming to New York and would like to meet him. "They invited me to dinner in their Chelsea room. I brought a gift of four forks that I had wrapped in a package with a hand-lettered label that said FEAR FOUR FORKS. They didn't open the package. She made sausages. I don't know how we ate them, maybe with our fingers. They had been eating barbecued chicken with scissors, which were the only cooking implements in their room." A mutually lighthearted spirit prompted an immediate rapport.

Christo's easy smile and friendliness spoke more eloquently than his few thickly accented utterances. Although most people needed help in order to un-

Manhattan, 1964: Christo and Jeanne-Claude in their room at the Chelsea Hotel. (Photo: Ugo Mulas)

derstand him, Johnson later claimed to have understood every word. Some who met the young couple became ruffled by Jeanne-Claude's assertive articulation of her husband's status as an artist. Writer Jesse Kornbluth later described her as a witty, engaging woman who could sometimes come across as "a domineering, driven, humorless shrew."[3] Jeanne-Claude traced that characterization to first impressions of her in New York. "Americans found me too aggressive because I would answer for Christo. They had no way of knowing he didn't understand the language. I should have taken the time to translate their questions for him, get his answer, and then translate his answers."

Christo recalled his frustration: "I was absolutely furious with myself for not learning any language. I became involved with so many things that there was no time to learn. I felt like an idiot. We stayed only four months and I felt very embarrassed. The most infuriating thing was not being able to buy materials for my work. I remember going into a hardware store on the Bowery near Houston Street to buy screws and things like that. Of course I had to take Jeanne-Claude with me, because I could not just point. I had to ask some questions. That was my biggest handicap. It was terrible." Neither was Christo's French sufficient, even by the mid-1960s—it made some people laugh, others cringe. Nevertheless, it was the only language in which he and Jeanne-Claude could communicate.

Christo prepared for the May group exhibition at Leo Castelli's gallery with single-minded determination. His goal was to create one large work. Throughout March and April, he constructed his first life-size *Store Front* in their Chelsea bedroom.

Christo called the storefront a "recuperation," since "many of the components literally came from demolished storefronts, the old-fashioned kind. They project the quality of real things, not fabricated by me, even though I put them together." *Green Store Front* grew out of several preparatory studies. In its enlarged, life-size scale, a glass showcase trimmed with thin aluminum edges was placed on either side of set-back door. Rectangular blocks framed with molding were used to support and cap the showcase. What appears to be a wrapped air conditioner was mounted above an inoperative door. Enhancing the door was a large masked glass window and a brass doorknob that Christo had appropriated from his Chelsea bathroom, replacing the hotel doorknob with a cheaper one. Interior neon lights, orange velvet, a barely visible freestanding package, and other materials were obscured by beige cloth hung over the inside of the showcase windows, while brown paper obstructed the view through the door's glass panel. Fully assembled, the replica storefront measured ten feet high by nine feet wide by three feet deep.

One day, while Christo worked on the *Store Front,* now in the Hirshhorn Museum collection, the phone rang. John and Kimiko Powers were downstairs, calling from the reception desk. "We collect contemporary art," John announced. "I heard you were staying at the Chelsea. Can we come up?" Jeanne-Claude replied, "Of course." The couple looked at the finished pieces and work in progress, then unhesitatingly selected a wrapped bottle. They said in unison, "We like it." Christo's first New York sale yielded slightly over one hundred dollars, enough for several weeks' rent and a few luxuries. Shortly afterward, another visitor, Richard Bellamy, a respected dealer, bought *Wrapped*

Magazines. The plastic-covered bundle bound in rope had *Seventeen*—"America's Teenage Magazine"—showing through its transparent skin. On the cover, an exotic-looking female face seems to express the discomfort of entrapment.

Christo's ambition went far beyond domestic-scale *Packages* and *Store Fronts* "wrapped from the inside."[4] He also thought about wrapping New York skyscrapers. By chance, Jeanne-Claude and Christo ran into Raymond de Seynes, a Paris-based photographer who had documented the *Rue Visconti Project* and many early packages and barrel constructions. They convinced him to join them on the Staten Island ferry to photograph lower Manhattan. Later, he also took pictures of Christo's recently completed scale models depicting high-rise buildings located at 2 Broadway and 20 Exchange Place. Composite images of these wrapped structures and the downtown skyline yielded a series of striking photo collages and photomontages. Sometimes drawn and painted over, these were neither surrealistic exercises nor visual puns, but studies that envisioned mammoth, realizable projects. The notion of a city panorama accented by one or more shrouded buildings had its roots in *Project for the Wrapping of the Ecole Militaire* and *Project for a Wrapped Public Building* done three years earlier in Paris. In each instance, Christo had employed techniques that prefigured much of their subsequent work.

The first few months in New York delighted Christo and Jeanne-Claude. They were invited to every art-world party. They were an attractive couple, a novelty, and as tourists, they were not viewed as a competitive threat by artists—despite the fact that Christo had an upcoming Castelli show. Jeanne-Claude recalled, "Even though he really wasn't a Castelli artist, he became known as one. In those days there were five important contemporary galleries in New York: Sidney Janis, Leo Castelli, Betty Parsons, Martha Jackson, and Dick Bellamy's Green Gallery—that's it! The real king was Leo Castelli."

The Christos were baffled by some of the offbeat gatherings they attended, none more so than George Kleinsinger's soirees. Jeanne-Claude remembered the eccentric composer: "We never knew him well, but we often went to his large apartment on the top floor of the Chelsea. There were usually lots of people there. I recall him playing the piano with a live boa constrictor around his neck. When he was too drunk to stay awake, he put his finger in the piranha tank. Their bites woke him, and he would go back to the piano. The entire living room and bedroom had over a foot of soil on the floor. A real jungle was growing there."

On May 2, 1964, "Four" opened at Leo Castelli's gallery. The reviews were mixed. *New York Times* art critic Brian O'Doherty observed that these four new talents, "manipulate ideas with such aplomb that their work becomes a kind of performance." He referred to Christo's "pet trick . . . wrapped packages prompting curiosity. He had extended the concealment idea to a lifesize shop-front, drapes covering the lighted windows and pearl-pink window linings, the air-conditioner suitably bandaged above the door. It has some of the effect of a 3-D Edward Hopper, and redeems an old trick with an inventive new performance."[5]

By now, any lingering doubts Christo and Jeanne-Claude had about moving to New York dissolved. The only uncertainty concerned the logistics and timing of the move. There were still many things to do in Europe: resolving matters with their landlord, arranging for storage or shipment of Christo's art and their few possessions, raising money, contacting friends, family, collectors, and dealers, continuing to produce work for coming shows, and retrieving Cyril, who had been left in France. On May 11, Cyril celebrated his fourth birthday with his grandparents in Toulouse. His parents had not seen him for nearly three months. They arranged to store a group of storefronts and packages, including *Dolly*, at the hotel. Surprisingly, there was no charge. In early June, their first flight together brought them back to Paris.

After a brief trip to Toulouse to visit with Cyril and the Guillebon family, they returned to Paris to attend to all the details that required attention. They had less than two weeks in France before going to Venice for the Biennale, still the world's preeminent exhibition of contemporary art. It was a frantic time. Like Leo Castelli, they arrived a week prior to the June 20 public opening of Biennale. Rumor had it that every detail, from curator Alan Solomon's choice of American pieces to the intense behind-the-scenes lobbying, was part of an attempted American coup masterminded by Castelli, with the goal of capturing the international art market.

No one had done more to promote European interest in recent American art than Leo Castelli and the Sonnabends. The growing vitality of the New York art scene and the emergence of Pop Art as a dominant force focused attention on the U.S. representation in Venice. Throughout the twentieth century, the Biennale had crowned a succession of European masters, including Braque, Miró, and Matisse. But in 1964, for the first time, the International Grand Prize for Painting went to an American: Robert Rauschenberg. Alan Solomon remarked to the press, "Anybody can see that the center of international art had shifted from Paris to New York."[6] Not everyone was thrilled. Art critic Hilton Kramer saw evidence of a Castelli-led conspiracy and a pattern of "cultural imperialism."[7] Italy's *ABC* complained, "Everything is lost, even a sense of shame."[8] Writing for *L'Express*, Pierre Schneider saw "hyperidealism" giving way to "hypermaterialism."[9] Ileana Sonnabend recalled, "There was a tremendous reaction against the 'American imperialists' taking over—where were the humanistic values? French people came to me saying I brought the Trojan horse, crying because Rauschenberg had won the prize. And Alan

[Solomon] said to me . . . 'You should say, "Yes, I did that because it was worth doing."'[10]

While in Venice, the Christos had completed arrangements for an August exhibition at Galleria del Leone that would include one life-size storefront, smaller preparatory collages, drawings, and sizable constructions. He planned to produce the work at army headquarters in Toulouse, where he and Jeanne-Claude would stay a month with the Guillebon family before moving to the United States. Christo described his in-laws' official residence as "an incredible, early nineteenth-century palace and gardens. Adjacent to it was a stable which had been converted into carpentry and cabinetmaker shops. I was given one full room equipped with carpentry tools."[11]

In Toulouse, Christo began work immediately. He and Jeanne-Claude scavenged demolition sites for discarded doors, moldings, and building remnants. He added missing pieces and reassembled two freestanding life-size *Store Fronts,* designed with interlocking elements that could be detached for shipping. Jeanne-Claude said, "I helped by bringing him wood and nails, running errands, and at the same time looking after Cyril." In little more than a month, Christo produced enough work for his exhibitions at Galleria del Leone in August and Galerie Schmela in December. Fortunately, both galleries were relatively small. The two largest pieces were *Red Store Front* and *Purple Store Front,* consisting of wood, metal, fabric, Plexiglas, electric light, and enamel paint. In addition, Christo created a group of elaborate three-dimensional cutout drawings and constructions. In each work, windows, not their uneventful views, became the focus of attention. Writer David Bourdon later described the facsimile storefronts: "They were so generalized as to be universal—a kind of 'everystore.' There are no goods or activities to be glimpsed through the undraped margins of the windows. And there are no signs, emblems, or addresses to particularize their location or function. . . . Like Hopper, Christo distills specifics to arrive at a generalization, creating a mood of detachment, loneliness, and vacancy."[12]

Leo and Toiny Castelli went to Toulouse that summer to see Christo and Jeanne-Claude. Their whirlwind tour included brief stops at museums, historical buildings, and landmarks. Castelli also visited Christo's makeshift studio, inspected the latest storefronts, and discussed a possible future exhibition.

In the second week of August, Jeanne-Claude and Christo disassembled *Red Store Front* and packed it and about a dozen smaller constructions and collage drawings into their run-down Renault. Then came the good-byes. For some time, Précilda had been concerned by what she perceived to be a steady erosion of Cyril's rich French heritage. As the family prepared to leave for

Venice, 1964: Christo, Cyril, and Jeanne-Claude eating lunch in a trattoria. (Photo: Gian-Enzo Sperone)

Venice, she burst out crying at the thought of her only grandchild someday forgetting French or, worse, speaking it with a Bulgarian accent. "What if he forgets everything?" she sobbed. Christo tried to sound reassuring. He looked into her eyes and gently uttered the fractured French equivalent of "Eh, madame, not worry, at home French always speak." Précilda shrugged in despair and cried even harder.

The family was caught in a major traffic jam at the Italian border. A customs inspector determined that the disassembled parts of *Red Store Front*, covered with plastic and tied to the roof of their battered vehicle, and other pieces—packed tightly inside the car—represented taxable commercial goods, not art. While Christo tried to explain, Jeanne-Claude encouraged Cyril to play with the inspector's rubber stamps. As the child began stamping everything in sight, the man demanded that Jeanne-Claude restrain him. She pretended not to understand. Finally, a chorus of car horns behind them persuaded the beleaguered official to relent and wave them through.

The gasoline gauge hovered near empty as they puttered into the outskirts of Venice. Making matters worse, they were almost broke. "We parked on the open roof of a garage," Christo recalled. "One look at our car and the attendant sent us to the last row on the top floor. He knew there would be no tip. We didn't even have money for the vaporetto into Venice. Jeanne-Claude called the owners of Galleria del Leone and told them they wanted to sell the whole exhibition. Later, they met us on the roof."

Jeanne-Claude said, "When a garage worker saw two well-dressed men approach us, he came closer, thinking there might be a tip after all." Jeanne-Claude began negotiating with Giovanni Camuffo and Attilio Codognato. By now, they knew one another well enough to haggle. She proposed selling everything for a bargain price of 2 million lira—$3,240. Camuffo snapped, "You're crazy," and offered 1 million. "We started screaming at one another," Jeanne-Claude recalled. "The attendant probably thought we were selling a carful of drugs." At stake were the life-size *Red Store Front,* three elaborate three-dimensional works, and seven or eight collaged drawings. Camuffo smiled when he recalled the scene: "I offered to buy the large storefront for five hundred dollars. Jeanne-Claude said, 'No, it's worth much more!' Christo cut in, 'Let me deal with Camuffo. I am Christo.'"[13] At last, they agreed on a price.

Christo designed a poster for the exhibition, installed the work, veiled the gallery window with fabric, and wrapped a sixteenth-century church carving that Codognato owned. He and Jeanne-Claude were almost two thousand dollars richer than when the show opened on August 19. They would need every penny to get started in New York.

The couple planned to leave for the United States in less than a month. Meanwhile, they had unsettled business in Paris and with galleries in Italy, Germany, and Holland. The family drove from Venice to Torino, hoping to retrieve or, better yet, to sell some or all of Christo's art still at Galleria G. E. Sperone. They and Sperone reached an agreement whereby Sperone paid for some work and held the remainder on consignment. This was a pleasant interlude in what proved to be an otherwise-frustrating tour of European galleries.

The next stop was Rome. They called G. T. Liverani, the elegant director of Galleria la Salita, who suggested meeting at Rosati's, a well-known café and artists' gathering place on Piazza del Popolo. The afternoon passed slowly as Christo and Jeanne-Claude nursed two coffees into the evening hours, but the dealer still had not arrived. Telephone calls went unanswered. Someone reported having sighted Liverani at the beach. Christo confessed, "We had no receipts for anything." They finally left Rome without payment or an explanation for the unkept appointment. Christo said, "We tried to call him and later asked people to talk to him." Nothing helped. *Wrapped Candelabra, Wrapped Magazines, Wrapped Shoes, Wrapped Chair, Wrapped Statue on a Pedestal, Wrapped Portrait,* and two 1961 packages were never returned.

Back in France, Christo assembled *Red Store Front* and *Purple Store Front* for the show scheduled to open at Galerie Schmela on December 5, 1964. In early September, the fatigued family managed its last art delivery—to Düsseldorf, where Christo, Jeanne-Claude, and Cyril were guests at Alfred Schmela's home. Since he would be in the states during the show, Christo helped plan its installation. Before leaving, he wrapped several store mannequins, as well as the king-size bed on which they were placed for Charles Wilp.

Christo and Jeanne-Claude then drove to Antwerp, expecting to pick up the unsold artwork from Christo's February exhibition with Galerie Ad Libitum. As in Rome, they recall being given the runaround, starting with a series of telephone calls to John Trouillard. When Jeanne-Claude gave her name, he hung up. She tried again, with the same result. Then Christo dialed, announced himself, and heard the dealer mumble something, which was followed by a click and a dial tone. Frustrated, they drove to Trouillard's residence.

Trouillard had apparently sold seven pieces. Eight others remained: *Wrapped Road Sign, Blue Package, Wrapped Table, Wrapped Road Lamp, Wrapped Shoes, Wrapped Mirror, Gray Package,* and *Wrapped Painting*—a veiled portrait of Jayne Mansfield. Earlier that summer, Christo had seen Trouillard and had managed to get paid for those pieces, which the dealer said he had sold. At that time, Trouillard had insisted on holding the remainder, since some collectors were still interested. Christo described the scene in September: "We went to recover the work. I thought it would be good to have those pieces in New York. We walked up several floors. He opened the door, came out on the landing, and said, 'What do you want? You have no appointment. Go away!' Jeanne-Claude tried to talk to him. He pushed her."[14]

"When we tried to go in, he pushed me so hard that I fell down the narrow stairway," Jeanne-Claude explained. "Christo wanted to call the police. I said, 'No. Dealers are very important people; young artists are not.'"

Christo's problems in Cologne, Rome, and Antwerp began to look less like isolated incidents and more like part of a pattern of expropriation. Despite precautions, he and other artists remained vulnerable to those on whom they most relied for help. The Christos had neither the time nor the resources to challenge Trouillard. Before leaving Belgium, they visited their friends and collectors Mia and Martin Visser. Martin offered them two high-quality mattresses from his factory to take to the United States. Jeanne-Claude gladly accepted. "I knew we would never have enough money to buy mattresses in New York."

Back in Paris, they began preparations for moving. There was much to do: settling the disposition of their room at 24 rue Saint-Louis-en-l'Ile, squaring their bills with local merchants, taking inventory and photo-documenting Christo's art, arranging secure storage for his work and other pieces acquired as gifts or through trades with other artists, updating their travel visas, booking passage, trying to sell more art, informing friends, family, dealers, and collectors of their New York address, and packing. Jeanne-Claude notified Philippe Planchon of their plans and requested that he forward her modest but desperately needed divorce-settlement allowance to the United States.

Harry Shunk and Janos Kender were enlisted to photograph Christo's work. Shunk recalled, "His art was housed in different parts of the city, and in each place we had to carry everything out to a courtyard or the street." On Christo's last visit to the photographers' apartment, he outlined his future plans with captivating sincerity. Shunk listened in disbelief. "I remember him sitting on the floor with Kender and me. He told us he was going to America to do big projects, things that couldn't be done in Europe. Except for the *Iron Curtain,* which wasn't very big, he hadn't done anything monumental yet. Well," Shunk recalled, laughing, "I didn't believe him."[15]

Pierre Restany did not laugh. "I think Christo already had everything in mind when he left for Europe. America gave him a sense of scale. Paris was the turning point, the fermenting period, but in America he would reach his potential. He was absolutely prepared when he went to New York."[16]

A farewell get-together with Ileana and Michael Sonnabend yielded names, addresses, and phone numbers of people to meet in New York. Christo presented Ileana with *Hand Cart.* She later reflected, "I was very touched when they were leaving Paris and asked for advice. I said, 'It's really very simple. When you get to New York, invite everybody in the art world for dinners. What you're going to do is call Rauschenberg, Johns, et cetera, and say I send my love.' I introduced Christo to all of our artists."[17]

Claes Oldenburg, one of her artists, happened to be in Paris in September 1964. He was busy creating his October Sonnabend exhibition. At Ileana's urging, the Christos visited Claes and Patty Oldenburg. "I first met Christo in the summer of 1964," Claes recalled. "His work always impressed me. There were definite connections. I had seen photographs of *Iron Curtain.* And his storefronts related to my *Store* on East Second Street."[18] They visited each other's studios, and Oldenburg received a small painted *Store Front* collage he admired. Subsequently, he gave Christo several painted plaster constructions, including *Ham and Eggs* and *Steak.*

The two artists made the gallery rounds and, with Jeanne-Claude translating, talked about Paris and New York. They were gentle provocateurs, gritty scavengers of the "imprecious," who shared an admiration for Jean Dubuffet's work. Both had discovered the evocative power of fabric, and they were inclined to envision large-scale projects. Oldenburg used burlap, canvas, and muslin to assemble facsimile foodstuffs. In 1962, he had begun producing oversize everyday objects made of vinyl; six months later, he created his first drawings of proposed public monuments. After Claes's October Sonnabend show and a working trip to Italy in November 1964, the Oldenburgs were to return to the Chelsea Hotel. Both couples vowed to renew ties there.

Christo and Jeanne-Claude sublet their room to Earl Brown, a musician. They made this arrangement not to maintain a foothold in Paris but to make some money. Jeanne-Claude said, "Mr. Cointreau set a date, many months in the future, by which we had to get out. We saw an opportunity: someone paying us more than we had to give the landlord." With family affairs apparently in order, she and Cyril visited Carole Weisweiller. "I remember Jeanne-Claude telling me they were going to live in the United States," Carole recalled. "When

I asked what kind of tickets they had, she answered, 'One-way.' I suggested round-trip tickets and offered to help pay for them. She insisted, 'One-way is just fine.'"[19]

In September 1964, Christo, Jeanne-Claude, and Cyril boarded the *France*. They took only a few suitcases and their Rietveld chair, comfortably sandwiched between the two mattresses they had been given by Martin Visser. Perhaps because they were young and accustomed to relocating, the significance of this pivotal move escaped them. "Nothing is traumatic at that age," Jeanne-Claude said. "Many of our things were stored at the Chelsea, and it was like going home. We didn't even realize we were changing our lives." After five days at sea, the family stood on the deck as the *France* sailed into New York harbor. Jeanne-Claude and Christo lifted Cyril up so he could see the imposing skyline.

Christo sensed unlimited possibilities. America offered a stage large enough to accommodate any drama unreserved ambition could fashion. His natural gifts and his capacity to reinvent himself would serve him well. This connoisseur of cloth and master of weathered oil barrels, nostalgic storefronts, and recycled packages of industrial urban discards would now immerse himself in a stimulating new environment of architecture, advertising and TV images, and every form of vanguard art.

Christo and Jeanne-Claude had the imagination, adaptive skills, and inner strength to deal with adversity and cope with relocation. However, their aim transcended coping. Working in tandem, they shared a vision of soaring, riding the winds of dynamic change that were now altering the face of contemporary art.

The mercurial, ever-buoyant Jeanne-Claude had become thoroughly knowledgeable about the art world's nuances. But it was love, not art, that motivated her. The physical chemistry that had drawn this couple together remained strong. In retrospect, she confessed, "I could tell you it was art, but he was a hell of a lover."[20]

8

New York

In September 1964, the Christo family checked into the Chelsea Hotel. Their modest lodgings consisted of a bedroom, kitchen, and such luxuries as a television, telephone, and a fully appointed bathroom.

Jeanne-Claude and Christo always thought of the Chelsea as temporary quarters. By October, they began an energetic search for a combination studio and living space. While they trudged about Manhattan, hotel staff and residents looked after Cyril. The couple inspected over fifty lofts and apartments. They walked everywhere to save subway fare. "We'd be walking and see LOFT FOR RENT signs and go up," remembered Jeanne-Claude. "They were all too small, too expensive, or too horrible." Once, they responded to an ad for seven rooms at eighty dollars a month in Hoboken, New Jersey. When they emerged from the train, Jeanne-Claude took one look around and declared, "I don't even want to see the place." They did an about-face and returned to Manhattan.

For Christo, who still spoke only fractured French, English represented a major obstacle, but four-and-a-half-year-old Cyril grasped the new language with surprising ease. Jeanne-Claude, newspapers, and television were Christo's language instructors. However, reading, understanding conversation, and, particularly, learning to speak, even at the most elementary level, were painfully slow processes. As in the past, he compensated for the handicap with a warm smile, attentive listening, expressive gestures, and his gentle good nature.

Claes and Patty Oldenburg arrived at the Chelsea Hotel from Europe on November 22, 1964. The two couples immediately renewed their acquaintance. Claes suggested they visit his former studio on Howard Street. Jeanne-Claude remembered him saying, "Let me introduce you to my landlord. He's got three floors that have been empty for years. The space is cheap."

The next day, Christo and Jeanne-Claude strolled downtown. They arrived at 48 Howard Street, one block north of Canal Street. Here, near Chinatown, they found a textile district teeming with fabric wholesalers, retailers, and manufacturers. Max Rosenbaum and his brother Ben owned the five-story loft building on Howard Street. Like their father before them, they operated a tin-roofsmithing business on the street level. Oldenburg, their only tenant, had a studio on the first floor. While Cyril occupied himself with the plastic toys that served as models for Oldenburg's work, his parents were guided through the three dilapidated upper floors by Max Rosenbaum. Layers of dirt, heaps of old machinery, hardened oil patches, and disagreeable odors explained the long vacancy and bargain monthly rent of seventy dollars per floor. After a short conference, Jeanne-Claude and Christo announced that they would take the top two floors, one for his studio and the other for their home. "The price was so reasonable, we didn't negotiate. Max seemed appalled that we intended to live there," said Jeanne-Claude. "He asked, 'Are you going to make that beautiful child live upstairs in that filth?' I said, 'We're going to fix it up first, of course.' Max turned out to be the best landlord in the world."

Moving out of the Chelsea Hotel, however, posed a new money problem. By early December, their tab had grown to about fifteen hundred dollars. Added to this were the monthly rent at Howard Street, the substantial cost of renovations needed to make their new space habitable, and living expenses. Despite their negative cash flow, the couple remained upbeat. Christo sold a small package. A child-support payment from Philippe Planchon—his last—finally arrived. However, significant help came from an unexpected source. Henri Rustin, a friend of the Guillebon family, frequently visited New York on business, and he learned of the couple's financial straits. He happily loaned them fifteen hundred dollars to renovate their loft space. In gratitude, Christo gave Rustin a small wrapped Brigitte Bardot portrait he had admired.

The last days of November and most of December were devoted to the cleaning, repair, construction, and painting of their new home. Jeanne-Claude remembered the wintry chill: "It was like a refrigerator. Our hands were stiff from the cold." Their backbreaking work began on hands and knees. Bundled in layers of clothing, she sopped up tacky oil patches in ammonia-soaked sponges and rags while Christo scraped thick areas of encrusted oil residue. They removed loads of debris.

After cleaning the top floor, which would serve as Christo's studio, they concentrated on converting the story below it into livable space. Some embossed tin sheets had fallen or were dangling from the high sheet-metal ceiling. Each had to be nailed back in place. The rotted floor presented a greater challenge. Using reject pieces of galvanized metal given to them by their landlord, Christo methodically patched in missing or deteriorated sections of the floor. Painted with thick layers of battleship gray, the surface soon looked almost presentable.

By the time they were ready to paint, the loft had become so cold that Jeanne-Claude retreated to the Rosenbaums' shop. Shivering beneath layers of clothing, she lamented, "What are we going to do? It's freezing up there." Max smiled and explained, "All you have to do is call Con Edison and they'll turn on your gas meter." She said, "We had no idea it was that simple. We thought they would have to install equipment and it would be very expensive. The same thing happened with the telephone."

With the heat turned on and construction complete, the energetic couple turned to painting. Their first target was the brick wall between their entry door and bedrooms. Jeanne-Claude said, "One night, we tipped the Chelsea maid to look in on Cyril, took the Eighth Avenue subway downtown to Canal Street, and worked until almost four in the morning. The wall looked so beautiful, so white. We returned to the hotel, found Cyril asleep, slept three or four hours, and rushed back to Howard Street. We were amazed to find all the paint peeling off. I ran downstairs and brought Mr. Rosenbaum to see what happened. He asked, 'Did you use shellac first?' Christo and I looked at each other. We had never heard of it. He told us to scrape everything off that big wall and use shellac before painting it again."

Twenty years later, Cyril tried to recall the move to Howard Street: "I don't remember much except being in charge of painting the bottom foot of the loft. My parents did everything else. There were rats everywhere."[1] Jeanne-Claude disagreed: "There were no rats when we arrived. There were mice. The rats came later."

By mid-December 1964, cleaning, construction, and painting were finished; in three weeks, the wretched space had become hospitable. Their few belongings were trucked over from the hotel. Some furniture and a few finishing touches were needed to make the place livable. Jeanne-Claude said, "In Manhattan, Thursday and Friday mornings were bulk-collection days, so Wednesday and Thursday nights, people could legally dump their unwanted oversize furnishings." She and Christo scavenged downtown sidewalks and Dumpsters for furniture and art materials. One good find was a castaway couch, which Jeanne-Claude later covered with black fabric. One evening, they harvested an intact but slightly burned wooden desk. The next night, they spotted an abandoned wooden chair on the sidewalk. When Jeanne-Claude approached it, Christo, still shy about foraging, crossed the street, pretending not to know her. On one of their nocturnal excursions, Christo confiscated a red lantern, which he subsequently transformed into *Wrapped Lantern*. "We stole it on the streets," Jeanne-Claude declared. "It was not stolen," Christo insisted. "It was thrown away."

Christo gathered enough discarded wood to build an ensemble of related furnishings: a dining room table and two benches, a coffee table, and four square multipurpose pieces that served as chairs, benches, or minitables. Each piece followed the severe lines of De Stijl. After considerable bargaining, Jeanne-Claude purchased a secondhand green leather sofa from a Canal Street merchant and then charmed or badgered him into delivering it at no additional charge. Claes Oldenburg provided a final piece of living room furniture: a large chunk of foam rubber from one of his works, which Jeanne-Claude covered in fabric to make a comfortable seat.

Jeanne-Claude said, "Even though our loft was ready, we were sleeping at both places—one night at Howard Street, the next at the hotel—to give the impression that we still lived there. We couldn't pay the bill [now seventeen hundred dollars] and we couldn't just disappear, so we acted like full-time residents."

Jeanne-Claude and Christo put aside their financial worries long enough to host a small Christmas Eve dinner. They invited the Oldenburgs and Claes's brother Richard, and their parents, who were visiting for the holidays. A recent sale helped pay for the dinner and Cyril's Christmas present. When the Oldenburgs arrived, Jeanne-Claude looked stunning in a floor-length Christian Dior black velvet dress, which she later described matter-of-factly as "magnificent, fit for a queen." She and Christo knew that Cyril wanted a bicycle. They couldn't afford it, but there it stood, gift-wrapped in colorful paper and tied in red ribbon. A three-foot-high Christmas tree brightened the room. Christo had purchased it, decorated it with lights, a few ornaments, and bottles of Coca-Cola—Cyril's favorite—then wrapped the festive tree in transparent polyethylene and bound it loosely in rope. Installed on a counter, his son's glittering package stood in front of a twelve-foot-high mirror on which Christo had sprayed CYRIL in large white letters.

Jeanne-Claude said, "That was our first Christmas in America; we had no idea that it was such a big celebration. Jim Dine and other people we met dropped by, each leaving a few presents for Cyril."

The dinner went smoothly: pleasant conversation, food, drink, and camaraderie. After Oldenburg's parents left and Cyril went to sleep, the two couples sat around chatting and drinking. They were all more or less intoxicated when Jeanne-Claude mentioned their recent good fortune in selling a piece. Suddenly, the evening turned sour. Claes screamed at Christo, "Why don't you go back to France! There are already too many artists here and too few collectors." Patty tried in vain to calm him, then apologized before they left. The next morning, Oldenburg returned and apologized.

Christo qualified as an outsider in every way; his six-month tourist visa was due to expire in two months. Neither American nor French, he remained a stateless refugee, since he had renounced his Bulgarian citizenship. Jeanne-Claude observed, "If he'd become French, he would have had to serve in the army, and that's the last thing we wanted. When someone asked where he came from, Christo would say, 'I'm free. I don't have any nationality.'"

New York has a way of both energizing and humbling its inhabitants. It provides a grueling testing ground where artists are expected to keep proving themselves. Christo had earned a slight reputation in Europe, but one known only to a small group of American artists, curators, dealers, and writers. "When we arrived here," Jeanne-Claude said, "even though Christo had already had more one-man shows and group exhibitions than most artists, his work was dirt cheap and almost unknown." One day, a Chelsea artist asked him, "When will you be having your first show?" When Jeanne-Claude translated the comment, Christo simply smiled and shrugged. Later, he said, "Okay, we'll start all over again at zero."

If Christo's visibility as an artist had diminished in the United States, his level of production had not. By late December, his Howard Street overflowed with work brought from the Chelsea Hotel and a substantial number of new pieces. There were various packages, including *Wrapped Lantern, Wrapped Telephone, Wrapped Iron,* a few indecipherable bundles, and a scale model, *Wrapped Building, Project for Lower Manhattan.* There were also collages and drawings at different stages of completion: *Wrapped Tree, Wrapped Table and Two Chairs,* and *Two Wrapped Buildings, Project for Lower Manhattan.* An array of storefronts, ranging in size from small studies and to large-scale three-dimensional constructions—some complete, others in progress—occupied most of the walls and work space.

Ivan Karp, manager of Leo Castelli's gallery from 1959 to 1969, recalled a visit to the Howard Street studio with Leo Castelli. "Christo's work was not alien to the basic temperament of the moment. The storefronts had a certain poignancy about them, and they had an American character that I admired. We thought the work was in an interesting private zone of activity. He was a modest, innovative, enjoyable presence, not terribly aggressive or vividly ambitious. She made up for that. Jeanne-Claude had a rather fierce style of promoting his art."[2]

Arman had moved to New York one year before Christo. "In France, one is always in some boring revolution," he said. "They do not make churches out of their movements here. . . . I got to know everybody here at once . . . like the museum people—Selz, Seitz, Hopps, Geldzahler, Alloway—you find that are working with you and helping you. They are not so official and conservative as in France."[3] Christo and Jeanne-Claude attended Arman's opening at the Sidney Janis Gallery on December 29, 1964. Many of the fifty works on view were accumulations—large quantities of a single industrial product, suspended and hermetically sealed in clear plastic. Inspired by piles of garbage, assembly lines, and window displays, Arman purchased or appropriated objects in bulk—screws, drills, ball bearings, Matchbox cars, toy boats, strainers, metal dowel pins, teapots, glass lenses, prisms, rivets, washers, fan blades, valves, springs, cog wheels, telephones, nuts and bolts, gauges—and encased them permanently in polymer boxes.

Christo shared Arman's distaste for Parisian exclusivity. In a mid-sixties interview, with Jeanne-Claude translating, he spoke of "dealers and critics and very arrogant museum people—such bureaucrats. . . . The real snobs are the painters. . . . A [French] painter who has had one show would not like to receive a painter who has not shown. He does not have children like an American painter because [he] might be mistaken for a dentist. Same reason a French painter will not take a second job, nobody would know he was an artist. He would rather starve. What a difference here." In the same article, Christo offered an early assessment of New York: "It is the most human city I have ever lived in. It is unstable, and that is good for creating. It is the most ruthless and rootless city, and when we are all so rootless it becomes the only place which gives us a true image of life."[4]

Many in the art world were sensitive to the startling contrasts between the two cities. After closing his Paris gallery in 1963, Daniel Cordier wrote, "The dimensions of Paris are not compatible with the scale of modern civilization; it has become a holiday resort, a place of entertainment, and is becoming less and less a center of creative activity. In order to interpret our period, an artist has to be familiar with its realities, its sensibilities. These can be felt better and more intensely in New York."[5] Tumbling sales, defecting artists and dealers, and the growing economic and cultural magnetism of America added up to an ongoing crisis in Parisian art circles. Arman stated, "It's hard to believe, but there are not more than a half dozen French collectors of avant-garde paintings."[6] With an article called "Paris Post Mortem," the *London Observer* joined a chorus of observers prompted to dismiss the French scene.[7] Marcel Duchamp had no doubt about New York's superiority: "There's more freedom here, less remnants of the past among young artists. They can skip all that tradition, more or less, and go more quickly to the real. Also people leave you alone here."[8]

In early 1965, Pop Art had reached its crest, and a new style vied for the spotlight. The Museum of Modern Art ushered in 1965 with "The Responsive Eye," a jazzy, full-blown introduction to Op Art organized by curator William Seitz. Leo Castelli provided Christo and Jeanne-Claude with an invitation to the MoMA opening. "It all seemed very familiar," said Jeanne-Claude. Christo could be forgiven for not getting excited. He had been friendly with Rafael Soto in Paris and was acquainted with the work of Julio Le Parc, Victor Vasarely, the Galerie Denise René stable, and the German Group Zero artists.

The exhibition itself presented an array of flat, impersonal, mechanical-looking surfaces capable of producing visual sensations of relentless vibration. Op-Art affected many viewers physically with its jarring retinal assault; meanwhile, the general public was deluged with fabrics, fashion, utilitarian objects, window displays, and accessories echoing the latest fad. The *New York Times* pronounced Pop Art "finished," an exhausted gimmick, and dismissed the trompe l'oeil geometric abstraction of Op Art as no more than "a fascinating eye game."[9] Nonetheless, both art genres fed a growing media-driven appetite for novelty.

Christo and Jeanne-Claude attended a decidedly unfashionable opening on January 8. Nam June Paik's first American solo exhibition, at the New School for Social Research, looked more like an appliance shop than an art display. The show, "N. J. Paik: Electronic TV, Color TV Experiments, 3 Robots, 2 Zen Boxes and 1 Zen Can," consisted of altered television sets and other mechanical apparatus displayed neatly on large folding tables. Christo and the feisty Korean-born avant-garde artist had developed a warm rapport in the late 1950s at Mary Bauermeister's Cologne studio. Paik had settled in New York several months before Christo.

The couple also attended other avant-garde shows. Writer David Bourdon found himself drawn into their lives. His earliest memory of them harkened back to the time they had had an animated conversation outside the Pocket Theater. "Jeanne-Claude spoke English, but her vocabulary was not large. It was a pretty limited discussion. She had very strong opinions about what was modern and what wasn't. I was impressed that she had such a definite take on things without the background and experience New Yorkers had," said Bourdon.[10] He recalled going with Ray Johnson to see the 1962 "New Realists" show at the Sidney Janis Gallery. "There were two packages lying on the floor," Bourdon said. "They looked as though somebody had bundled up old newspapers and left them on the floor. They were extremely provocative. I was taken with them and discussed them with Ray." In early 1964, Johnson introduced Bourdon to Christo and Jeanne-Claude during their first New York stay. "I knew the Christos before I started writing for the *Village Voice,* but I don't think they took me seriously until I became a weekly published critic. Then I was on their hit list, to be pursued."

Bourdon became a regular visitor to Howard Street. "They had such high spirits, and she has that wonderful sense of humor, telling all those terrible jokes. We saw a lot of each other, but for years I couldn't understand a word Christo said. When I began visiting Howard Street, he was doping storefronts. I didn't understand them at all. I just liked them. In his studio, there was an entire wall covered with three-dimensional storefront drawings and collages. I used to go up there to see dozens and dozens of pieces that I liked, priced from two to five hundred dollars, and I would shake my head, thinking, Poor guy, he's never going to sell any of these. I had no money. But there was a great positive attraction. There was spark. I don't know that I recognized it as a spark of genius, but I realized that these were very unusual, very committed, very brave people. I had great admiration for them because they had uprooted themselves and come from Paris to a New York that was very hostile to foreigners. I admired their chutzpah."

In mid-January 1965, the Christo family's masquerade as full-time Chelsea tenants came to an abrupt end. Their unpaid hotel bill was approaching two thousand dollars. For some time, manager Stanley Bard had observed their pattern of staying every other night at the Chelsea. One morning, he stopped them in the lobby. "When will you be moving out?" he asked. "Everybody knows your loft is finished." Jeanne-Claude blushed and said, "It's not quite ready yet." Bard smiled knowingly. "Come on, Jeanne-Claude, why do you keep running up the bill?" She confessed. "We can't pay it." The story had a familiar ring. "Don't worry," he assured her, "you'll pay me when you can. Just leave one of your husband's works here." Christo selected an elaborate three-dimensional storefront construction with interior lighting as collateral for their debt.[11]

In February 1965, the couple launched a methodical campaign to lure artists, writers, dealers, collectors, and curators to Howard Street. Jeanne-Claude recalled, "So many people had invited us on our first trip to New York and afterward, that I had to do the same. They became our first guests. It was the only way for us to get to know people and get them to invite us. They seemed to have a lot of fun here." They began giving dinner parties, which quickly became the talk of a gossip-hungry art world. The couple brought together key figures in the arena of contemporary art, some of whom they already knew to one degree or another. The evolving invitation list of art celebrities included Leo Castelli, Jasper Johns, Robert Rauschenberg, William Rubin, Sidney Janis, Marcel Duchamp, Frank Stella, Barbara Rose, Dick Bellamy, Henry Geldzahler, Jim Dine, Lawrence Alloway, James Rosenquist, William Copley, Tom Wesselman, Claes Oldenburg, Ellsworth Kelly, Leo Steinberg, and Saul Steinberg.

Ivan Karp recalled that "Jeanne-Claude reached into the art community with tremendous conviction. They invited everyone they considered luminaries, whoever she imagined would be of significance to Christo's career. They made a lot of mistakes. Part of the problem was the fault of their guests; because she is of French origin, they anticipated some culinary skills." Karp described the initial gathering as "a disastrous, bleak evening with some of the worst food served in a private home, ever!"[12] One regular guest, who insisted on anonymity, offered a review of Jeanne-Claude's typical cuisine: "The meals could gag a starving dog." With European art and artists in general disfavor, the substandard meals provided an excuse for veiled hostility from some quarters.

David Bourdon recalled, "They were not liked by the New York hierarchy. People were contemptuous of them. They were perceived as being very pushy. The Christos didn't hesitate to invite these very famous figures, who were legendary to me. And then they served these god-awful meals. A lot of the unpopularity they met in the early days was directed against Christo's art; the rest was directed against Jeanne-Claude and her flank steak. She was charming, and the dinner parties were very political. Before or after eating, the guests would have to trudge upstairs to see Christo's work. You see, in those days, people didn't behave that way in the New York art world. As a result, they were unpopular and had a very hard time. If it hadn't been for a steady stream of European visitors who offered so much support, I'm sure the Christos would have felt like they were surrounded by Apaches."[13]

Of course, there were guests who cared more about intellectual stimulation and having a good time than about the menu. Holly and Horace Solomon fit that category. He worked in the family business, selling lotions. Holly was an actress and would later become one of the city's most influential art dealers. They had been collecting Pop Art before turning their attention to Christo's work. Jeanne-Claude longed for a sale. She and Christo were in debt and desperately needed money. When Holly arrived for the first time, wearing tattered jeans and playing the part of Pop princess, Jeanne-Claude burst into tears. While Horace and Holly examined the work, she took Christo aside and whispered, "She's well intentioned but obviously not rich enough to buy a *Store Front.*"

The Solomons were drawn to the brightly painted *Orange Store Front,* a massive piece. Cloth draped inside a large window and inside a Plexiglas area of the door masked much of the shallow blue interior. The orange facade was accented by two sheets of galvanized metal over the door and window. The Solomons studied the imposing work before announcing that it would be too big for their apartment. They conferred, then unexpectedly commissioned a yellow store front. The vividly painted *Yellow Store Front* incorporated wood, Plexiglas, galvanized metal, fabric, paper, Peg-Board, and electric light. Holly said, "I think I understood the work immediately, the nature of hiding, of showing a little bit, of pleasure and negation of pleasure. Christo's work is really about the freedom of the human spirit."[14]

The price for *Yellow Store Front* was a lifesaving $3,500. The Solomons also purchased several collages and drawings. Like previous and subsequent collectors, they were attracted both to the artists and the work.

Holly also commented on the notorious dinners; "We watched them entertain and mix people. Even though they had no money, there was food on the table, good, bad, or indifferent. We always joked about what a lousy cook Jeanne-Claude was, but the point was getting to know one another. They didn't have matching plates or silverware. Everyone sat at a long table, had dinner, and saw Christo's work. We met engaging people from all over the world. I don't think we sat around discussing art. It was always zestful, rather than ponderous, talk. Poverty is a state of mind. I think Christo is wise. He doesn't see money as something for bank accounts, but as something to use."

Manhattan, 1965: Christo and art writer David Bourdon in the Christos' living room. (Photo: Jeanne-Claude)

.   .   .

Christo had shown his first life-size *Store Front* construction in a May 1964 group show at Castelli's gallery. Despite tentative plans for a 1965 one-man exhibition, his long-range relationship with Castelli remained uncertain. Unlike the typical American dealer, Castelli paid monthly stipends to most of his artists; some ran up large debts against future sales, forcing Castelli to take out bank loans each summer to meet off-season expenses. As a result, adding another artist to his stable represented a major financial consideration.[15]

Castelli's gallery manager, Ivan Karp, felt warmly toward Christo. Unfazed by the language barrier, Ivan portrayed the artist as "a very affable character" and said, "I enjoyed his company. In fact, I was so affected by him as a person that, at Christo's request, I visited his brother, Anani, in Bulgaria. Anani was a movie actor of some renown, a rather prominent personality. We visited his home and transmitted his brother's good wishes and affection."[16]

Although Christo and Jeanne-Claude could not afford it, on one occasion they took the extraordinary step of inviting Ivan and Marilyn Karp to a good restaurant. It cost them a month's rent. "Ileana Sonnabend had told us in Paris how important Ivan was," Jeanne-Claude explained. "So we invited him to dinner, but not at Howard Street, because she said he liked only lobster and steak. I couldn't possibly do lobster here. We had never been in that kind of restaurant. Of course, we didn't have a credit card in those days. We had some cash, but I had to borrow some money from Ivan because the bill was so much."

It was a buoyant time for some artists. "Pop Art awakened high spirits and optimism," said Karp. It also fostered pride in all things American. Jeanne-Claude recalled, "When we arrived in New York, Ivan treated us very nicely. One day, he took us to Leon Kraushaar's Long Island mansion. He had a large collection of Pop Art. I don't know if Ivan wanted Mr. Kraushaar to tell us what he told us—'I only buy American artists. When I say "American," I mean American passport.' After six months in the United States, Christo and I were illegal aliens with expired visas. I don't know if Ivan was trying to help or make us understand how things really were."

Karp insisted that the American art establishment and the artists themselves were not exclusionary. "I don't think that they felt jeopardized at all, he said. "The emergence of American art was so powerful, with the sequence of events that came out of Abstract Expressionism, that we felt great muscle. The most disconcerting element was the arrogant French posture about keeping the banner. I'm not sure that Nouveau Réalisme ever really existed as it applied to a group of artists. There were a few whom we enjoyed. Tinguely was very much appreciated, and Arman, but not across the board."[17]

Not everyone shared Karp's analysis of the situation. Foreign artists working in New York were not about to capitulate. They were, after all, part of a community of artists, part of a historical period of change, and contributors to the driving spirit of innovation that energized the moment.

The efforts of individual artists, whatever their nationality, revealed a growing international partiality for urban/industrial materials, consumer objects and imagery, and large-scale environments. Daniel Spoerri, for example, held a Duchampesque exhibition, transforming his hotel room into an environment. The show, "Chelsea Hotel Room 631," sponsored by Richard Bellamy's Green Gallery, opened on March 3, 1965. Spoerri's unconventional "trap-pictures"—chance arrangements of soiled plates, dirty cups, cigarette butts, bottles, napkins, food residue, and other everyday objects—were affixed to trays, boards, and panels that filled his small room. A sign announcing I AC-CUSE MARCEL DUCHAMP offered the only explanation for the strange assembly of art.

Three floors above Spoerri, Arman had begun planning to invite artists to join his Artists' Key Club. The invitation read:

As—says the poet—the forbidden poetic, the Artists' Key Club invites you to gamble on March 13, 1965. For a bet of $10 you can win a signed work of art by one of 13 artists: Arman, Ayo, George Brecht, Christo, William Copley, Niki de Saint-Phalle, Robert Filliou the poet, Alberto Greco, Allan Kaprow,

Roy Lichtenstein, Dieter Rot, Daniel Spoerri, Andy Warhol. The odds are 1 to 2. The rules simple:

At 6 P.M., March 13, 1965 come to the desk of the Chelsea Hotel—222 W. 23rd Street, New York City—and ask in which apartment your Penn Station locker key is for sale, and a drink is offered. Each key costs $10—each gambler can buy but one key.

Once in possession of a key, go to Penn Station and locate the corresponding locker. Inside the locker you'll find either a signed work or a small gift.

Each artist contributes 4 works; 104 keys are on sale; your odds of winning are 1 to 2.

And if you win, your odds of having your favorite artist are 1 to 13.

And astrologically, your odds are according to your date of birth.

And regardless, your odds of having fun are 104 to 1.

For the forbidden is fun, says the poet.*

Allan Kaprow vividly recalled his participation: "One of the issues in the art world at that time was whether to stay in the gallery/museum ambiance or not. In 1965, Penn Station was undergoing renovations. Large sections of wall space, including some banks of lockers, were curtained off with painting drop cloths. When we first checked out the station, we saw those lockers and together hit on the idea of secreting small works of art."[18]

On the evening prior to the Artists' Key Club gathering, Barbara Moore took detailed notes on the preparations:

FRIDAY, MARCH 12, 1965

7:30 pm   Meet in Arman's room #930 at Hotel Chelsea. . . . Great disorder. Arman's art collection plus the 104 objects and art works. George Brecht has contributed 8 containers of snuff in different aromas—peach, tobacco, etc.—4 signed (to be considered works of art), 4 unsigned (to be considered gifts). . . . Roy Lichtenstein has given 4 signed drawings plus 4 anonymous toys. Christo arrives late.

8:50 pm . . . Great care in packing works into cartons, shopping bags and grocery cart. . . . Everything counted—there are 52 art works, 52 gifts. Nobody wants to carry Dieter Rot's cheese pieces because they smell so much.

9:00 pm   Piled into elevator with objects, Kaprow pushed against Rot's cheeses. Elevator stops at each floor on way down, 1 or 2 people manage to squeeze in. . . .

9:10 pm   Stuff loaded into Kaprow's car. Once again the cheeses are almost left on the sidewalk, since no one will touch them.

*Later March 13 the 13 members of the Artists' Key Club will go on together to have a dinner—greater or smaller according to their gambling odds of selling all the keys.[19]

9:15 pm   Arrival at the 8th Avenue entrance to Penn Station. Kaprow stays in the car while we each take an armful of objects. We fan out in all directions, armed with quarters, and place the pieces in lockers. . . . We are aware that 2 policemen and a Penn Station guard regard us suspiciously. . . .

9:45 pm   Arman and Christo report they have finished. They shake hands on a job well done. . . .[20]

Peter Moore photographed the action: Close-up photos reveal a smiling, then reflective Christo, a scarf wrapped around his neck, his face gaunt, like a young Alberto Giacometti. Allan Kaprow, his eyes sparkling, sports a full beard and wears a suit and tie as he works alongside Christo. Other snapshots record a cheerful camaraderie. One of Christo's packages is visible amid stacks of art objects headed for the lockers: *Esquire* magazines, wrapped in clear plastic, tied and mounted on a wooden board. In another photograph, taken on Saturday, March 13, a middle-aged blond woman looks admiringly at a small bundle wrapped in plastic.

Allan Kaprow recalled, "A friend of mine bought several keys. One opened a locker containing a Christo. It was rolled-up *Esquire* magazines wrapped in plastic. He took it home and called me a day or two later to say that the magazines were really wonderful reading. After I explained what he had done, he said he'd wrap it up again. Later, he called back to say he didn't do a good job and asked if I could help. It had been wrapped with heavy string. I rewrapped it as I remembered it and the piece stayed with me until he picked it up."[21]

Childish or exquisitely irrational, playful or irreverent parody of the stifling commerce defining the establishment, the Artists' Key Club's sole event resonated with the spirit of the moment. The club came and went in a flash, its thirteen members having lightheartedly engaged in just one of many actions taken outside a gallery system that seemed propelled increasingly by money, not art. Claes Oldenburg complained that even Happenings and avant-garde performances had turned chic. "The whole thing had become totally commercial. People were arriving in Cadillacs."[22]

Two weeks later, Christo and Jeanne-Claude hosted a large gathering at their loft. Instead of the usual eight, ten, or twelve dinner guests, they invited a huge crowd of artists, collectors, curators, and dealers. It was one of only two times they dared entertain such a large gathering. "It was full," Jeanne-Claude recalled. "You had to squeeze between people to walk." The rotund Henry Geldzahler, curator of American painting and sculpture at the Metropolitan Museum of Art, arrived with painter Frank Stella and his wife, writer Barbara Rose (one year earlier, this prominent couple had invited Christo, Jeanne-Claude, and Geldzahler for a rooftop picnic luncheon at their home). Most of the Artists' Key Club participants were among the throng of art-world luminaries at the Howard Street party. The day also happened to be Daniel Spoerri's thirty-fifth birthday. About 10:00 P.M., Arman slipped out of the noisy mob scene and picked up a large birthday cake. When he returned, the placed the cake on a coffee table, and everybody starting singing. Jeanne-Claude said, "Spoerri was so surprised, he didn't know what to do. I think he felt he had to do something. So he jumped up on the table and landed in the cake with both feet. It splashed all over and none of us could eat it. The next day while I was cleaning up, I thought, No more big parties, only dinners."

A few weeks after the Artists' Key Club event, Christo received a much-needed boost. The April issue of *Show* magazine contained a handsomely il-lustrated ten-page article about European artists at the Chelsea Hotel. Titled "The Left Bank of the Atlantic," it spotlighted seven recent residents, including Arman and Christo. Writer Marvin Elkoff portrayed "the tattered old Hotel Chelsea" as an "avant-garde Ellis Island" with twenty or more newcomers "cur-rently holed up there."[23]

Photographs of two large storefront constructions were reproduced, along with a half-page photograph of Christo wrapping a freestanding wooden coatrack. In the article, Christo lamented the arrogant, snobbish French art scene. Elkoff mentioned Christo's "Parisian wife, Jean-Claude [*sic*] . . . It was something in the nature of very elegant Pop art, the mingling of real and make-believe, to see her in a chic *après-ski* outfit and bouffant hairdo in a downtown loft."

The article led to at least one sale. The buyer, Harrison Rivera-Terreaux, became one of the Christos most trusted friends and collaborators. Harrison, who created window displays for Bergdorf Goodman, Bloomingdale's, and other stores, and designed curtains and furniture patterns for fabric makers, had been captivated by the article. He said, "There was a photograph of a storefront that I fell in love with. I had never heard of Christo. I just had to have a storefront, so I called him up and we made an appointment. I looked at some small storefront pieces that I liked, but I also saw these little bundles ly-ing on his worktable. They fascinated me. I didn't know what they were or why I liked them, but we made a deal for a small *Package*."[24]

Christo and Jeanne-Claude prospered in April. About the time of Harri-son's purchase, an unexpected check arrived from Galleria la Salita in Rome. The partial payment, a final one, seemed to them a rationalization of the gallery's having sold work from Christo's 1963 exhibition. Christo also under-took his last portrait commission, and Jeanne-Claude landed a brief but lucra-tive job as an interpreter for a visiting French art dealer, Aimé Maeght.

.   .   .

That month, both Christo and Jeanne-Claude were on hand at Leo Castelli's gallery for the first public showing of James Rosenquist's brash protest painting, *F-111*. "We never missed one of Leo's openings," said Jeanne-Claude. "*F-111* was a very ugly thing." The garish Day-Glo work measured ten feet high by almost eighty-six feet wide—thirteen feet longer than the largest actual *F-111* supersonic-jet fighter-bomber. Fifty-one sections depicted light-bulbs, spaghetti, cake, a nuclear blast, a young girl with a saccharine smile under a hair dryer, and other images set against a background of the plane's fuselage. It qualified as the largest—and some said most vulgar—Pop artifact. David Bourdon recalled, "I can't say I loved it, but I was bowled over. Now, we all realize it is a great work of art."[25] *New York Times* art critics John Canaday and Hilton Kramer did not concur. Canaday characterized Rosenquist's effort as "pretentious" and "juvenile," while Kramer dismissed *F-111* as "slick, cheerful, overblown, irredeemably superficial . . . leaves the spectator feeling he ought to be sucking a Popsicle."[26]

The nature of art openings had changed in 1962. Castelli's gallery replaced the traditional Tuesday-night opening, which tended to be an intimate social gathering where few people looked at the art, with an all-day Saturday, no-invitation-required, alcohol-free event. By 1965, many galleries followed this example. One consequence of this change was the emergence of postopening loft parties. Holly Solomon said, "In the sixties, we all went to loft parties. Networking went on there. It was the lifeblood of the art world."[27]

Harrison Rivera-Terreaux had little money, so after purchasing his second Christo piece, he began trading baby-sitting for art. "Christo and I went to every Saturday opening and then to wild parties afterward," Jeanne-Claude recalled. "If you did three or four openings, there would be three or four parties. Not that we liked parties, but it was important that people see us there. You had to listen for the address. We were invited to every party on our first trip to New York as tourists. After that, once people knew we had moved here, it was different. You didn't get invited, because you had become the competition."

"There was a certain amount of crashing," said Ivan Karp. "People came unannounced, but I don't remember any real difficulties."[28] Jeanne-Claude observed, "Ivan Karp was very precious to Leo. Because Leo always said yes, yes to everybody. Then he would send Ivan to say no. We went to Castelli's gallery every Saturday, even between openings, to see who was there and try to meet everyone. Leo would introduce us to people, and Ivan would make sure we didn't meet anyone."

Karp commented, "Jeanne-Claude gave her whole life to fiercely promoting Christo's art. I felt put-upon. Her dinners were an ongoing scandal. There was a kind of endless beseeching for his cause. It isn't unusual to find a dedicated artist's wife, but this was more intense. . . . I didn't want to be in the same room with her. It was as if she were on the wall, part of the exhibition. I don't think that any rejection of her presence bothered her at all. Had I been the gallery director instead of second in command, I might have been disconcerted to the point of discontinuing the relationship." David Bourdon offered another viewpoint: "Ivan just wasn't interested in them or in the art. The Christos were relentlessly campaigning to get Castelli's attention. Leo was flattered. His European charm masked any apprehension that he had. Ivan, being a bystander, could see the shameless flattery. Since he wasn't the one being flattered, I think he developed a very cynical attitude about it."[29]

Ivan Karp and others who shared a distaste for Jeanne-Claude's meals and her overly transparent promotion of Christo's art recognized her captivating charm nevertheless. Everyone agreed that both she and Christo were beguiling and unusual. They regularly appeared at avant-garde performances and a variety of museum and gallery openings. They frequented the Sidney Janis Gallery; in April, they saw nineteen of Ellsworth Kelly's imposing minimal paintings, and in May, they attended a group show of recent works by Arman, Dine, Fahlström, Marisol, Oldenburg, and Segal. Oldenburg exhibited two sculptures and eight of his first "Colossal Monument" sketches. Among them were such playful subjects as various enlarged foodstuffs, two versions of *Colossal Teddy Bear for Central Park*, *Vacuum Cleaner for the Battery*, *Ironing Board for the Lower East Side*, and *War Memorial for Canal Street and Broadway*—an enormous concrete block envisioned as halting traffic at the intersection around the corner from 48 Howard Street. Christo no doubt took note of his friend's whimsical studies. For the past year, Christo had been producing collages, photomontages, and models depicting his plans to wrap several New York skyscrapers.

In May 1965, the couple also attended Ray Johnson's first one-man show, at the Willard Gallery, where they saw a large number of his drawings, collages, and paintings. David Bourdon recalled, "Some of the collages were composed of intricately arranged pieces of cardboard, glued together like tile mosaics with lots of painterly color."[30] Johnson said, "I exhibited a collage titled *Christo*. It depicted a cross-shaped figure, a stylized Christ holding a round object—a bowling ball. I was thinking, Christ/Christo. I also showed a drawing of the De Stijl chair in his living room. I did it at their place and, over the years, used offset printings of it in many of my artworks."[31] Like Christo and Jeanne-Claude, Johnson and Bourdon crashed loft parties. Bourdon viewed the past nostalgically: "There couldn't have been more than two thousand people interested in contemporary art, so word spread. It's really hard to underestimate the importance of all those parties, because that's where everybody met, exchanged gossip, and started their feuds."[32]

"The end of that period coincided with the appearance of drugs," Holly Solomon observed. "At first, the parties were good-natured, fashionable, fun. We danced and wore wonderful paraphernalia. I remember one party in the

Manhattan, summer 1965: Jeanne-Claude and Cyril on the roof of their home.
(Photo: Christo)

late sixties at the place of a very famous person. Someone gave me LSD and I became very ill. Horace, Jeanne-Claude, and Christo took care of me all night. That was really the end of an era, not only for me, but for everyone."[33]

Shortly after their thirtieth birthday on June 13, Christo and Jeanne-Claude endured their first sweltering summer as loft dwellers. New York's unique appeal dissolved in a heat wave. Jeanne-Claude described that time: "There was no air conditioning, so we opened all the windows for cross-ventilation. The place turned black with pulp and soot from the garment industry. It was disgusting. The summer became so steamy, we couldn't sleep at night." "It was very, very hot," Christo added. "I have pictures of me working on a *Store Front* completely naked."

One look around Christo's studio revealed a transition in his work. Old-fashioned, weathered-looking storefronts of all sizes were giving way to more streamlined versions. The earlier pieces, their windows and doors veiled, had a handcrafted charm about them and the look of Constructivist stage sets. The inaccessible, ungainly reconstructions of commercial facades served as prototypes for *Four Store Fronts Corner,* a mechanical-looking installation with built-in lighting, designed to fill three-quarters of one room at Castelli's Gallery. "We tried to arrange a Castelli exhibition for 1965," Christo said, "but Leo said, 'No, wait until 1966.'" Built with wood, Formica, galvanized metal,

Manhattan, 1966: Christo, Jeanne-Claude, and Cyril in front of a *Store Front*. (Photo: Thomas Cugini)

lacquered Masonite, clear and colored Plexiglas, and highlighted with red, yellow, and blue, the unadorned, modernized *Four Store Fronts Corner* appeared to be the progeny of Gerrit Rietveld's De Stijl architecture.

Just as the summer heat seemed unbearable, Christo and Jeanne-Claude got lucky. Robert and Reth Delford-Brown, who had a large home in Great Neck with a swimming pool, tennis court, and orchard, asked them to house-sit. "We said we would be kind enough to spend a heavenly month with Cyril at their house," recalled Jeanne-Claude.

In mid-August, just after they returned to Howard Street, Allan Kaprow phoned with a proposal for *Calling,* a two-part Happening scheduled for Saturday, August 21, and Sunday, August 22, 1965. Kaprow wanted the artists to participate, particularly Jeanne-Claude. "Allan asked if I would mind being wrapped," she said. "I agreed."

Kaprow recalled, "Each participant was a friend or colleague. I admired the Christos. He was a lively character and they made a good team. I think everyone shared that perception. They needed each other."[34] *Calling* involved twenty-eight participants. Kaprow plotted the initial action in Manhattan, featuring two women and a man who would be subjected to wrapping, rewrapping, and other indignities. The other participants acted as drivers, carriers, telephone operatives, and so on. Kaprow's scenario began promptly at 4:00 P.M. on Saturday. Jeanne-Claude and two others with similar roles were instructed to wait at three different locations. Peter Moore photographed Jeanne-Claude—who was wearing black pants and a black sleeveless T-shirt, her black hair hanging in two braids—standing on the northeast corner of Hudson and Christopher streets. In the photo, she is carrying a paper bag containing aluminum foil, muslin, and a roll of cord. At 4:30 P.M., a car pulled up, someone called Jeanne-Claude's name, and she got in. Moore's pictures show Peter Zimmer, a handsome young artist, wrapping an openmouthed Jeanne-Claude in foil as they sit in a vehicle. Kaprow's instructions read: "The car is parked at a meter somewhere, is left there, locked; the silver person sitting motionless in the back seat." Passersby, accustomed to the bizarre aspects of city life, glance at the silver-swathed occupant and go about their business. According to plan, "Someone unlocks the car, drives off. The foil is removed from the person; he or she is wrapped in cloth or tied into a laundry bag. The car stops, the person is dumped at a public garage, and the car goes away. At the garage, a waiting auto starts up, the person is picked up from the concrete pavement, is hauled into the car, is taken to the information booth at Grand Central Station."[35]

Another series of Moore's snapshots show Jeanne-Claude, covered from head to toe with muslin, loosely bound with rope around her neck, arms, and legs, being carried by two men into the railroad station. Pedestrians on Lexington Avenue barely break stride as the corpselike package passes. She is carried into the massive rotunda, attracting scarce attention from scurrying commuters. Then she is placed alongside two similarly clad figures, each with their legs outstretched, their backs propped up against the round information booth in the center of the cavernous space. Kaprow said, "After they deposited her, she and the other two were tagged, like packages that had lost their way."[36] The three human packages attracted a throng of curious onlookers, who formed a semicircle around them. Several tourists' cameras sprang into action, joining Moore in documenting the Happening. At this point, Kaprow's directions were: "The person calls out names, and hears others brought there also call. They call out for some time." And the crowd builds. "Then they work loose from their wrappings and leave the train station."[37] Several hundred spectators watched Jeanne-Claude and the others escape their confinement. Another photograph captures Jeanne-Claude in a telephone booth, smiling, wide-eyed, listening to fifty designated rings before someone says, "Hello," then ends the first day of *Calling* with a click.

On August 22, gray skies and occasional scattered showers failed to discourage a hard-core group of vanguard artists, as well as their friends and relatives, from packing into cars and driving to North Brunswick, New Jersey, to witness the conclusion of Kaprow's *Calling* at George Segal's farm. Segal said later, "We were shocked when almost four hundred people showed up. Allan invited several artists to help organize an afternoon of Happenings. Yvonne Rainer and Trish Brown did their own modern dance on the roof, Chuck Ginnever made giant Chinese dragons—sculpture sewn together over a framework of sticks and wire—La Monte Young and Marion Zazeela did a concert of Young's music with the musicians lying on high, unmown grass, Dick Higgins performed *Lots of Trouble,* and Wolf Vostell blew up a television set and buried the pieces."[38] Christo's face beamed as he said, "I remember Yvonne Rainer silhouetted on the edge of Segal's roof. It was fabulous."

Calling, part two, began in the late afternoon. Kaprow offered some last-minute instructions before sending everyone into a thickly wooded area behind the farmhouse—everyone, that is, except the three who had been wrapped the previous day. There seemed to be no paths in a wall of greenery. Kaprow's plan called for people to wait at five prearranged locations where a "heavy sailcloth with a hole in the center dangled from ropes attached to the branch of a tree." At his signal, volunteers climbed into a canvas sling and were suspended upside down. None of the groups could see one another. "Come on!" Kaprow called out to the trio who had been left behind when everyone entered the forest. The three "searchers" began shouting names as they set foot in the damp, overgrown wilderness. Each person hanging from a tree and the group sitting nearby answered, "Here, here, here. . . ." Later, Kaprow described the scene: "The three who were wrapped the day before, including Jeanne-Claude, were given large shears."[39] Kaprow's brief choreography read: "In the woods, they come upon people dangling upside down from ropes. They rip the people's clothes off and go away. The naked figures call to each other in the woods for a long time until they are tired. Silence."[40]

Calling embraced no rational discourse, no conventional plot, no climactic ending. It resonated with the alogical feeling of a dream sequence. Because of the numerous locations, no one perspective could take in more than fragments of the overall scenario. Kaprow sought to involve the audience, and he expected his outline for specific actions to activate the observer and provoke spontaneous, accidental events as players and viewers mingled in one physical space. Kaprow insisted, "The word *audience* is no longer appropriate. We're not dealing with a passive spectator in my case. You have active participants whose most important roles are to take responsibility for what's going on."[41]

Despite obvious differences, there are striking parallels between Kaprow's Happening and Christo's later projects. Both men shared a desire to engage the public: Everyone is—or should be—part of the art. They also incorporated real-life settings as active elements in their work, as if to proclaim, The only way to see art is to be physically involved with it. Each artist viewed their ephemeral undertakings as singular, unrepeatable events. Kaprow's and Christo's large-scale, seemingly irrational, quasi-theatrical experiences announce both a disregard for art as a precious, salable commodity and an urge to meld art with everyday life.

For Christo, 1965 ended on an upbeat note. Guido Le Noci agreed to publish a monograph on Christo's work. David Bourdon, Otto Hahn, and Pierre Restany had been enlisted to contribute essays. The small book, *Christo*, would appear in mid-1966 with *Dolly* (1964) reproduced in color on the cover. In gratitude, the artist presented the ever-supportive Le Noci with a group of artworks to help defray expenses. The new year brought a rush of opportunities: The artist had been selected to participate in eight prestigious American and European group shows,[42] Leo Castelli finally set a May 1966 date for Christo's *Store Front* exhibition, and the Stedelijk van Abbemuseum in Eindhoven, Holland, scheduled Christo's first one-man museum exhibition. Guggenheim Museum curator and Pop Art advocate Lawrence Alloway agreed to write a brief introduction for the Eindhoven show catalog. Alloway, a confident observer of American popular culture, joined a growing group of writers and collectors who addressed Christo's art, including Martin Visser, Martin Friedman, and Jan van der Marck.

Christo worked intensively and his productivity coincided with a growing sense of expectation, if not anxiety, over the Eindhoven and Castelli shows. The labor and logistics involved were formidable. Each exhibition would feature an enormous *Store Front* construction: *Three Store Fronts* was designed to bisect a large gallery at the museum, while *Four Store Fronts Corner* would fill the larger of the two rooms at Castelli's gallery. Both works were constructed between July 1965 and January 1966 in the artist's congested studio. Photographs show Christo walking past the eight-foot-high, forty-six-foot-long *Three Store Fronts*, which stretched diagonally across the length of his high-ceilinged work space; the seemingly endless expanse separated a wall lined with large show windows masked with fabric from another wall, this one crowded with small *Store Front* studies. The massive thirty-six-foot-long right-angle corner facade of *Four Store Fronts Corner* added to the congestion. Older

Manhattan, 1966: Christo in his studio. (Photo: Ugo Mulas)

works, recent packages, a scale model for an outdoor piece envisioned for Eindhoven, and various art materials were part of an organized clutter that still left enough room to accommodate other sizable undertakings.

Christo's plan for the Stedelijk van Abbemuseum exhibition went beyond simply shipping a body of work to Eindhoven. The event demanded his presence. He would construct several pieces on-site, including the monumental *Air Package,* which would be stationed just outside the museum's entrance, reassemble *Three Store Fronts,* and install the show. Getting to the Netherlands presented a challenge, since Christo and his family were residing illegally in the United States on expired six-month French visas issued in September 1964. Jeanne-Claude's mother offered to help. In a 1965 letter, Précilda wrote, "I will do everything humanly possible to help. If necessary I will seduce the American Ambassador. Too bad for your father."[43]

Jeanne-Claude recalled, "Christo, Cyril, and I could not leave the United States. We didn't even have our passports. Anita Streep, an attorney specializing in immigration, had them. Streep finally got Christo special permission to go. He received temporary travel papers, but they said, 'He can go for a few days, but the wife and child can't.'"

As soon as Christo arrived at the Stedelijk van Abbemuseum, he began uncrating work and assembling *Three Store Fronts.* There were also collages drawings, packages, and wrapped objects like *Wrapped Armchair,* a comfortable push-button reclining chair that Christo had bound in cloth and clear plastic and rope in New York. In addition, there were three large pieces yet to be done. *Wrapped Tree*, a 1964–1965 collage drawing, served as model for Christo's first life-size *Wrapped Tree* in 1966. "I did a big wrapped birch tree," he said, "where the roots were wrapped in opaque fabric and the branches with clear plastic . . . like the wrapped nudes: some parts were visible, some invisible." The trunk remained uncovered, stretching between the cloth and plastic packaging at either end of a seemingly in-transit thirty-three-foot long tree, which was incongruously reclining on a four-foot-high white pedestal. A second on-site sculpture, *56 Barrels*, had initially been constructed at the home of Martin and Mia Visser; it was then reassembled on the museum grounds. Fifty-five weathered oil barrels of different sizes were stacked vertically in five tiers, capped with one barrel lying horizontally on the top.

Lawrence Alloway's text for the Eindhoven catalog stated:

> Christo is an important artist at this time of the pursuit of objectivity in art, of investigation into the esthetics of familiar objects and working procedures that are, in terms of handling, impersonal. . . . The familiar object and the familiar facade are presented literally. The reactions that they generate are based on the objective acts of making a package or screening a window, so that the factual basis of his work is neither transcended nor undermined. It is the source of the mystery.[44]

Alloway's description of the artist's detached presentation of commonplace objects hardly prepared one for the imposing outdoor *Air Package*. Hovering over the museum entrance, it consisted of a manufactured rubberized canvas balloon, seventeen feet in diameter. Filled with air, the balloon was covered with transparent polyethylene, bound securely with rope, and held aloft by steel cables and guylines. The massive spherical package had a pitted surface that might have concealed a small moon with thick craters. *Air Package* barely moved. However, suspended above the treetops, neither free nor earthbound, its eerie presence asserted itself. The free-floating nature of a balloon, like the function of other objects that had fallen into the artist's grasp, was denied.

Two days before the opening, Christo phoned Jeanne-Claude and explained that in Holland artists usually select the music to be played at their openings. "I want the *Batman* record," he said. "The soundtrack for the TV series had just come out," Jeanne-Claude recalled. "I bought one, went to the airport, stopped a KLM pilot, and pleaded, 'Please take this record to the Amsterdam airport. My husband is waiting there to pick it up!" On May 6, 1966, Christo's one-man exhibition at the Stedelijk van Abbemuseum opened to the blaring sounds of *Batman*.

Later in May, Christo's first American solo show opened without the benefit of music. *Four Store Fronts Corner* nearly filled one room at Leo Castelli's gallery. Since it occupied most of the space, the area for viewing it was cramped and afforded only partial views of the entire work. Jeanne-Claude described the public's reaction. "It made people feel very uneasy because they couldn't enter the space. They could only walk to one corner and back to the door and then to a dead end at the other corner. They were cornered."

Lawrence Alloway enjoyed the Castelli show. He said later, "For me, the most appealing storefronts were the later, modern ones with new fixtures, like the Castelli one; they had no texture or nostalgic charm. I also liked Christo's concept of a corridor leading nowhere. His storefronts spread out like some of the Pop Art environments. They projected a sense of scale that extended beyond the object. I see the storefronts as a very important turning point in his career, bridging the gap between various-size packages and his later environmental pieces. Going from packages to storefronts was a step in that expansion. From the storefronts, which still had a sculptural finesse about them, he went on to produce the large-scale projects with their enormous environmental spread."[45]

Many important collectors of contemporary art, such as the Sculls, the Tremaines, Richard Brown Baker, Leon Kraushar, Count Giuseppe Panza, and Dr. Peter Ludwig, frequented the Castelli gallery. Collector and connoisseur Victor Ganz remarked, "There were times in the mid-1960s when you felt that if you didn't get to Leo's every other day you were going to miss out on something."[46] Barbara Rose suggested that what Castelli was really selling "was a sense of art history being made right there and then."[47]

For the opening, Jeanne-Claude was wearing a facsimile Paco Rabanne designer dress composed of hundreds of highly reflective thin, pink, plastic circles, each about two inches in diameter, hooked together by wires. The sparkling ensemble was handmade by Harrison Rivera-Terreaux while babysitting Cyril.

That fall, school tuition for Cyril, art materials, imminent travel costs, and other expenses weighed on the family. Several timely sales provided them with enough money to pay the bills. Christo produced four wrapped portraits: two of Holly Solomon, one of her sister-in-law, Muriel Ribner, and one of Horace; a study and a large final version of each subject were realistically painted, veiled in clear plastic, and tied in rope. He also created the evocative *Wrapped Portrait of Jeanne-Claude,* an oil painting on canvas, which was partially covered with fabric, separated from the viewer by one or more layers of clear plastic, and securely bound with rope and cord. The moody portrayal offered a stark contrast to Jeanne-Claude's buoyant public persona.

In October, Annina Nosei, a former assistant to Ileana Sonnabend who had sublet the Christos' Paris room in early 1964, paid a visit to Howard Street.

Annina and her fiancé, Los Angeles art dealer John Weber, had come to New York for *9 Evenings: Theatre and Engineering,* and, more importantly, to get married. The Christos offered their loft for the wedding reception.

That same October, the family flew to Minneapolis for two significant events: Christo's first major American museum group exhibition and the execution of his first ambitious project in the United States. "Eight Sculptures: The Ambiguous Image," a provocative show organized by the Walker Art Center, opened October 22; it featured the work of Christo, Donald Judd, Robert Morris, Claes Oldenburg, Lucas Samaras, George Segal, Ernest Trova, and H. C. Westerman. Christo's contributions included *Dolly* and *Pushcart*—1964 works containing an enigmatic package—along with *Four Store Fronts Corner.* The catalog contained illustrations of and insights into Christo's work. Museum director Martin Friedman's introduction cited Christo and Oldenburg as artists who utilize psychological as well as physical space to transform ordinary objects.[48] Curator Jan van der Marck saw in Christo's art "a statement of mystery, ambiguity and paradox. The package, the exponent of that statement has become the artist's visionary obsession. . . . Its expressive power is related to use and wear and is further enhanced by an ominous contour and an excess of strangulating knots." Van der Marck stated that "the artist's familiar yet disquieting storefronts are packages without contents that "further expand Christo's treatise on the absurd."[49]

Christo had developed considerable support in Minneapolis. In addition to Martin Friedman and Jan van der Marck, David Johnson, president of the Walker Art Center's Contemporary Arts Group, and Arnold Herstand, director of the Minneapolis Institute of Art, marveled at the artist's innovation and contagious enthusiasm. Herstand had previously invited Christo to design a project that would involve all of the school's first-year students. Encouraged by the success of his *Air Package* in Holland, Christo proposed constructing a sixty-foot-long airborne package. He envisioned a see-through inflatable structure filled with colorful balloons that would be lifted by helicopter from the lawn of the Minneapolis Institute of Art and transported across town to the roof of the Walker Art Center. Most of his preparatory studies depicted a round, rather than oblong, form; in one collage, the package is seen carried aloft by two helicopters. "I discussed the project with Jan van der Marck, who knew the Christos before I did," said Herstand. "Jan reassured me that the idea was feasible. Christo provided a list of materials needed. We ordered a lot, but the budget exceeded what we had initially planned and required additional financing."[50]

Christo's startling offspring, *42,390 Cubicfeet Package,* was to be erected between October 24 and 29 with the help of 147 students. Four U.S. Army high-altitude research balloons, each measuring eighteen by twenty-five feet when inflated, and 2,800 brightly colored balloons, each twenty-eight inches in diameter, would be sealed in 8,000 square feet of translucent polyethylene and tied with 2,700 feet of quarter-inch rope.

On Monday, October 24, Christo held the first of many meetings with students and faculty. Despite his limited vocabulary, he communicated his complete commitment to the project. At first, many students looked at one another as if to say, Is he kidding? Herstand recalled, "The real excitement began once the work started. Students were used to doing interesting projects, but nothing like this. There was a genuine rapport, with teach-ins going on all night, lit by bonfires in the school courtyard, where they were putting this thing together. Soon a gigantic package took form, on the scale of the houses surrounding the school. At first, there was some opposition, but most students and staff quickly got caught up in the whole thing. They helped work out the logistics. It wasn't a high-tech operation; there were no professionals involved, no engineering team. All kinds of problems came up during the construction, like how do you fill this huge volume with air? I think they eventually did it by reversing two industrial vacuum cleaners. We always needed to send out for additional things. Christo spent his days and nights working and checking up on everyone. Some students became very close to him. Staff supporters from the Walker and the Minneapolis Institute of Art came every day to help and see the progress. I remember the first night it was inflated, some neighborhood kids punctured the skin and let the air out. The next morning, it was repaired and reinflated. After that, the students guarded it. During the last few days, a large percentage of the freshman class built fires and camped around the package all night to protect it. People kept coming around. In fact, there were calls coming to the police saying that a flying saucer had landed. At night, spotlights lit the package, this huge translucent object with colored objects floating inside. It did seem to pulsate, even after being inflated and tied down. Every breath of air would move the thing. It was almost alive!"

Herstand recalled a growing excitement and uncertainty. "Every Christo project has terrific crises because he goes beyond what people think possible. We had trouble getting a helicopter. The first people we contracted refused. That wasn't surprising. We finally arranged for a helicopter. After one look around, the pilot became uneasy. He said that any liftoff would depend on the winds. If the winds were under five mph, it could happen on Friday.

"Jeanne-Claude worked on publicity. She called reporters from *Time*, *Life*, the *New York Times*, and stringers from the New York papers, tempting them with the prospect of a Fellini-esque event, a mammoth package being airlifted across the city to the Walker. I remember a *Life* reporter saying, 'If you can get it high enough so that we can see the skyline of Minneapolis under it, we'll feature it on the cover of *Life*.' Putting thousands of inflated colored balloons inside was an interesting touch. As the wind rolled the package about, all the balloons tumbled and bounced inside. That added color and mystery.

"On Friday, the pilot returned. We attached ropes from the package to his helicopter. He tried; however, the winds were too strong. He was nervous because this tremendous package acted like a sail when the wind hit it; the pull could be very very dangerous. We had a crisis, and Christo became sort of hysterical. His emotionality and Jeanne-Claude's coolness under fire made a good combination. There was real danger and we were all concerned."[51]

David Johnson said, "Friday morning the weather was so bad that it appeared the project would fail. The *Life* magazine photographer had left town. I received a telephone call from Jeanne-Claude saying that Christo was beside himself. When I arrived at their hotel, I found out the helicopter had left and the newspapers, magazines, and TV had been told that the project was canceled. I agreed to pay for the helicopter and immediately made several telephone calls arranging for media coverage on Saturday."[52]

Christo and Jeanne-Claude repaid Johnson's kindness with several works of art. Christo also designed *Wrapped Boxes,* an edition of one hundred small square cardboard boxes, which were then sent to the members of Johnson's Contemporary Arts Group. "Christo never touched those boxes," Jeanne-Claude explained. "Inside each was a certificate signed by him that said 'You have just destroyed a work of art.' The only thing Christo did was sign the certificates. They were then placed in boxes by the students who wrapped and mailed them."

"The word got out," said Arnold Herstand. "On Saturday, students, faculty, museum staff, and hundreds of neighborhood people were on hand. The weather was borderline, but the pilot said he would try." At 12:30 P.M. on October 29, Christo's ungainly, glistening *42,390 Cubicfeet Package* was airborne. Herstand described the carnivalesque atmosphere: "People were cheering because it was an exciting moment. You could see the helicopter behind the school struggling to get off the ground. People on their bellies—a lot of them—were trying to photograph the sky underneath the piece so that it would look as if it were way off in the distance. Jeanne-Claude communicated by radio with the helicopter operator. He tried to lift the package and actually had it off the ground for a few minutes before being forced down by strong winds. The pilot was surprisingly daring, but the air currents were too strong. A decision to go ahead would have meant taking a terrific risk. Obviously, Christo was disappointed, but I think it was still quite an achievement. There were many people who thought it was a great experience. Within a few days, the object was destroyed. I think in the end it was very mysterious. There is a history going back thousands of years of artists doing temporary events. That kind of tradition is often forgotten. In the past, artists frequently did ephemeral pageants. For example, Leonardo and other Renaissance artists created extravagant festivals. That's what Christo's projects are about."[53]

Christo had proved capable of rallying a dedicated team of coworkers and, with Jeanne-Claude's help, raising financial support. Later writers would blame the Federal Aviation Agency, a fearful pilot, and nervous city officials for blocking the crosstown journey. The real villain was Christo's lifelong adversary and strongest ally: nature. In retrospect, *42,390 Cubicfeet Package* represented an early skirmish in an ongoing engagement. In the future, the artist would unhesitatingly sacrifice the luxury of complete control to allow the unpredictable energies, the beauty, and the awesome strength of nature to play electrifying roles.

9

At Work Around the World: 1967–1969

The absence of any completed major project in 1967 only belied Christo's intense contemplation and production. That year, he mounted three one-man exhibitions, participated in eleven American and European group shows, and produced numerous drawings, collages, and a few scale models, envisioning and preparing at least a dozen large-scale projects. Christo and Jeanne-Claude's trademark activities continued to be erecting walls or barriers—as with barrels or storefronts and exploring the expressive possibilities of wrapping. The results demanded that viewers reexamine familiar imagery in a revised context.

Both Christo and Jeanne-Claude devoted considerable time to garnering support for their bold, technically feasible visions. If anything, at this stage there were too many dreams. Most went unrealized. In 1967, he created drawings and a scale model for *Wrapped Whitney Museum of American Art;* between 1964 and 1966, images depicting various Manhattan skyscrapers wrapped; and in 1966 and 1967 studies of wrapped groups of trees for Washington Park in Saint Louis; and the Maeght Foundation in Saint-Paul-de-Vence, France. In addition, he designed oil-barrel structures for sites in France, West Germany, and New York's Central Park, as well as an audacious project to blockade the Suez Canal with 10 million oil drums—his response to the Arab-Israeli six-day war. Other proposed projects were for wrapping the Ponte Sant'Angelo and the National Gallery of Modern Art in Rome. There were also projects that would come to fruition the following year: their largest, most spectacular air package, another massive *Store Front,* and their first wrapped buildings.

In January 1967, Christo's father visited New York for the first time. Among the unfamiliar sights, one pleased him the most: his grandson. Vladimir Javacheff had never met Cyril or Jeanne-Claude. He was impressed by his daughter-in-law's charm and by the striking physical resemblance between his son and grandson. In April, Jeanne-Claude's parents also paid their first visit to Howard Street.

The dinner parties attended by well-known guests continued unabated. Christo and Jeanne-Claude were particularly fond of Teeny and Marcel Duchamp. Christo said, "We saw him often in New York. He was always very encouraging. I remember his home. It was humble but very lovely. Christo recalled Duchamp's disinterest in wealth and the salable art object: "He seemed genuinely amazed at how people put value on an object. Not only art. How can you calculate with money how rich the life and energy of a human being is? Money is only some kind of relative identification, but what does it actually mean?" Duchamp did indeed denounce what he termed the "terrific commercialization" of art in the 1960s.

"So many artists, so many one-man shows, so many dealers and collectors and critics who are just lice on the back of the artists. . . . And with commercialization has come the integration of the artist into society, for the first time in a hundred years. In my time we artists were pariahs, we knew it and we enjoyed it. . . . The only solution for the great man of tomorrow in art is to go underground. He may be recognized after his death, if he's lucky. Not having to deal with the money society on its own terms, he won't have to be integrated into it, and he won't become contaminated, as all the others are."[1]

To varying degrees, Christo and some of his contemporaries had resisted the contamination of a "money society" by producing unsalable art. One artist influenced more by Duchamp than by the dollar was the vanguard composer Nam June Paik, a friend of Christos and Jeanne Claude. Paik would later credit Christo for being the only artist ever to send collectors to his studio. In early 1967, Paik and Charlotte Moorman desperately needed money. Unable to sell his video or musical creations, Paik pleaded with Christo to wrap a black-and-white portable TV set Paik had been working on. Paik said that no one would buy his work, but if Christo wrapped it, Charlotte might be able to sell it. "Christo gladly agreed," Jeanne-Claude recalled. "Those two could ask almost anything from him. We had great admiration for them." This quasi-collaboration, *Wrapped Television,* a cubelike form veiled in plastic and tied with twine, left only the antenna exposed. It was signed twice: "Christo for Paik '67," and "Paik '67."

Nineteen sixty-eight was one of Christo and Jeanne-Claude's busiest years, but their increasing art production tells only part of the story. Attaining artistic goals required that an enormous amount of energy be expended in non-studio activities. The demands of various projects would eventually fill, and in a real sense become, Jeanne-Claude and Christo's life. "They are our children," she said of their projects, each of which became another member of their extended family.

Christo had long been intent on wrapping a large building. "As early as

1964," he said, "I understood that the only chance I would ever have to realize the wrapping of a building would be within the museum world. This is why, in 1967, I proposed to wrap the National Gallery of Modern Art in Rome. I made a scale model, drawings, collages, and a photomontage of this proposal because there was a chance I could realize it simultaneously with an exhibition there." The idea and the show never materialized, but, he said, "We came very close."[2]

During 1968, the Christos developed plans to wrap five museums: New York's Museum of Modern Art and the Whitney Museum of American Art, the Kunsthalle in Bern, Switzerland, the National Gallery in Rome, and Chicago's Museum of Contemporary Art. Two of these projects would come to fruition. They also targeted other structures: the three-story Teatro Nuovo opera house in Spoleto, Italy, New York's twenty-three-story Allied Chemical Tower, and a free-form opera house and the Harbour Bridge in Sydney, Australia. Another new goal was to wrap vast stretches of a coastline.

Money was needed for these ambitious projects and for the couple's day-to-day expenses. Selling art became imperative. By then, however, Christo and the Castelli gallery had parted ways. Ivan Karp recalled, "They wanted to progress very, very rapidly. I don't think that Leo's facility was the right platform for that. Jeanne-Claude had much larger ambitions."[3] "I couldn't really go on representing him," Castelli explained. "I already had what seemed like too many artists. One thing that helped me feel not too bad: his incredible wife, Jeanne-Claude. Already it was quite apparent that she would do much better as a free agent than if he stayed with the gallery."[4]

Indeed, the Christos were moving ahead at full speed. His first of five one-man shows in 1968 opened at New York's John Gibson Gallery. The mailer announced, "Projects of Packages, Store Fronts and Barrels," illustrating his scale model of the wrapped National Gallery of Modern Art in Rome. Many pieces found buyers. The Museum of Modern Art purchased the 1963 *Package on a Wheelbarrow.* Added to his intense studio activity were the usual dinner parties, openings and postopening gatherings, appointments with collectors, curators, and writers, and all the complex logistics related to forthcoming exhibitions and potential projects. A cursory examination of the family calendar for 1968 reveals the very large number of support activities required to advance all the projects. On January 8, Priscilla Morgan, director of the eleventh annual Festival of Two Worlds in Spoleto, Christo, and Jeanne-Claude initiated discussions regarding Christo's participation in the festival; they agreed that he should wrap a town landmark. On January 15, Harald Szeemann, director of the Bern Kunsthalle, invited Christo to join eleven other artists in an exhibit marking the museum's fiftieth anniversary; rather than show a group of typical pieces, Christo offered to wrap the edifice and the exhibition. Szeemann responded enthusiastically. On January 16, Christo and Saul Steinberg finalized a trade of their works. That same day, curator Robert Doty asked Christo to participate in the Whitney Museum's 1968 "Sculpture Annual," scheduled to open on December 17; Christo proposed wrapping the museum. Doty offered no help.

In addition to their discussions with the Whitney, the artists were busy with repeated visits from collectors and dealers, selecting photographs, and worrying about the cost and transport of helium for another air package. Jean Leering, director of "Documenta IV," had selected Christo's work for inclusion in the 1968 show in Kassel, Germany. After several meetings, Leering agreed that Christo would show a life-size *Store Front* and a mammoth outdoor air package. A number of artists were allocated five thousand dollars for developing their projects, a sum that would prove wholly inadequate for covering the cost of constructing a twenty-eight-story-high inflatable. Horace Solomon helped by providing Christo with his factory supervisor from Solo Products in Englewood, New Jersey, to help build *Corridor Store Front*.

On February 1, John Gibson, Christo and Jeanne-Claude, and Museum of Modern Art's William Rubin met to discuss the possible wrapping of MoMA. The following week, Harry Shunk and Janos Kender, photo-documenters of the Paris art scene who had recently moved to New York, delivered photos of the museum to the artists. By February 10, Christo and Jeanne-Claude had convinced Lawrence Alloway to write an article on Christo's contribution to "Documenta IV" for *Art International* magazine. Alloway also agreed to begin work on a Christo book scheduled for publication by Abrams the following year. On February 21, Christo and Allan Kaprow discussed *Transfer*, a Kaprow Happening staged at Wesleyan University.

The frantic schedule continued in March: on the ninth, plans were drawn for a late 1968 Christo show at the Institute of Contemporary Art in Philadelphia, and discussions continued with the Whitney, MoMA, Kunsthalle, "Documenta IV," and Spoleto officials. Apparent diversions, such as visits on March 16 and 18 to Andy Warhol's studio to see movies, were, like keeping abreast of the art scene, work-related. After dismantling *Corridor Store Front* and preparing it for shipment, and attending the March 25 black-tie opening of "Dada, Surrealism, and Their Heritage" at MoMA, Christo had some last-minute meetings with William Rubin before leaving for five busy weeks in Italy, France, Holland, and Germany.

Christo and Jeanne-Claude had proposed wrapping the six-story MoMA to memorialize the June 9 closing of the "Dada, Surrealism" show. Rubin appeared receptive. In his mind, the artists' work either embodied the spirit or reflected the heritage of Dada and Surrealism. The wrapping of MoMA promised an exciting final note to a major exhibition. After considerable deliberation, however, the museum administration chose caution rather than the daring vision attributed to Dada and Surrealism. David Bourdon cited the museum's fear that the spectacle surrounding the wrapping of the building would lead to civil disorder. Current events supported his concerns. On April 4, Martin Luther King, Jr., had been assassinated, triggering riots in four cities. Later that month, protesting students took over Columbia University, and in May, student unrest and general strikes nearly toppled the government of Charles de Gaulle.

Christo and Jeanne-Claude had also advanced several related proposals to MoMA: wrapping the Abby Aldrich Rockefeller Sculpture Garden, setting up a wall of barrels that would block traffic on the Fifty-third Street side of the museum, wrapping trees inside the main hall, creating a mastaba of oil barrels in the lobby, and wrapping women who would be placed on pedestals for the closing night. Instead, Rubin offered Christo the first "Project Room" and the first of what would become regular "Project Shows" on the museum's first floor. The exhibition, scheduled to open June 5, consisted of six scale models and ten drawings and photomontages. In the catalog, *Christo Wraps the Museum . . . a Non-Event,* Rubin wrote, "It is not surprising that he should have dreamed that it was time to wrap up the Museum—and for that matter the trees, the sculptures, and even some spectators in the garden. The Museum staff found this a potentially lively and poetically strange project. But the more practical heads of the fire department, police department, and insurance agencies prevailed."[5] One writer complained that MoMA had "chickened out," adding, "pity."[6]

On Saturday, June 1, 1968, John Gibson mounted "Christo II—Scale Models, Photomontages and Drawings," featuring preparatory materials for upcoming projects. The show sold out. Gibson recalled, "We took it down, put up another and sold out again, extended the exhibition, and then put up a third, and sold half of that. The first year I represented Christo we sold fifty works of art. . . . It was a great, much-deserved success."[7] On June 5, Jean and Dominique de Menil purchased almost everything in Christo's MoMA show, then donated the pieces to the museum.

The following day, Christo flew to Frankfurt, and Jeanne-Claude and Cyril traveled to Rome. Then on June 8, Jeanne-Claude and Cyril boarded the train from Rome to Spoleto. While Christo struggled to prepare his massive air package for "Documenta IV" in Kassel, Jeanne-Claude would attempt to wrap the Teatro Nuovo. Christo had thoroughly briefed her and produced drawings, collages, and a scale model to clarify his intent. Awaiting Jeanne-Claude was Priscilla Morgan.

"After I arrived, they told me that we could not wrap the theater because the firemen had forbidden it. So I called Christo in Kassel and he said, 'Okay, look around the town and call me back tomorrow,'" Jeanne-Claude recalled.

The next day, June 12, Jeanne-Claude studied the town's landmarks, spoke to officials, and had lunch with Gian Carlo Menotti, the founder and guiding spirit of the festival. That night, she reported to Christo by phone, "They proposed an abandoned church. People thought it was a very funny idea, an abandoned church, Christo."

"I won't touch a church," he replied. "No way! Have you seen anything else?"

Jeanne-Claude described an old fountain and medieval tower. "Do you want me to try to get permission?" she asked. He said he did.

On June 13, the day Jeanne-Claude and Christo turned thirty-three, Jeanne-Claude and Priscilla Morgan approached various town officials. Jeanne-Claude said, "We went to the city council, the chamber of commerce, and the mayor for a permit. Priscilla did most of the talking. It was done informally. We just walked around, had lunch with them, and explained everything while Cyril played with their kids. They were pleased because they thought Christo might say, 'I want the theater or nothing.' We already had fabric, rope, and a crew ready to work."

On Friday, June 14, Jeanne-Claude and a group of workers tried to wrap an old stone tower on the edge of town. Her agenda told the sad story in large letters: "TOWER—NO. TOO MUCH WIND." The wind subsided, and early Saturday morning, Jeanne-Claude led a successful assault on the tower, resulting in an enormous vertical package. On Monday morning, June 17, Jeanne-Claude and the same workers shrouded a Baroque fountain on the facade of an ornate four-story building facing a central market square. The result was a curious merger of old and new. These structures and the contemporary gestures visited upon them seemed entirely in the spirit of the Festival of Two Worlds. Jeanne-Claude took a number of striking photographs. They showed neatly draped, carefully tied white structures glistening in the sunshine. Few of the curious onlookers noticed the absence of Christo's obsessive signature knotting. Using Jeanne-Claude's photos, Christo produced, for the first and only time, a series of drawings after, not prior to, a project. The two Spoleto packages remained in place for the three-week duration of the festival. One writer later reported, "An irate woman gasping for air in her plasticized apartment reached out her window with a butcher knife and slashed Christo's package."[8]

When Jeanne-Claude, Cyril in hand, arrived in Kassel, she sparkled with the elation of success in Spoleto. Her glow was to vanish quickly because of the Kassel air package. Four herculean efforts to erect a spectacular twenty-eight-story-high phallic-shaped air-filled structure were to result in weeks of agony, tears, improvisation, and suspense. "That air package," she remembered, "was a disaster, the most nightmarish project in my life. Everything went wrong. Each time, all the time, day and night, we were in total panic."

The project had evolved from their 1966 air packages in Eindhoven and

Minneapolis. To research the possibility of realizing their latest and largest in-flatable, Christo had set up a meeting with Mitko Zagoroff, now a mechanical engineer at MIT, in November 1967, and the two men collaborated in plan-ning the installation. By the time Christo arrived in Kassel on June 7, 1968, Zagoroff had just completed work on a number of concrete foundations for the air-filled column. Zagoroff smiled as he later called to mind the hazardous venture. "At the time, I was very interested in ballooning. We had an initial technical choice to make: whether to have it lighter than air or not, whether it should be a balloon or an inflatable structure. At first, we used both concepts. We thought with helium it would rise and stay up. The problem: The slightest wind could bring it down, parallel to ground level. The other approach was to make an inflated structure like a tennis ball—that is, to inflate it rigidly with air, then treat it as if it were a solid body and lift it with a crane. I did all the de-sign on that score."[9] Whatever the method of installation, Christo and Jeanne-Claude's *5,600 Cubicmeter Package* had been designed to tower over Kassel, visible for over fifteen miles in every direction.

The first try at raising the monster package took place in a large park meadow on a rain-swept morning of June 24, three days before the official opening of "Documenta IV." David Bourdon described the scene: "The rain turned into a storm, and the polyethylene skin, after three hours of inflation, was suddenly rent by a ten-foot rip. Having burst its seams, the shimmering, polyethylene colossus, which had been erect a mere ten minutes, thrashed slowly on the ground, collapsing with the majestic throes of a dying whale."[10]

Zagoroff remembered this all too clearly: "During the project we went through four erections. The first one was inflated with air as a rigid body. When we started to tip it, the skin burst; it was a combination of skimping on the thickness of the skin and the German authorities requiring heavier anchor cables than we had reckoned with. It was so close to the opening that Christo said, 'We've got the helium. Why don't we just repair the tear and try again with helium?' The Christos had insisted from the beginning on having helium ready. So that was the second approach."[11]

This attempt was also short-lived. On June 26, the repaired inflated ob-ject, almost the length of a football field, left the ground for a few minutes, but before coming upright the wind whipped it around, a rupture developed, and the package collapsed. Forty-two thousand cubic feet of helium, along with the artists' meager financial resources, dissolved in air. The media had a field day. Headlines ridiculed the very public failure; large photos underscored the point. Most writers alluded to sexual connotations, with much of the humor focused on Christo's inability to "get it up."

Because he spoke German, French, and English, art dealer David Juda had been hired as the artists' liaison for "Documenta IV." He spent weeks working with Christo and supervising a crew of local art students. Juda re-

Kassel, 1968: Jeanne-Claude and Christo during the installation of *5,600 Cubicmeter Package,* "Documenta IV" (Photo: Klaus Baum)

called the June 26 fiasco: "Just as the balloon was going up—it was half upright, like a bent penis—it buckled under extreme pressure and burst at the seams. Jeanne-Claude was extremely upset and crying. Christo just took her in his arms and said, 'Did you see how beautiful it was? Don't worry, it's only a sculpture.' I think he was probably upset later."[12]

It seemed as if the artists had tried everything. At one point, they had contacted the German army, hoping to utilize a giant helicopter. A former Luftwaffe pilot and war hero arrived to help. "It was a horrible experience," said Jeanne-Claude. "In the end, he said it couldn't be done. If the rope is very long, it's much too dangerous for the pilot. If the rope is too short, as he tries to fly, the air motion beneath him pushes the balloon down. After that, Mitko discovered that the mathematical equation he had been using to fill the balloon with air stopped becoming multipliable at some point. It was a calculation never used before because there was never a need. He had to invent a new formula. We found a famous scientist, Professor Trostel, to work with him."

Zagoroff recalled the frustration of June 26: "We had a failure on our hands. Everybody slept on it and then Christo made the decision, 'Goddamn it, we've done all the hard part. All we need is a new skin.' At that point, we had built all the foundations that were going to anchor the structure. We had built an enormous cradle for the bottom. We had bought a blower to inflate it. We even bought a spare generator that would keep the blower going if there was a power failure. The Christos had spent a lot on all the peripherals. It turned out that the right kind of fabric manufacturer happened to be there in Kassel, a small company in the business of building tennis halls."[13]

The artists were determined to salvage the situation. The "Documenta IV" show ran from June 27 through October 6. Jeanne-Claude would somehow raise the money for a new envelope while Christo gathered the remnants of five thousand dollars' worth of polyethylene, packed it on a train, and set out to wrap the Kunsthalle in Bern. *New York Times* art critic Grace Glueck had seen him struggle to raise the "beautiful bratwurst-like object" and watched it crash to the ground. Glueck also witnessed the start of act three. "I remember driving with Jeanne-Claude—not just his wife and project partner, but the other half of Christo—to the manufacturer of the polyethylene material. She wanted to negotiate a new skin for the balloon. As we drove up to the factory she drenched herself with perfume as an added attraction to her persuasive rhetoric," Glueck noted.[14] To pay for the fabric, the artists sold the enormous *Corridor Store Front* to Belgian collector Isi Fiszman.

Much of the groundwork for wrapping the Kunsthalle had been prepared by Harald Szeemann. Once Christo arrived, he and eleven construction workers spent six days fitting remnants of the 27,000 square feet of polyethylene salvaged from the Kassel debacle and tying the material with 10,000 feet of nylon rope. They attached fabric to a series of wooden supports that were installed around the squat nineteenth-century structure to prevent any damage to the building. At one point, fire department officials facilitated the process by making a hydraulic ladder available. David Bourdon reported, "Insurance companies refused to underwrite the Kunsthalle and its valuable contents during the period it was to be wrapped, so to guard against possible fire and vandalism . . . Szeemann had six watchmen posted around the building at all times. As this proved quite expensive, the building was unwrapped after one week."[15] An English magazine offered another explanation for the premature dismantling: "Visitors [to the museum], entering through a slit in the plastic, were almost overcome by the heat and the stagnant air inside."[16]

Nonetheless, the Christos had at last wrapped an entire building. Suddenly, everything seemed possible. After seven years of dreaming and planning, they had transformed a public facility in dramatic, unexpected ways. The oversize parcel tucked into the center of a neatly manicured Swiss city appeared incongruous. Like the smaller *Packages,* it revealed through concealment. Under wraps, part sensual, part enticing gift, part prisoner, the softened contours of the museum had attracted attention, aroused feelings, and evoked mystery. Jeanne-Claude never saw the luminous, billowing fabric tied firmly about the Kunsthalle, and Christo never saw the shimmering veils that covered the fountain and tower in Spoleto. Each act created new, disquieting forms. Each intervention bestowed a sense of wholeness while remaining ambiguous enough to suggest possession, freedom, or any number of other interpretations.

Christo returned to Kassel in early July. Buoyed by their Bern project and by Jeanne-Claude's timely sale of *Corridor Store Front,* they, Zagoroff, and David Juda prepared to raise the uncooperative balloon. The new synthetic textile envelope, spray-coated with water-resistant polymer and heat-sealed, had been completed in record time. On July 14, a reconfigured Christo team tried again. Joseph Beuys and other artists lent a hand. The inflated monolith lay stretched out on the ground, snared in twelve thousand feet of rope and connected to an adjustable cradle, two large cranes, and six concrete foundations set along a circle nine hundred feet in diameter. Pumped full of air, the monumental oblong column weighed 180 tons. Photographs show lines of young men holding the thick guylines in place while other figures secure ropes atop the precarious horizontal structure. The cranes were not up to the job. "When we tried to pull it up by its midsection," Zagoroff recalled, "it sagged and the skin broke open. Too much pressure inside. The embarrassing thing for me as engineer is that we were meticulous in monitoring the pressure." After giving a long technical explanation illustrated by charts and photos, he added, "Let me say it simply. The skin elongated readily on each panel. However, at the seams, where it overlapped, it was twice as strong. So it didn't expand as much. What I hadn't calculated was that the cross seam, where it crosshatched, caused double loading along the longitudinal seam. That did it. It split along one seam."[17]

The German press documented the new failure in detail. Pictures showed what looked like a knife wound running lengthwise through the midsection of the sinking balloon, and the dejected artist, his head slumped down like the wounded air package. "The whole thing didn't explode," Mitko Zagoroff explained. "It was a localized burst. The repair was easy. What we really needed was a different way of erecting it. Christo decided to get taller cranes, more cranes."[18] Jeanne-Claude said, "It was a very tough time for us. We stopped caring about the time deadline. At that point, it was not for the public; it was for us. There had never been an inflated structure of that size on earth. So we couldn't ask anybody how to do it."

Christo, *Wrapped Bottles and Wrapped Cans,*
1958–1960. (Photo: Eeva-Inkeri)

Christo, *Project for a Wrapped Public Building, 1961.*
(Photo: Harry Shunk)

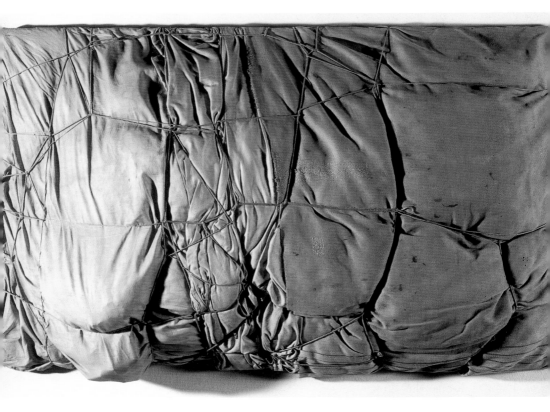

Above: Christo, *Package, 1961.*
Museum of Modern Art, New York.
(Photo: Wolfgang Volz)

Left: Christo, *Purple Store Front, 1964.*
(Photo: Wolfgang Volz)

Opposite: Christo and
Jeanne-Claude, *Iron Curtain-Wall
of Oil Barrels, Rue Visconti, Paris,
1961–1962.*
(Photo: Jean-Dominique Lajoux)

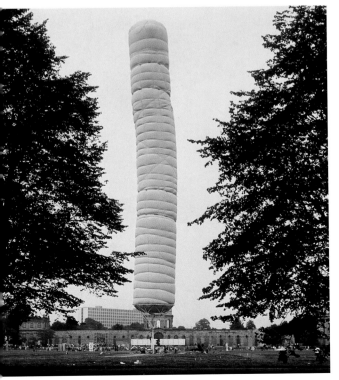

Above: Christo and Jeanne-Claude,
*Wrapped Kunsthalle, Bern,
Switzerland, 1968.*
(Photo: Balz Burkhard)

Left: Christo and Jeanne-Claude, *5,600
Cubicmeter Package, Documenta IV,
Kassel, Germany, 1967–1968.*
(Photo: Klaus Baum)

Opposite:
Christo and Jeanne-Claude,
*Wrapped Coast, One Million Square Feet,
Little Bay, Sydney, Australia, 1968–1969*
(Photos: Harry Shunk)

Above: Christo and Jeanne-Claude, *Oceanfront, Newport, Rhode Island, 1974.* (Photo: Gianfranco Gorgoni)

Opposite: Christo and Jeanne-Claude, *Valley Curtain, Rifle, Colorado, 1970–1972.* (Photo: Harry Shunk)

Below: Christo and Jeanne-Claude, *Wrapped Roman Wall, Porta Pinciana delle Mure Aureliane, Rome, 1974.* (Photo: Harry Shunk)

Above: Christo and Jeanne-Claude,
*Wrapped Walk Ways, Jacob L. Loose
Park, Kansas City, Missouri,
1977–1978.* (Photo: Wolfgang Volz)

Opposite (above and below):
Christo and Jeanne-Claude,
*Running Fence, Sonoma and Marin
Counties, California, 1972–1976.*
(Photos: Wolfgang Volz)

Right: Christo and
Jeanne-Claude, *Wrapped
Vestibule, The Art Gallery of New
South Wales, Sydney, 1990.*
(Photo: Wolfgang Volz)

Above and below: *Christo and Jeanne-Claude, The Pont Neuf Wrapped, Paris, 1975–1985.* (Photos: Wolfgang Volz)

Opposite: Christo and Jeanne-Claude, *Surrounded Islands, Biscayne Bay, Greater Miami, Florida, 1980–1983.* (Photo: Wolfgang Volz)

Above: Christo and Jeanne-Claude, *The Umbrellas, Japan/USA, 1984–1991*: Ibaraki. (Photo: Wolfgang Volz)

Below: Christo and Jeanne-Claude, *The Umbrellas, Japan/USA, 1984–1991*: California. (Photo: Wolfgang Volz)

Above and below: *Christo and Jeanne-Claude, Wrapped Reichstag, Berlin, 1971–1995.*
(Photos: Wolfgang Volz)

Above and below: Christo and Jeanne-Claude, *Wrapped Trees, Foundation Beyeler and Berower Park, Riehen, Switzerland, 1997–1998.* (Photos: Wolfgang Volz)

Opposite: Christo and Jeanne-Claude, *The Wall, 13,000 Oil Barrels, Gasometer, Oberhausen, Germany, 1999.* (Photo: Wolfgang Volz)

Christo, *The Gates Project for Central Park, New York City.* Drawing, 1991. (Photo: Wolfgang Volz)

Christo, *The Gates Project for Central Park, New ork City.* Collage, 1996. (Photo: Wolfgang Volz)

Christo, *Over the River, Project for the Arkansas River, State of Colorado.* Drawing, 1997. (Photo: Wolfgang Volz)

Christo, *Over the River, Project for the Arkansas River, State of Colorado.* Collage, 1997. (Photo: Wolfgang Volz)

With money borrowed against future sales, the artists frantically engaged the services of two of Europe's largest cranes. It took weeks to orchestrate their simultaneous arrival, one from Hamburg, the other from Spain, each wide load escorted front and rear by motorcycles. The eventual bill was nine thousand dollars. When the first giant crane pulled onto the Auepark meadow, it started sinking. "It had been raining all summer," Jeanne-Claude said. "We needed army steel mats like the kind they use in the desert." Zagoroff and Juda somehow convinced the British Rhine army to help.

Finally, before dawn on Saturday, August 3, 1968, with five cranes in place and workers assembled, the artists made a final attempt. Alfred Barr, senior curator of the Museum of Modern Art, had come to offer moral support. Jeanne-Claude stood quietly in the darkness, holding his arm. She recalled, "We didn't know each other very well, but that morning we became best pals. Barr arrived at five A.M., when there is a lull in the wind. Five in the morning is the same all over the world. The wind is usually zero between five and six, because the night wind is starting to die before the day wind picks up."

"There was a very scary moment," remembered Zagoroff. "We were in a situation where, had there been any wind, the structure could have toppled the cranes. The cranes were capable of raising the balloon in quiet air quite easily. But if there had been any kind of wind, either they would have had to let the structure fly or it would have toppled them. So we did it early in the morning, when there is no wind at all. The erection proceeded little by little by little, until it was nearly complete. At eighty degrees, there was a slight wind. That started a flutter in the structure. It began weaving to and fro, left and right, up and down . . . left, right, up, down. The cranes were shaking and the whole structure rose out of its bottom cradle like a rubber ball, bouncing. The tether tube that inflated it almost dislocated."[19]

Jeanne-Claude recounted the moment: "At one point, the balloon became unbalanced and started banging on one crane and then another. The crane operators had never done anything like this in their lives. When one crane began to tip, I ran toward the man in the cabin, yelling, 'Jump!' He shouted back at me in German. I later found out that he had said, 'Woman, go back in the kitchen and let me do my job.' If he had gotten killed, there would have been no more Christo. Both cranes were tipping and the banging sounds were horrible."

Zagoroff described the dramatic conclusion: "It was a very tense moment, but somehow the balloon got past eighty degrees and the crew tied down the guylines left and right, which stopped it from weaving. They tied down the front, and we were really over the hurdle. I almost threw up, I was so relieved. We were over the hump, and a jubilant mood set in with the workers. At this juncture, the artists were furious. There were still ten or twelve ropes to be secured, and they wanted everything tied down before any celebration.

There was really nothing to worry about. Some harsh words were said to the students. I was just amazed. For the Christos, the project is the important thing; it takes the highest priority, and all civility is put aside. I felt threatened. After all, we all have feelings. I also feel closer to them when things go badly. Christo manages to establish an urgency for the project. Always. So that everybody involved becomes committed to the project and believes in the urgency. It becomes their urgency. Christo has a knack of posing that urgency, and both Jeanne-Claude's and his personalities drop out of the picture. The act becomes the important thing."[20]

What mattered was the *5,600 Cubicmeter Package* towering triumphantly over Kassel. The fourteen-thousand-pound colossus held gentle sway over the city for over two months before it and the rest of "Documenta IV" were dismantled. Lawrence Alloway described the package as "huge—about the height of Mies van der Rohe's Seagram Building—but as nervously responsive to air pressures as a tendril of seaweed to water currents."[21] The financial outlay seemed not to matter. When all the bills were paid, the project's cost reached seventy thousand dollars, an enormous amount for a controversial, temporary work of art. "I still have nightmares about that project," Jeanne-Claude said.

Christo and Jeanne-Claude learned a great deal in Kassel. The *5,600 Cubicmeter Package* clarified a dynamic method of operation, one that would reemerge in subsequent large-scale works: extensive planning with a team of technical advisers, obtaining permission from authorities, selling working drawings and models to finance the project completely, temporary installation by a team of motivated workers, site cleanup, and in-depth documentation of the experience.

Joyce Alazrachi, who traveled to Kassel for the event, suggested a reason that people were drawn to Christo: "It's his sincerity coming through. He really loves what he does. It's not showmanship or showing off. It's not competitive spirit. He does it because he feels like doing it. I don't think he compares himself to anybody. I remember in Kassel people called his air package a phallic symbol. I asked him about that. He said, 'Oh well, if that's what they see. It really doesn't matter.'"[22]

On September 6, Jeanne-Claude and Cyril had an early lunch with Jacques de Guillebon before leaving Paris for New York. The following day, Christo left Cologne to join them. The prolonged effort in Kassel accounted for a staggering amount of work awaiting their attention. Among stacks of mail was a feature article in *Du* magazine; it contained full-page photos of their loft building, the studio, Christo, Jeanne-Claude, and Cyril posed between two shop windows, and Christo on the roof of 48 Howard Street, wrapping the skylight to prevent leaks in his studio.[23]

Kassel, 1968: Dimiter (Mitko) Zagoroff, Jeanne-Claude, and Christo during the final installation of the *5,600 Cubicmeter Package*. (Photo: Klaus Baum)

On September 11, Cyril returned to school, and Christo and Jeanne-Claude attended the first meeting with the management of the Allied Chemical Tower. He had prepared scale models showing a wrapped wedge-shaped skyscraper at 1 Times Square. Using Harry Shunk's photographs as a point of departure, Christo created over a dozen dramatic drawings and collaged photographs. His plans included material samples of a thick white woven cloth. The project called for "several thousand feet of Dacron rope" and "16,000 linear yards of woven, synthetic fabric," sewn at a factory into a one-piece slip-cover. "The wrapping of the building will take between 5 and 7 days. The installation of the fabric will be done from the top of the building, slowly unfurling the slipcover and tying the ropes."[24] In the end, the owners cited insurance requirements as the reason for turning down the project.

By mid-September, Christo's attention focused on "Monuments and Projects," his one-man exhibition opening October 4 at the University of Pennsylvania's Institute of Contemporary Art. It included earlier work and three on-site projects. ICA director Stephen Prokopoff and a small band of collectors had followed Christo's development and become ardent supporters. Prokopoff linked the work with a "general sense of alienation that pervaded European intellectual life during the post–World War II era." He characterized the storefronts as "allusions to an unremittingly faceless present" and "so depersonalized, they stand as metaphors of alienation, monuments to a civilization barren of inner life."[25]

Suzanne Delehanty, an art historian with a background in ancient art, remembered, "The ICA was a small organization. Stephen was director, I was his assistant, and there was a part-time installation crew. That was it." Delehanty, who subsequently became director of the ICA, recalled her vivid first impressions of Christo: "You just had to like the man. You know, he's wired energy. There is a kind of intensity about him and a warmth. His eyes sparkled. I had to round up fifteen hundred–plus oil barrels, the equivalent of five freight cars full. They were to construct a truncated pyramid in our large fifty-by-fifty-foot gallery. Getting them wasn't easy. It meant disrupting oil companies' operations, since drums are needed at every stage of the delivery cycle. The materials Christo chose engaged this invisible system. Negotiations for loaning barrels were made with various companies by Stephen and Nathaniel Lieb, an ICA board member. I remember that one company wouldn't lend, but insisted on selling their barrels to us; after we returned them, they would give a refund—it was their way of doing a loan receipt. I had to convince the university business office not to worry about a ten- or fifteen-thousand-dollar invoice. We borrowed oil barrels from several companies: some did a straight loan based on an exchange of letters; others used their own systems of inventory control. It was fascinating."[26]

Delivery workers laid Masonite sheets over the stairs to form a ramp, then covered the surface with tarpaulins. Large tarps were also placed throughout the building so that barrels could be rolled without causing damage. "ICA had to return each oil drum in good condition," Suzanne explained. "During the installation, there was always some kind of crisis. We all loved working with the Christos, but there were moments when it got tense. There was a lot of 'How are we going to get this done?' and 'We've got to do it.' There was a lot of—and I use the word affectionately—fireworks. It was a very intense experience. One night, some architecture students who were perplexed with the piece snuck into the gallery. During the setup, they took some barrels. I think the work violated their concept of architecture. Maybe because the structure was so architectural in scale, they felt it impinged on their territory. Anyway, we retrieved the barrels."

While the multicolored oil barrels were stacked to form a massive mastaba in the ICA ground-floor entry gallery, another work, *Two Tons of Stacked Hay*, took shape on the level above. The installation crew, paid M.F.A. students, alternated between unloading barrels and making forays into the countryside to gather bales of hay. Suzanne Delehanty reflected, "The bales of hay were stacked, creating a bulky structure, covered with tarpaulin and tied with rope. *Two Tons of Stacked Hay* stood alone in a room about sixty by thirty feet. Ed Flynn, one of our workers, came down with hepatitis. After that, we all had to get gamma globulin shots."

Another ICA work lasted only a few hours. When dinner guests—Holly and Horace Solomon, John Gibson, Mitko Zagoroff, and artist Robert Indiana among them—arrived, seven wrapped female nudes awaited them. Each had been placed on a pedestal. Harry Shunk and Janos Kender documented the process and photographed Jeanne-Claude, Christo, and Cyril alongside a wrapped woman. Delehanty observed, "Some people thought that the packaged women were absolutely phenomenal. Others were quite distressed; they didn't think it was art and called it an outrage. Some were amused. A few guests were concerned about the women perspiring too much. They had no ventilation. Lots of attention was given to bringing them drinks—you know, ginger ale with a straw. They remained wrapped, reclining on pedestals all through dinner."

On October 2, 1968, two days before Christo's ICA opening, Marcel Duchamp died in Neuilly, France. Several months earlier, he and Christo had completed a trade. Christo recalled, "We saw him and Teeny often at the end. He visited my studio just before leaving for Europe, looked at everything, and loved the studies for the *Wrapped Coast* project in Australia. We exchanged some things from his *Valise*, made by Teeny's daughter, for a *Wrapped Coast* collage. I don't know if he knew what I was trying to do, but he was very encouraging."

Although some of the Christos' projects found support and were realized, a greater number met with rejection. Within the next sixty days, their proposals to wrap the Allied Chemical Tower and the Whitney Museum were effectively terminated. Christo proposed an exhibition to the Los Angeles

County Museum that would have extended beyond their walls to include an enormous air package and fifteen miles of wrapped California coastline. The museum saved and later published Christo's letter, but it never acted on the proposal.[27]

One small success took place in Connecticut. It could be traced back to a conversation over coffee between art dealer John Gibson and collector Vera List, a few months earlier at "Documenta IV." Gibson said:

"She remarked that she would like to have a large outdoor work by Christo for her sculpture garden. I suggested a wrapped tree. She agreed, stipulating that it be no more than twenty feet long. That fall, Christo and I went look-ing for trees near Greenwich, Connecticut. . . . Christo fell in love with an enormous fallen oak tree; it must have been at least fifty feet long, but he had to have it."

Gibson described what happened next as "an experience out of an old Buster Keaton film." A bulldozer loaded the tree onto a truck, which was far too small for its load. They managed, however, to balance it precariously and, with Christo and Gibson following behind in a car, began the ten-mile trip back to Greenwich. The tree stuck out so far that it forced on-coming cars off the road, sending everyone into hysteria. Still crying from laughter, they reached the List estate, and found Vera List, sitting in her study, absorbed in a pile of art mailings. Remembers Gibson, "I told her, simply, that the tree had arrived. Without going out to look at it, she suggested that we dump it by the side of the garden. The next day, completely nonplussed by the tremendous size of the tree, Vera ordered a crane to lift it onto a site overlooking Long Is-land Sound and ordered a concrete base to be built for it. Over the next several days, Christo wrapped the branches in plastic and the roots in burlap, and then polyurethaned the trunk.[28]

"I visited the List Collection years later with a group from Brussels," Gib-son said later. "I led them around the house, looking for the Christo tree. It was no longer there. I said, 'Vera, what happened to the tree?' She said, 'Well, the dogs started frequenting it too often. Albert cut it up for firewood.'"[29] Like much of the Christos' ephemeral work, photographs and a collage drawing— *Wrapped Tree (Project for Mrs. Vera List)*—provide the only evidence of the work's existence.

On January 11, 1969, Christo arrived in Chicago to prepare to wrap his first American building—Chicago's Museum of Contemporary Art. MoCA and the neighborhood were anything but distinguished. Built in the early

1900s, the former bakery and past headquarters of Playboy Enterprises was described by David Bourdon as "a banal one-story edifice (with a below-ground gallery) having about as much charm as an old shoe box."[30]

Jan van der Marck, now director of MoCA, had laid the groundwork for *Wrap In Wrap Out*, an attempt to shroud MoCA's exterior, its gallery space, staircases, and assorted contents. By January 15, six student volunteers from the Chicago Art Institute and Institute of Design were ready to work, and sixty-two pieces—ten thousand square feet—of sturdy tarpaulin and four thousand feet of heavy manila rope were in place. Curious onlookers asked if the museum was being remodeled or perhaps conserving heat. In *The New Yorker*, Calvin Tomkins reported "a chorus of outraged protests from American museum directors."[31] Sherman Lee, respected director of the Cleveland Museum of Art, called the project a "catastrophe" and denounced van der Marck as a "cheerfully self-exploding museum director."[32] The MoCA press release asked, "What more appropriate object to mummify than a museum?" It quoted van der Marck: "With the whole idea of a modern museum and its usefulness somewhat up for grabs, Christo succeeds in parodying all the usual associations with a museum: a mausoleum, a repository for precious contents, a desire to 'wrap up' all of art history."

After outfitting the chunky structure with a dark brown warm winter garment that contrasted with its snow-covered surroundings, Christo wrapped a vertical signpost in clear white plastic. He then proceeded to cover the gallery floors with 2,800 square feet of rented painters' drop cloths, wrapped the staircase, an exit sign, a public telephone, a twenty-foot tree, and assorted furniture. Jeanne-Claude remembered the January 17 opening; "People were asked to remove their shoes. Not at Christo's request, but for security reasons. We were afraid that the women with high heels would trip, especially on the wrapped stairway. It was very lovely to see everybody in bare feet. The next day, we read in the newspaper that a guard who had locked the museum and thought everyone had left heard a noise and found a young couple making love underneath the wrapped stairway on the wrapped floor."

Time magazine contained photos of the artist fastening a knot and of MoCA transformed. The unattributed article said that onlookers didn't know "whether they ought to laugh or snarl." It credited "the bespectacled Bulgarian-born artist" with knowing "how to muffle a rampant motorcycle so that it acquires the petrified dynamism of a stuffed buffalo or a blindfolded rhinoceros. He can embalm a slender sapling so that it lies with the mute pathos of Pearl White bound and gagged on the railroad track."[33] A *Newsweek* article reported: "Museum guards have had to unwrap spectators who insist on bundling themselves up in dropcloth." The piece quoted MoCA public-relations director Karin Rosenberg as saying, "'Since Christo wrapped us up, young people have been coming in and sitting down to talk, as if the museum were a park. Some people have even said they thought it was very sexy.'"³⁴

A number of ambitious projects failed to materialize in 1969. Christo made a striking series of collages and drawings depicting hundreds of wrapped trees along the Champs Elysées; one year after the 1968 riots, Parisian authorities had no appetite even for this mild subversion. His proposal to wrap fifteen miles of California coastline fared no better. A barrel project, *Houston Mastaba, Project for Texas,* the glass *Closed Highway,* and a scheme to wrap public walkways in Ueno Park, Tokyo, and Sonnsbeek Park in Arnhem, Holland, simultaneously, also met with rejection. However, in May, Christo traveled by himself to Europe and realized two projects. He produced the modest *Wrapped Floor* and *Wrapped Staircase* in conjunction with his solo show at Wide White Space Gallery in Antwerp.

Throughout this time, Christo and Jeanne-Claude increasingly focused on one monumental vision: *Wrapped Coast,* whose full title was *Wrapped Coast—One Million Square Feet, Little Bay, Sydney, Australia.* John W. Kaldor, an employee of Universal Textiles in Sydney, played a key role in getting the project moving. Kaldor recalled, "On a visit to New York in 1968, I saw Christo's work from "Documenta IV" reproduced in a magazine. I had recently become interested in international contemporary art and decided to ring him up. Jeanne-Claude invited me to the loft. I was a young textile designer, not earning much money, but I bought a small *Package.*"³⁵

Three years earlier, Kaldor had convinced his company to sponsor an annual Australian sculpture competition. The winner would be given the funds for overseas study and a museum exhibition in either Sydney or Melbourne. The idea proved so successful that other firms adopted the practice. On February 12, 1969, Kaldor wrote Christo that he had obtained permission from Universal Textiles to invite an outstanding young foreign artist to Australia each year. "I asked if he would like to have a show or give lectures," Kaldor said. "Christo wrote back that he would love to come to Australia but that he wasn't any good at lecturing and didn't want an exhibition. He wanted to wrap a coastline!"³⁶ On April 11, Kaldor wrote, "I'm doing everything possible to get a coast! Next week I will be seeing the Premier of New South Wales as the only way we will get there is to go to the very top." He advised Christo not to worry about labor: "I am sure we will get a lot of art students. The first and main problem is to get a coast." He inscribed in pen beneath the typed note, "I am really very excited about this project and am doing all I can."³⁷

An April 28 letter from Minister of Lands T. L. Lewis rejected the project. It "would not be an appropriate use of Crown land," he stated. "The only thing I can suggest is for you to seek an area of privately owned land for the purpose you have in mind." Kaldor did just that. He sent the artist a telegram on May 8. "HAVE RECEIVED PERMISSION TO USE COASTLINE IN SYDNEY ITSELF 9 MILES FROM THE CITY CENTRE FOR YOUR PROJECT STOP WILL SEND AS SOON AS POSSIBLE PHOTOGRAPHS MAPS SURVEY ETC STOP PLEASE ADVISE PROSPECTS FOR SUPPLY OF PACKAGING MATERIAL FROM AMERICA OR SHOULD I TAKE STEPS TO INVESTIGATE LOCAL SUPPLY?" Prince Henry Hospital owned the property. John Clancy, the chief executive officer, and the hospital directors had given permission to use their stretch of rugged coastline "for the purpose of a 'packaged coast.'" But there were certain conditions, including: "The name of the hospital is not to be used for any purpose whatever in any press, radio, or television statement or publicity material . . . and under no circumstances is it to be suggested that the hospital is sponsoring the project"; the public would be admitted only with hospital consent; Christo and workers could enter the area only at "a point and by a route" determined by the hospital; costs and liabilities would rest with Christo; no part of the site would be damaged; and utilization dates would be October 1 through November 30, with restoration of the site completed by December 14. In addition to delivering a coast, John Kaldor convinced insurance underwriters to donate the cost of their services to provide broad liability coverage, and he induced the Bureau of Meteorology to supply all weather information concerning past October and November records for pressure, rainfall, sunshine, and wind velocity.

Jeanne-Claude, Christo, and Cyril arrived in Sydney on September 25. Christo remembered, "From the moment John Kaldor leased the land and from our arrival in Sydney, we were confronted with furious people. There was a lot of confusion; people thought that Prince Henry Hospital was financing the project instead of curing the sick! While we were still surveying the land, one man was carried onto the site by stretcher as a demonstration about the frivolity of the hospital. Even the nurses believed the hospital was financing the project and threatened to go on strike! Finally we had to make a radio statement that the project was entirely paid for by us, that we were not getting any money from the hospital or other government agency."[38]

The Aspen Center for Contemporary Art paid the ten-thousand-dollar bill for 1 million square feet of Sarlon Erosion Control Mesh, a synthetic, highly reflective, open-weave, opaque straw-colored fabric. What appeared to be a charitable donation was in fact a sale. As Jeanne-Claude explained, "John Powers, through the Aspen Institute, bought a large number of drawings. He bought because we begged, not because he wanted to."

Early on the morning of October 5, the artist met at Kaldor's house with Ninian Melville, a retired major in the Australian Army Corps of Engineers, who had been appointed site supervisor. "We have one hundred and twenty men and women ready to die," Melville announced.

Jeanne-Claude said, "We know it's dangerous, but don't talk like that."

Confused, Melville replied, "You told me you wanted them to die." Finally, they realized his Australian accent made the word *today* sound like "to die." The work crew consisted of students from Sydney University and East Sydney Technical College, as well as a number of local artists and teachers. During the next twenty-three days, 15 professional mountain climbers and 110 workers expended seventeen thousand hours attempting to impose Christo and Jeanne-Claude's audacious fusion of art and landscape.

John Kaldor recounted an early incident:

> Part of the site was a garbage dump. There were typical city employees working there, simple, tough manual laborers. When Christo arrived, they were dumping soil in that area. They thought the project was a joke. . . . [But] within a day they were helping Christo. He didn't even say that much. It's his art, his charisma, his communicating—sometimes in nonverbal ways. Many students became really committed to him. There were even a few architecture students who gave up architecture to become artists.[39]

In October 1969, Imants Tillers, now Australia's leading avant-garde artist, and nine other architecture students eagerly joined the project workforce. Soft-spoken and unpretentious, Tillers said, "I was thrilled to contribute to this amazing work. Knowing art could be like this gave me a great feeling of excitement. The project offered a new perspective on art and convinced me to become an artist. I worked near the waterline—you know, down below—with a gun that fired threaded nail fasteners into the rocks. That's how we would fix the ropes that held the fabric down. Once we decided on which direction the material should go, sheets were dropped and we would fix them down below. Then a climbing guy would come down a rope and fix the fabric onto a vertical surface. It was fun. Jeanne-Claude was very vocal, very assertive. Christo was quieter. I thought she was a great force on location. When things went wrong, she shouted orders.[40]

Wind, water, surf, rocks, 1 million square feet of fabric, and thirty-five miles of rope slowly became part of one vast, living, breathing organism— *Wrapped Coast.* Restless air currents rippled under its undulating skin like land-borne ocean waves. Christo and Jeanne-Claude understood that their large expenditures on an unsalable work of art appeared irrational. They also knew that aside from aesthetic issues and whatever people thought of them and the project, the safety of people and animals was paramount: Years later, Christo stated, "We would never pull off these projects if we behaved with an arrogant, confrontational attitude. If we have succeeded in doing a few projects, it is because we have been able to create the right chemistry of willingness, understanding, and expectation."[41]

Little Bay, Sydney, Australia, 1969: Christo at the *Wrapped Coast.* (Photo: Harry Shunk)

"The concept of art was so narrow at the time that *Wrapped Coast* appeared to be the work of a madman," Tillers recalled. "The press made a joke of it. . . . As the wrapping took place, it became an incredible environment to be in. The transformation took place on such a large scale. It was just so sculptural, with every surface and volume articulated."[42]

Christo and Jeanne-Claude arranged for Shunk and Kender to photograph everything. Shunk gave his account: "*Wrapped Coast* was really extraordinary. I think it was Christo's best project. The enormity of it. I remember a terrible storm destroyed the fabric. We took photos of John Kaldor trying to hold down the material. He nearly got blown off a cliff. Then he tried to repair everything by himself. They had to do the whole thing over again."[43]

"It was the most beautiful storm," said Jeanne-Claude. "The winds came about halfway through the project and we lost about one-third of the fabric." The unexpected one-hundred-mph gale wreaked havoc, lifting three- and six-hundred-foot-long billowing sheets into the dark sky. Kaldor called to mind the evening of October 15: "The few of us working closest to Christo were absolutely devastated. We didn't know how to get on. Obviously it hurt Christo more than us. He had such strength, such charisma, that by the next morning he convinced everyone around him that this is the nature of his work and we had to go on. Within hours, everybody was enthusiastic and working harder than ever. He is really a leader."[44]

Raising money to buy replacement fabric became the immediate challenge. The architecture students continued working dawn to dark, refusing to be paid. Two exhibitions generated some needed cash.

Daniel Thomas, then curator of the Art Gallery of New South Wales, recalled the dangers; "The fabric might be draped over a crevasse between rocks, not over soil. One could step unwittingly from wrapped rock or earth onto wrapped air."[45] There were weathered pockmarked boulders, salt-stained jagged stones, and an eighty-four-foot-high cliff to contend with. One of the most experienced mountain climbers had a frightening fall; the next morning, he returned to work wearing a wide neck collar, insisting, "It's nothing." On October 12, the Outpatient Department at Prince Henry Hospital billed "Christo Christo" $7.35 for an X ray. "It was a stupid thing," Christo said. "While wrapping with the mountain climbers, I fell between two slippery rocks and dislocated my right shoulder. They fixed it right away." Jeanne-Claude watched from a distance. "I could see Christo clearly. I didn't see him fall, so I didn't understand why a worker punched him. I ran over, thinking there was trouble. Christo was thanking the man for punching his shoulder back into place. Then we went to the hospital, which was not very far away. I remember a young doctor bandaging Christo and telling him not to use his arm for a few weeks. Afterward, the doctor went around Sydney bragging, 'I wrapped Christo!'"

The project was completed on October 28. For some, *Wrapped Coast* suggested a rejection of the art establishment's rampant commercialism, yet for Prince Henry Hospital, it represented an economic opportunity. On one weekend, 2,500 sight-seers paid twenty cents each to see Christo and Jeanne-Claude's sprawling oddity. It took about an hour to stroll along the mile-long stretch of wrapped coastline. Every step across fabric-covered rock, scrub, and soil was a tactile adventure filled with surprise. The curious, artificial landscape seemed part surreal, part lunar, part last frontier, on the edge of an unreal world. Christo observed, "The most enjoyable part of *Wrapped Coast* was probably the 'promenade' that visitors were able to make; people would take time to walk from one side of the project to the other. For me, that element of time was the most significant and influential."[46] Once again, Christo and Jeanne-Claude's gentle intervention spoke volumes about impermanence and artistic freedom.

On Wednesday, October 29, one day after completing *Wrapped Coast*, Christo and Jeanne-Claude flew to Melbourne. By Thursday, materials and labor were on hand for installing *Wool Works*, a site-specific sculpture at the National Gallery of Victoria. Two large shipments of wool bales were stacked into a monolithic form reminiscent of *Wrapped Hay* at the Chandler Coventry Gallery. Dark tarpaulin, tied more gently than usual, covered the top three-quarters of the structure. The enormous package, with bales still visible along its base, filled the museum's large Keith Murdoch Court. An additional seventy-five bales of opened, partially opened, and unopened wool were stationed in rows around the massive form. Wool, central to the regional economy and part of the local folklore, proved to be an apt choice for the installation. The lamb-quiet indoor environment projected little of the vulnerability, obvious danger, and notoriety associated with *Wrapped Coast.* The exhibition opened October 31. The Christos left the following morning for three final days in Sydney. They bid farewell to the Kaldors and a band of Aussie admirers before departing November 4 to complete, with Cyril—who during their stay in Australia had lived at John Kaldor's house and gone to school with his children— their round-the-world trip. *Wrapped Coast* still had a four-week life span before removal and site restoration.

John Kaldor, like the coast of Little Bay, had been transformed. "My relationship with Universal Textiles had become strained because I gave six months to the project and very little to them. I thought, 'If I can coordinate *Wrapped Coast,* hundreds of students, mountain climbers, and everything else, I can run a small company. I'm grateful to Christo for giving me the impetus to start my own textile company."[47]

Daniel Thomas observed:

> [The] most magical thing about Christo's *Wrapped Coast* may not have been the experience of the work itself by the many thousands who visited it. There was also an extraordinary response from the millions who knew it only through the Australian media. At the first announcement there was scoffing, but it seemed to me that as soon as the project became sufficiently visible the public overtook the media and fell in love with the *Wrapped Coast*'s spectacular, wonderful absurdity and beauty. . . . I believe that the wide public took Christo's work to its heart not merely because commonly-shared Australian experience was recognized, not because great size and strange beauty are wonders in themselves. I believe that the *artistic practice* of Christo was also appreciated: his over-the-top concept, his easy perseverance, his collaborative work processes, the generosity of his intentions."[48]

Edmund Capon, director of the Art Gallery of New South Wales, said, "That momentous event in 1969 . . . did more for contemporary art in Australia than any other single event."[49]

10

Valley Curtain: An Eagle with Two Heads

Cyril's godmother—Jeanne-Claude's close friend Carole Weisweiller—followed the couple's adventures from afar, but she had held a negative view of most vanguard artists, including Christo. That changed by 1969. "I was absolutely amazed at the success of *Wrapped Coast.* They are an extraordinary couple, like an eagle with two heads."[1]

Anyone who knew Christo and Jeanne-Claude in the early 1970s knew they were capable of soaring to unimagined heights. As if invisibly coupled, they seemed to sense each other, communicating through the smallest gesture. With the passing of time, it became increasingly difficult to picture them separately, or to imagine a project not driven by their dual force. Just as Christo's work began to command growing attention, the unheralded collaboration of Jeanne-Claude and Christo became the operational reality. Among famous couples in art history, it is rare to find one who so completely shared identical goals.

However, it was not until April 1994 that they announced and publicly clarified their long-standing artistic interdependence, acknowledging their past and present coauthorship of the projects. Henceforth, they were both to be credited as a single artist. They stated that he had produced all of the drawings, collages, prints, and models, while she had prepared the taxes unassisted. Jeanne-Claude said, "I don't draw, and he doesn't do the taxes."[2] However, even though Jeanne-Claude had fronted all business dealings for decades, giving the impression that she alone managed financial matters, they maintained that every decision—including all economic, social, political, and aesthetic ones related to the projects—was always arrived at jointly. "The drawings are the scheme for the project," said Christo. "After that, we do everything together: choose the rope, the fabric, the thickness of the fabric, the amount of fabric, the color; we argue, and we think about it. Everybody knows that we have worked together for over thirty years. There's no point in arguing about who does what. The work is all that matters."

The news raised some eyebrows. Skeptics felt that designating Jeanne-Claude as an artist was inappropriate. They viewed her as no more than a spunky superdealer. Writer Albert Elsen's observation was typical: "[She] would make a better chief executive officer than most who run our big corporations."[3] Art dealer Rosa Esman echoed that sentiment: "We always thought that Jeanne-Claude would make the best president of the United States or the world. She is a most extraordinarily effective businesswoman. Her tremendous warmth and appeal is very persuasive, sometimes overly so."[4] If there had been any misrepresentation of Jeanne-Claude's role, no one deserved more blame than the couple themselves. Beginning in the mid-1960s, they nurtured public personas that were as effective as they were misleading.

When they returned triumphantly from *Wrapped Coast* and their around-the-world trip, no one thought of Jeanne-Claude as an artist. In 1970, attributions were not an issue. All that mattered then and in the decades that followed was overcoming obstacles to subsequent projects. From the moment they first arrived in New York, they had carefully observed how people in the art world interacted, trying to determine what operational techniques best fit their own developing strategy. The "good cop, bad cop" approach had the most appeal. "We saw how well some people worked together," said Jeanne-Claude. "For example, Leo Castelli could say, 'Yes, yes, of course,' to everybody. Then he would send Ivan Karp in with the ax. So, Christo and I decided, Okay, Christo will be Castelli, the white angel, and I will be Ivan Karp. Christo was always saying yes and then coming to me to say no. It worked so well that people think I'm evil. We also thought, If collectors want to be mean about the price, then they'll have to deal with that monstrous woman, not the poor defenseless artist. But Christo was always involved. I only remember two times when he was not present for a sale. The funny thing is that I tend to give bigger discounts than Christo. He says, 'No way! You don't know how much time I spent doing that.' We wanted Christo to always be the 'good cop.' Once when he was out of town, I sold the same collage to two different collectors. It was very embarrassing. If people got the impression that I did business alone, it's not their fault, but the truth is, we always sell together."

In their silent partnership, Jeanne-Claude and Christo brought to each other and to the art indispensable elements that have fused together in the formulation and consummation of each project. Albert Elsen called their union "a wedding of socialism and capitalism. She has been crucial to conceiving and carrying out his unprecedented method of personally financing his projects, thereby taking advantage of the capitalist system. She is also vital in overseeing operational details of these daunting projects and to planning their realization."[5] In the twenty-five years between *Wrapped Coast* and their announced artistic partnership, Christo was seen as the genius, a visionary who reigned supreme in the top-floor studio of 48 Howard Street. Jeanne-

Claude, among other things, did everything possible to allow him enough freedom from time-consuming everyday details to produce the art objects that financed their mutual dreams.

The debate about Jeanne-Claude sharing the designation "artist" hinges on the definition of the word *art,* not on any argument about her central role. Long before she had been proclaimed an artist, Lawrence Alloway said, "I see her role as very much part of what Christo has achieved. I imagine the packages and storefronts were his product singularly, with her encouragement. Whereas *Wrapped Coast* and the big environmental works are absolutely as much Jeanne-Claude's as Christo's. I don't know if they would use a word like *collaboration.* But I can't see the major projects without Jeanne-Claude. She realized the potential of using the media to give form to the work. I think that's especially hers. Their art grows out of a thing that Christo was doing singularly as an artist. She had joined him and enhanced it."[6]

Arman observed, "I cannot separate Jeanne-Claude from Christo, Christo from Jeanne-Claude. They are a team that works perfectly. Now, it's fashionable for artists like Oldenburg and Kienholz to associate their wives with everything they do. But it's more their will than what their wives do. A team like Jeanne-Claude and Christo, that's different."[7] For Barbara Rose, Jeanne-Claude "is the other half of Christo. They're one person. Of course she knows she doesn't have the artistic talent. She's the support system: the business, political, administrative end, and much more. Unlike some artists' wives who have attended themselves and taken credit for art that isn't theirs, Jeanne-Claude has done the opposite. But she is really a full partner."[8]

Asked if Christo could function without Jeanne-Claude, Rosa Esman replied, "I think he could, but it would be hard. I would like to say that I feel he is independently creative enough, but she makes it all happen for him. She lets him sit back and do the work. I think the world perceives them as being incredibly effective, taking for granted that Christo is a genius. His ideas are innovative and have restructured the way we look at our industrial world. Jeanne-Claude contributes to these ideas. It is a partnership."[9] Could Christo manage without Jeanne-Claude? Her sister, Joyce, answered emphatically, "Materially and emotionally, he could not. She is really his source of inner strength. Not of artistic strength, but of inner strength that permits artistic strength."[10]

In 1994, Jeanne-Claude explained why they had waited so long to make things clear: "In the beginning it was hard enough trying to explain that each project was a work of art. Trying to explain that it was a work of art by two artists would have been out of the question." In the 1970s, the couple were perfectly content with the roles of artist and manager. However, over the years, Jeanne-Claude's participation in every aspect of the decision-making process became more evident. How are decisions made? "We scream a lot," she explained.[11]

The 1960s ended, leaving unrealized ideals and widespread dissent in their wake. Long hair, sexual freedom, antiestablishment ideas, and counter-cultural art had become omnipresent in America. Christo continued to employ strategies that both utilized and skirted the art establishment. Selling remained a necessity, but frequently he converted opportunities for conventional gallery or museum shows into provocative but unsalable projects. His impulse toward dispensable, subversive, out-of-frame art advocated freedom over captivity. One recurring strategy transformed the art of walking: fabric gently intervened between foot and ground. The artists' recent stopovers in Asia on the way back from Australia reinforced that approach. They had observed the cultural practice of removing one's shoes before entering a home and had witnessed a general sensitivity to ground surfaces in the ceremonial use of gardens.

To walk on inviting cloth-covered floors, stairs, paths, grass, rocks, or other familiar surfaces only slightly modified everyday routine, yet that seemingly minor adjustment dramatically altered a viewer's visual and tactile experience. Interiors, landscapes, and pathways were transfigured by cloth skins. The result blurred the line between art and nonart, allowing the preposterous, the mundane, and the mysterious to coexist. Reality and unreality collided in a willful merger of art and life.

In 1970, Christo developed four "underfoot" project proposals. The first was *Wrapped Island*, a collage drawing dedicated to John Kaldor; it depicted a neatly wrapped steep-cliffed island, five to six miles in perimeter, afloat in the South Pacific Ocean near Australia. *Wrapped Island* never advanced beyond the drawing stage. Next, considerable work went into planning *Wrapped Walk Ways*, an ambitious project designed for simultaneous installation at two sites six thousand miles apart—Sonnsbeek Park, Arnhem, Holland, and Ueno Park in Tokyo—although it was never realized. Variations on *Wrapped Walk Ways* and the concept of dual realizations at distant sites would be revisited in the future.

Christo did complete two floor-related projects in May 1970. Assisted by young staff members at Tokyo's Metropolitan Art Museum, he installed *Wrapped Floor*, using 1,476 square yards of fabric to transform a cavernous gallery floor and massive double staircase into one of the Tokyo Biennale's more memorable entries. The floor, a stark network of carefully arranged textures, resembled an Abstract Expressionist painting. Towering over the vast horizontal expanse of wrinkled fabric in an otherwise-empty hall was a balcony, draped in a sensuous cascade of sweeping folds and flanked by matching wrapped staircases. The untouched elements, a series of five tall archways connecting the balcony to the museum, long stretches of gallery walls, and a three-story ceiling, visually became part of the work; *Wrapped Floor* unified the space. Photos show visitors strolling or standing quietly as they contemplate the eerie environment.

On May 14, Christo traveled to Philadelphia, intent on appropriating another well-traveled staircase. "It was the end of the Vietnam War," he explained, "and a group of artists and students had received permission to use the Philadelphia Museum for a peace exhibition. These young people had come to New York to ask me to do a project for the show. Of course, there was this big stairway, and we still had all these drop cloths from the Museum of Contemporary Art in Chicago."

Jeanne-Claude arrived in Philadelphia during the installation. "Evan Turner, the museum director, took me around while Christo was working," she recalled. "The floors, steps, and surrounding walls were covered with fabric. He asked, 'How do you like it?' I said, 'It's beautiful. I love it.'" A Shunk and Kender photograph reveals a proud-looking Christo. Arms across his chest, wearing horn-rimmed glasses, a pressed suit with bell-bottom trousers, and a tie, he stands on the wrapped staircase, surrounded by young workers in the background.

Syndicated art columnist Emily Genauer's review, "Unclear Visions of an Antiwar Theme" began, "The grand, wide, sweeping staircase of the Philadelphia Museum covered, along with the soaring walls of the great hall it dominates, with thousands of yards of material has to be the most unforgettable art image anywhere in this international art year."[12]

June 1970 was a typically hectic month for Christo and Jeanne-Claude. In addition to their usual busy routine, they discussed a new project with Mitko Zagoroff—*Valley Curtain*. The artists enlisted Harry Shunk and Janos Kender to produce site photos in Colorado.

That June, in England, Joyce May Alazrachi wed Clive Henery, a British musician, while in Sofia, Anani Javacheff, Christo's older brother and now a rising star in Bulgarian theater and film, prepared to marry for a second time, this time to Daniela Sotirova, known as Didi. On June 27, the Christos began a monthlong whirlwind trip through Europe, while Cyril went to camp in Maine.

The *Valley Curtain* concept remained crude at this stage. Christo has often talked about the idea of "passing through" or "passage" in his art. "I was referring to an energy that the work creates," he explained, "an energy that is the essence of the culture's physicality. There is a dynamic inviting you to penetrate, to go beyond the barrier of a fence or curtain, to touch the surface, to see what is underneath or beyond. That energy comes from the evocative, the fragile. If the barrier is steel or concrete, you cannot do it. Perhaps you can pass through, but it is not teasing or inviting you. Fabric enhances that dynamic, tempting you to see what is beyond, and even if you know what is there, to go underneath, to recuperate and to return. The Great Wall in China is a fascinating case. The Mongols invaded China more often after the wall was built; it was inviting and made them more conscious. The mechanics or formality of my work has to do with this territory consciousness. More and more I love to manipulate space by making a gentle disturbance, by creating a new border. *Valley Curtain* is inviting, teasing, provocative, and, like other projects, almost suicidal."

The outline for the project stated, "It will be a curtain made of woven synthetic fabric, suspended on a steel cable, about 1,500 feet long, anchored to the two mountaintops with foundations. The Curtain will span 1,200 feet." "In the first drawings," Christo later recalled, "the curtain was white and the color of no importance. The fabric's attachment to the cable was absolutely clumsy. Later, the drawings refined the forms and clarified how the project would look." Jeanne-Claude asked, "Why does the *Valley Curtain* have to be white? It looks dead. You have to find a stronger color." Christo did.

On August 7, they arrived in Aspen for the opening of a Christo exhibition. He said, "We spent a lot of time driving, looking at eleven possible valley sites." On August 10, along with Tri-Co surveyor George Nelson and photographers Shunk and Kender, they began a three-thousand-mile journey by dune buggy and later by Land Rover, weaving back and forth across Colorado. Nelson prepared charts that showed eleven valleys, numbered in order of preference, indicating road accessibility, proximity to the nearest town, contour of the landscape, altitude, vegetation, and orientation to the valley. Rifle Gap ranked first, Canyon Creek second. On September 10, the artists wrote to Nelson that they had pared the original eleven valleys to four that interested them. They instructed him to find out who owned each property. By October, Chicago attorney Scott Hodes, the son of art collector Barnet Hodes, initiated contract discussions with three Rifle Gap property owners: Mr. and Mrs. Stanley Kansgen, Lloyd D. Wilson, and the U.S. government.

Christo explained their choice: "We chose Rifle Gap because it was on the western slope of the Rocky Mountains, dry, open, with great access to Route seventy going east-west. But there was also something special about the valley. Millions of years ago, a movement of rocks created a completely different, very rewarding vision looking at the valley from the Colorado River or from the back. If the valley had been a V shape or equal on both sides, it would have been very dull." Rifle Gap, an unusually narrow valley—twelve hundred feet wide—between two steep sandstone cliffs, lies seventy miles due west of Aspen and seven miles north of Rifle, then a small, dusty mining town that had seen better days. Jeanne-Claude added, "The inspiration for every project is different. We choose a place for personal reasons. Personal because it touches our mind and our heart."

Hodes set up an October 22 meeting in Washington, D.C., with the artists, their engineer from Zetlin Associates in New York, and John Crow, deputy director of the Bureau of Land Management, Department of the Interior. The other landowners appeared receptive, providing a fair rental could be agreed upon and that they would be absolved of any potential liability.

On November 19, Christo left for Europe. Jeanne-Claude remained in New York, handling preparations for the *Valley Curtain* project. Working with Scott Hodes, she helped finalize the most significant step taken during Christo's absence: incorporation. Her notes in the family agenda refer to establishing a corporation, with herself as president and treasurer, and Christo as assistant secretary. Hodes said, "He was the first artist, to the best of my knowledge, to create and do business through the corporate form. I organized the Valley Curtain Corporation. Through that structure, we achieved the ultimate, which was limited liability for the artist. The Valley Curtain Corporation executed all the contracts. In time, other artists copied Christo, and now many of them conduct business through the corporate form. We did not incorporate to avoid taxes or to shelter income. It was done to avoid liability. I think that the Christos were the first to recognize that the law could be used to protect their assets in the event of an unpredictable catastrophe. Christo is not interested in the accruements of wealth. He cares about his art, and that is all-consuming."[13]

There is a Russian proverb that says, "Never accept free wine; it's cheaper to buy it." To avoid the loss of artistic control that often comes with donors and grants, Christo and Jeanne-Claude devised a method of collecting funds in advance. In exchange for a sum of money, they would offer "purchasing subscribers" works worth considerably more. These subscribers could select these works—at their convenience—from Christo's studio. To deal with a projected budget in excess of $200,000, the Valley Curtain Corporation sought "cosponsors." After depositing ten thousand dollars in a bank account by December 29, 1970, these cosponsors were offered the following terms:

1. Christo's works in the amount of $14,290 (30 percent discount)
2. The cosponsors would have the first choice on all the preparation works for the *Valley Curtain* project (drawings, collages, diagrams, scale models).
3. The $14,290 could also be applied to a variety of earlier works by Christo (1959–1966)—such things as packages, oil drums, vitrines, storefronts, and preparation work for previous projects.
4. Cosponsors could, if they chose, commission a new and specific work.

5. Works could be selected by cosponsors immediately or until June 1971. Delivery of chosen works would begin in January 1971.

The vast majority of those who would eventually buy into the plan were part of the artists' European base of support: dealers, collectors, and institutions involved with vanguard art. For their ten-thousand-dollar check, Parisian collectors Denyse and Philippe Durand-Ruel selected *Wrapped Motorcycle*—they had been offered the same piece in 1964 for three hundred dollars but had thought it far too expensive.

While Jeanne-Claude continued discussions with Scott Hodes, fine-tuning the details of the innovative Valley Curtain Corporation's proposal, Christo worked frantically in Milan, preparing for a one-man show and for his part in the Nouveau Réalisme Festival that was to take place from November 26 to 29. His November 26 opening at Galerie Françoise Lambert featured drawings, collages, and studies for proposed Milan projects: *Arco della Pace Wrapped, Curtains for La Rotonda, Wrapped Monument to Vittorio Emanuele, Piazza del Duomo,* and *Wrapped Monument to Leonardo da Vinci, Piazza della Scala.*

"In the spring and summer of 1970," recalled Christo, "Guido Le Noci applied for permission to the city of Milano. Officials made a big fuss because the Arco della Pace is an important entrance to the city, too important for this type of activity. They rejected the idea." Undeterred, Le Noci obtained materials and authorization to wrap another landmark, the monument to Vittorio Emanuele II. The massive equestrian statue stands atop an enormous base in the middle of Piazza del Duomo, facing the ornate cathedral. Situated in the heart of the city, the statue can be seen from a number of busy vantage points, including the enclosed shopping street, or galleria. Vittorio Emanuele II was the symbol of a united Italy under constitutional democracy, and throughout the 1960s the monument to him had become a flash point for political demonstrations. Christo's choice of this public sculpture ensured both optimal visual prominence and rich symbolic content for his work.

Most participants in the festival conceived of actions or events designed to engage the public. The festival opened on a chilly Friday morning, with Christo's giant package dominating the Piazza del Duomo. Le Noci had obtained the fabric from the same supplier used two years earlier in Spoleto; he also hired construction workers to assist Christo. Overnight, the statue had been transformed. The artist's elegant oddity immediately aroused the public. Christo preferred active rather than passive viewers, but in Milan he found an overly activated audience. The project became a focal point that initially attracted protesting factory workers and the curious. Christo recalled, "There was a strike at Pirelli, the tire manufacturer. Members of their all-Communist union marched around with flags and signs, using the wrapped monument as a platform to make speeches. It was a perfect place. It became political. That

Milan, 1970: *Wrapped Monument to Vittorio Emanuele the Second.* (Photo: Harry Shunk)

made the mayor, even the Milano Socialists, very nervous." Pierre Restany remembered, "Some conservatives, especially veterans, were upset. Vittorio Emanuele the Second is the father of Italy, and they took the wrapping as an insult. They sent cables to Rome and picketed, so we had to ask Christo to remove the fabric. It lasted only one day. I told the mayor, 'If Christo has to unwrap it, you should give him another monument.' He said, 'Instead of Vittorio Emanuele the Second, a political figure, take the statue of Leonardo in Piazza della Scala. Culture is not like politics. Nobody will care.'"[14] Christo had already targeted the Leonardo da Vinci memorial; several *Wrapped Monument to Leonardo da Vinci* drawings were among his Milan project proposals on view at Galerie Françoise Lambert.

That night, Christo unwrapped the bronze image of the Italian king. He and his crew gathered the fabric and rope and made arrangements for a crane to meet them before dawn on Saturday, November 28, at the Leonardo monument in Piazza della Scala. "It was pitch-dark and cold," recalled Christo. "We started about six A.M., before it became too busy with morning traffic and people going to work. We finished by noon." Fabric, rope, and knots traversed a barely recognizable contour. Bundled in cloth, the statue—concealed, protected, imprisoned—offered a mysterious dialectic between past and present. "The disturbance is important. It makes a new, very abstract form," Christo observed.

On Saturday evening, Christo and other artists gathered in the normally crowded Piazza del Duomo to witness Jean Tinguely's well-publicized disruption, *Victory*. Constructed only steps away from the Vittorio Emanuele monument, Tinguely's latest machine stood loosely covered in fabric on a nine-foot-high platform. Just before 9:00 P.M., with fifty policemen standing guard, three television crews in position, and eight thousand people lined up behind metal barriers and stacked on the steps of the Vittorio Emanuele monument, Tinguely drove a flower-covered van to a prearranged place beneath the draped, floodlighted structure. A group of mortars fitted with large fireworks rockets was mounted on its roof rack. The crowd gasped as the draped facade collapsed, exposing an enormous golden phallus with two gold testicles decorated with plastic fir cones, grapes, and bananas. The sound system bellowed a drunken version of "O Sole Mio" as the phallus ejaculated a cloud of smoke, accompanied by a barrage of earsplitting fireworks that drove thousands of resident pigeons into confused flight. The crowd in the square roared with laughter. Someone on the supporting platform, clad in an astronaut's gleaming asbestos suit, operated a large wheel that regulated the step-by-step destruction of *Victory*. Within thirty minutes, the massive phallus was reduced to ash and smoke. By 10:00 P.M. the police, firemen, TV crews, and crowds, like Tinguely's machine, disappeared into the night.

After the noisy demise of Tinguely's contraption, Christo, Ettore Sottsass, noted architect and a founder of the Memphis Style; Lisa Ponti, the editor of *Domus* magazine; and several friends strolled over to Piazza della Scala to see *Wrapped Monument to Leonardo da Vinci* at night. Christo's work again acted like a lightning rod. This time, right-wing protesters had invaded the site, their anger fueled by the wrapped monument. Christo said, "Ettore Sottsass tried to reason with these young men, saying, 'We are all Italians. Why are you so upset? This is art.' Suddenly, someone hit him. He was bleeding from the nose. His ear was bloody. I can still see that as if it happened today. Lisa Ponti and I pulled him away. There may have been other people hurt, but I only remember Ettore. Everyone was screaming. The police came quickly because it was in front of City Hall. We ran to Ettore's apartment. It was not far away. It was a very, very ugly time."

The next night, the *Wrapped Monument to Leonardo da Vinci* again attracted a disapproving segment of the public. Restany explained, "A neo-fascist squad arrived, sang the fascist hymn, and, after a speech saying that the work offended the deepest Italian values, they set fire to the fabric. When firemen arrived, they climbed a large ladder and accidentally chopped three fingers off the statue with an ax. Those fingers are still missing."[15] When Christo heard about the incident, he rushed to the deserted plaza, only to find a heap of charred fabric and rope next to the unwrapped monument. Photographs are all that remain of his two ephemeral Milan projects.

Although Christo and Jeanne-Claude worked on various projects in 1971, most of their energy was focused on *Valley Curtain*. With each new step, the logistics became increasingly complex. Jeanne-Claude smiled as she recalled that time. "We are naïve people. You have to be to believe you can hang a curtain like that." In 1970, they had hired an attorney, surveyor, contractor, engineers, and others. Their first key decision of 1971 was to employ a project director to help them deal with the challenging task of suspending a curtain comparable in size to the Brooklyn Bridge's main span. Jan van der Marck had resigned his position at Chicago's Museum of Contemporary Art in early 1970. "As of January 4, 1971, I took responsibility for all para-aesthetic aspects of the *Valley Curtain*," he said. "As no European or United States museum was willing to take *Valley Curtain* under its institutional auspices, this working association with a museum professional may have helped the *Valley Curtain*'s credibility in the art and business communities"[16] Van der Marck recognized that certain kinds of vanguard art, including Christo's major projects, could exist only outside the traditional confines of museums.

On January 4, 1971, Lev Zetlin Associates, a New York engineering firm experienced in bridge and airplane-hangar design, completed a *Valley Curtain* structural-feasibility study commissioned by Christo the previous October. The estimated budget and twenty-one pages detailing specifications were daunting. On January 8, Scott Hodes secured a certificate of incorporation in Illinois for the Valley Curtain Corporation. Five days later, van der Marck signed the first land lease with Mr. and Mrs. Stanley Kansgen. It called for $2,400 in eight monthly rental payments for use of their uninhabitable Rocky Mountain tract. A photograph shows the beaming middle-age farming couple: he in well-worn overalls and she in a flowered blouse and apron. A pending contract with the other private landowner, Lloyd Wilson, calling for more than twice as much rent, did not trouble the Kansgens. Van der Marck's first written report states, "The contract was signed and a $300 deposit was left. No secret was made of Mr. Wilson's insistence on $5,000 and the very idea that we would have to match that amount was rejected out of hand."[17]

With a population of 2,300, Rifle is located in the Grand Hogback Range in Garfield County, Colorado. On January 13, before their joint presentation to the Chamber of Commerce, Christo and van der Marck met with William J. Tadus, mayor and proprietor of Harris Jewelry Company; Stanleigh Megarger, city manager; Jimm Seaney, head of the local radio station and president of the Chamber of Commerce; Jim Le Donne, golf pro and manager of the Rifle Golf Club; and Ina Lamont and Jim Drinkhouse, editors of the *Rifle Telegram*. While the community had no history of embracing avant-garde art, *Valley*

Curtain promised to pump up a sagging economy with jobs and an influx of tourists. The financial, if not aesthetic, logic convinced most business leaders. Questioned by a *New York Times* reporter, Anthony Macchione, a fifty-year-old rancher, builder, and café owner, broke into laughter. "I don't get the real point of the thing," he said. "But it's not going to cost you anything so you got nothing to lose. My final word is, 'It's wonderful—whatever it is." Jimm Seaney added, "I wouldn't know a Wyeth from a Mondrian. The question we asked was 'Why?' And they came back with 'Why not?'"[18]

Writer Calvin Tomkins examined the unique small town and its economy:

> The local Chamber of Commerce likes to describe Rifle as the Oil-Shale Capital of the World, but the only local oil-shale plant . . . closed down three years ago, throwing a number of Riflians out of work. The town, in fact, has been in something of an economic depression for several years. Although a Union Carbide vanadium refinery just outside town provides a number of jobs, the big-game hunting that is Rifle's other major industry had not been as good as usual in recent years.[19]

"Although Christo's English is still a little erratic, his obvious sincerity and his beautifully considerate manners seemed to captivate nearly everyone in Rifle, including those who thought he must be off his rocker. . . . [Mr. and Mrs. Kansgen] were so startled at first by the whole idea that for several weeks they were afraid to mention Christo's proposal to anybody," Tomkins wrote. However, after meeting the artists, they were totally charmed. "Christo promised to give Mrs. Kansgen, who runs a small historical museum of Western artifacts a good-sized piece of the *Valley Curtain* . . . [after] the project was terminated."[20]

The real opposition to this artistic enterprise surfaced two hundred miles away, in Denver, first from environmentalists and then from Colorado State Highway Department bureaucrats. Ecological concerns and a potential restraining order prompted Christo and van der Marck to contact scholars at Harvard and elsewhere before meeting with the Rocky Mountain Center on Environment and the Colorado Open Space Council. Professor William Weber, head of the biology department at the University of Colorado, responded to fears that the curtain could harm plant or animal life, particularly unsuspecting birds that might be snared in flight. Weber contended, "Any bird that could not manage to fly over the curtain would have to be in pretty bad shape to begin with."[21] Another criticism concerned the potentially injurious effects of a shadow cast by the *Valley Curtain* for three months. Van der Marck noted, "Anxious to refute the Colorado Council's 'very strong feelings,' we learned from a properly scientific source that the shadow of the curtain—very slight, since the curtain is diaphanous—would slow down the dehydration of the soil, actually benefiting plant and animal life."[22] These pronouncements from academia seemed to quiet initial concerns.

Nearby nuclear testing and nuclear-fuel processing presented a far more dangerous environmental hazard than Christo's temporary landscape alteration. A full page of the *Valley Curtain* insurance policy listed every conceivable exclusion regarding nuclear-related liability. Van der Marck noted:

> Between the planned 60-90 kiloton nuclear underground detonation at Rio Blanco—35 miles away—and the foul smoke-belching uranium processing plant of Union Carbide—10 miles from Christo's Valley Curtain, this proposed art project will be an innocent to pollution and ecological tampering. Not a single tree will have to be cut, no wildlife other than possibly snakes and jackrabbits make their living on the bare terrain, covered with sparse low bushes, tumbleweed, and an occasional tree. Birds, sensitive to moving objects and surfaces, won't crash into the curtains as they crash into the steel and glass sides of office highrises in New York or Chicago. . . . For low flying aircraft navigational warning lights may have to be installed in compliance with FAA regulations.[23]

On the evening of February 17, while Jeanne-Claude remained in New York to meet with collectors, Christo flew to Denver. The next morning, Christo, van der Marck, and Janos Kender arrived at the state capital at 11:00 A.M. for a press conference to announce the *Valley Curtain* project. A reluctant host, Lieutenant Governor John D. Vanderhoof, edged into a corner. On hand were three national TV crews, United Press International and Associated Press, a *New York Times* stringer, and local Colorado media. Environmental issues with political overtones dominated the questioning. Also on hand were Rifle supporters: William Tadus, Jimm Seaney, and First National Bank president Allen Koeneke. Following the session, Vanderhoof's press aide asked Christo not to communicate that the lieutenant governor in any way endorsed *Valley Curtain*.

After lunch, an appearance on an afternoon talk show, and a slide talk followed by art students' questions at the University of Denver, Christo and van der Marck heard a disturbing report. Van der Marck wrote, "Governor [John] Love, that day, was quoted as saying that he didn't know about the curtain (I had written him a long explanatory letter a month before and he could have read the papers or seen TV coverage!), that he didn't think much about it as a work of art, and that he was afraid it might interfere with the highway. . . . It was clear that we had taken Colorado's highest officials by surprise and they now felt stuck with a politically hot potato."[24]

On February 19, Christo and van der Marck discussed the project with art students in Aspen. The next day, the two men taped a half-hour TV interview in Grand Junction and then drove to Rifle, where they campaigned at Mc's Café and at the annual banquet of the Rifle Gap Land Company stockholders. An enthusiastic Mayor Tadus predicted that *Valley Curtain* would spur the local economy and put Rifle on the map.

Perhaps taking their cue from Vanderhoof's or Love's misgivings, the State Highway Department presented its first set of obstacles. Christo's eight-thousand-pound curtain, designed to hang from a cable support system spanning about 1,250 feet across Rifle Gap and State Highway 325, included a twenty-five-foot-high-by-fifty-foot-wide arch-shaped opening to allow cattle herds, horses, and normal vehicular traffic. Naturally, a permit would be required. In an unsolicited letter dated March 2, officials made some reasonable demands that had to be met before they would consider issuing a permit: detailed engineering drawings, copies of all property-owner easements, insurance policies covering a minimum of $1 million for public liability and $100,000 for incidents of property damage, procedures that would allow normal traffic during the erection and removal processes, and sufficient bond to ensure restoration of the site. That initial salvo and other unforeseen events were to escalate a projected budget already in excess of $250,000.

The Valley Curtain Corporation obtained releases from the Graham Mesa Ditch Company and the Silt Water Conservancy District regarding irrigation ditches that passed through the site; it also offered to pay for placing existing telephone and power lines underground.

As more and more people became involved, the project took on its own life, obstructed by incidents, miscalculations, and diverse personalities, hurtling toward an uncertain fate. The artists felt the weight of mounting bills. They urgently needed additional sales. While they had raised a staggering $180,000 in cash, the unruly *Valley Curtain* budget had mushroomed to almost twice that amount.

Jeanne-Claude tried to enlist additional scientific, moral, and financial support. She coordinated *Valley Curtain* production schedules and dealt with Rifle citizens, slow engineers, fabric specifications, bids on the foundation and steel cables, insurance, legal matters, public relations, photographic needs, shipping arrangements, business and personal correspondence, and more. The ongoing effort to quiet environmental concerns, for example, is evident in a list of scientists inscribed on April 6 in the family agenda.

On April 7, Christo flew to Denver for three days of talks with students, teachers, journalists, and environmentalists. Van der Marck noted, "The meeting with the Open Space Council dragged on for a long time—we could, of course, not convince everybody, but the upshot of it was that somebody made a motion stating that with the dangers of air pollution, underground atomic explosions and the 1976 Winter Olympics, the proposed Valley Curtain was a minor matter of concern and should be allowed to happen as planned."[25]

On April 24, Christo departed for three frantic weeks in Europe, high-lighted by a handsome but unheralded project in Krefeld, ten miles northwest of Düsseldorf. He appropriated Mies van der Rohe's landmark structure, Haus Lange, an architectural appendage of the Kaiser-Wilhelm Museum. The aim of the architect and his client had been to integrate the house with its surround-ings, offering inviting views of the building's interior from the park grounds and of nature's panorama from within. Christo loved the structure and its set-ting, but, nonetheless, his *Wrapped Floors, Covered Windows, and Wrapped Walk Ways* nullified van der Rohe's intentions. He wrapped the floors with fab-ric, covered the windows with brown wrapping paper, and covered the exterior footpaths with fabric, thereby divorcing the house from its normal environ-ment. Nothing could be seen inside Haus Lange from outside vantage points, and visitors strolling through the entombed two-story building found every vista blocked. Shadows shifted across the paper-sealed windows, hinting at swaying trees or passing figures in the park.

During Christo's absence, Jeanne-Claude settled on Morrison-Knudsen as the *Valley Curtain* contractor. Their $229,000 bid was substantially the low-est. Workers would be hired from the tritown area: Carbondale, Glenwood Springs, and Rifle. On the morning of May 3, Jeanne-Claude and representa-tives of Morrison-Knudsen signed the contract. She called Scott Hodes and arranged an eighty-thousand-dollar down payment, expressing confidence that all the money would be raised promptly.

That afternoon, the Houston Museum of Fine Arts's director, Philippe de Montebello, visited Howard Street, where he and Jeanne-Claude finalized plans for a comprehensive *Valley Curtain* exhibition. They worked with With-ers Swan, a New York public-relations firm, on preparing a press release that named the museum cosponsor and announced an opening on July 25, 1971, five days before *Valley Curtain* would be hung in Rifle, Colorado. The show would be an overview, tracing the project's evolution from conception to real-ization with drawings, collages, scale models, surveys, records, blueprints, cor-respondence, and photographs.

Valley Curtain was to be a striking orange. By early May, 250,000 square feet of white nylon polyamide were dyed in a Putnam, Connecticut, plant. At a May 6 meeting in Rifle, Leon D. Stoddard, vice president of Morrison-Knudsen, re-layed Colorado Highway Department fears that the bright orange would dis-tract motorists. Stoddard also indicated that a considerable area around the site was radioactive and heated by underground-mine fires.[26] On May 12, tele-phone lines extending three hundred feet north and south of the curtain's axis were placed underground at the artist's expense; twelve days later, with a per-mit secured, power lines were also given a proper burial.

Christo returned from Europe on May 13, having completed his *Wrapped*

Floors, Covered Windows, and Wrapped Walk Ways at the Haus Lange, mounted several exhibitions, including a solo show at Galerie Yvon Lambert in Paris, and secured loans, pledges, and sales amounting to ninety thousand dollars. The incoming cash barely kept pace with escalating costs, in light of demands from the Colorado Highway Department. Officials were fuming over the failure of Christo's engineers to respond to their May 2 letter requesting information on the project. On May 13, van der Marck discovered the oversight and tried to set up a meeting with the highway department's chief engineer, Charles Shumate, in Denver.

In a letter dated May 28, 1971, Shumate expanded the requirements, stating, "It is impossible for the Division to give any assurances as to whether or when State authorization for the project would be forthcoming. Please be assured we are not attempting to delay the project. This Division must be assured that the construction, display and removal of the Curtain will not jeopardize the safety of the traveling public."[27]

On May 20, Bureau of Land Management officials in Denver rejected a petition from van der Marck because he was not an American citizen. He saw no malice in the action but complained, "How heavy they felt their responsibility weigh on their shoulders and how much tax-supported time they have to waste on trifles."

Van der Marck stated:

Test borings began on June 14 and proceeded at snail's pace since equipment had to be carried piece by piece up the slopes on a steep, rocky trail. . . . On June 25, the boring results—cores that looked like sticks of dynamite—were all neatly stacked in boxes to be shipped to Denver for analysis. The outcome was devastating. The top anchors, designed to go straight in, each to be weighed down with seven tons of concrete, would have pulled themselves clear out of the mountain.[28]

Discussions with Ken R. White resulted in a new anchor design by Lev Zetlin Associates, increasing construction costs by $62,000. Two hundred tons of concrete would be needed to secure another anchor. In addition, the complex assembly and cable connections required fifty-nine stressed steel rods and ten-ton steel caps. Van der Marck blamed Lev Zetlin engineers for the delays: "They were not registered in the state of Colorado—an oversight discovered eight months after the contract to design a curtain had been signed. Consequently, all of their drawings had to be sent through a Chicago engineering firm licensed to work in Colorado." Van der Marck's list of complaints about Lev Zetlin included overengineering, poor planning, and failure to carefully inspect the site. He also blamed the contractor for "taking his sweet time."[29]

At the site, Morrison-Knudsen workers greeted Christo warmly. Tomkins said, "Cyril . . . gave each man a brisk, European-style handshake and asked about swimming."

By June, the projected budget had soared to $400,000. The artists had already raised $370,000 and felt confident they would have the balance by late July. The vast sums of money had no apparent impact on their frugal lifestyle; cash, like permits, fabric, or wind, was simply another essential element in the project's evolution. They took pride, however, in not accepting business donations or government grants. Every cent came from motivated supporters paid in full with Christo's art.

The late July target date fell victim to bureaucracy and circumstance. However, determined Riflians pressed on, and a conference call between Governor Love, Jimm Seaney, and other prominent local citizens no doubt helped move the Colorado Highway Department to grant Christo's permit, which they did on July 12. The sixteen-point agreement letter allowed forty-five days to complete construction and called for site restoration by September 30. A July 15 press release prompted a letter to Scott Hodes from Leon Stoddard, who stated that Morrison-Knudsen needed additional time to complete the project. He also offered reasons why there would be substantial additional costs. Throughout the summer, Christo and Jeanne-Claude brushed off reports of incompetence and deliberate delays by Morrison-Knudsen. To meet the August 15 deadline, workers were assigned overtime schedules—sixty hours a week instead of forty, but this was not enough. The Valley Curtain Corporation filed for an extension, with a new goal of the first week of September. The Colorado Highway Department granted it.

Engineering miscalculations and mechanical failures became commonplace. One accident resulted in tangled steel cables, which took an entire day to rectify. Shortly afterward, an enormous cable plummeted from its cliffside mooring, nearly killing workers in the valley. Then the custom-made cart designed by Morrison-Knudsen to ride above the cables spanning the valley proved unusable. It would have allowed workers to attach, adjust, and repair the curtain. In its place, the crew devised a makeshift platform, suspended by pulleys from the highest cable. Each mishap caused further delays. The Valley Curtain Corporation asked for and received a second permit extension from the Colorado Highway Department. With a growing sense of alarm, the artists telephoned Mitko Zagoroff and explained the ongoing technical problems; he agreed to join them in Rifle.

In the midst of this prolonged period of uncertainty, Christo and Jeanne-Claude received an image of the Brandenburg Gate, a postcard of the Reichstag, Germany's once and future parliament building, and a note from Michael S. Cullen, a young American architectural historian and fledgling art dealer living in Berlin, who proposed that the artist wrap the Reichstag because he had seen the 1961 Christo proposal for wrapping a public building, which Christo indicated would be a parliament building. So was launched a twenty-four-year odyssey.

In Rifle, work picked up momentum in early September. Two hundred and two tons of concrete were hand-carried in buckets and poured into excavated sloping forms on the west side of the valley. An additional 174 tons were used on the eastern slope. The Colorado Highway Department granted another extension of the work period to September 30 and extended the maximum display period to October 31. The ever-changing schedule presented potential visitors with serious problems regarding travel plans.

Repeated delays in Rifle made van der Marck uneasy. "Labor Day came and went with a rodeo and country fair at which Christo juried the floats—one of which carried a model of the Valley Curtain—and I selected the Garfield County Rodeo Queen. It did not cheer us much," van der Marck observed.[30] A Harry Shunk photo shows a deadpan downtown crowd observing a man driving a small tractor, pulling the Chamber of Commerce's *Valley Curtain* float. The colorful depiction of the anticipated work included a sign reading IT'S CURTAIN TIME IN GARFIELD COUNTY. CURTAIN GOING UP ON A WORLD OF RECREATION, SPLENDOR AND ENCHANTMENT. YOU HAVE TO SEE IT TO BELIEVE IT.

On September 13, a quarter of a million square feet of vibrant orange material left West Virginia for Colorado. On September 17, Shunk photographed Christo and a group of construction workers loading long bundles of tied fabric. The curtain's arrival at Rifle Gap lifted spirits. Despite continuing postponements of the unfurling date, a steady stream of art-world visitors had started to trickle in. On the eighteenth, Pierre Restany joined some of Christo's other European supporters. Rifle warmly welcomed curiosity seekers, dealers, collectors, curators, writers, artists, students, teachers, journalists, a Rice University student film crew, and Rainer Crone's German filmmaking team—now buried in miles of footage accumulated since July. Jan van der Marck's phone kept ringing, causing him to observe, "Never had any project been so thoroughly covered."[31]

A few days later, Mitko Zagoroff arrived and immediately immersed himself in the engineering nuances of the project. *Valley Curtain* was constructed of 15 percent more fabric than was needed to fill the space, allowing the cloth to billow as much as forty feet in any direction. Scale-model wind tests reinforced expectation of the billowing effect one associates with large sailboats. On October 1, Mitko sent a letter and sketches to Ken R. White, suggesting an improved lacing system for attaching the curtain to the cable.

Even before Zagoroff's arrival, the artists' relationship with the Morrison-Knudsen project boss, Wes Hofmann, had seriously deteriorated, By early October, they rarely spoke. Hofmann had devised a plan for unfurling the bundled fabric with a series of "magic knots." The artist and Zagoroff doubted the magic. The tightly rolled curtain had been attached to a pickup cable. Tied to each knot were long ropes that would hang from the furled curtain and, once yanked, untie the knots, allowing the material to drop into place.

Tension mounted as the curtain lifting approached on the weekend of October 8. As word spread, a mélange of diverse personalities, supporters, and skeptics converged on the town. Rifle had never seen anything like it. Normally clear roads were clogged with traffic. Every room for miles around had been booked, and there was standing room only at Mc's Café and the Rifle Golf Club. One enterprising young man sold *Valley Curtain* jewelry from the back of his pickup truck. The eagerly awaited economic boom had arrived. On hand were scores of students and others anxious to help, cowpokes and tourists, Scott Hodes, David Juda, curator Germano Celant, Robert Urie from the fabric manufacturer, David Bourdon, Pierre Restany, dealer Michael Sonnabend, artists Gilbert and George, TV crews from NBC and CBS, reporters from the Associated Press, United Press International, the Colorado media, and hundreds of others. "It was a round-the-clock party," Sonnabend recalled.[32]

With the curtain's climactic moment near, Jan van der Marck wrote: "Saturday, October 9th, promised to be another day filled with delays and aggravations. The phone began to ring again with the familiar question from reporters and network people: 'When will the curtain go up?' "[33] At midday, the Morrison-Knudsen crew slowly began raising the cable-supported curtain to its final position. Hundreds of ropes streamed down. Calvin Tomkins observed that plans called for the gigantic curtain to be raised high above the valley, where it "would be left overnight in its furled state. Then on Sunday, it would be unfurled gradually and secured to its thirty ground anchors."[34] At 4:15 P.M., however, with the curtain and support cable raised to only two-thirds of their full elevation and still unsecured, Wes Hofmann announced that work would stop at 4:30. Jeanne-Claude and Christo angrily confronted Hofmann. They contended that failure to tie the curtain assembly to the four main cables risked losing everything. They pleaded with Hofmann to secure the curtain before dark, insisting that his crew was ready and willing to do the job. Hofmann refused to budge. He argued that there wasn't enough time, and besides, he said, the lives of his men meant more than Christo's curtain.

Mitko Zagoroff recalled, "It was a fiasco. We couldn't believe the inept planning. . . . The Christos were livid."[35] At about 5:30 P.M., the Christo entourage reassembled at the nearby golf club for drinks. Shortly afterward, two friends of van der Marck arrived from Salt Lake City. "Before it grew darker, I decided to walk with them the quarter mile to the site to show them where we stood with the work," van der Marck later wrote. "It must have been 6:20 by now—the curtain started to come loose and billow out, in agonizing slow motion, two hundred feet below the east-slope anchor. We couldn't believe our eyes."[36] A large section of brilliant orange material had been set free by a slight breeze and the "magic knots." At the golf club, Pierre Restany glanced toward Rifle Gap and saw the artists' dream unraveling. "I will always remember that. I called Christo over. He stood silently at my side, with a single tear running down from his right eye."[37]

Alexandra de Guillebon, who had been at the site since mid-July, watched in disbelief. "I think everyone cried. It was unbearable," she recalled.[38] As the wind intensified, the convulsive fabric lashed out, unfastening itself from its knots in agonizing jolts. Van der Marck remembered:

> As the evening advanced, hundreds of dispirited people stood around, unable to intervene, watching the curtain fall prey to everything obstructing its course. . . . The most sinister sound was the curtain catching on rocks and trees and ripping as it struggled to free itself. When it caught on the trolley car and then pulled away, a huge vertical rip appeared. Like a giant tongue, split up the middle, the better part of the curtain's east half, or a hundred thousand square feet of fabric, licked through the valley. The bright orange made it fiery, and against the darkening sky the torn curtain gesticulated like leaping flames. Even the sounds resembled that of a huge crackling blaze. . . . People stood perplexed, some weeping and some confused as to what was happening. Nobody had anticipated a catastrophe of this magnitude. For Christo, this came as the worst blow of his career. It had never occurred to him that our enormous effort might come to nothing.[39]

That night, the restless curtain lifted a car into the air and tossed boulders about. Fortunately, no one was hurt. By daylight, Sunday morning, much of the shredded curtain hung absolutely still. Torn sections were strewn about the valley. The sun-bathed orange cloth offered striking contrast to a solid blue sky. TV, radio, and newspapers pounced on the misfortune. Police cars descended on the site, joined by many Rifle citizens, curious visitors, and Christo supporters. Jeanne-Claude held back her tears and came to the same conclusion as Christo: to try again.

The curtain was a total loss, but the costly concrete foundations and cable complex remained intact. So, too, did community support. At a Sunday-afternoon press conference, the artists, van der Marck, and Hodes put on their best faces, fielding questions before a battery of cameras. Calvin Tomkins recalled:

> The press conference was well attended by Rifle citizens, most of whom joined in a standing ovation for Christo after his statement, in which he promised to return the following June to finish the project. One woman, a member of the Rifle City Council, got up and said that until the accident most people had tended to look on the curtain as a crazy idea that just might

help the town, but that since they had seen how beautiful it looked, even in its death throes, the *Valley Curtain* had become *their* project as well as Christo's, and they all looked forward impatiently to his return next year. Christo was moved. It was as though the town of Rifle had become, through his efforts, a community of artists.[40]

By October 13, the fabric had been removed and the foundations and cables secured. Christos and Jeanne-Claude paid their outstanding bills and left without a word to Wes Hofmann.

In retrospect, the artists had perhaps been too good at luring collectors, dealers, other artists, critics, curators, friends, and the media to witness the long-delayed and ultimately unsuccessful performance at Rifle Gap. The highly publicized failure was devastating. Unresolved engineering questions were to haunt the artists until work resumed. Meanwhile, bills kept arriving: $4,500 for Shunk and Kender photos; $4,200 for Mitko Zagoroff's engineering services; monthly payments to the Kansgens and Lloyd Wilson; and premiums to extend bonding and insurance contracts. Just how this star-crossed venture would affect Christo's sales remained uncertain. At this point, most collages were priced at $980.

Although much of the hardware remained usable, an entirely new curtain had to be designed and manufactured. Mitko Zagoroff's company, Unipolycon, and the Ken R. White Company assumed reengineering responsibilities. Naturally, this cost money. On November 11, 1971, while Christo tried to elicit support and sales in Europe, Jeanne-Claude noted in the family agenda that the Valley Curtain Corporation account was overdrawn by $1,800, though $4,800 in checks for works Christo had sold in Italy were on the way.

On November 12, Michael Cullen visited Howard Street. Jeanne-Claude relayed Christo's interest in wrapping the Reichstag, urged Cullen to obtain permission, and arranged an initial meeting between the two men in Zurich on December 4. "We met at the Hotel Savoy," Cullen recalled. "I brought maps and photographs of the Reichstag for his drawings. He was affable and excited about doing the project. That carried over to me, but I had no idea how incredibly energetic one has to be in order to keep up with him. Christo rarely sleeps, and he is very impatient. That's understandable when he wants to realize a dream. There's a time pressure, his own internal pressure, and the thing he's done in his head has to come out."[41]

A few days after meeting Cullen, Christo returned to New York. On December 8, he, Zagoroff, and Zagoroff's partner, John Thomson, conducted wind tests on Christo's *Valley Curtain* scale model, which had been sewn by

Jeanne-Claude. Christo and the engineers cheered as the miniaturized drape easily withstood high winds generated by an electric fan.

Thomson remembered Christo and Jeanne-Claude regrouping in late 1971: "After the October 1971 fiasco and a lot of hysterical shouting, they asked us to help them mount another effort. Mitko and I dropped everything and began planning ways to manage the fabric, making it into a bundle and putting a cover over it so it could be managed like a package. Mitko and I did engineering drawings for the new curtain and supervised the manufacture and transport. The projects are a real adventure. Christo is wonderful to work with. The only trouble is that I can't understand what he says."[42]

As Cyril prepared to enter junior high school, Christo and Jeanne-Claude decided to send him to the Dalton School on the Upper East Side, although it would require a giant financial sacrifice.

Though *Valley Curtain* loomed large in Christo's mind, in 1972 he produced drawings for other projects, including his *Wrapped Reichstag Project for Berlin,* collages, studies for a giant mastaba to be constructed from 200,000 oil barrels outside of Houston, and *Wrapped Bridge,* a project for Pont Alexandre III in Paris.

Meanwhile Riflians debated whether Christo and Jeanne-Claude, as well as the army of tourists, would ever return. Some true believers awaited the curtain's resurrection like the Second Coming. Others argued that the artist's enormous economic loss and corresponding loss of credibility meant it was all over. On May 25, 1972, after separate trips to Europe, Jeanne-Claude and Christo returned to Rifle. Word spread quickly that they had returned, affirming their commitment to drape *Valley Curtain* across Rifle Gap. So much remained to do in so little time.

By late May 1972, the project again began to pump up the local economy. Engineer John Thomson called Christo a modern-day Robin Hood. "He scatters money around like confetti. He takes it from collectors, galleries, wealthy people who pay hundreds of thousands of dollars for his art. Then he hires itinerants, engineers, factory workers, lawyers, and people who do things. It's a wonderful arrangement, very progressive, like a taxation scheme where the rich pay more."[43] Any money from art sales was immediately snapped up by an endless line of vendors: installment payments for fabric manufacturers and sewing, rope, assorted materials, engineers, builders, construction workers and ironworkers, project staff, other salaries, legal costs, insurance, photographers, airfares, housing, car rentals, food, leases, fees, and more fees.

After the 1971 fiasco, the Christos replaced Lev Zetlin Associates with Unipolycon. They also hired highway department engineers Ernest Harris and

Sargis Safarian, asking them to recommend local contractors who might give the project the personal attention necessary. One person interviewed for the job was Theodore Dougherty, head of A & H Builders. "The Christos were looking for a smaller contractor to complete the work. At first we refused. Morrison-Knudesn, one of America's biggest contractors, had failed the year before. How could we do the job? The Christos asked again. We said we would have to think it over. You could see that he was a sincere, intelligent man. She was all dolled up, very haute couture. They looked, and they are, very uptown people."[44] Eventually, Dougherty and the Christos hammered out an agreement.

Fieldwork under the supervision of Henri Leininger had begun on June 21, 1972. The curtain arrived in Rifle on July 31 and was elevated on August 4. By August 6, students and part-time workers were on-site, ready to begin training sessions the next day. Jeanne-Claude said, "We had all kinds of workers. Local ironworkers and construction workers with dark suntans and tattoos working alongside carpenters and longhaired hippies smoking marijuana. We had hundreds of arms and legs. We don't use volunteers, and we don't pay very well—only a little over minimum wage—but everyone had fun."

The Guillebon family arrived from France on August 3 to see Christo's anticipated triumph and, perhaps more important, to spend some time with their grandson; their son, twenty-three-year-old Norbert, accompanied them. "It was fantastic, impossible to be uninvolved," Norbert said later. "I joined one of the student teams. The work was very precise. We rehearsed pulling and tying ropes quickly and accurately."[45] Joyce May Henery, her husband, Clive, and their son, Jonathan, drove to Rifle Gap after visiting the Grand Canyon.

Everyone familiar with the 1971 *Valley Curtain* disaster had reason to feel uneasy during the early hours of Thursday, August 10, 1972. An anemometer recorded wind speed; workers watched it like sentries certain of imminent invasion. Thirty-five construction workers and sixty-four students and art teachers stood ready to unfurl the giant curtain. By 9:00 A.M., hordes of visitors and most Rifle citizens had arrived at the site. At 9:05 A.M., with a near-zero wind reading, teams of workers watched as the artists, he in a white hard hat, she in a yellow one, gave the order to unfurl. *Valley Curtain,* a film by the Maysles brothers, shows Harrison Rivera-Terreaux pulling a cord, and suddenly the brilliant curtain bolted open, east to west, nine hundred feet in ten seconds. Three-quarters of the enormous drape sprang into view before a release chain jammed high over the valley. A gasp was heard from the crowd. Ironworker Donald Jenkins and his crew prepared to board their cable car on the east peak to undo the snag. Few observers recognized that the curtain was once again in jeopardy.

In the film Christo is seen running, screaming, "Pull, pull, pull, pull, pull!" as workers tried to anchor ropes being whipped about by billowing fabric. Again he shouted, "Pull! Pull! Where is the blue truck operator?" Watching the giant cloth billow, Donald Jenkins, on the east peak, asked, "What could be holding it back with that much pressure behind it?" After a walkie-talkie exchange, Jenkins and his crew ventured out precariously over the valley in their improvised cable car. Before they reached the blockage, the fickle wind changed direction, allowing the monster curtain to swiftly assume its full form. Applause broke out. Christo suddenly beamed and said, "Beautiful." Jeanne-Claude's wide grin gave way to laughter. Her father hugged and kissed her as the workers cheered. A Denver skydiving group floated down on the site in brightly colored parachutes.

The next hour and a half was spent frantically securing twenty-seven sets of anchor lines designed to contain the magnified power of a vast expanse of billowing cloth animated by the slightest breeze.

In the *New York Times,* Grace Glueck called the curtain "one of Christo's most beautiful works. . . . It swayed and billowed in the wind as if about to reveal a Wagnerian spectacle staged by the artist. The crew was ecstatic. They passed around champagne and gave Christo a dunking in Rifle Creek. Anthony Macchione, Rifle's big-wheel businessman and rancher, paraded up and down on his brown quarter-horse. 'I think it's beautiful,' he said." Glueck also quoted Ernest Harris: "'The project's ephemerality worried me. But I think you can look at it as an orchestra concert. You hire musicians and you pay them a fortune to perform and then it's over. What you have left is memories, tapes and so forth.'"[46]

Donald Jenkins mingled with celebrating workers. Looking up at the curtain, smiling, he said, "I've never seen anything so beautiful in all my life."

At that moment, a journalist thrust a microphone in his face, "Were you skeptical the way most people were at first?"

Jenkins answered, "No. I can't see any reason for being skeptical over it. They built the Golden Gate Bridge, they built the Space Needle, the Empire State Building. It's not the erection of it, it's the thought. This is a vision. I would have never thought that anyone would have ever thought of doing something like this."

Valley Curtain dazzled many observers, among them, museum professional Thomas Garver, found the experience moving: "It's the transmission of light and color through fabric." The light under *Valley Curtain* reminded me of standing beneath a grove of New England maple trees in the fall. There was this intense orange light."[47]

In the late afternoon of August 10, the Maysles brothers filmed Christo, his left arm around Jeanne-Claude's shoulder, as they viewed the curtain from afar. She says, "That's the best view of all." Christo responds, "Beautiful! Incredible! Just like the drawings."

Jeanne-Claude later recalled, "When I heard him say that I thought, 'My

Rifle, Colorado, 1972: Christo in front of the *Valley Curtain.* (Photo: Harry Shunk)

God, that sounds so corny. The Maysles brothers knew how I felt and said, 'If you don't like it, we'll remove it.' I told them, 'No, no, he said it.' Now it's one of my favorite lines because it shows how pure his heart is." Albert and David Maysles's *Valley Curtain* was nominated for an Academy Award. Calvin Tomkins called *Valley Curtain* "by far the finest film I have ever seen about an artist and his work."[48]

The Maysles brothers captured *Valley Curtain*'s memorable birth and brief life. However, the film does not show the curtain's sudden demise. On August 11, twenty-eight hours after the curtain's installation, a gale estimated in excess of sixty miles per hour destroyed it. David Bourdon arrived in Rifle, only to find the curtain gone, as did others. Jan van der Marck recalled:

> Starting halfway up the west slope, the curtain tore in an eastward direction over a five-hundred-foot length, then zipped straight up to the cables. The wind reclaimed the curtain as fast as the eye could follow its devastating effect. What had been likened to a giant butterfly peeling from its cocoon, was now more like a whale thrashing in its death throes. A sight of overwhelming beauty was transformed in seconds into a paroxysm of ripping fabric. . . . Nobody but Christo and the engineers had quite anticipated the awesome pressures of the curtain; it strained and groaned in the gentlest breeze. At twenty knots, the wind load on the curtain equaled the force needed to propel two ocean liners at full speed.[49]

The project's short life span had a sobering effect on most observers. One week after the winds prematurely cut down the colossal animated fabric, townspeople reached out to the artists. A metal plaque with a key to the city read PRESENTED TO CHRISTO AND JEANNE-CLAUDE BY THE CITIZENS OF RIFLE FOR THEIR DEDICATED EFFORTS IN CONCEIVING AND ACHIEVING 'THE VALLEY CURTAIN.' A PURE AND BEAUTIFUL TRIBUTE TO THE IMAGINATION OF MAN. It was signed by Mayor John B. Scalzo and dated August 18, 1972.

Priscilla Morgan remembered a dinner she later attended at Howard Street with Isamu Noguchi, Saul Steinberg, Richard Lindner, Gian Carlo Menotti, and others. "When Christo described *Valley Curtain* being blown down, I could see Isamu listening in amazement. He and Lindner admired Christo's work and were astonished to hear about the curtain's short life span. Richard painted ten or twelve hours a day, making art to last forever; Noguchi whacked away at tons of marble or granite for posterity. Then you have this amazing man, a singular artist, who works like hell for long periods of time, only to see the work disappear. That just took their breath away."[50]

Mitko Zagoroff, Albert and David Maysles, Jan and Ingeborg van der Marck, Harrison Rivera-Terreaux, Wolfgang Buggenhagen, photographer Wolfgang Volz, and other Christo supporters converged on Amsterdam's Stedelijk Museum for the January 19, 1973, opening of the *Valley Curtain* exhibition. Harry Shunk developed film, printed contact sheets, and produced enlargements for the Stedelijk. His partner, Janos Kender, had disappeared shortly after returning to New York from Rifle, leaving Shunk despondent. Kender had also faded away after the aborted attempt with *Valley Curtain* in 1971.

Christo recalled, "After *Valley Curtain,* there was a huge drama. Harry was in total despair. He asked Jeanne-Claude to call Kender. They came to Howard Street and, like psychiatrists, we told them they must stay together. 'You can't risk an enormous archive of many artists' photographs because you have emotions. Be reliable. We need you.' They had lived together for almost seventeen years, but things became worse when Kender disappeared for a long time with a woman." In an effort to help Shunk keep the photo archive intact, the Christos engaged attorney Harry Torczyner.[51]

The celebrated collaboration between the photographers finally came to an end. Janos Kender would marry an American divorcée. Harry Shunk continued working for Christo for another year before gradually cutting his ties. Years later, he would bitterly reflect, "None of this would have happened if Christo had not hired a lawyer. He was afraid Kender would take the negatives. I liked Christo a lot. Actually, he is one of the best artists to work with, but he and Jeanne-Claude caused a lawsuit." Shunk not only blamed them for destroying his relationship with Kender but also complained that "all Torczyner cared about was the negatives. He offered Kender the cameras and told me, 'We can buy new ones. You can never buy the negatives.' Torczyner was very, very difficult."[52]

Torczyner's *Christo versus Kender* file reveals a September 10, 1973, settlement, finalized by Shunk, Kender, and Christo and Jeanne-Claude at the attorney's Fifth Avenue office. In her agenda, Jeanne-Claude noted, "Bring $5,500 for Kender." It was seventeen years before Shunk learned of the artists' financial sacrifice on his behalf; however, that did little to alter his view of their intervention as a well-meaning but destructive act.

Harry Torczyner had represented Christo and Jeanne-Claude on several legal matters. Perhaps the most complex one concerned 48 Howard Street. Jeanne-Claude recalled, "Ben and Max Rosenbaum informed us that we had thirty days to leave because they had found a buyer for the building. We were shocked. I asked them if they would sell to us if we could match whatever the price was, plus one dollar. They said we could certainly have preference. So we called everyone we knew to raise the deposit money." Family friend Henri Rustin wrote a check for $12,500 in exchange for some of Christo's art. Jeanne-Claude said, "We still owed a lot of money to Ted Dougherty. I called Ted and explained that we had the money we owed him but needed it to buy our house. He insisted we make the purchase." The price for the narrow five-story structure was $175,000. The Christo family occupied the upper two floors; their seventy-five-dollar-per-floor monthly rental became the basis of mortgage payments.

To shield the new owners and to avoid an expensive tax reassessment, Torczyner devised a strategy that utilized two corporations owned by Ben and Max Rosenbaum. He said, "It was a tricky operation. At no time could you reach the Christos. Whatever you checked, there was no trace of them." Torczyner's note to Chase Bank on April 2, 1973, simply referred to unnamed "clients." He had been given power of attorney to sign checks, leaving Christo and Jeanne-Claude, who were still not U.S. citizens, in the shadows. "We never bought the building. We bought Dapaul Realty Corporation and Danjedan, Ltd., which owned the building," said Jeanne-Claude, smiling.

When Christo and Jeanne-Claude traveled to Tunis that summer, a routine passport check proved to be a nightmare for Christo. An intense customs officer became agitated by the "stateless" designation on Christo's weathered refugee document. "Stateless? What country is that?" he demanded. The answer did little to soothe him.

"I was arrested at the airport," Christo said. "That was the moment I decided to become an American citizen." The artist had long harbored magnified fears of just such an incident.

Jeanne-Claude tried to help. She said, "Even though he had a valid visa, they kept asking, 'What kind of passport is that?' and 'What is stateless?' They seized all his papers. Christo was so scared. He was green with terror. Making things worse, there were three Bulgarian Communists in line behind us, listening to all that." Airport security insisted that his visa was invalid without a recognized passport or other papers showing a country of origin. The couple was ushered into a small room and interrogated for over an hour, then taken into Tunis for more of the same. That night, Christo was released and ordered to report the next day to the Passport Control Office in downtown Tunis for further questioning. "The authorities held his papers until we left the country," Jeanne-Claude said. "For a refugee, that is traumatic."

Back in New York, Christo immediately called attorney Anita Streep and began the application process for citizenship.

11

Running Fence: Part One

On June 17, 1973, Christo and Jeanne-Claude flew to the West Coast, where they were to spend almost a month trying to determine a site for their latest obsession, *Running Fence.* Accompanying them were Harry Shunk, thirteen-year-old Cyril, and his best friend, Ludmil Pandeff. Shunk complained, "We drove up and down the coast and back again to find a place for the *Running Fence.*" Jeanne-Claude grumbled, "I drove 3,000 miles. Elvira Pandeff never told me that her son easily became carsick."

The genesis of *Running Fence* can be found in *Three Store Fronts,* 1965; a 1970 collage called *Curtains for the Wall;* several 1970 studies called *Curtains for La Rotonda;* and a 1972 prototype called *The Divide.* "The first collages were not called *Running Fence,* but *The Divide,*" Jeanne-Claude explained. "And the fabric wasn't white. It was a salmon color." "Jeanne-Claude didn't want to say 'divide' because it was an unfriendly word," Christo added. "That's why we changed it to 'the fence.'"

The inspiration for *Running Fence* was thirte-foot-high snow fencing. "The idea came as we drove across the Continental Divide in 1972. I saw this metal fence along the crest of the mountains. It seemed to be running and hiding behind trees as we drove down the mountain. I did a collaged drawing over photographic images of an Irish landscape with rolling hills. We showed the drawing to Dr. Ernest Harris. Ernie said, 'You should go to Northern California. It's not too busy there, and it has these ranches with beautiful rolling hills.'"

Christo's specifications called for the fence to rise out of the ocean and cross rolling hills that were largely bare of trees. He also wanted nearby access roads, a freeway to cross, and, to provide visual interest, contrasting types of fences for farm animals. Finally, after an exhaustive search up and down the West Coast, Christo and Jeanne-Claude reached a consensus. The ideal route they selected for what would end up being a twenty-four-and-a-half-mile-long *Running Fence* ran through Sonoma and Marin counties, north of San

Francisco. Christo recalled his initial impression of the gentle landscape; "The first time there we saw this huge mist roll in and cover the land. We worried that nobody would see the fence. But it became so beautiful. In the end we liked it." Jeanne-Claude said, "There was another place farther south that we both loved. It had a village called Harmony. It would have been wonderful to say 'the Fence at Harmony.'"

The town of Petaluma was to become the artists' California headquarters for the next three years. "It was very much like Rifle, only bigger," said Jeanne-Claude. A richly atmospheric community of about 25,000 people, Petaluma is located on the southern edge of Sonoma County, forty-five minutes north of San Francisco. The main street is a clutter of small businesses set against a backdrop of low mountains. Two-lane roads snake through downtown, flowing into a countryside of grazing cows some horses, pastures, and mostly bare rolling hills. The region is a thoroughly American dairy and ranching center. One writer has observed that Petaluma "has gone down in history as the only place in the United States that had a chicken pharmacy, a drug store devoted solely to the health of poultry."[1] Calvin Tomkins noted Petaluma's "strongly agricultural flavor, with feedstores and big, rambling hardware stores coexisting peacefully with brand-new shopping plazas and taco stands and twenty-four-hour liquor stores. . . . [Christo] needed the social texture and rich contrasts of America in the 1970s, and he got them, in full measure."[2] On July 13, 1973, the artists commissioned surveyors to map the *Running Fence* route. On October 5, and again on November 4, Christo and Ted Dougherty met with members of Petaluma's Chamber of Commerce at Sonoma Joe's Lunch.

That fall, Christo prepared for his forthcoming citizenship examination. In New York, Jeanne-Claude, Anita Streep, and others drilled him on what to expect. He had been told repeatedly that the first question would be, "Who was the first American president?" After many rehearsals, he impatiently snapped, "Yes, I know, George Washington."

Christo's crash course in American history and government was put to the test on November 7, 1973. At 8:30 A.M., he, Anita Streep, and witnesses David Bourdon and Steve Gianakos arrived at the U.S. Courthouse at Foley Square in downtown Manhattan. The naturalization officer looked over the application and said, "I see that you married a divorced woman. Were you the cause of the divorce?" Everyone held their breath, expecting Christo to answer, "George Washington." Instead, he replied, "No, her first husband was." The Certificate of Naturalization, Petition No. 821516, Alien Registration No. A13 952 386, had affixed to it a photograph of Christo Javacheff, with dark horn-rimmed glasses and shoulder-length brown hair. It noted that he was five feet seven, had brown eyes, weighed 131 pounds, bore no distinguishing marks, and that his former status was "stateless."

"Christo was perfectly happy for seventeen years with no passport," said

Jeanne-Claude, "only traveling documents. He enjoyed being stateless. I was unhappy with his refugee status because every time we had to travel, even in Canada, he needed a visa. When we were going to many countries, I had to start weeks ahead of time getting visas. Christo's U.S. passport made my life easier."

Decades later, Christo reflected, "I can't say that I don't have Bulgarian links. Of course I have. But I can't say I have any affection for Bulgaria, even though I was born there and I lived there for twenty-one years. I'm not nationalistic. When I escaped from Eastern Europe, I displaced myself; that can be disorienting, but it can also be inspiring. Since then, I have been permanently displaced. Even as an American citizen, I don't pretend to be American. I feel very much like a refugee."

On December 13, the couple were back at work in California. Jan van der Marck, *Valley Curtain* project director, had recommended a colleague for the same position on the *Running Fence* project: fifty-four-year-old German-born Peter Selz, curator of painting and sculpture at New York's Museum of Modern Art from 1958 to 1965 and founding director of the Berkeley Museum.

A December 14 meeting at the Berkeley Museum included van der Marck, Christo and Jeanne-Claude, Selz, and his assistant, Lynn Hershman. Hershman felt a contagious enthusiasm. She watched wide-eyed as Jeanne-Claude turned on the charm, and she tried to follow Christo's words.

Hershman was both a writer and a promising artist. After the December 14 drive through the *Running Fence* site, and then dinner, the artists visited an environmental exhibition that Hershman had installed in a San Francisco hotel room. They liked it and developed an immediate rapport with the young woman. "We had the same kind of mental vernacular," Lynn said. Indeed, the Christos were to rely on her to handle the day-to-day operations. As she put it, "Selz was there for the sizzle. You know, he would make a few appearances, the photo opportunities. He was a very good public speaker. He had a reputation and a name, but he wasn't there for the day-to-day stuff."[3]

The Christos expected more than "sizzle." On December 27, 1973, Scott Hodes sent Selz a four-page agreement that specified a fifteen-thousand-dollar salary, plus expenses, to commence on January 1. The agreement provided for Selz to "devote as much time and effort as is necessary for the successful performance of his duties and the completion of the Running Fence Project." In retrospect, Jeanne-Claude would unflinchingly disparage Selz's contribution. Selz projected a kinder image of Jeanne-Claude, and he took pride in his association with the project. "People attribute each project's conception to Christo, but all the projects are really by Christo and Jeanne-Claude," he said, a prescient statement, given that they did not formalize their artistic partnership until 1994.[4]

In December, Jeanne-Claude sent cosponsorship contracts to one hundred collectors, dealers, and museums, inviting them to purchase $33,500 worth of Christo's art for $20,000—a 40 percent discount. About 80 percent of the sales were to European collectors. She also sent a December 20 letter to Lynn Hershman, authorizing eight hundred dollars to print stationery "with the words Running Fence *Project* (not Corporation). "The image of the running fence we wanted to put at the top should be dropped," Jeanne-Claude wrote. "It looks too much like advertising for a ski resort?!!" Instead, she enclosed what she described as "a map of our hills," to be reproduced as shown in a layout done by Christo.

On January 16, 1974, Christos and Jeanne-Claude assembled their team of engineers to test a prototype section of *Running Fence* in a muddy field near Soda Lake on the western edge of Denver. On hand were Christo, Jeanne-Claude, Harry Shunk, John Thomson, Ernie Harris, Ted Dougherty, Lynn Hershman, and a small corps of reporters and photographers. A 184-foot-long life-size model, costing ten thousand dollars, had been constructed under the supervision of A & H Builders and Ken R. White's engineering company to determine, among other things, the fence's ability to withstand high winds. The tests were instructive, and the Christos and the engineers went back to the drawing board in an effort to discover better ways of installing the fabric panels. Peter Selz arrived in Denver on January 17.

On January 20, Mr. and Mrs. Hans Raven organized a dinner meeting with a group of approximately two hundred property owners at the Sonoma County Fairgrounds building in Petaluma. The *Running Fence* speakers had a tough sell. Many of the landowners were ranchers who had never seen the inside of a museum, let along examples of vanguard art. Some of those present had never ventured farther than nearby San Francisco. When Selz opened by saying, "The fence will rise from Bodega Bay, will go along the shore, move to the crest of the hills, cross a good many roads, go through Valley Ford, and finally cross Highway One oh one north of Petaluma," most guests had no idea what he was talking about. Halfway through his two-page statement, Selz said in his slight German accent, "Once you agree to participate, you will be sent an easement agreement or contract." He presented a target date of late August or early September for completion of the project. No one showed any inclination to embrace this proposition. Christo's heavily accented explanation of the project, the showing of the Maysles' *Valley Curtain,* and the introduction of the *Running Fence* team, including the very French Jeanne-Claude, were all part of a curiously foreign presentation that raised more questions than it answered.[5] Few onlookers knew what to make of that evening's meeting. However, the daunting task of building community support had begun.

At breakfast on Monday, January 21, the Christo entourage discussed the previous night's presentation. That strategy session was followed by an interview with the artists on a local radio station, as well as a conference that included Christo, Jeanne-Claude, Scott Hodes, Hans Raven, Ted Dougherty, and attorneys representing several property owners. Nobody said so, but the notion of completing the *Running Fence* project by August or September of that year began to appear somewhat optimistic.

That same day, Christo left for Rome, followed on the twenty-fourth by Harry Shunk. Christo had targeted a 49-foot-high, 850-foot-wide section of wall at the end of via Veneto, one of the city's most active streets. The two-thousand-year-old wall also bordered the famous Villa Borghese gardens. The massive structure contained four arches, three for vehicular traffic and one for pedestrians. Guido Le Noci had done all of the groundwork for the project, a major contribution to "Contemporanea," the highly touted exhibition organized by its founder, Achille Bonito-Oliva. Le Noci had assembled large quantities of polypropylene and rope and a crew of construction workers to cover both sides of the wall, the top, and the arches. Christo financed the project through sales of his art, including a group of *Wrapped Roman Wall* studies done in the previous year.

"I thought Guido would get approval to wrap the wall," Christo said, "but he actually never got permission. Everybody—all these bureaucrats—was signing papers, sending them to somebody else. Nobody wanted to take responsibility. In the end, there was no permission. Guido said, 'Even though we don't have permission, I will make sure the president of the republic comes for the project.' The president of Italy did come.

"The installation took two or two and half days," Christo recalled. "It was sunny, cold, and dry. I remember Guido at the top of the via Veneto, feeding the workers at very posh restaurants to keep them around." If wrapping the ancient stone wall was meant to provoke unrest, it failed. Rome took the event in stride. The piece did, however, incite discussion. The phantomlike presence reawakened history as it entered contemporary folklore. Art historian Dominique Laporte contemplated the work and asked, "What does it mean to drape cloth over stone? What is he doing, this man who shrouds a monument of stone that defies time? . . . Insofar as art is a religion without referents, veiling a wall, wrapping the stone . . . that spans and defies time, raising a great wall of cloth, [these] are religious acts, reverse sacrifices."[6] The eerie transformation remained in place for forty days.

Reminiscing, Harry Shunk smiled mischievously and confided, "In Rome, I discovered that Christo doesn't like it when things work out too well. He liked problems. He likes excitement. It's strange, because in Rome everything went very well. The people weren't against it. There were no angry letters in the newspapers or protests. The students were for it." He laughed, adding, "It was difficult to work with Christo with no tension."[7] *Wrapped Roman Wall* was the last project that Harry Shunk photographed. It was agreed that Wolfgang Volz would later replace Shunk.

On February 12, 1974, Christo went to Colorado to refine a five-post prototype of *Running Fence* set up near Ted Dougherty's home outside Denver. During his absence, Jeanne-Claude juggled Peter Selz, Lynn Hershman, Petaluma citizens, fabric suppliers, attorneys, museums, galleries, magazines, publishers, writers, photographers, collectors, not to mention her dentist, her travel agent, the Dalton School in New York (where Cyril was a student), friends, and family. Jeanne-Claude found herself dealing with the increasingly bureaucratic tangle evolving in California: town, county, state, and federal agencies that might have a say in regulating portions of the fence, obstacles to the property easements, and so on. Engineers Ernie Harris and Sargis Safarian had just sent the artists a chart outlining the sequence of permits and licenses needed, with estimates of the time that would be required to secure them. On February 16, Christo and Jeanne-Claude and Scott Hodes agreed to assemble a legal team on-site. The agenda for the day noted, "Ask Scott about Nemerovski!"

San Francisco lawyer Howard Nemerovski vividly recalled meeting Christo and Jeanne-Claude a couple of months earlier while tagging along with his wife, Jackie, on a tour of New York artists' studios. "I saw a drawing of this *Running Fence* thing in Christo's studio," said Nemerovski. "I remember saying to the Christos, 'Here's my business card. If you ever need any legal help in California, call me. My firm will do it for nothing because I'm very excited about the idea.' Our law firm did a lot of pro bono work. I didn't think it would be a big deal. Some time later, Hodes called and asked me to help. I said, "Gee, Scott, that's great! Then, obviously, they told you about me.' He said, 'No. I'm sure they don't know you at all.' Imagine, I thought they would never forget my generous offer and our studio encounter. I guess I made no impression on them. You know, if they met Moses on a street corner, they'd try to sell him a collage and not pay much attention to him. Needless to say, the work was complex; it lasted for years, and it sure as hell wasn't free."[8]

There would come a point where the artists were forced to employ nine attorneys. To help put together the legal team, Nemerovski approached Edwin Anderson, a conservative tax attorney in Sonoma County, regarded by many as a pillar of the community. "In a way, I was endorsing Christo by representing him when a lot of people thought the whole thing sounded goofy," said Anderson."[9] At this stage, Christo and Jeanne-Claude needed all the help they could get. None of the landowners was rushing to support the project or to sign a contract. As an art authority, Peter Selz spoke a different language than did the bewildered farmers and ranchers. "I would go up there and tell them about the project and show them some work Christo had done," Selz said. "It meant absolutely nothing to them. They thought it was some kind of real estate gimmick, somebody trying to get their land. It was very, very difficult to get across what we were trying to do. Where was the profit? Why was he doing it? It took a long time before we got the first signature."[10] Lynn Hershman worked longer and harder and fared a little better. However, alarm bells were ringing in New York. Jeanne-Claude knew that she would have to spend considerable time getting to know the landowners and then use all of her powers of persuasion face-to-face.

On February 17, Christo flew to Copenhagen, the second of five European trips he would make in 1974. Jeanne-Claude followed three days later with Peter Selz. They had come for the opening of the *Valley Curtain* show at the Louisiana Museum, on the coast just north of the Danish capital. On the twenty-fourth, the couple flew to Paris for the February 25 wedding of Norbert de Guillebon and Anne de Clermont-Tonnerre

Christo's third trip to Europe came in April, when he installed the *Valley Curtain* documentation exhibition at the Sonja Henie-Niels Onstad Foundation in Hovikodden, Norway, and had a one-man exhibition of various works at Galerie W. Aronowitsch in Stockholm. When he returned to the United States, awaiting him was an invitation to participate in "Monumenta," an outdoor exhibition of work by forty contemporary sculptors in Newport, Rhode Island. With the *Running Fence* project encountering unexpected delays, Christo seized on the opportunity to realize a less daunting project. On May 8, he flew to Providence, showed the *Valley Curtain* film, and lectured at the University of Rhode Island's Fine Arts Center. On May 10 and 11, he and Sam Hunter, the "Monumenta" curator and Princeton University art professor, inspected the sprawling site for the projected exhibition. Christo found himself drawn to a quiet piece of coastline, a cove at King's Beach, along Newport's Ocean Drive. A meeting of land and water had been the premise of *Wrapped Coast* in Australia, and *Running Fence* had been visualized as rising out of or terminating in the Pacific Ocean. Christo immediately began a series of collage drawings that envisioned a white fabric floating over the coastal inlet. He also called Mitko Zagoroff and his associate at Unipolycon, Jim Fuller, asking them to help engineer the fabric's flotation and anchoring.

On May 22, Christo returned to Europe. After a brief stay in Milan, he flew to Paris and joined Jeanne-Claude and Cyril, who had arrived on the morning of May 25, just in time for the wedding of Alexandra de Guillebon at Essertaux. Christo went on to Düsseldorf, Zurich, and Stuttgart, while Jeanne-Claude and Cyril returned to New York after spending only twenty-nine hours in France.

In New York, the fourteen-year-old Cyril inadvertently became part of a playful interview conducted by Ray Johnson for *Art in America.* The six-page article, "Abandoned Chickens," consisted of eleven lighthearted "interviews" with artists about their childhood memories, toys, and pleasures. Illustrating the piece were photos of the artists as children, childlike drawings, the author's amusing sketches and diagrams, and an image of Christo's 1964 *Wrapped Easter Bunny.* The article ended with a brief dialogue characterized by Johnson's penchant for the farfetched:

> Christo's favorite childhood toys were soldiers and trains. When I went to interview Christo, I was greeted by his son Cyril, who offered me a glass of orange juice. It was not wrapped in a plastic bag. I asked Cyril what his favorite toys were. Cyril: "Basketball!" Cyril was very interested in his current interests—mammals, science and exobiology. The Christos arrived. I mentioned Christo's childhood in Yugoslavia. I made a mistake; he corrected me. He is Bulgarian. He presented to me a very long History of Bulgaria. I asked about unwrapping childhood Christmas presents. They didn't wrap presents in Bulgaria, he said. He mentioned a favorite cat named Gladys. Also dogs. The favorite dog was called Charo. He had three brothers. I asked Jeanne-Claude Christ [*sic*] what her favorite childhood toy was and she replied "Trees." I asked "What do you imagine Joseph Beuys's favorite childhood toy was?" She answered, "Probably a hammer."
>
> Christo was not sentimental:
>
> I was.
>
> I was sentimental about *Citizen Kane,* Rosebud the sled, Patty Hearst's childhood toys and unwrapping Christmas-wrapped presents.
>
> Christo was not.[11]

On June 3, 1974, Jeanne-Claude flew to San Francisco. Her thoughts were focused on the more than fifty families that owned land along the projected path of *Running Fence.* What could she say or do to convince these ranchers and farmers to sign easements allowing the project to go forward? The next six days would be devoted to winning support, or at the very least, discovering the cause of their stubborn resistance.

With Lynn Hershman as her guide, Jeanne-Claude set out immediately with characteristic determination. She recalled, "On the very first night, I visited a family at around nine-thirty in the morning. I thought it was early in the day. Little did I know that they had to get up at two-thirty A.M. to start milking at three A.M. I had no idea. I asked the woman who came to the door, 'When can I speak to your husband without disturbing him?' She said, 'He milks at three A.M. and finishes at five, so come back at five.'" At five A.M. on June 4, a stone-faced farmer listened politely to her appeal, said he would think about it, and went about his business. "During the first year we were constantly being turned down by the farmers," Hershman recalled. "I can still see Jeanne-Claude in tears."[12]

"Obtaining permission presented new problems on each project," she explained. "There's no routine. With different people in different countries we have to learn the best way to approach these problems. Christo says each project is like a university education."

Finding the right approach proved elusive. Calvin Tomkins described Jeanne-Claude's tenacity: "She would try to pick a time of day when the rancher's wife was home alone (telephone calls were useless; people simply hung up on her), and she learned to wade through packs of furiously barking dogs and other fauna without flinching, to drink endless cups of coffee, and to show a keen interest in milking, fertilizers, and other country matters."[13] Years later, Jeanne-Claude chuckled and said, "By the time we finished *Running Fence*, I had become one of the leading international experts on artificial insemination. That doesn't help when you're talking to the mayor of Paris. I also learned a lot about making butter and milk and pasteurization. Christo always says the projects are like a university for us. We have to learn about cowboys in Colorado, ranchers in California."

The artists promised each cooperating family a gift. At the conclusion of the project, landowners would receive all the steel poles, cables, and fabric that had crossed their property. Then they sweetened the offer: Sign on and have a choice of a color television set, a refrigerator, or a freezer. Jeanne-Claude recalled, "Scott Hodes suggested that idea. We were so naïve. My God, all those ranchers had TVs, refrigerators, and giant freezers with whole sides of beef in them." There were no takers. They changed the offer to $250 for land rental. "The biggest attraction was the rental and the materials," Christo said. "Not so much the fabric as the steel poles and cables. That's why when Ted Dougherty bought army-surplus poles in Dallas, we quickly had them shipped, even before permission, to a yard near Petaluma. The ranchers were very excited to see them. They would come and look and touch. They could see real value."

On June 23, four men with specific tasks flew west for the *Running Fence* project: photographer Gianfranco Gorgoni, Albert and David Maysles, and writer Anthony Haden-Guest. In the bitter aftermath of the split between Shunk and Kender, the artists had enlisted Gorgoni to document the *Running Fence* project. In the wake of their critically acclaimed *Valley Curtain* film, Albert and David Maysles joined the dynamic couple to begin shooting the *Running Fence* process. Anthony Haden-Guest, the artists hoped, could help convince area residents of the merits of the fence.

"One of our first signatures was that of Hans Raven," said Jeanne-Claude. "He was a rich rancher with properties in different states. We thought, That's great, because he's a wealthy guy who will influence the others. We introduced him to some landowners, but not everybody liked him. In fact, that signing hurt us. After awhile, we realized it was a mistake." Christo added, "There were many things to consider. First, we had to learn about a family, whom they talked to, whom they respected. We tried to see who had influence. For example, our lawyer from Santa Rosa, Edwin Anderson, was very helpful."

Anderson reacted cautiously to Howard Nemerovski's request that he represent the artists' interests at forthcoming Sonoma County hearings. "I hadn't heard about *Running Fence* and didn't know anything about Christo and Jeanne-Claude. I said I was reluctant to get involved because I didn't have any particular goodwill with the county Board of Supervisors." A meeting at Anderson's office left him unenthused.

"I had spent about an hour more than I expected with the Christos. When I told my wife, Jeanne, about the project I might become involved with, she responded, 'That's really stupid. Don't you know you're really being taken?' Her honesty was helpful, because I knew that would be everybody's reaction. I asked Anthony Haden Guest whether he really thought that Christo was on the level. He said that he had followed his career closely and thought he was. Based on his comments and my own observations, I felt fairly confident that I wasn't going to be surprised with some unexpected agenda."[14] Anderson took the job, and Jeanne quickly became a dedicated *Running Fence* supporter.

Anderson's motivation for getting involved had nothing to do with art and everything to do with the individual freedom and property rights of local landowners. "I thought Christo had a right to build his fence as long as the ranchers agreed," said Anderson. "My real interest was a private property issue. The ranchers ought to have the right to grant an easement for this kind of project across *their* land. It was that simple." Despite the controversial "goofy idea," the Andersons hosted three gatherings of area board members, politicians, community leaders, and ordinary citizens. "We showed the *Valley Curtain* film, and Christo answered questions," Anderson recalled. "It is a very impressive film. We also put on some other public programs. We had one at the library, and I vaguely remember one in a banquet room with a good crowd. I was really taken by the Maysles' film. When we showed it, few people were convinced to come over and support the fence, but it did convince people who were uncertain not to oppose us."

Some of the first *Running Fence* footage taken by the Maysles brothers shows Jeanne-Claude driving Christo down a long dirt driveway leading to a farmhouse. Inside, the Maysles shot the couple talking to Mr. and Mrs. Spirito Ballatore. The gruff, weathered-looking Italian-born sheep and cattle rancher leans over his kitchen table, studies a map, and says, "If a lot of people are not so careful—they throw a cigarette."

Jeanne-Claude responds, "Mr. Ballatore, I'm just as scared as you of those people, because this is our *Running Fence*. Everything we have in the world we put up to build it." Unconvinced, Mrs. Ballatore questions the wisdom of opening the project to the public. Next, the camera captures Christo and Jeanne-Claude crammed into a phone booth. She smiles, trying to explain the urgent need for a meeting; the person she is calling is unavailable. Christo looks exasperated. The next sequence shows Jeanne-Claude talking to a woman outside a farmhouse while Christo paces nervously in the distance. Moments later, they both get into their car. Christo says, "You cried. Why'd you cry? It's ridiculous. Why'd you cry?"

"Let's go," Jeanne-Claude responds quietly.

He repeats, "Why did you cry?"

She lights a cigarette. "Because I cried."

Frustrated, Christo growls in French, "I won't have it! I could change the whole route of the fence if I wanted."

The complex approval process had become far more lengthy than originally thought. The target date for completion had shifted to 1975. After spending ten days in New York, the couple returned to Petaluma from July 18 through August 14, then headed to Newport for "Monumenta."

In August 1974, fifty-three large works by forty sculptors began to sprout in Newport parks and malls, along the rocky shoreline, in front of mansions, and in other accessible places. There were also small pieces, scale models, and drawings shown in a traditional gallery setting, backed up by a series of artists' lectures, symposiums, and films. The exhibition included work by Claes Oldenburg, Alexander Calder, Donald Judd, Richard Serra, David Smith, Tony Smith, Isamu Noguchi, Henry Moore, Barbara Hepworth, Sol Lewitt, Barnett Newman, George Rickey, Louise Nevelson, Alexander Liberman, Beverly Pepper, and Christo.

Christo, Jeanne-Claude, and Cyril arrived on August 15, two days before the exhibition's official opening. They, Mitko Zagoroff, and Jim Fuller began with the anchoring of a wooden boom that would mark the outer edge of Christo's *Ocean Front* on a cove at King's Beach, along Newport's Ocean Drive. Even before the couple arrived in Newport, *Valley Curtain* was being shown, and a local radio talk show had aroused considerable curiosity regarding what promised to be "Monumenta"'s most unusual sculpture.

Christo's use of relatively fragile fabric offered a dramatic contrast to works assembled from steel, stone, and other durable materials. "The project is more than fabric," he explained. "It includes the ocean, the coast, the sky, the wind, and the people." In an interview with Princeton graduate student Sally Yard, he addressed the profound decision to utilize cloth in much of his work, "Fabric exists like our skin, or like the leaf on a tree. The leaves on the tree fall off, and our skin can be broken. All the elements of tension—sometimes involving real fears and serious technical problems—are normal because we are dealing with very fragile but at the same time powerful material. In a way you can find that quality in sailors, who fight the sails and the ocean's force."

High winds and rough seas caused a weekend delay for dozens of workers poised to install *Ocean Front*. Other pieces in the show fared even worse. One work was dropped off a cliff, one sculpture was assaulted by a car, and ten others suffered graffiti scratches or unintended alterations.

At 5:45 A.M. on Monday, August 19, 1974, the high waves having subsided, work began on *Ocean Front*. Six thousand pounds of white polypropylene fabric, sewn into a specific pattern and folded into a cocoon, were loaded onto a rented truck. Fuller and Zagoroff had completed exhaustive technical calculations and done much of the physical preparation; skin divers had charted the water's depth and recorded shifting tides; twelve anchors stabilized the 420-foot-long boom that drew a line along the outer edge of King's Beach Bay; forty-two rebar stakes were driven into coastal rocks ringing the inlet cove; Jeanne-Claude distributed life jackets. (As usual, all material and labor costs were paid for through the sale of Christo's art.) Then pairs of workers, spaced at six-foot intervals, carried a seemingly endless intestinal-shaped package toward the shore. Those leading the strange procession quickly became merely heads bobbing in the water alongside the submerged serpentine form. Jeanne-Claude, "Monumenta" president Bill Crimmins, and others were waist-high in water as they helped guide the packaged material toward the boom, some 360 feet seaward. Once the polypropylene was laced securely to the boom, swimmers began unfurling the long cocoon; they spread the untied fabric toward the shore, where teams of young people pulled the ends taut and tied the prepared edges to preinstalled stakes along the beach. Christo, clad in blue jeans, a bright shirt, and thick industrial gloves, bounded in and out of the surf, pulling ropes, tying knots, and barking instructions.

Ocean Front outwitted the elements for over a week. Then stormy weather, waves, and strong winds caused the once-pristine surface of the fabric to be tarnished with seaweed and debris. Jeanne-Claude blamed the boom: "It wasn't high enough, so the tide brought in all kinds of things. After eight days, someone telephoned, saying, 'It looks like diarrhea instead of white fabric.' Christo said, 'Remove it immediately.'"

Back in Petaluma, Christo and Jeanne-Claude spent considerable sums of money on whatever seemed necessary to realize the *Running Fence* project. As de facto contractor and corporate manager, forced to keep an eye on costs, Jeanne-Claude did everything possible to control spending. "Does the fence really have to be that high?" she might ask. Plans called for an eighteen-foot height—or, as Christo once said, "five cows high," roughly the height of a barn. Jeanne-Claude also asked, "'Why does it have to be twenty-four and a half miles long? It would be just as nice if it were five or ten miles." "Christo explains the reasons," she said. "We argue. Thank God he always wins. But I have to try."

On September 19 the artists and a team of skilled workers began two arduous weeks of plotting the exact path of the fence. The long trek to the Pacific started at Meacham Hill, the eastern extremity of the fence's path. Periodically, Christo took a wooden stake from a bag and placed it on the ground to indicate the fence's general direction. Trailing him, a crew supervised by Ted Dougherty hammered stakes into the undulating terrain at precise sixty-two-foot intervals—the length of each fabric panel—numbered each marker, and topped it with a red plastic ribbon. Christo said, "We were walking through the hills pinpointing the position of each pole in relation to the roads and houses." Then Jeanne-Claude picked up the story: "I remember a surveyor behind us saying, 'You're not walking straight.' We laughed. 'Of course we're not.'"

The circuitous route had already been divided into twenty-three segments. "Christo," wrote David Bourdon, "laid the path nonsequentially at the convenience of ranchers. . . . Through mutual agreement, they charted a course that would not interfere with livestock and vehicles. In addition to the ranchers' requirements, Christo also had to make adjustments to satisfy his engineers. . . . Among the occupational hazards were numerous barbed wire fences and several intimidating bulls.[15]

The Running Fence Corporation (RFC) applied for building permits on November 5 in Sonoma County and on November 19 in Marin County. The target date for completion was now spring of 1975. Voices of a still-unorganized opposition were increasingly heard, but work moved forward. By November 5, Rubber-Crafters in Smithville, West Virginia, had completed sewing 220 of a projected 2,217 panels. Each section measured seventeen and a half by sixty-eight feet—six feet wider than the space between poles, in order to allow for movement in the wind. In 1973, 165,000 yards of white nylon had been purchased from J. P. Stevens in New York for $130,000; the fabric, designed for General Motors, had mistakenly been made too wide for its originally planned installation as inflatable vehicular air bags. Sewing, packaging, and shipment to California would cost another $188,445. Unipolycon engineer John Thomson coordinated design and production of the fabric panels, each outfitted with grommets on four sides. Ernie Harris and Sargis Safarian assumed responsibility for the fence's hardware, including ninety miles of steel cable, 350,000 steel hooks, and 14,000 earth anchors. By year's end, the original budget of $400,000 looked naïvely optimistic.

Running Fence became an instrument for gauging the interaction between artist and public in a variety of uncharted situations. Bay Area art critic

Allan Temko disparaged Christo and his art, saying, "Christo is the Evel Knievel of modern art. These museum people who praise him are in that too-too, chic-chic, *Vogue* and *Harper's Bazaar* idea of art."[16] The Christos had expected and encouraged strong reactions, but the vehement opposition to the project exceeded anything they had previously experienced. Yet they had always contended that the entire process was part of the work:

> Any art that is less political, less social, less economic is less than contemporary art. . . . The American system, society, the way the whole big machine works—I find perfect to use for my projects. To grab American social structure and make it work, this is what I learn in America. I think all the power and force of art comes from real life, that the work must be so much part of everyday life that it cannot be separated. It is because *Running Fence* is rooted in everyday life that it gains so much force.[17]

At fifteen public hearings in 1975, the artists' vision would collide with reality. During one meeting, the camera caught one man gesturing emphatically, screaming at an older man, "It's a bunch of garbage. That's art? Some lousy curtain coming through here with a bunch of city slickers looking at it. To hell with it. I'm against it. I think it's stupid." Women looked on, amused. The older man talked quietly about jobs and money coming into the county. His adversary, still fuming, said, "What kind of art is that? Hanging a piece of rag up for fifty miles. I could hang a rag up. I bet he can't even paint a picture. He's an idiot." Clearly, the artists had a great challenge ahead.

The year began with a major setback. The Christos, lawyers, art historians Sam Hunter, Tom Garver, and Peter Selz, contractor Ted Dougherty, engineer Ernie Harris, Stan Picher of the Audubon Society, several researchers, and a group of ranchers came together for an important January 20 hearing before the Marin County Planning Commission. For four days, Jeanne-Claude had been urging ranchers, museum people, and friends to attend. Only six of the seven commissioners were present, with a majority vote needed to approve any action. Three Christo staff members had prepared an in-depth report for the commission, recommending that an environmental-impact report (EIR) need not be undertaken, and that the RFC be granted a use permit. The RFC had already agreed to protect the environment, control traffic, provide insurance, prevent fires, and so on. No one spoke against the project, but, with the media in evidence, there was no shortage of questions. Someone asked if birds might fly into the fence and die. Picher answered, "No bird unless it's ill will fly into an opaque fence." Even an ailing bird, he added, would bounce off. Commissioner Marie Sessi worried about animals tripping over the guylines that supported each pole. Chicago researcher Marty Abel offered to tie ribbons to the wires so that deer could see them. Commissioner William Long feared fire, and his colleague, Gloria Duncan, questioned the noise level of the fabric flapping in the wind. The staff admitted to not having thought of that. A reporter observed, "Christo . . . looked confused, like a man struggling to make some connection between what he has on his mind and what is being discussed."[18]

Issue one—not requiring an EIR—passed by a vote of four to two, with Sessi and Long voting no. The solidly pro-Christo audience breathed a sigh of relief as the environmental concerns seemed to be resolved. Then the hearing turned its attention to the fence. One commissioner good-naturedly began waving his hands, gesturing toward the drawings, the aerial photos of the route, and the staff reports, then turned to Christo and asked, "Why?" It had been agreed earlier that Christo would not speak. Curators Tom Garver and Sam Hunter spoke enthusiastically about the proposed fence. The *New York Times* quoted Hunter and an exchange that followed: "'The fence is a temporary monument. It is an artistic process of great complexity involving an artist, engineers, students, landowners and governmental bodies. The process is part of the product. And when the product finally emerges, like a butterfly from its cocoon, it is a thing of beauty.' 'Sure, sure,' said Commissioner Marie Sessi, 'but what about all the cars and the parking and all that jazz?' 'I seriously doubt,' responded Commissioner Jerome Friedman, 'that too many people would drive all the way out here to watch a fence.'"[19]

Despite doubts, Chairman Friedman voted yes, as did Becky Watkin and Gill Murphy. Aesthetics were not to be the issue. Murphy said, "These people are serious." Duncan saw no value in the project and thought it "a waste of time," something offended her sense of aesthetics. She voted no, along with Sessi and Long. A tie vote failed to gain the necessary majority. Christo, backed up by attorneys Howard Nemerovski and Steve Tennis, said, "We appeal." The *New York Times* quoted rancher Edward Pozzi, "'My father said, "The rocks are hard wherever you go."'"[20]

An appeal hearing was scheduled for February 4 before Marin County's Board of Supervisors. Attorney Steve Tennis said that this time Christo's battery of lawyers and experts would make a more forceful presentation. Christo would also be turned loose to pitch his ideas. The day after being rejected by the Planning Commission, the artists appeared on a local radio talk show. Asked about the snag, Christo observed that officials seemed satisfied with environmental and safety issues. However, smiling broadly, he admitted, "They doubt the artistic quality of the project." Jeanne-Claude added, "They won't accept that it is art."

There were many other doubters. By this time, the opposition had begun to organize the Committee to Stop the Running Fence. Mary Fuller McChesney, a sculptor and writer, and her husband, Robert, a painter and teacher, helped organize the group. Mary echoed a complaint heard elsewhere. In an article she wrote, McChesney asked, "How do Mr. and Mrs. Christo pay for their Mercedes Benz? And their color TV? And their French wines? Do they write these off as business expenses? Nothing unusual about that and why not? Jeanne-Claude is the president and treasurer of the corporations at salaries unspecified and she runs the books."[21] The facts were that Christos and Jeanne-Claude spent very little on themselves, had no color TV set, owned no Mercedes or any other car, and poured every penny back into their work. Two days before the appeal hearing, the *San Francisco Examiner* published a photo of the artists surrounded by hundreds of Vietnam War–surplus poles, purchased at forty-two dollars each. In the accompanying article, Jeanne-Claude spoke of money and the uncertain future of the fence: "We're not interested in money, we're interested in projects." She added, "Every time Christo does a project, he does it with his own money. You understand that."[22]

Mary Fuller McChesney did not understand. Her letter to the editor appeared in the *Press Democrat* on the day of the appeal hearing. It said in part, "It's a money making proposition, a deal, not art. . . . A public relations snow job is not the same as fine art. . . . It will bring tourists into the county and make it into a crummy Coney Island kind of event. . . . It's old hat already."

Speculations about the Christos' wealth persisted. Board of Supervisors Chairman Gary Giacomini paid a visit to Howard Street. To his surprise, he saw the sparse, run-down four-story walkup they called home. He left New York a confirmed supporter of the fence. At 3:00 P.M. on Tuesday, February 4, 1975, he called the five-member Marin County Board of Supervisors to order.

Once again, no one spoke against the project. Christo addressed the commission with obvious sincerity. There were also presentations by a parade of attorneys, experts, and landowners. They tried to address every conceivable concern. A sour Commissioner Robert Roumiguiere felt the project inappropriate for Marin County, fearing an influx of sight-seers that would damage property and create a disturbance. A one-page summary of the proposal added concessions to the long list previously agreed upon. In response to the fear of crowds, the document anticipated "comparatively little sightseeing activity." The last sentence stated, "It is important to stress that no effort will be made to encourage viewing of the *Running Fence*." In fact, of course, the press would take care of that.

Lester Bruhn, a leathery-skinned landowner in Valley Ford, a community of just over one hundred people, urged the board to overrule the Marin County Planning Commission. "I've talked to an awful lot of ranchers and haven't found one rancher against it. We're all gettin' compensated for puttin' this thing up. They're gettin' the material, plus compensation for it. I can't see takin' that away from the ranchers. Thank you." Citing the creation of jobs, rancher consent, and a lack of environmental danger, Chairman Giacomini called for a vote, saying, "It may well provide us with the opportunity of a life-time." The vote was four to one for granting a use permit. However, only about four of the fence's twenty-four and a half miles were regulated by Marin County; Christo still needed approval from Sonoma County, the Coastal Commission, the State Lands Commission, and the Army Corps of Engineers. He expressed relief at the decision, hoping it would set the tone for forthcoming hearings.

At 4:00 P.M. on February 13, entering the jammed hearing room of the Sonoma County Board of Zoning Adjustments in Santa Rosa, the seat of county government, one could feel the tension. At stake was a conditional-use permit. One commissioner said, "We don't have a provision in the zoning ordinance for a twenty-four-mile-long, eighteen-foot-high fence." As a result, the application was submitted under an unfamiliar clause covering "carnivals and outdoor festivals." Ed Anderson had worked overtime preparing for a lively confrontation. "My responsibility was Sonoma County, where most of the fence would be constructed," he said later. "I talked to members of the Planning Commission, the Board of Supervisors, and county staff to familiarize them with the project."[23]

Anderson received permission to start the meeting by showing the Maysles brothers' *Valley Curtain* film. Then the public had an opportunity to speak. The opposition had followed the Marin hearings, then started to organize, hoping to block once and for all what they felt to be an insane scheme. Mary Fuller McChesney, the outspoken opposition leader, wearing a white sweater and floppy black hat, said, "If we allow the Running Fence Corporation to use agriculturally zoned land for what amounts to advertising for their books, movies, Happenings, and theatrical gestures, I submit that it will be very difficult to logically refuse permits to other temporary activities: carnivals, rock concerts, motorcycle races, whatever." A sprinkle of applause followed her departure from the podium.

Lois Raymond, another opponent, condemned "pseudo–art lovers and pseudointellectuals who've come from urban areas to brutalize Sonoma County," and she urged the locals to "bid this carpetbagger adieu." Toni Novak-Sutley, a member of the Peace and Freedom party, called the project an "elegant hustle" and "another exploitation of our dwindling natural resources." Frank Musetter, a telephone company executive, echoed Allan Temko's comparison of Christo to Evel Knievel, cautioned about potential crowds, then unfolded a white handkerchief, waved it, and asked, "Is that art?" Artist Byron Randall minced no words. "It's obviously fraudulent," he said. "It's not art." Another artist, Bernard Kroeber, said what colleagues must have been thinking: "This guy in the last three months has had more publicity on a project that has not yet been done than most Bay Area artists have had collectively in the past five years." Kroeber added, "After this, Christo could sex a chicken in a park in Petaluma and make money."

Traffic, crowd, fire, and environmental questions were answered by

Christo supporters and county staff, while Bay Area museum staff and art faculty spoke favorably about the aesthetics of the project. Christo repeated his contention that everyone was part of the work: "The work is not only the fabric, the steel poles, and the fence; the art project is right now, here. Everybody here is part of my work. If they want, if they don't want, anyway they are part of the work." Few if any minds were changed, but the hearing showed democracy grinding along, working its imperfect path.

Ed Anderson later said, "The thing that stayed with me about the hearing was the involvement and enthusiasm of the ranchers. I thought they were quite eloquent, which surprised me. They made so much common sense. It was their land. They really trusted this guy."[24]

The temporary nature of the project troubled several speakers, but not a hefty gray-haired rancher's wife who stepped to the podium, smiled, peered through her glasses, and said, "I'm Mrs. George Mickelson from Petaluma. The fence goes through our property. We welcome it. There was one thing said about the art being temporal. Some of the meals I prepare aren't much. The rest of you can all say that, too. But sometimes I go to a lot of work to prepare a meal that I think is art. It's a masterpiece! And what happens? It's eaten up, disappears, and everybody forgets it." Still smiling, she sat down to loud applause and laughter.

The board voted four to one to issue a conditional-use permit. Lois and Ron Raymond decided to file an appeal with the county Board of Supervisors.

Mary Fuller McChesney began working on an article,—"What's in the Package?"—for *Current* magazine.[25] She wrote, "Who did Christo buy and how much did he pay and where is the money coming from are questions frequently asked. . . . How the hell did Christo get 35 of those salty characters out on the coast to go along with his scam and let the fence cross 57 parcels of their land?" She quoted an unnamed businessman as saying, "'He muscles in like the syndicate.'"[26] Calvin Tomkins observed, "The fence's detractors had to believe that Christo's real objective was money (in addition to fame); the other possibility—that he was building the fence for its own sake, and that the process was the sole reward—seemed an idea too threatening to entertain."[27]

Jeanne-Claude looked nervously at her watch. She had been on the phone for hours, reminding ranchers and others of the 7:30 P.M. hearing before the Sonoma County Board of Supervisors. Pacing back and forth, puffing on a cigarette, she checked off names as the crowd trickled in. March 18's one-item agenda was the Raymond's appeal to overturn the Board of Zoning Adjustment's issuance of a conditional-use permit to the RFC. Like the RFC, the Committee to Stop the Running Fence had spent the last month lining up speakers. Both sides had marshaled their forces; men, women, and children sat on the floor amid a standing-room-only crowd, awaiting the anticipated fire-works.

In recent days, Christo had used his powers of persuasion, addressing Rotary clubs in Los Robles, Oakmont, and Hillsborough, speaking to students at four regional colleges, lecturing at three area museums, and appearing on two radio talk shows. On the day of the hearing, Petaluma's *Argus-Courier* ran an editorial entitled, "Running Fence Is Commercial Venture That Will Be Harmful."

When Chairman Charles "Chuck" Hinkle convened the packed meeting, he and four other board members looked out at a sea of unsmiling faces. Large Christo photomontages lined the side walls, obscured by people standing three deep in the aisles. A podium and microphone had been set up in front of the room, facing the board. The parade of speakers began. Eric Denton, captain of the California Highway Patrol in Santa Rosa, stated that his men could cope with a "reasonable amount" of increased traffic. A supervisor suggested a new condition: The fence should be promptly removed if vehicular traffic was disrupted. The artists agreed. Ronald Raymond read a strong, reasoned statement outlining the basis for his appeal. Ranchers, art-world personalities, and people from all walks of life had their say, and then some. Delicately phrased, wistful, outraged, the comments varied wildly in tone. Opposition to the fence proved fiercer than anticipated, ranging from pragmatic questions to embittered demands.

Attention was riveted on Christo as he stepped to the microphone. "Everybody here is part of my work," he began. "Even those who don't want to be are part of my work." He portrayed the fence in heavily accented English, saying, "The fabric is a woven nylon and conductor of light, and at sunset it will appear as an incredible ribbon of light traversing all the ranchers' fences. It can never be seen in its entirety." Then he addressed the question that wouldn't go away. "I know there's a lot of outrage at the considerable cost of my project and at the effort that is going into it. But all my money is mine. We haven't a cent from any foundation or government agency." To underline the point, he held up a collage drawing of the fence. Pointing at it, his brown eyes flashing, he stated emphatically, "This is what I sell."[28]

The wrangling went on for six hours. Late in the hearing, a speaker brought up the 1972 *Valley Curtain* project. He accused the Christos of not living up to their agreements with Rifle, a serious charge, given the many conditions imposed on the RFC. Attorney Ed Anderson began to squirm. "After that testimony," he recalled, "a fellow got up in the back of the hall and started walking down the aisle. I asked Jeanne-Claude, 'Who is that?' She said, 'My God! He was the mayor of Rifle when we did the project.' Apparently, he had moved to Cloverdale, a town about thirty minutes north of Santa Rosa. He said, 'I want to tell you people that the Christos did everything they committed themselves to and a lot more.'"[29]

The hearing ended at 1:30 A.M. Four members voted to sustain the permit issued by the Board of Zoning Adjustments; one voted no. The *Running Fence* supporters still present congratulated one another.

The next few weeks would have ups and downs. On March 31, the RFC won unanimous consent to erect the fence from the three-man State Lands Commission after pledging a meticulous cleanup and no environmental damage. "When the project's done, it's gone," Nemerovski assured the commission. Then came a hearing on April 24 before the thirteen-member North Central Coast Regional Commission, a branch of the California Coastal Zone Conservation Commission. The RFC was approved, but the regional commission added fourteen more conditions to those already agreed upon with Marin and Sonoma counties, and they all put discretionary power in the hands of Joseph Bodovitz, the executive director of the California Coastal Zone Conservation Commission, who had a distinct bias against the project. Opponents quickly appealed the RFC's April 24 permit victory. The California Coastal Zone Conservation Commission put aside the permit issued to the RFC by their North Central Region and set a June 18 public hearing to consider the opposition's appeal.

Christo and Jeanne-Claude, Peter Selz, and others began contacting art authorities, environmentalists, landowners, politicians, and community leaders, asking them to lobby on behalf of the project. Howard Nemerovski recalled the 9:00 A.M. hearing in San Diego: "Bodovitz dug up a couple of environmentalists who talked about the damage that was going to be done. You'd have to be an idiot not to understand the dedication that the Christos had to leaving the area totally unspoiled after the project. The commission kept loading us up with ameliorating steps we would have to take. For example, someone asked, 'When are you going to put this fence up? You have to have moonlight.' 'Why?' we asked. 'Because night-flying birds could injure themselves if they don't see the fence.' We said, 'Fine. We'll put it up at that time of the month.' Someone else said, 'You can't do that. That's the mating season of elk.' Elk want to fuck each other, and if they were doing it, they might get their dingus caught in the guy lines. Every environmental concern that was raised was answered instantaneously by the Christos. There wasn't anything the commission wanted done they didn't say yes to—which, of course, frustrated Joe Bodovitz. He clearly wanted this thing killed because he had a bug up his ass."[30]

Three commissioners voted for the permit, nine against, dealing the project a severe setback. Some blamed the failure on an overzealous lobbying campaign; a blizzard of letters from influential people simply irritated commission members and staff. An art critic observed, "Sometimes it seems as though

Christo and his backers—perhaps his backers alone—are their own worst enemies. . . . Too much pressure had been brought to bear on officials."[31]

Things got even worse the next day. Superior Court Judge John Golden in Santa Rosa rescinded the RFC's permit for Sonoma County, ruling that an environmental-impact report (EIR) should have been filed. With little money and dogged persistence, an elated Committee to Stop the Running Fence had finally blocked the project, at least for 1975. With two crushing blows in two days, plans for a September realization were no longer feasible. Since an EIR would take seven weeks, the artists were forced to set a new target date—September 1976. "That was the worst moment for me," said Ed Anderson.[32] Everything he had worked so hard for was suddenly undone.

On June 25, the RFC filed an appeal with a San Francisco judge, and on July 15, Sonoma County commissioned Environmental Science Associates to prepare an EIR—at Christo's expense.

Opponents were to discover that the legal process had not yet run its course. Christo worked harder than ever in the studio; Jeanne-Claude worked equally doggedly, making phone calls, selling art works, and managing RFC business. The 1976 target date for construction required new permits from various Marin and Sonoma county boards, the U.S. Army Corps of Engineers, the State Lands Commission, and other agencies. Renegotiated leases with each landowner were also necessary.

Lynn Hershman said, "For me, the process became a kind of armature. I refer to it a lot, inside, like a psychological, sculptural armature. When I'm having difficulty, I think back to what the Christos would have done."[33]

On September 17, 1975, Christo and Jeanne-Claude looked on as three appellate judges of the District Court of Appeals reversed Judge Golden's earlier ruling. The victory came too late. To avoid giving antagonists an issue for future hearings, however, the artists decided to proceed with the expensive EIR.

Later, Christo beamed when describing the two-volume EIR, written by fifteen scientists at a cost of $39,000. "This is the first artwork with an environmental-impact report," he stated proudly. Printed on 100 percent recycled paper, the bewildering document had been prepared by Dr. Richard Cole of Environmental Science Associates. Christo viewed the weighty report, like the diverse people drawn into the process, as part of the *Running Fence* project. The final draft—replete with foldout maps, diagrams, time charts, an archaeology report, legal history, a fabric sample, lists of amphibians, reptiles, mammals, and birds found in Sonoma County, as well as of rare and endangered native plants, and reports on marine biology, soils, geology, seismology, waste-disposal issues, air quality, noises, traffic contingencies, parking, ocean engineering, rainfall means and extremes, and dust emissions from unpaved roads—also included statements from supporters, opponents, and uncommitted observers.

The study saw no significant danger of irreversible environmental damage. Under the heading "Impact Overview," it sounded a philosophical note: "The large-scale irreversible environmental change may very well be in the ideas and attitudes of people. *Running Fence* is an idea, as well as a physical object. Because of this idea, different people may become more aware of the dairy farm environment of southern Sonoma County and northern Marin County, and more sensitive to its beauty and preservation. As an idea or an event, *Running Fence* will remain in the memories of all those involved with the idea, whether they are sympathetic to the project or not."[34] Clearly, the writers had come to understand the Christo's intent as the artists.

The winter was spent obtaining permit extensions and combating lawsuits. Step by step, the RFC legal team had been moving the permit process toward a climax. Two December hearings were to prove decisive. At 9:00 A.M. on December 3, the Sonoma County Board of Zoning Adjustments (BZA) convened at Santa Rosa's County Administration Center. The artists and their attorneys, Ed Anderson and Paul Kayfetz, endured an agonizing session, one that gradually took on the belligerent tone of an inquest.

Dr. Richard Cole tried to answer questions from commissioners and the public as the analysis and counteranalysis of minutiae dragged on. Finally, the assault on the fence ended with a motion to certify the adequacy of the EIR. With five votes in favor, none against, the document was approved. By a vote of two in favor, three against, the indispensable use permit was denied, however.

The RFC filed an appeal and tried to regroup. The last chance to reverse the BZA decision would take place at a December 16 Sonoma County Board of Supervisors hearing. Christo and Jeanne-Claude were used to high-stake gambles. Their enormous investment of time, money, and energy was now on the line for one fateful spin of the wheel. They frantically took turns calling supporters to ensure a strong turnout. Once again, they needed the ranchers and a little luck.

At 4 P.M. on December 16, the Christos huddled with their legal team at Ed Anderson's office. Christo seemed agitated. Relentlessly long, tense days had finally gotten to him. Calvin Tomkins reported that the "main effort" was to calm Christo down.

Most of the 120 people filling the meeting room at Santa Rosa City Hall on December 16 were proponents of the project. Ranchers and their wives turned out in force. One supervisor who had supported the fence in March was no longer on the board. As a result, with only four of the five members of the board present, it would take three votes to win; a tie would uphold the BZA denial. Supervisor William Kortum, a veterinarian, had a strong distaste for the project. Making matters worse, the chairman, Charles Hinkle, stated that although he had supported an RFC permit in March, he now might vote either way.

As in the BZA hearing, the first, albeit less compelling, agenda item called for certifying the EIR. Not surprisingly, Dr. Joel Hedgpeth had discovered a burning new issue: He feared an influx of small planes might encounter a "very dangerous updraft area" along the coast, and he called for more study of the matter. In defending the report's lack of precise information on the topic, Dr. Cole responded with veiled exasperation, saying, "People may bring light planes to look at the fence. If they are careless, they may come too low, and they may crash, and that's it." After a brief discussion of this and several other questions, certification of the EIR carried, three votes in favor, Kortum against. A hush of nervous uncertainty settled on the assembly as the moment came to address the real issue: the RFC's use-permit appeal.

The first speaker, Rick Seifert of Sebastopol, launched the public forum quietly, "I have come to other hearings before, and I have not spoken. . . . I think it is an exciting project, and I am very much in favor of it." Outspoken Bay Area art critic Allan Temko minced no words: "I was the first to call Christo the Evel Knievel of modern art." Temko likened the fence to such "commercial stunts" as "flagpole sitting" and "the environmental devastation of Woodstock. . . . If you want to see something big and great, just go out and look at the Golden Gate Bridge, in which things are done permanently, for the greater enrichment of the community, not for temporary rip-offs."

In answer to questions about the RFC's total assets and ability to cover liability claims, attorney Steve Tennis explained, "This corporation consists of works of art and cash." Christo added, "Mr. Chairman, we have the tax returns from our tax man, and up to now, for two years, the Running Fence Corporation, we have spent $1,600,000. The tax attorneys are all here."

Mr. J. Deaton from Petaluma urged granting a permit: "One thing that nobody has spoken on is the amount of money that is being put into this county." Then rancher Leo Ielmorini marched forward. "I am a resident of Valley Ford, and this fence is going through my property I lease," he stated.

Hinkle asked, "How much are you getting paid?"

Ielmorini replied, "I'm getting the material. It is several posts and whatever material is on it."

"How many acres of land do you have?" asked Hinkle.

"One thousand."

"One thousand acres. Quite a few poles?" responded Hinkle.

Ielmorini replied, "It is not going across the thousand acres, just catching one corner of it. . . . I am just beginning to wonder what happened to plain common sense. . . . I'm for it. . . . It's been a lot of enthusiasm with everybody involved. This is something you have never seen before and we want to be, to get this in."

After a string of pro-fence speakers, opponents hoped that an elderly woman making her way to the microphone would shift the momentum. She did not. Seventy-two-year-old Bessie Gaven Steitz spoke briefly and softly: "Part of the fence will go over land that has been in my family for over one hundred years, and I approve very much of this project, and I want to see it happen."

Such heartfelt testimony on the part of the ranchers reflected their determination and that of the artists to see the project realized.

The last public speaker, Ed Pozzi, addressed the board at nearly 1:30 A.M. "I have heard a lot of talk, and they are not going to pull one over on me," he stated. "Majority rules, and if that isn't the case, something must be wrong. . . . I am for it."

Before the long-awaited vote, Supervisor Kortum said that he was uncomfortable with only $1 million insurance coverage for each occurrence. "We ought to make it at least one million and a half," he said. Instantly, RFC attorney Kayfetz accepted, and a twenty-sixth condition was attached to the proposal.

Then an unidentified voice called out, "In all seriousness . . . someone in the opposition told me that this was going to be . . . a McDonald hamburger—"

Christo jumped up. "I have never had any contact with any company in America," he said.

Hinkle then said, "To clear the record up, let me ask you, plain and simple. Do you plan to place anything along the route, do you plan to sell anything?"

Christo replied, "No."

"Do you plan to erect lemonade stands?" asked Hinkle.

"I don't have any," said Christo.

Supervisor Theiller responded to the increased insurance bond, "With all those conditions, Mister Chairman, I would like to move that we adopt those conditions and the use permit."

Supervisor Johnson added, "Second it."

Then Supervisor Kortum said, "I can't vote for this."

Johnson explained his position, saying, "I think one of the disturbing things that has come out of this hearing, to me, is the way we are losing something in Sonoma County, that I have grown up in, and enjoyed, and that is the willingness of the residents to welcome new people, who have possibly different lifestyles, into this community, and to give them the benefit of the doubt. . . . People are willing to do this, and I see no reason that we should treat people that come into our county . . . as outlaws, or [as people] to be castigated. I therefore vote in favor of the *Running Fence*."

Johnson and Theiller were known supporters; the real suspense concerned Hinkle. Christo and Jeanne-Claude studied Hinkle for a sign of victory or disaster. The chairman said, "This is especially a difficult decision for me tonight. . . . I probably am going against Dr. Kortum and Mr. Rinehart, who are very close personal friends. The McChesneys and so on, I think we agree on most things in life, but I don't see on this project that there is going to be that damage to that land. I think we have all the guarantees that we can possibly think of, to protect the citizens of this county. So help me, if something goes wrong, I will wring his neck myself. . . . On that basis, I feel miserable about it, but I'm going to vote for the project."

The roll was called at this point and the final vote recorded: three in favor, one against.

12

Running Fence: Part Two

The *Running Fence* project activated many people. Christo and Jeanne-Claude were greatly encouraged by the support they received and by the fact that their art was recognized not as an imaginary construct but as part of the real world. However, their capacity to endure government bureaucracy, legal controversy, and the endless public meetings that this entailed was sorely tested in California. *Running Fence* had encountered fiercer, more sustained opposition than had any previous project.

In January 1976, there was yet another appeal, but the Marin County Planning Commission denied it by a vote of five to two. It was time to get to work. Jeanne-Claude tended to a host of essential tasks. Raising cash topped the list. By early 1976, the RFC had spent over $2 million. Jeanne-Claude asked her mother for a substantial loan: $110,000, to be repaid with 14.8 percent interest. Précilda agreed. Jeanne-Claude also approached her sister Joyce, who declined. "At that point, my inheritance had gone down the tubes," Joyce explained. "I told her that I expected some money from Morocco soon, and if it came in time, I would loan it to her and come to see the project."[1] Six months later, Joyce added a thirty thousand-dollar loan to the family investment in the project. At one point, Jeanne-Claude went so far as to leave the country for one day to borrow $100,000 from Dr. Carolina Molinari, a wealthy collector. "She was an elderly lady with homes in Barcelona, Madrid, Caracas, Paris, and Mexico City, and a big apartment in New York. I flew from New York to Mexico City, picked up a check, signed papers, and the next day took a flight to Chicago and deposited the money in our Running Fence account. It was a loan that we paid back with interest," said Jeanne-Claude.

Christo produced a group of handsome *Running Fence* collages and drawings before taking off on a rapid European tour. On February 12, he visited Berlin for the first time and, joined by Michael Cullen and photographer Wolfgang Volz, inspected the Reichstag, Germany's former parliament building. That same day, Christo held his first press conference to discuss wrapping

California, 1976: Jeanne-Claude working at the *Running Fence*. (Photo: Wolfgang Volz)

the Reichstag; he also discussed progress on *Running Fence*. When asked how he put up with the tedious bureaucracy, Christo patiently explained that the process was really less a matter of red tape and more one of red paint. "Some painters," he said, "mix red and yellow to get orange." He had mastered a different kind of chemistry, stirring politics and people to obtain startling results. The lively social dimension, central to the work, made up in vitality whatever it lost in predictability. Christo genuinely felt that everyone was a part of his art.

By March 1976, realization of the *Running Fence* project seemed within reach.[2] While Christo spent most of his waking hours drawing, Jeanne-Claude worked overtime on the phone. She pleaded with supporters to attend the April 8 permit hearing of the Coastal Commission (North Central Region), called writers, lawyers, and engineers, and prodded dealers, collectors, and friends to buy art. She dispatched a four-thousand-dollar partial payment for steel cables, rented a Petaluma farmhouse, paid RFC expenses and taxes, ordered frames, worked with photographers, helped arrange exhibitions, and still found time to attend openings, do the banking, serve jury duty, and provide regular dinners for eight to twelve guests—with an ever-improving menu.

On March 16, Jeanne-Claude telephoned Ted Dougherty. He and his crew chief, Hank Leininger, had just established the RFC's new field headquarters on Leo and Rosie Ielmorini's property in Bloomfield, a Sonoma County community of five hundred people, located near the midpoint of the fence's projected path. Jeanne-Claude and Ted discussed the workforce, strategy, insurance, and the construction timetable. Dougherty had begun hiring local workers and had subcontracted a San Leandro firm, Underground Construction, to install the cable. "I didn't want the Christos to pay union wages," said the veteran contractor. "We were fifty miles from San Francisco, and if the unions moved in on that job, it would have been hell. Instead, we offered to pay the ranchers to build the fence across their own property. Only one agreed, but we did hire lots of grandkids, nieces, nephews, sons, and daughters. We kept the unions out by saying it was a rancher project, building a fence across their own land."[3]

Bloomfield had no galleries or museum, but the tiny hamlet began to talk, think, and *be* art. Were Dougherty's supply lists really art materials? "L-B units, strut-guys and trawler winch" had an unusual ring, even for the initiated art lover. Did Dougherty's work charts—"prefabricate pig tails, move ladder-boom units and punch holes with anchor drivers"—suggest art activities to even the most astute art expert? Perhaps not, yet a complex, unprecedented art continued to evolve, step by arduous step. It came together in a rich tapestry of legal papers, engineering notations, prodding phone calls to and from Howard Street, maps, charts, scientific reports, photographs, drawings, and, most important, aroused people.

On April 8, the artists and a loyal band of supporters were cheered when the California Coastal Commission's North Central Region voted to renew the RFC permit. The Committee to Stop the Running Fence appealed immediately. The only remaining major roadblock appeared to be the statewide Coastal Commission, which would hear another appeal. In the meantime, work proceeded on schedule in Bloomfield. Part of the Ielmorinis' farmhouse became Dougherty's field office. The rancher's large fenced-in yard bristled with activity: Young workers in yellow hard hats neatly stacked odd-shaped metal pieces, large rolls of wire, five-thousand-foot cable spools, and various barrels and containers amid an assembly of cars, Jeeps, flatbeds, and a fleet of specially designed power wagons and ladder trucks.

Finally, on April 29, 1976, three days after securing insurance coverage, over twenty trucks rolled out of the Ielmorinis' cluttered yard to begin the first stage of construction. Installation of 2,050 steel poles and over ninety miles of steel cable took most of the summer. Four specially designed trucks (costing thirty thousand dollars each), held aloft on flotation tires to avoid damaging the soil, had been outfitted with machinery to drive anchors, punch postholes, install poles, and dispense cable. The peculiar-looking vehicles carried an assortment of fire-prevention equipment; after a year's drought, any spark could ignite the parched hills. Other trucks carried poles, cable, tools, supplies, water, and up to sixty field-workers. Hundreds of charts outlined the specifications of every pole and anchor. Workers bolted two thirty-inch supporting steel "shoes" three feet from the bottom of each twenty-one-foot pole and planted the first of fourteen thousand anchors attached to "pigtails" (short lengths of steel cable), which would eventually be clamped to aboveground cables. The initial weeks of painstakingly accurate installation moved along on schedule, despite complaints lodged by Lois Raymond, the leader of the Committee to Stop the Running Fence, and other residents. Inspectors—hired by the county but paid by the RFC—found no serious violations.

The summer of 1976 had its share of potential catastrophes. Joseph Bodovitz, executive director of the California Coastal Zone Conservation Commission, seemed determined to abort the project. On June 18, his staff compiled a four-page report that began by urging a two-thirds vote, instead of a majority, to approve the coastal segment of the fence. Adding that, the additional burden appeared to be an unnecessary precaution, given the emphatic staff recommendation to deny a permit. A negative judgment ensured that the statewide body would once again overrule its North Central Region, uphold an appeal by the Committee to Stop the Running Fence, and deny the RFC a permit. The staff document voiced concern about "the impact of visitors," concluding, "the project would pose too great a risk to a delicate coastal area." When word of the staff recommendation reached the Christo camp, it became clear that something had to be done. The ocean portion was an integral part of the fence in the artists' minds. To avoid almost certain defeat, they and their lawyers devised a delaying strategy. The attorneys requested a postponement of the permit hearing until Christo could attend. A note in the family agenda stated that if anyone from the Coastal Commission called, "Christo *is* in Europe"; another memo reminded Christo not to answer the phone.

On June 21, Christo flew to Berlin for meetings with representatives of the CDU, the SPD, and the Freedom Democratic Party, as well as two Reichstag administrators. On June 23, he met with Annemarie Renger. Also present were Michael Cullen, Wolfgang Volz, and Paul Baumgarten, architect for the Reichstag reconstruction, who welcomed the project.

On July 21, Jeanne-Claude received a disturbing call at Howard Street from Ted Dougherty. Some "aesthetic terrorists" had sabotaged several trucks. Dougherty described the vandalism. "They slashed tires on a number of trucks that had been parked in the fields overnight. It was no teenage prank. In the worst case, tires were slashed on one of our big thirty-thousand-dollar anchor trucks, and the hydraulic controls were broken with hammers. They hot-wired the engine and left the throttle full open; then somebody took a crowbar, punched holes in the radiator, and knocked the drain plug off the bottom of the crankcase so that the engine would burn itself to death. Now that's insidious."[4]

On July 22, Christo and Gianfranco Gorgoni flew to California. The situation had worsened overnight. Ted's wife, Phyllis, and a local newspaper had received bomb threats. Dougherty recalled, "Phyllis told me she had answered the phone and that someone said, 'I want you to know we've placed four or five plastic bombs along the length of the fence. It won't kill a man, but it will tear his legs off.' Phyllis asked, 'Is this the opposition?' He said, 'You bet it is, and we're going to keep this up until the project is stopped.'"[5]

Workers were shocked and angered by the ugly turn of events. Their jobs had become deadly serious. Deputy Sheriff Ed Wilkinson, a demolition expert, gave the crew a short course on how to recognize explosive devices and what to do about them. He suggested security measures to Dougherty: (1) three low-level helicopter patrols between 5:00 and 9:00 P.M. daily, with a deputy sheriff and "one of your people" aboard; (2) thirteen fixed-wing patrols between 5:00 and 9:00 P.M. daily, with a deputy sheriff and "two of your people" aboard; (3) an explosives specialist to walk specified routes prior to work crews. The recommendations were accepted. Also, vehicles would no longer be left at work sites, but parked in the guarded Bloomfield yard.

Newsweek reported the incident, "Officials of Sonoma County say they can't guarantee protection against further acts, but Christo, who has maintained from the start that *Running Fence* is not just an esthetic project, but a process involving social, political and economic forces, refuses to give up. 'It's all part of the power of the project,' he says."[6] Jeanne-Claude was later quoted as having said, "There are crazy people in California. I am worried about my Christo. Maybe they think if they kill him they will stop *Running Fence*—but they don't know me."[7]

After the bomb threat, Jeanne-Claude instructed the Petaluma Inn to change Christo's room every night. "I told them not to tell anyone which room he was in," she said. "I even told Gianfranco Gorgoni, 'When you start the car, do it before Christo gets in.' He said, 'Thanks a lot!'"

On August 12, four trucks loaded with fabric panels arrived on site from Smithville, West Virginia. Ted Dougherty recalled, "We had been hearing rumors that some shadowy group was threatening to burn the fabric. When these four large semitrailer trucks arrived, Christo asked what I was going to do with them. I said they were going to our Bloomfield yard. He said, 'Good. Put guards on every corner, and if they come around, shoot at them.' I said, 'Christo, you can't do that.' He said, 'What will we do?' The best way to hide something is to put it with a bunch of other stuff so that you can't tell what it is. So I said, 'Let's put these trailers in a yard full of trailers in San Francisco so they can't see them.' "[8]

On August 18, another near catastrophe occurred. Dougherty remembered it vividly. "Some of the Committee to Stop the Running Fence lived in a little burg called Happy Acres. We tried to stay away from there as much as possible. No one living in Happy Acres had given us permission to build except the subdivider who owned it; we could go down his streets, but not on any private property. That day, Christo, Mitko Zagoroff, Tex Aycock, and everybody else was out there working. We had developed a machine that didn't drill but punched holes in the ground. If we hit something, we could just stop. In Happy Acres, we hit something hard. Tex reached into the hole and said, 'It's just rock. Go through it.' Christo and everyone else agreed. So they pounded away and up comes a geyser of water! We had broken through a six-inch water main that supplied Happy Acres."

Lois Raymond happened to be in the middle of her wash when the water stopped. Dougherty telephoned residents and sent a runner around to explain and apologize. "Of course we were not very well received," he said. "One cantankerous old gal had the most foul mouth you've ever heard. One of the friendlier townspeople went to turn off the water pump. The repairs took a few hours. We called people to tell them everything was okay, but we said, 'Let the water run awhile to get the dirt out.' Hank Leininger went to see this cantankerous woman. She met him at the door with a barrage of abuse. He said, 'The water's on.' She dragged him inside and showed him that it wasn't. Hank knew something was wrong. He drove to the pump house, looked in, and saw the pump was cherry red. The guy had turned on the discharge but not the intake. So there was no water going through while it was running all the time. It was really dangerous. It could have been a disaster."

On August 20, having completed the first stage of construction, work quietly began on the ocean extremity of the twenty-four-and-a-half-mile-long area. The ocean portion of the fence had been planned to extend 558 feet farther, terminating at a peculiar-looking barge designed by Jim Fuller, John Thomson, and Mitko Zagoroff. Two navy mooring buoys were welded into a ten-ton steel raft measuring sixteen by twenty-four feet. Plywood sheets pro-

Bodega Bay, Marin County, California, 1976: Jacques de Guillebon, Christo and Henry Leininger working at the ocean portion of the *Running Fence*. (Photo: Wolfgang Volz)

vided a deck for the ungainly floating platform. To keep a low profile, the barge's construction took place in Marshall, a coastal town fifteen miles south of the more expedient Bodega Harbor. The Committee to Stop the Running Fence heard about the work. They were informed that it was an offshore structure for photographers.

The engineering plan called for a three-thousand-pound anchor installed 2,536 feet seaward, thus maintaining a stable line between the barge and the fence. One of the most difficult technical problems concerned the design of the fabric panels. The intention was for them to seem to rise out of or disappear into the ocean; how could they maintain the appearance Christo wanted when subjected to strong winds and changing tides? "When it's practical and simple and costs nothing," Jeanne-Claude reflected, "you can bet it's John Thomson's idea." Thomson's solution was to tie metal buckets to the underside of the fabric. Small-scale tests proved the technique could keep a portion of the material beneath water while the visible fabric maintained the characteristic look of the fence.

By mid-August, Christo and Jeanne-Claude had given up commuting between New York and California and had settled at the Petaluma Inn. "They didn't get a lot of sleep, or seem to need any," observed Thomson. "They were always on the dead run. Jeanne-Claude is an energetic, terribly effective, nearly ferocious girl. They make a very powerful pair."[9] Ted Dougherty said, "They work so hard on these projects. It's just go, go, go. Where they get the drive from, I don't know."[10]

The countdown clock ticked faster. A wave of anticipation could almost be felt stirring in the rolling hills. On the morning of August 29, over three hundred people filled the stands of the fairgrounds in Petaluma. All were applicants for RFC jobs paying $2.40 an hour.

A few days later, forty A & H construction workers, aided by a helicopter, positioned and reinforced poles along the coastal section. At 3:00 A.M. on September 4, the barge was surreptitiously towed into position in Bodega Bay. The artists had decided to complete the westernmost portion with or without a permit. Several weeks earlier, they had invited Dougherty and Ed Anderson to dinner in Petaluma to discuss the possible consequences of going into the ocean without a California Coastal Zone Conservation Commission permit. Anderson explained that even with authorization from the North Central Region, that illegal act could result in fines and other court actions. Anderson recalled, "Dougherty wanted to know what I thought his exposure was. Was he committing a criminal act? Was he facing imprisonment? My sense was that there would be a big hullabaloo but that it would amount to nothing. I added, 'With one exception—if we have an earthquake and the coast falls into the ocean, then we'll have one hell of a problem. They'll say the fence did it!'"[11] Given the potential liabilities, Christo proposed relieving Dougherty of his responsibility through some type of reorganization. Dougherty declined. "What the hell," he said, "if they put me in jail, I'd just be a martyr, which is the last thing those people want."[12]

Dealers, collectors, curators, TV and radio reporters, press, friends, family, and the curious began arriving to witness the event. Engineers, lawyers, and ranchers all studied the influx. Guido Le Noci, Pierre Restany, David Juda, John Kaldor, and other supporters streamed into a string of small towns in Marin and Sonoma counties.[13] Cyril arrived in late August. Joyce May Henery with her baby, Julia, and Précilda and Jacques de Guillebon came to help and perhaps witness something extraordinary. And, of course, the Maysles brothers and others wielding cameras roamed the countryside, trying to document the once-in-a-lifetime spectacle.

Poles and cable marked the path of a fence ready to bloom. Just before the Labor Day weekend, Christo and Dougherty were to arrange the last-minute delivery of the fabric, which had been secretly stored in San Francisco. Dougherty, however, had misplaced the name, location, and phone number of the truck lot. "Christo had told me to make sure I didn't leave any papers around that might be found by those people who vandalized our trucks and threatened to burn the fabric. He asked, 'Where did you put the note?' I couldn't find it. I had hidden it where nobody could find it. The office was about thirty feet long. He walked to one corner, turned around, and stared at me. He'd walk to the other corner, turn around, and stare at me. I kept looking through my papers, trying to remember where I'd put it. It must have been fifteen minutes. Christo never said a word. He was distressed but never blew his top. I finally found the note. Thank God he never started screaming like he does with Jeanne-Claude. She can get him hysterical."[14]

The fabric delivery, scheduled for Labor Day, September 6, 1976, at 6:00 A.M., required the shipment to leave San Francisco before 5:00 A.M. Christo decided to lead the four-truck convoy to Bloomfield. Jeanne-Claude drove him to San Francisco. Dougherty chuckled as he recalled this event: "They went to the truck yard and found nobody there. The Christos came back in a panic. A little later, three trucks rolled in. I asked a driver what had happened. He said, 'You don't think we were going down there at four in the morning to pick up trucks. We took 'em home Friday night and parked in front of our houses.' If Christo knew they were unprotected all that time, he would have had a fit."[15] The fourth truck arrived at 10:30 A.M. an embarrassed driver explained that he had picked up his girlfriend the previous night. While they were drinking beer inside his cab, he was arrested, thrown in jail, and fined for having an open container.

Now the workers were ready. The artists watched forklifts transfer huge boxes of fabric panels from the four large delivery vans to their fleet of smaller trucks in Bloomfield. Dougherty outlined distribution plans at an afternoon foremen's meeting. Each box contained several bags. Each nylon bag held a sixty-eight-by-eighteen-foot custom-made piece of cloth weighing fifty-six pounds. Beginning that afternoon, 2,100 carefully marked bags were placed alongside designated poles at the last possible minute to minimize any chance of sabotage. While the rest of the country enjoyed the holiday, the Christo entourage felt a growing sense of excitement. A 3:00 P.M. a barbecue for the workers provided a final interlude before another frenzied period of activity—the next day's unfurling, which would bring *Running Fence* to life.

Lynn Hershman and a handful of others were troubled by talk of ongoing construction activity along the coast. Would Christo defy the Coastal Commission? Not without a permit, she thought, and certainly not without telling her. Hershman had always considered the artists' eagerness to operate within the legal framework, one of their great strengths. However, now all signs pointed toward a violation of the law. Paul Kayfetz had been hearing the same reports. He explained that any coastal work would not only be illegal but could subject her and other people on the staff to criminal prosecution.

All the rumors were true. The thousand-yard coastal tract in question snaked through an isolated parcel of land three miles from the nearest country road. Calvin Tomkins described the covert operation:

Christo and a band of trusted workers had been going out to the ocean, driving their trucks overland across the treeless hills and down to the edge of a bluff overlooking Bodega Bay, which at that hour was usually shrouded in fog. Until about nine o'clock, when the fog lifted, they sank ground anchors, attached cables, and dug postholes. When they talked over the citizens-band radio that linked several of the trucks to the Bloomfield headquarters, Dougherty and Christo referred to the work in the coastal zone as "special preparation," in case anybody happened to be listening in. Ed Pozzi and some of the other ranchers who lived in that area heard Christo's trucks going by at five each morning on their way to the ocean. "I knew what they were doing," Pozzi confided to me later. "I just thought more power to them."[16]

With Christo working in the field, Hershman decided to confront Jeanne-Claude at the Labor Day buffet dinner. Jeanne-Claude had been in overdrive since 3:00 A.M. She had little patience for another problem in a day of wall-to-wall entanglements. A few days earlier, Steve Tennis had asked her the same question. Jeanne-Claude coolly assured Tennis that engineers were simply testing the soil while awaiting issuance of a permit. "Was it true?" Hershman asked. Jeanne-Claude suggested that if the possibility of coastal-zone work worried her, she could resign and avoid liability.

Lynn had hoped for a more positive, open response. After three and a half years of dedicated work, she felt entitled to information on this vital issue. She believed she had done most of Peter Selz's work, yet she felt repeatedly pushed into the background. "On Labor Day," Hershman said, "I had a flare-up with Jeanne-Claude. When I asked what was happening on the coast she wouldn't tell me. She got very upset. A lot of very difficult tasks fall on her. She stayed controlled, convincing, and manipulative. In retrospect, what they did was absolutely right, but at the same time, there was so much confusion. Later, they said they were protecting people by not letting them know. After years of living and working on-site, I was upset, not being able to prepare for the press and public. There was a lot of resentment when I voiced my opposition. Nobody backed me up."[17]

The day seemed interminable. That night, monitors guarded the materials. The Bodega Bay crew worked for fourteen hours. The fourteen heavier, thicker, well-anchored poles nearest the ocean had been airlifted into position by helicopter. At 6:00 P.M., workers cheered as the first panel billowed in the fading sun. The attorney general's office, the Coastal Commission's office, and the courts were closed for the holiday; by the time they reopened on Tuesday, the coastal section would be complete. At 9:00 P.M., a moonlit trail of fabric rippled in the breeze, a tiny sample of what the morning might bring. Christo moved along the steep incline, caressing the cloth as he walked. From a distance, Jeanne-Claude pointed to her coconspirator and said, "Look at Christo flirting with his fence."[18] The ocean portion of fabric between the shore and the waiting barge would blossom on Tuesday morning. So, too, would another twenty-four miles of fence.

Crews were scheduled to report at 4:30 A.M. on Tuesday, September 7, 1976. By 4:45, over three hundred workers were gulping down coffee and doughnuts at the fairgrounds. For the past two weeks, six test panel sections, set up between the pigpens and sheep corrals, had been used to provide training on how to hook, hang, and unfurl fabric.

One worker, Elizabeth Whitney, later wrote, "It was like hanging a giant shower curtain, [but] "it would be different 'out there,' what with the wind and uneven terrain." She and the other trainees had seen the *Valley Curtain* film and knew that one reason they were starting early was to avoid high winds. "Christo knows something about the wind and his art," Whitney said. "In a schedule rivaling that of the Normandy Invasion, various crews were to be deployed to various key high-wind locations, then picked up and moved to other sections of the Fence."[19]

At 5:00 A.M., workers began piling into five waiting buses. Everyone was issued a white hard hat, a flashlight, and a sleeveless yellow T-shirt emblazoned with the *Running Fence* logo.

On the shore, there was no sign of the usual morning fog. The sun rose into a bright blue sky, announcing a scorching day, when the temperature would exceed one hundred degrees. Standing on a boulder, Christo shouted instructions into a bullhorn. "Pooool! Poooool!" he exhorted workers on the raft anchored offshore. The final length of fabric, suspended from a cable and held down by a long line of attached buckets, gradually made its way from the rocky coast toward the westernmost point of the designated area. Suddenly, the panels installed the previous night along the steep cliffside were linked to the ocean segment. It created an illusion of a fence rising out of, or settling into, the choppy waters. Jim Fuller beamed at the successful engineering exercise and said what all of the engineers and the artists knew: "There's no book to tell you how to build a twenty-four-mile-long nylon fence."

Watching the material bob up and down on the water, Jeanne-Claude said, "It looks so beautiful." Knee-deep in the surf, Christo, excited by how the waves animated the fabric, called out to Jeanne-Claude, "Look! Look! Look!" He smiled broadly as a wave swept over him. A helicopter hovered overhead as still photographers and TV and film crews scrambled over the rocks to record the action. One of the Maysles brothers' cameras caught a glimpse of General de Guillebon carrying buckets to the shore. An assembly of European and American dealers, collectors, and museum personnel enjoyed the spectacle.

Soon, however, numerous problems arose: Chartered buses left work crews stranded all along the route, materials and supplies were unavailable, packaged lunches never reached most workers, and large water jugs were soon

California, 1976: Christo during the installation of the *Running Fence*. (Photo: Wolfgang Volz)

emptied, not to be refilled. A toilet truck had a mishap, depositing waste in Happy Acres.

Whitney wrote:

> In the afternoon wind, what we had in our hands was no longer just a 59-pound piece of white nylon, but a raging beast, an untamed stallion leaping out into the air, tearing at out hands, wrenching itself from our grasps.

Sometimes the fabric ballooned out like a spinnaker; other times it flew free like a silk scarf. As we watched we could see billowing panels in the distance marching up hillsides like sailing ships, "Those guys up there are having a hell of a time, too," we commented. . . . Our hands were sore, our backs were sore, our feet were blistered, our faces sunburned, our knees shaky. The Christo jokes started coming thick and fast; the Christo accents gradually perfected, the Running Fence taking on a more familiar name, namely the F__ __ __ing Fence.[20]

Angry, exhausted, disillusioned workers drifted into the fairgrounds late Tuesday night. Some had waited hours for a bus; others walked. Blistering weather and botched planning set the stage for rebellion. The Christos had wasted hours while concealing themselves in a eucalyptus grove to avoid an injunction that had not been issued. That night, he, Jeanne-Claude, and Ted Dougherty huddled for two hours with the men responsible for feeding, supplying, and transporting workers: Dennis O'leary and Harrison Rivera-Terreaux. They finally hammered out a plan for improved logistics, hoping the disenchanted workforce would return before dawn on Wednesday.

Paul Kayfetz had reason to feel uneasy. "I had been left out of the loop and made no effort to pry because I would have felt uncomfortable knowing more about it," he said. "Then I received a call from Burr Heneman, an acquaintance who confirmed my suspicions. I had been put in a position of making repeated representations that he would not make the illegal jump. I had promises from Christo that he would honor that commitment. Once he went into the ocean, for reasons that I don't particularly quarrel with, he left me with egg on my face and with broken promises that he had made directly to me. At the last Coastal Commission hearing, when Christo was still trying to get permission, Bodowitz expressed concern that if the permit was denied, Christo might do it anyway. I had been assured by my client that the entire project would be in compliance with the law."[21]

In Christo's mind, he had simply challenged the system and was prepared to pay the consequences; his allegiance was to his art. Calvin Tomkins later asked Christo if going into the ocean would mean losing his good name. "Ah, my good name," Christo said, smiling. "But what about my good name as an artist? It is more important I cheat the law than I cheat my art."[22]

Christo and Jeanne-Claude talked about their legal and labor problems during Wednesday morning's predawn hours. Less than half of the fence had been unfurled. He would have to motivate the workers and avoid a process server until the project was complete. About 300 of the previous day's 350 troops returned for another punishingly hot endurance test. Elizabeth Whitney recalled Christo's 5:10 A.M. pep talk: "On the whole the same faces were there again, the same sleepy looks, the same rumpled clothing." Christo apologized and promised that lunches and plenty of water would be delivered by helicopter. She mimicked his accent: "Yesterday we haf terrible trouble with ze buses.' . . . This time there was one simple plan: half start on the east and half start on the west and 'Ve meet in ze meedel.' "[23]

The media had a field day. On Wednesday, September 8, the *San Francisco Chronicle* ran an article headline, THE RUNNING FENCE'S ILLEGAL LEAP. Photos showed "the immense conversation piece." that "materialized out of nowhere, illegally." The article stated that work had proceeded without benefit of the California Coastal Commission's final appeal hearing. Executive Director Bodovitz responded, "We'll treat it the same as any violation of the Coastal Act and ask the attorney general to take appropriate action." Deputy Attorney General Christopher Ames indicated his intention to move immediately for injunctive relief and punitive damages. "Some of Christo's enthusiasts were baffled and unhappy over the turn of events," the article observed. Lynn Hershman commented, "Many of us believe that Christo would never deviate from the law in this project, and we certainly hope he hasn't." An unnamed source stated, "He decided he would see his art work finished, even if it could mean fines or jail."[24]

Within hours, California's attorney general sought a temporary restraining order on behalf of the Coastal Commission. The artists urgently needed legal representation. Ed Anderson got the last-minute call. "It was late, and they couldn't reach Howard Nemerovski or Paul Kayfetz," he said. "Kayfetz had called me the day before, reporting that the fence was going into the ocean; he said people there were told that I had approved it."[25] Although Anderson had little familiarity with the environmental questions or the Coastal Act and generally practiced in Sonoma County, he agreed to represent the RFC before the Marin County Superior Court while Christos and Jeanne-Claude tried to locate Kayfetz.

On Wednesday morning, Christo finally tracked Kayfetz down. "Christo asked me to appear before the judge with Anderson. I explained that I didn't feel comfortable going into court on behalf of a client who had not told me the truth and had embarrassed me in front of the Coastal Commission by having me make representations that he didn't honor. I felt Anderson could do a fine job. The Christos were annoyed but not angry. He accepted what I said. There were no harsh words, no big scene; they didn't fire me."[26] Nevertheless, the RFC's high-powered legal team seemed to be unraveling.

That morning, Christo supervised determined crews working their way east from Meacham Hill. One young woman's long blond hair flowed out of a hard hat that proclaimed PEOPLE'S FENCE. By 10:00 A.M., an arabesque band of cloth snaked several miles closer to a linkup with its other half. Elizabeth Whitney and other foot soldiers worked their way slowly eastward from the coast. She felt the fence coming to life. "It was becoming not 2050 panels of nylon attached to 90 miles of steel cable with 312,000 hooks, but one thing—one undulating, rippling, billowing creature, a friendly land serpent, emerging and disappearing over and around hilltops, sneaking up behind us and disappearing in front of us, " Whitney wrote.[27]

Not everyone shared Whitney's aesthetic experience. "The student work force is dwindling as the second day of scorching heat takes its toll," Calvin Tomkins reported. He also observed Jeanne-Claude on the phone to Switzerland, trying to sell a drawing "so they can meet their next payroll"; a quarter-mile-long paper and string miniature fence made by two adolescents—it terminated in a toilet bowl alongside a sign, OUR FENCE LEADS TO THE WATER TOO. With reference to an aborted Christo press conference at the Bloomfield headquarters, Tomkins noted, "Everyone wants him to talk about what this morning's San Francisco *Chronicle* calls his 'illegal leap' to the ocean. But Christo refuses to discuss it. He refers them to his lawyers. He answers two questions, loses his temper, and slams out of the room."[28]

Ed Anderson and Scott Hades cheerfully faced the State of California, the Coastal Commission, and the Committee to Stop the Running Fence at an afternoon hearing. Anderson later described the proceedings: "Superior Court Judge David Menary snapped, 'What the hell is all this about? So this young prosecutor says, 'Well, they've violated this and built that.' The judge asked, 'What's going to happen?' The kid says, 'We think thousands of people are going to come and cause all kinds of environmental damage, harm the coast, do this, do that, and blah, blah, blah.' So Menary says, 'Wait a minute! I thought the purpose of the Coastal Act was to protect the coast *for* people. Now you're telling me the people will damage the coast. That doesn't make any sense to me.' The judge concluded, 'Anyway, I'm not doing anything. That's all. No injunction!' He scheduled another hearing for October 14, after the project. I never said anything!"[29]

At about 3:00 P.M., Jeanne-Claude, coordinating operations at the Bloomfield headquarters, received the good news. Anderson jovially related Judge Menary's response to a request to remove the work done in the coastal zone. Menary had said, "Why order him to take the fence down? He's going to take it down anyway. We'll have a hearing in a month or so. If there's any damage, it's the same now; it doesn't matter. If we have to fine, we'll fine him then. That's it!" A Maysles crew filmed Jeanne-Claude calling Christo as he worked frantically in the field. Other footage shows him listening to the crackling mobile phone. You can see the tension leave Christo's body as he smiles.

Morale remained a problem. The fence was far from finished and, because of the nonstop drive to complete work in Marin County before a possible injunction, meals had been cut short and defections continued. A combination of brutal heat and strong afternoon winds added to the toll. September 8 ended with efforts to keep the workforce intact. Committee to Stop the Running Fence leaders had a well-attended press conference on Lois and Ronald Raymond's back deck, facing a portion of the fence. They were disappointed by the Superior Court's nonruling and no less adamant in their opposition. Mary Fuller McChesney recalled, "The press was very sympathetic. The project was a tasteless, cheesy, artistic joke, environmentally inappropriate, you know, all the usual things. I remember they couldn't get the crews going and there were many technical problems getting it up. The Christos were very arrogant, expecting hard physical labor from those students at a minimal wage. I heard workers really bitching about it at the local bars. The work was way behind schedule. I thought it looked like Jean Harlow's nightgown."[30]

For most people, *Running Fence* offered an entertaining diversion from the impersonal swirl of world events. On September 10, as work resumed on the project, halfway around the world 800 million Chinese stood silent for three minutes as sirens announced the death of Chairman Mao Tse-tung. A *Time* magazine reporter posed the question, "Is [the fence] another Great Wall of China?" A smiling Christo replied, "No, it is not a Wall of China! China Great Wall built with purpose, therefore not a work of art. Work of art must be unusable! This fence is unusable!"[31] The accent quoted resembled mock Chinese rather than the artist's elusive Franco-Bulgarian. The superficial Great Wall/*Running Fence* comparison rested on their elongated, serpentine paths. The ephemeral fence, however, sat lightly on the landscape, animated, breathing with each air current, reflecting a quivering band of light. On September 9, the still-incomplete project was not yet a *running* fence.

As work crews gradually closed the gap between the eastern and western portion of the fence, the largest artwork ever created seemed poised to leap into the record books, art books, and the chronology of the twentieth century. Later in September, New York's Metropolitan Museum of Art would pay a record $3.25 million for a Rembrandt painting; the cost of *Running Fence* rapidly approached that figure.

Elizabeth Whitney's crew continued their drive eastward on day three. "I came to the ridge overlooking the area where people were still working, a long straight stretch on the valley floor," she wrote. "Scores of workers were there, at least ten per panel, opening and securing one panel after the other. From the top, a straight line of poles could be seen, and from each one flew out a billowing panel. It looked like a row of brides, I thought, their veils flying in the wind." Despite strenuous effort, the fence, "racing to find its other half," remained divided on Thursday night.[32]

On Friday, September 10, Day Four, there was a noticeable tension as the gap between the converging halves began to shrink. Whitney described Christo driving her crew toward completion: "Pleez. Moof now. We must moof now. We haf much more to do. Plees. Bring thees ladderz. Plees. Who iss doing thees panel?" At one point, dazzled and distracted by the fast-moving fence, Whitney found herself walking alongside Christo, wondering, "When will he stop to look at the Fence, or has he already seen it in his mind's eye?"[33]

By noon, the startling, evanescent *Running Fence* became whole. Bewildered, enchanted, skeptical spectators found release in the consummation of the unlikely, unrepeatable vision. Whitney reported, "A wonderful pandemonium of tourists, press, workers, monitors, passing motorists, cyclists, and locals shared the blazing hot sun making this the theatre event we all knew it really was." The hungry media fed on an orgy of relieved tension, leaping into print and onto TV screens in living rooms around the world. Workers poured water over one another, lapped at cans of beer, "letting ourselves be photographed to pieces." The three major American networks, German television, the Maysles' film crews, and legions of still photographers recorded the festive conclusion of a forty-two-month effort. "All of us who labored on it and loved it and hated it and laughed at it began to see it," wrote Whitney. "We saw the early morning sunlight turn it to quicksilver and the hot light of noon blaze down on it and outline its shadow in black."[34]

About two-thirds of the original workforce survived the grueling four-day effort. Exhausted but exhilarated, they gathered in Bloomfield to celebrate. Someone doused Christo with beer; he smiled broadly and said, "I'm very sorry that I was shouting so much." His wiry frame seemed to uncoil after the unremitting pressure. "Thank you. Thank you," he added, then gladly autographed an assortment of hard hats and T-shirts.

Many ranchers saw *their* fence for the first time. Some became tour guides. Charlotte Zwerin, a filmmaker working with the Maysles, said, "The ranchers . . . didn't understand that the Fence was a work of art until they saw it. Then . . . saw that all that effort produced something that they could admire and thought was beautiful."[35]

A Maysles crew filmed rancher Edward Pozzi approaching the fence. In the film, he greets a female worker and says, "I better see what's goin' on on my ranch. I'll never have this chance in another lifetime." Another sequence shows Lester Bruhn, wearing a cowboy hat, as he crouches in a quiet fog. Blowing a whistle, he calls his sheepdog. You can hear windblown fabric and metal clips making *pings* as sheep pass through an opening in the fence. Smiling, rancher Armand Mazzuchi says, "I think I'm going to come up and sleep here, right next to the fence." The camera finds Spirito Ballatore watching the fence disappear in the water. A straw hat casts a patterned shadow over his weathered face. Almost involuntarily, he whispers, "Beautiful. I can hardly believe it."

Christo later recalled sounds "like Buddhist monks in the hills" and "cows using poles to scratch themselves." In the fading light of September 10, he and Jeanne-Claude stood silhouetted against a saccharine sunset overlooking Bodega Bay. Christo, his face in shadow, laughed. "It looks like a giant scale model," he said.

She replied, "It's ready to take the slightest wind."

"Okay, Mrs. Christo?" he asked. Then they kissed.

Ecstatic contemplation of the epic project coincided with such mundane matters as mounting bills. Thirty-five sheriffs, three helicopters, and eighty round-the-clock monitors working twelve-hour shifts provided surveillance, maintenance, and traffic/trespass control. Christo and Jeanne-Claude estimated security costs at nine thousand dollars a day.

On Saturday, September 11, Christo and Jeanne-Claude were already in high gear before dawn. Their *Running Fence* quietly sprang to life in the morning mist. A gentle wind was like blood in its veins. The first and last of an endangered species rustled, flexing its muscles peacefully from Bodega Bay through two counties. It would grow more restless throughout the day. The hills, too, were alive with people. Everyone knew that the strange, inviting thing that hugged the ground was finite. The fence was to be terminated in twelve days or less; the Highway Patrol had authority to remove all or part of it at any time if, in their judgment, it posed a safety hazard. That Saturday, "thousands of people drove by in cars," Christo said. "The Fence was visible to sightseers on the beach two miles away. I loved the way the fabric shimmered in the wind, in the morning mists. It caught and reflected the changing light; it responded to the colors and contours of the landscape."[36]

Art collectors Dorothy and Herbert Vogel were thrilled to see the fence. Dorothy said, "I'll never forget walking along *Running Fence* because it was one of the most moving experiences we ever had. It was like being inside a work of art! The part near the water was most memorable—so exquisite. Photographs can't replace seeing it at different times of day as the light changed. We learned that you have to experience a project firsthand. Photos don't do it justice. The fence went on forever. Your eyes just didn't believe it. Actually seeing the project is like owning a work of art, because we own the experience of being there."[37]

Running Fence had a way of making friends; a surprising number of skeptics were quickly won over. The converts were seduced not by words or aesthetic theory but by the sprawling project's unexpectedly pleasant reality. John Walker, director emeritus of the National Gallery of Art in Washington, D.C., had real questions about whether *Running Fence* even qualified as a work of art. Seeing the realization of it made a believer of him. "The beauty of the curtains blowing in the wind as the Fence comes out of the sea and runs across the hills and meadows of California is to me one of the most moving sights I have seen," he said. "I must say I was moved quite literally to tears. I came to the conclusion the Fence is a work of art."[38]

David Bourdon harbored no doubts. "*Running Fence* was the most spectacular work of art I have ever seen. The movement was incredible. I remember seeing it from a car driving along winding roads. The road would be winding one way and the fence would be winding another. Sometimes the two were parallel. The fence literally did appear to be *running*. When it veered away from the road, it seemed to gallop off over a hilltop. Other times it would come rushing toward the road. It was an incredibly kinetic work."[39]

On Saturday, September 11, ranchers threw a dinner party in honor of Christo and Jeanne-Claude. Several hundred high-spirited friends jammed Freestone House, just north of Valley Ford. A former train station, brothel, and hotel—it was owned by Thomas Golden. Christo and Jeanne-Claude were recipients of an enormous *Running Fence* cake. Harry Milden, a Petaluma dairy farmer, presented the smiling couple with a bronze plaque. There were remarks by a number of landowners, inducing Ed Pozzi, who predicted the next project would be wrapping the moon. Ed Anderson sounded an eloquent note while addressing complaints that vast sums were wasted, given the ephemeral nature of the fence. "Life is temporary too," he said. "A moment between two eternities. And Christo has made that moment for us a lot brighter."[40]

All predictions of doom suddenly seemed as far-fetched as the fence itself. Crowds and traffic were manageable, low-flying planes did not drop from the skies, the coast escaped environmental damage, the parched hills did not explode into flames, deer, horses, dogs, cattle, sheep, chickens, and even a buffalo passed through numerous openings in the fence without becoming entangled, birds found it a convenient perch and managed to avoid fatal crashes into the fabric, vandalism was limited to a few souvenir hunters cutting patches of material, crime and trespass were nonproblems, people refused to litter, none fell victim to fence-related injury, and the visual pollution feared by some proved to be visual elation, bordering on the sublime for most.

Of course, there were some who continued to view the project as a moneymaking scam, an affront to art and the environment. However, Ed Anderson never met them. He maintained, "I have never been able to find anybody in Sonoma County since the fence went up who said they opposed it. In fact, everybody was a dedicated supporter right from the beginning. People think of it now as one of the greatest events in Sonoma County history, a positive experience in every way. Someone once said, 'Defeat is a bastard child, but victory is shared by God knows who' "[41]

The fence proved more engaging than forbidding. On September 14, Marin County's Board of Supervisors passed a resolution commending Christo and Jeanne-Claude for the "majestic" *Running Fence*. That afternoon, Jeanne-Claude noted "strong winds" in the family agenda. They certainly were. From afar, the convulsive calligraphic line asserted its unrestrained energy. Up close, it raged loudly, projecting real sculptural volume without solidity, given frenzied form by the rampaging wind. Neither barrier nor enclosure, the fence reflected sunlight and moonlight, rode and revealed the waves, embraced cascading hills and valleys, and, Christo liked to say, "gave shape to the wind."

Jeanne-Claude called the rolling hills the most beautiful anywhere. The free-flowing ribbon of fabric enhanced and emphatically underscored a quiet beauty that for some had become invisible through benign neglect. Art historian Werner Spies wrote, "The high, bulky curtain is transformed into lines that trace a drawing across the tawny land faded by heat and drought. An autonomous drawing, which sometimes follows the contours of the ground but for the most part changes them, lopping off hilltops, inscribing a softer, dreamlike landscape over the existing one."[42] English writer Lady Marina Vaizey observed that the meandering fence "sculpts the land, and is in turn sculpted by the wind and light. It intensifies the characteristics, physical and emotional, of the way in which we apprehend the meeting points of man and landscape. And it has cost nobody, except Christo, anything."[43]

Some art-world observers called the *Running Fence* one of the most surprising, spectacular works of the century. A few added the word *spiritual.* During the fence's final days, imminent removal only underscored the poignant urgency of experiencing its quicksilver beauty, wavering between reality and abstraction. Ranchers, visitors, and workers counted down the remaining hours. Christo spoke of the "suicidal nature" and "the involuntary beauty of the ephemeral." Then it was gone.

On September 21, two weeks of billowing spasms ended in premeditated, inevitable removal. The memory phase of *Running Fence* began. Sonoma County would celebrate the achievement, designating pole 7-33 a historic landmark. The Coastal Commission had other ideas; on September 23, it voted to deny a permit for the by-then-removed ocean segment. On October 14, it instituted a suit against the RFC, seeking ten thousand dollars in civil penalties and five hundred for every day the fence had violated the coastal zone. Ted Dougherty recalled, "To avoid further legal expenses, the Christos offered to settle for a total of ten thousand dollars. When the Coastal Commission accepted, the Committee to Stop the Running Fence finally disbanded."[44] Their relentless opposition had cost the artists an estimated $300,000 in legal expenses, or 10 percent of the project's eventual $3 million price tag. Christo and Jeanne-Claude left California deeply in debt. Many people were forced to wait for payments.

By October 23, 1976, most materials had been distributed to the ranchers, trucks and other specialized equipment were being sold, and no physical trace of *Running Fence* remained other than in people's memories and in the extensive documentation of every facet of the project. "Everything was recycled," Jeanne-Claude said. "Fifty-nine families used the poles to build cattle guards, the fabric to cover stacks of hay, piles of manure, and tractors. Some ranchers made curtains, even two wedding dresses."

Running Fence left an afterglow in its wake, resonating in photographs, books, drawings, film, and in the memories of those who had seen it evolve. The work also lived on in a large documentation exhibition that started its world tour at a museum in Rotterdam. When former project worker Tom Golden heard about the opening, he immediately began to organize a group trip to the Netherlands. "I kept calling ranchers and supporters," Golden recalled, "telling them, 'It's going to be wonderful.' "[45] On June 30, 1977 a troupe of twenty-five enthusiastic Marin and Sonoma county adventurers boarded a flight for Europe.

The ranchers arrived in Rotterdam on July Fourth. Christo was already there, busy installing the exhibition at the Museum Boymans-van-Beuningen. Tom Golden said, "There were hordes of people. I remember the Mayor of Rotterdam threw this big party. The ranchers and the Christos were guests of honor."[46]

Albert and David Maysles and Charlotte Zwerin's upbeat *Running Fence* film contributed to the project's afterlife and mythology, capturing the sense of urgency people felt in the face of such quicksilver beauty. Their hour of mesmerizing footage followed the artists' near-impossible dream, from negotiated leases through packed, interminable hearings, construction, and realization. The film culminates with a series of incredible vistas, the couple and their majestic fence framed in a glorious sunset. Lynn Hershman, who went on to become an independent filmmaker and artist, critiques the happy ending: "I think it would have been stronger if it showed the whole process, including the end of it. The destruction—death—is part of the process. There is more to the story, including the effect it had on people's lives. The fence still exists."[47]

The film drew both lavish praise and bitter attacks. *Village Voice* film critic J. Hoberman complained about the artist and the documentation: "How the maestro raised $3 million is apparently a subject which didn't interest the Maysles brothers. . . . [They] are grievously lax in following up on their subject's repeated assertion that his art is a 'very deep political, social, economic experience.' "[48] In contrast, reviewer Michael Florescu gave it a rave review: "The film succeeds precisely because the image of the Fence overwhelms all attempts to explain it, and, what is more, transcends all of the emotions it aroused." The fence, Florescu wrote, is Christo's "art *hors catégorie*" and a "powerful manifestation of the free spirit."[49]

For forty-two months, Christo and Jeanne-Claude had watched the fence gather energy and develop its own reality. It grew beyond anything they had imagined.

13

Team Christo

Art critic Harold Rosenberg, moderating a panel whose topic was "Time and Space Concepts," speculated that very few in the audience had seen Christo's *Running Fence* or *Wrapped Coast* but suggested that everyone present had probably seen photos or films of them. Rosenberg stated that since "the transitory nature of certain types of works makes them inexpedient for the gallery," in the case of environmental art "the gallery is replaced by the media."[1] However, few in the media could deal with the complexities of *Running Fence* with anything more than tongue-in-cheek commentary, questions concerning the artist's motives, and short sound bites expressing utter amazement.

Situated in the real world, energized by real people and real controversy, Christo and Jeanne-Claude's most recent project had proved to be among the most political, most publicized artworks of the twentieth century. Looking back, Christo said, "*Running Fence* grew like a child, beyond anything I could imagine. It built its own reality."[2] A number of publications quoted Christo as saying, "Every project is bigger than my imagination." Jeanne-Claude also talked about the expansive, energy-gathering nature of the fence; her comments rarely appeared in print, however. After all, she was regarded as simply the artist's wife and dealer, an attractive foil for a self-proclaimed prophet whom *Time* magazine called "a small wiry man with an intense stare and a manic thirst for promotion."[3] Ted Dougherty remembered, "Jeanne-Claude was lost in Christo's shadow. She doesn't like to be out in the spotlight. After working so hard, I don't think she got much satisfaction out of *his* success. She needs recognition, too."[4]

The artists found themselves in what became a familiar state following each project: perpetually threatened, if not by outright bankruptcy, then by a critical cash-flow problem. Raising the stakes on each new effort forced the couple to take a year or more to become solvent again. Fortunately, any highly publicized, realized project stimulated purchases. Christo produced art objects; Jeanne-Claude produced sales. Each knew exactly what the other was doing and freely offered advice on how to do it. In 1977, operating without benefit of studio assistants—an increasingly rare occurrence for an established artist—Christo developed plans for a number of complex projects, including *Wrapped Reichstag* for Berlin, *Wrapped Walk Ways* for Saint Stephen's Green in Dublin, *Wrapped Monument to Cristobal Colón* for Barcelona, *The Mastaba of Abu Dhabi* for the United Arab Emirates, *Wrapped Bridge* for Paris, *Wrapped Floor* for Munich, and *56 Barrels* for the Kröller-Müller Museum in Otterlo, the Netherlands.

In 1977, with more time for studio work and travel, Christo supported the airline industry with seventy-nine flights to scores of cities, including Berlin, Barcelona, Dublin, Tel Aviv, and Tokyo; he installed exhibitions, gave lectures, and examined potential project sites. A typical highly focused tour began on January 9 with a flight to Düsseldorf. The next day, Christo met with Werner Spies, who was preparing an essay for a small *Running Fence* book. Jeanne-Claude tended to remain in New York, but even she accrued thirty-five days of foreign travel that year, with additional stops in a number of American cities.

In Berlin, on January 15, 1977, Christo convinced Mayor Klaus Schütz to endorse the *Wrapped Reichstag* proposal. Two days later, the plan suffered a setback in Bonn when the Bundestag Presidium rejected the idea. President Karl Carstens informed Christo that he personally favored wrapping the former parliament, but as president of the Bundestag, he had to oppose it. The artist also met with Willy Brandt; the Social Democratic party chairman, former chancellor, and Berlin mayor offered his support. Christo returned to Bonn and Berlin three more times in 1977.

On January 24, while Christo installed an exhibition at the Jerusalem Museum, Swedish art dealer Carl Flach called Jeanne-Claude in New York to report a collector's interest in a large *Running Fence* drawing priced at fourteen thousand dollars. "Christo had an enormous effect on newcomers to art who were frightened by the highbrow attitude of the traditional dealer," said Flach. "His work offered a marvelous bridge for bringing them into the art world. The Christos operate outside the art system, which is something of a private club. Christo has a way of making people feel they are joining him on a daring voyage. Through it all, he has humility. It's marvelous to see a human being indulge himself in something irrational. We all secretly dream of doing that. He gives people hope that they can do what they really want to in life."[5]

Flach's client, Torsten Lilja, bought the large *Running Fence* drawing and bought into the Christo mystique. On February 15, he and his wife, Kerstin, visited Christo's studio. Enthralled by the art and the artist, they began what was to become the largest, finest collection of Christo's work: their own—the Lilja Art Fund Foundation. Lilja became a powerful ally. In the future, his commitment to Christo and Jeanne-Claude was to translate into major purchases at critical junctures. "In raising large amounts of money, Christo and Jeanne-Claude sometimes gets into a bind," Lilja said. "Then you can get a telephone call in the middle of the night asking for immediate help. But I don't mind that. Christo is charming, generous, and loyal to people. When he promises something, he does it."[6]

Torsten Lilja called his new friends "Team Christo." Impressed by their creative process and artistic integrity, he said, "I have come to regard them as not only preeminent artists, but also as a team with a unique natural talent for entrepreneurship. . . . They may not do everything in the most efficient and professional way, but what they lack in efficiency they make up in enthusiasm. . . . The Christos have initiated a whole new development in the art world."[7]

"All of our projects," Christo said, "have this fragile quality. They will be gone tomorrow. They will be missed. These projects are absolutely irrational. Nobody needs a *Valley Curtain* or a *Running Fence.* They do not exist because the president of a republic would like to have them, or some mayor or representative of the National Endowment for the Arts. They exist because *we* want them. They have total freedom. This is why they cannot stay. Because freedom is the enemy of possession, and possession is equal to permanence. You have to have freedom with no strings attached. This is why we pay for our projects. What is really exciting is to borrow space that has never been part of the art experience. In a gallery or museum, that space is absolutely serene, pristine. Outside, in the real world, everything is owned by somebody. Twenty-four hours, around the clock, we are funneled through highly controlled space, designed by urban planners or politicians. That space is owned by so many people, with so many jurisdictions. We love that space and want to borrow it for a short moment to create a gentle disturbance."

Reminders of mortality were everpresent. On April 2, 1977, Jeanne-Claude wrote in the family agenda, "Mia is no more." Both she and Christo felt a profound sense of loss at the death of Martin Visser's wife. Another close acquaintance, the artist, Oyvind Fahlstrom, had died several months earlier of a brain tumor. William Saroyan wrote that every real artist takes a position on death: Some remind you of it; others help you forget about it. Christo and Jeanne-Claude's work does both.

That summer, after the Rotterdam opening of the *Running Fence* exhibition, Christo, Jeanne-Claude, and Cyril spent a few days with the Guillebon family in Tunisia. After a pleasantly uneventful stay, they proceeded to Nice, Paris, and Hamburg, where Christo produced an edition of six packages of *Die Zeit Newspapers, Wrapped;* each bundle contained eight folded copies of *Die Zeit,* capped by a photograph of one of the tabloid's six cultural editors, visible through clear polyethylene tied with rope. They then made a final stop in Berlin. On July 22, the Christos engaged Mayor Dietrich Stobbe in "constructive discussions" regarding the *Wrapped Reichstag* proposal.

Back at Howard Street, Christo resumed work. An ongoing body of carefully crafted art objects reflected his unique working process. He explained, "I draw in a different way. When I travel to sites or work in real physical space, that is part of the drawing. I never start from zero. I use maps, photography, technical drawings, diagrams, and other things. All that is combined to produce a small sketch, elaborate collage, or scale model. In the studio, I work on many, many things. I make connections. Starting or finishing drawings is not only done on paper. They connect the formal elements related to the locations."

Christo often thought about his parents. Images of his mother lingered: Tzveta Yavachev, at their tearful 1956 farewell in Sofia's airport; that last embrace was half a lifetime ago for the forty-two-year-old artist. In 1977, still enduring the bleak routines of a repressive Communist regime, Tzveta, age seventy-one, suffered from a litany of medical problems, including cataracts in both eyes and severe troubles with her knees. She was nearly blind and crippled.

Christo's brothers, Anani and Stefan, were not allowed to leave Bulgaria other than for rare visits to other countries in Eastern Europe. Separation from Anani had been particularly painful for Christo; his older brother had remarried, had a son, and continued to win national recognition as an actor, despite roadblocks by petty Party bureaucrats aware of Christo's defection.

The Christos sent money to Tzveta and Vladimir whenever possible and repeatedly tried to arrange for them to travel to the West. Jeanne-Claude recalled, "We desperately tried to arrange for them to leave. Every petition we made was rejected." Christo said, "The Carter administration demanded that Communist countries allow a fixed number of their people with relatives in Western Europe or America to travel. I remember we talked to Vice President Mondale's wife, Joan. She helped us." Joan Mondale had seen and been enormously impressed by the Maysles' *Running Fence* film. She felt it portrayed American democracy at its best and wanted it shown worldwide. After conversations with Christo and Jeanne-Claude, Mrs. Mondale enlisted the U.S. ambassador to Bulgaria to facilitate visas for Tzveta and Vladimir Yavachev.

A breakthrough finally came in August 1977. Permission would be granted. The couple sent five hundred dollars to Bulgaria on August 19 and another five hundred four days later. Christo planned to see his parents in Paris that November. Jeanne-Claude said, "Our opthamologist friend, Dr. Patrice de Laage, and his wife, Elizabeth, made arrangements for Tzveta's eye operations at his clinic on the Riviera. Patrice also set up the operations on her knees."

Christo spent most of September meeting with German politicians, press, and others, installing the *Running Fence* exhibition and a small *Wrapped Reichstag* display at Bonn's Rheinisches Landesmuseum, arranging exhibitions in Zurich and Vienna, and mounting shows in Tokyo and Kyoto.[8] Meanwhile, in New York, Jeanne-Claude pursed other possibilities. On September 23, she telephoned her father to get advice on how to enlist Paris Mayor Jacques Chirac's support for the *The Pont Neuf Wrapped, Project for Paris;* the notion of wrapping the city's oldest bridge had intrigued the artists since 1975. As usual, they were moving at full speed on several fronts.

Before the long-awaited reunion with his parents, Christo flew to Minneapolis for an opening at the Walker Art Center and then on to subsequent discussions in Kansas City, where the Nelson Gallery's newly formed Contemporary Art Society (CAS) had invited him to come and propose a large-scale work. Christo arrived in Kansas City on October 29, 1977. CAS president, collector Byron Cohen; art dealer James Morgan; and the Nelson's curator of twentieth-century art, Ellen Goheen, provided a whirlwind tour. "We drove around and looked at the Missouri River and the parks," Goheen said. "The places we thought Christo might like didn't interest him. We proposed Penn Valley Park, a big public space with undulating hills near the heart of the city. He finally chose Loose Park. It was near the Nelson Gallery and had an appealing topography with English and formal gardens. It was doable and more focused."[9] Before finalizing his selection of Loose Park, Christo telephoned New York to describe the site to Jeanne-Claude. "What do you think?" he asked her.

"If you like it, I like it," she responded. *Wrapped Walk Ways* quickly became a high priority in their lives.

En route to Paris on Sunday, November 6, Christo spent much of the long flight in reverie, considering the prospect of seeing his beloved parents. He later described the cold evening of November 8, when they arrived at Orly Airport: "My mother was almost blind and could hardly walk. She was crying. We stayed in Paris for a few days, went to see Jeanne-Claude's parents, but the pain made it almost impossible for her to walk. My parents talked about the years of misery in Bulgaria. They and my brothers had suffered because I escaped to the West. It was a very nasty, nasty period. They could never write about all these terrible Communist characters who made life miserable. Idiotical things; no good heat, no good medical care. Her whole body ached because they refused to operate. They said, 'We only care about young people; old people can die.' My parents were not young, so we decided to have them stay in the south of France. It was warmer, and all her operations would take place there."

On November 12, Christo accompanied his parents to the Riviera. The next day, he flew to London for the opening of a one-man show at the Annely Juda Gallery, then returned to Nice. From Nice, he flew to Hannover, where, joined by Jeanne-Claude, he installed an exhibition at the Kestner Gesellschaft. When they returned once more to Nice, Jeanne-Claude finally met her mother-in-law. She and Tzveta spoke French. Christo communicated through expressive body language, an infectious smile, and a mixture of halting Bulgarian, fractured French, and a sprinkle of German. In a taxi, Jeanne-Claude noticed that Tzveta had no purse. "Christo's mother said she hadn't owned a purse since the 1940s," said Jeanne-Claude. "I asked her about Sofia. She pointed to the driver and said, 'Shush, shush.' 'Mama,' I told her, 'this is Nice. The driver doesn't give a hoot.' She insisted, 'They're all spies.' Two minutes later, Christo's father was shocked when he saw a butcher shop still filled with meat in the afternoon."

Christo and Jeanne-Claude met Anani's second wife, Didi, for the first time. She had also obtained permission to visit France for a brief period. Didi joined the Yavachevs at their hotel. Anani and their four-year-old son had been detained in Bulgaria to ensure her return. Didi also told of the horror stories that plagued everyday life.

On November 17, Tzveta's cataracts were removed. After the operations, Christo and Jeanne-Claude secured an apartment in Nice for her and Vladimir. Jeanne-Claude said, "It was a place we had rejected at first because the window looked right out on the street. We thought at their age it would be too much noise and they would want something quieter. Not at all! She adored the whole thing, looking at cars all day long." On January 4, 1978, Tzveta underwent two knee-replacement operations. "With all of the surgery, they stayed until June," Christo said. "Jeanne-Claude and I never knew the Riviera. We had only been to Arman's house in Vence one Christmas. By spending a lot of time showing my parents things, we discovered the Riviera and Provence."

Jeanne-Claude recalled that after Tzveta's successful operations, "Vladimir would playfully complain, 'What have you done? Now she sees everything, she's taller, and runs around so fast, I can't keep up with her.'"

The proposed *Wrapped Walk Ways* project for Kansas City represented a logical extension of earlier efforts involving horizontal surfaces. This interest dated from 1968, when the sight of vast expanses of fabric and rope stretched out on the ground between attempts to raise the *5,600 Cubicmeter Package* in Kassel suggested a range of expressive possibilities. The following year,

Wrapped Coast demonstrated the concept's viability. At that time, the artists had been impressed by people's sensitivity to garden paths in Japan, Cambodia, India, and Thailand. Other related projects in 1969 included *Wrapped Floor* in Christo's studio; *Wrapped Floor* and *Wrapped Staircase* at the Wide White Space Gallery in Antwerp; *Wrap In Wrap Out* at Chicago's Museum of Contemporary Art; and a series of studies depicting *Wrapped Walk Ways: Two Parks Project*, designed for simultaneous installation in Tokyo and Arnhem. In 1971, the process evolved with *Wrapped Floors, Covered Windows, and Wrapped Walk Ways* for Haus Lange in Krefeld, Germany. The more than three hundred feet of paths wrapped in a beige-gray synthetic fabric at Haus Lange were only a small fraction of what was proposed in 1976 as *Wrapped Walk Ways* for Saint Stephen's Green in downtown Dublin. Permission was denied.

Jeanne-Claude grimaced when she said, "We felt damn sure we were going to do Saint Stephen's. It was a great disappointment." Christo compared it to Loose Park: "Of Course Saint Stephen's was more famous, more poetic. It would have been exciting to do because every writer in the world had been there. Nobody knows Loose Park. But we wanted to realize the Kansas City project. In Dublin there was a small square, very convenient to do. The Loose Park situation was similar." The transient magic carpet they planned for Loose Park had the potential to transport everyday routine into extraordinary experience. It would demonstrate again how little had to be changed to alter conceptually everything viewers and participants took for granted. The intervention of fabric between walkways and the feet of pedestrians and joggers could do just that, transforming hard paths into a soft, sensual carpet.

Before Christo began his usual series of preparatory drawings and collages, he and Jeanne-Claude discussed at length aesthetics, choice and color of fabric, logistical considerations, and strategy.

On December 31, Christo and Jeanne-Claude boarded a train for Boston. They spent the waning hours of 1977 there with James Fuller, poring over plans that showed every tree and path in Jacob L. Loose Memorial Park. Fuller, a quietly thorough businessman who had worked with Mitko Zagoroff on other Christo projects, had been preparing fabric and installation options for *Wrapped Walk Ways* since mid-November. He relished the challenge. "I enjoy a process that brings so many diverse people together and gets them to look at familiar sights in totally new ways," said Fuller.[10]

The first formal presentation of *Wrapped Walk Ways* took place in Kansas City on January 11, 1978, as a bemused Parks and Recreation Department considered the proposal. Was it serious? Was it art? The artists, a handful of supporters, three commissioners, Parks director Frank Vaydik, assistant director Jerry Darter, and a few reporters filled the small meeting room. Ellen Goheen recalled the board's initially cautious response to the project: "Of course, part of Christo's deal is that he wants some controversy. We had the enthusiastic backing of the Contemporary Art Society, and director Vaydik was supportive in presenting the idea. Winning over the park commissioners was another matter. They were three distinct personalities jockeying for the spotlight. There were real concerns about public safety that had to be addressed." A preparatory work by Christo did not help. The collage depicted horizontal folds across some walkways, raising fear that pedestrians or joggers might become entangled or tripped up by the fabric. "They asked for safety assurances and more information before deciding," said Goheen.[11] The request was tabled until February.

Unlike *Running Fence*, however, the Loose Park venture failed to ignite a firestorm of protest. Initial opposition was muted. A few letters to the editor complained about the CAS's misguided elitism, the peculiar art, and the wasteful expenditure of an estimated forty thousand dollars. Letters pro and con created a civilized stir. However, measured criticism never escalated into a Committee to Stop the Wrapped Walk Ways or any organized opposition.

The Christos left town, not to return until the February hearing.

On January 20, 1978, Christo arrived in Munich to finalize plans for *Wrapped Floor*, a project for Galerie Art in Progress. Two days later, he flew to Copenhagen, where Jeanne-Claude joined him for the January 24 opening of the *Running Fence* documentation exhibition. That night at the Louisiana Museum, Dr. Jivka Langvad, a transplanted Bulgarian and a linguist, introduced herself. She not only knew Christo's older brother, Anani, but was Didi's best friend. Langvad recalled, "Christo was extremely shy. He had forgotten his Bulgarian. I tried to understand him. As a language specialist, I know that people think in either words or pictures. He thinks in pictures so much that he forgets languages. His French isn't fantastic, either. His Bulgarian is the worst. He never had a chance to speak his mother tongue after going to the West. The pronunciation is correct, but there's a loss of words and an inability to construct sentences properly. I felt sorry for him. It was painful to listen because he tried and really cared. You could see how embarrassed he was."

Langvad worked for an international health organization and traveled freely to and from Bulgaria. She briefed Christo on Anani and current conditions in the country. Not surprisingly, everyday life remained bleak there.

Jivka Langvad later reflected, "Anani used to be very temperamental. Once, he slapped an actress who missed a line or irritated him in some way. She went around for several months in a neck brace. Now he's really mellow. He still storms about and screams, but at those moments, we don't pay attention." Langvad portrayed Christo's younger brother Stefan as "an average, obedient citizen," unlike Anani and Didi.

"Anani had been persecuted because of Christo's defection," Langvad explained. "It remained a large stain on his biography. In the 1960s, Anani played only lead parts. Young schoolgirls went absolutely crazy over him, swooning every time he appeared on-screen. People everywhere recognized him. Despite his fame, he remained modest, congenial, unspoiled, and unsnobbish. Anani has a heart of gold. One day, he fought with a high-ranking Communist in the cinema world. Afterward, the man screamed, 'You're finished!' He actually stopped Anani from making movies, but since then, he's been a celebrated theater and television actor. He remained a star, but if not for that fight, he could have continued like a comet in cinema."[12]

Christo himself recalled that Anani's movies had been shown in Cannes, Venice, and Berlin. "Even though he was invited to those film festivals, they never allowed him to go—a punishment. Another thing, in a Communist country, a famous leading actor receives a title like 'Artist of the People.' The title is not so important, but it would have given him a higher salary. Because of my defection, Anani never received the title."

Christo and Jeanne-Claude returned to Kansas City on February 13, where they met with project director Jim Fuller. All three left the next day, after a snowstorm postponed the Parks and Recreation Department's board meeting.

The artists were not present on February 21, when the project hit a snag: the Kansas City Art Commission. Ellen Goheen said, "The Art Commission wasn't very interested, and I don't think they liked the project. We didn't need their approval, but approaching them added some more controversy."[13] The commissioners raised questions of access to the park, cost, and safety before a tie vote failed to endorse the proposal. One commissioner, Ileana Ingraham, grumbled, "It just doesn't do anything. If it were my money I'd rather see another contemporary artist."[14] However, most observers agreed that the commission had no jurisdiction over *Wrapped Walk Ways* because of its temporary nature.

Christo and Jeanne-Claude appeared at Atlanta's High Museum in February then went to Miami for the March opening of a Christo exhibition sponsored by the American Foundation for the Arts. They then returned to Kansas City on March 14 to present his proposal, which would cover every footpath in the park with golden-colored nylon fabric. Parks director Vaydik and three commissioners listened attentively. Their typical agenda and areas of expertise did little to prepare them for this unfamiliar brand of art. Most questions concerned potential safety hazards.

Jim Fuller assured the Board that no one would be denied park access. Fuller asked the commissioners to prepare a list of requirements, including insurance, and promised that each provision would be honored. He recalled,

"We had to convince park officials that we weren't talking about a trivial affair. And of course park officials are park officials. They're used to dealing with hard realities, and they were difficult to convince."[15]

The *Kansas City Times* quoted Christo as saying, "I think it would be a very beautiful work of art. . . . You will watch your feet." He likened it to reading: "It will take you time to see. It cannot be seen at once." Christo also reminded everyone that the work was temporary. Ralph T. Coe, director of the Nelson Gallery, stated that the gallery was "behind this 900 percent." Parks board president Richard L. Marr commented, "I think we're basically for the project." There were no opponents speaking against the project, although newspaper letters and letters and telephone calls to the board were running against the plan. Marr and board member Carl Magliazzo wanted to see a sample section installed in Loose Park before making a decision. Another unenthusiastic board member, Dr. Jeremiah Cameron, said that he would probably vote yes so that residents had a chance to see the project and make up their own minds. He confessed, "Personally I don't think it's much of a contribution to art."[16] Fortunately, the projected forty-thousand-dollar budget required no tax dollars. The board, however, would not vote on the proposal until its April meeting.

On April 11, one day before the fabric tests, Jim Fuller and Ted Dougherty arrived in Kansas City, as did the artists. Dougherty had finally put his credit in order and begun work on technical and contracting issues related to *Wrapped Walk Ways*. Christo and Jeanne-Claude had envisioned a highly reflective fabric, "golden, like the wheat." A sample covering a section of sidewalk seemed closer to beige. "Christo didn't like it," the *Kansas City Star* reported. City councilman Harold Hamil didn't like anything he saw. He drafted a resolution stating that the council "officially disassociates itself from the proposed plan" and warned park officials not to use public funds for the project. "Things like this are stunts this guy likes to capitalize on," Hamil said. "My personal opinion is that it is an absurdity."[17]

Byron Cohen, Ellen Goheen, Parks and Recreation Department commissioners, and staff seemed more concerned about safety than about color as they strolled along an abbreviated patch of fabric. "I liked it," said Richard Marr. He saw little danger of tripping over the careful horizontal folds that gave the path texture. Jeremiah Cameron found the demonstration more impressive than any preparatory drawing. "When the sunlight falls on that nylon and sets it sparkling, it's very beautiful." Christo told the *Kansas City Times,* "We hope when the leaves are falling over the *Wrapped Walk Ways* it will be very beautiful. . . . This is our aim, to make people aware they're putting their feet on something different."[18]

That night, a generally supportive crowd of over seven hundred jammed Atkins Auditorium at the Nelson Gallery to view the *Running Fence* film. The audience responded enthusiastically or with polite questions. One skeptic cited the possibility congested traffic and parking around Loose Park, saying, "This is all great if you don't have to live around it." He asked Christo, "Have you considered the impact on the surrounding neighborhood and on people just trying to get to work as part of your art?" People *are* part of the art, Christo replied, adding, "We are ready to remove the project in twenty-four hours if they cannot stand it."[19]

On April 14, Christo lectured in San Diego. The next night, he and Jeanne-Claude flew from New York to Paris. Then, on April 16, in Hamburg, they met with a group of distinguished Germans to found the *Kuratorium für Christos Projekt Reichstag*. The board, inaugurated to build support for the *Wrapped Reichstag* project, consisted of seventeen influential citizens. Christo, Jeanne-Claude, and Scott Hodes attended an organizational meeting at the home of Gerd Bucerius, publisher of *Die Zeit*.

On April 18, the Kansas City Parks and Recreation Department's board met to consider *Wrapped Walk Ways*. The turnout was sparse. Board president Marr called for project opponents to be heard. No one rose to speak. The minutes state that those favoring the idea expressed their support by acclamation. A motion to accept by Commissioner Migliazzo won unanimous approval quickly. About a dozen supporters clapped after the vote. Parks director Frank Vaydik said it was the first time he could remember his board being applauded. Everyone smiled broadly.

On June 13, the artists' forty-third birthday, Byron Cohen and Richard Marr signed an agreement outlining safety procedures and establishing a two-week display period in October. In addition, ten days were allotted for installation, as well as five days for removal. The artists would pay for materials, labor, and insurance.

The Christos' worldwide travels continued unabated, with trips to Zurich for the June 2 opening of the *Running Fence* exhibition at the Kunstgewerbe Museum and then to Nice to visit his parents before their return to Bulgaria. They then flew to Paris, Stockholm, Oslo, Zurich, Nice, Brussels, Düsseldorf, Frankfurt, Milan, and Sydney before returning to America.

The couple's attention remained fixed on *Wrapped Walk Ways*. Christo made several trips to the Putnam-Herzl Factory in Putnam, Connecticut, to finalize the choice of color and oversee the job with Jim Fuller. The fabric—136,268 square feet of it in rolls varying in width from 44 to 64½ inches—was pressure-dyed a radiant saffron. The material was shipped to Rubber Fabricators in Craigsville, West Virginia, where 52,000 feet of seams and side hems were sewn and 34,500 half-inch brass grommets were inserted at twelve-inch intervals along the hems.

Meanwhile, a few art critics, journalists, and letter writers were having a field day in the Kansas City press. Repeated assurances that Christo would pay all project expenses and even donate a collage to the Nelson Gallery did little to slow a torrent of suggestions for alternative ways to spend the money. One resident proposed, "For $40,000 we could put some . . . poets . . . in trees at Loose Park; park users could simply ring a bell on a low branch and the poet would read a poem. . . . [They] could tell the poet to get back up in his tree if they didn't like the poems."[20]

In a letter to the *Kansas City Star,* two residents sarcastically sympathized with those "well-educated, artistically sophisticated newcomers" being "stuck here in the boonies among us ill-educated, unsophisticated and unappreciative bumpkins." Without naming the CAS, they wrote that while they thought the project "harmless," they did object to anyone trying to convince the citizens of Kansas City that they would witness one of the greatest artistic achievements of the century. Great art, in their view, should speak for itself. Pointing out that someone once said that the more minimal the art, the more maximal the explanation, they concluded: "In view of the lengthy articles and other publicity surrounding this project, one can only conclude that this is indeed 'minimal' art."[21]

Christo rejected the word *minimal.* He repeatedly characterized *Wrapped Walk Ways* as "simple, direct, intimate—like chamber music," and, above, all "public." Loose Park's seventy-four easily accessible acres were actively utilized every day by a diverse public. On September 26, with preparations on schedule, materials in place, and fabric installation only a week away, Jeanne-Claude noted in the family agenda, "Take bullhorn, slides and film." A worldwide network of friends, family, and art-world figures was about to converge on an increasingly curious city. Letters and telephone calls invited or reminded supporters to come. On September 28, the *Wrapped Walk Ways* exhibition opened at the Nelson Gallery/Atkins Museum.

On Sunday, October 1, 1978, one day before beginning the fabric installation in Loose Park, workers assembled for an orientation session. Contractor August Huber had hired eighty-four people: thirteen construction workers, sixty-seven unskilled laborers, and four professional seamstresses. Howard Glover and C. D. Wigham, Jr., had spent the previous week as part of a Huber crew that prepared sidewalks and paths by cleaning, filling holes, and covering steps with wood. Both men had taken good-natured ribbing from fellow workers who accused them of being publicity hounds and, yes, even artists. The men smiled, admitting they were not always enthusiastic about the project. Wigham reflected, "At least it's something different. . . . We didn't volunteer for this job, but then I'm not sure we wouldn't if we ever had the chance again. I've got to say it's been fun."[22]

On Monday morning, October 2, Suzanne Richards joined her cleanup crew. "I haven't gotten up in the middle of the night to go anywhere in a long time," she said. "There was a great sense of urgency and no time for casual conversation at the onset, and within ten minutes of my arrival I was down on my knees picking rocks around the lake." By midafternoon, Richards had been given a crash course in adhering metal eyelets to the edge of the fabric. "I became known as the grommet lady," Richards said. Eventually, 34,500 steel spikes would be driven into the soil through brass grommets. Richards wrote, "I went home Monday, after ten hours of work and thirty minutes for lunch, utterly exhausted, and woke up Tuesday so stiff, I wondered if it was going to be possible to put in another ten. But as the morning chill and darkness disappeared, so did my stiffness."[23]

The workforce was made up of a diverse group of men and women. The youngest worker, Anselm Spoerri, the son of collector Elka Spoerri, had come all the way from Switzerland to help. Another unskilled laborer, Kansas City art dealer Susan Lawrence, had known Loose Park intimately since childhood. She and her crew were instructed on how to arrange and secure the cloth properly while hammering spikes into grommets. Lawrence recalled the Monday start:

> We were given yellow shirts, work aprons, and work gloves, hammers and nails. Dressed in blue jeans and denim work shirt, I felt that I looked professional in my first experience as a construction worker. Later I would add knee pads to my costume and decorate my sleeves with orange fabric streamers. I felt that the way I looked was part of the work of art. . . . After initial delays and confusions, the fabric began to flow like a river over the walks. As the sun rose higher, the saffron fabric began to shimmer and glow as the light hit the folds. Sometimes it looked like velvet.[24]

Freelance writer Rosemary Smithson, aglow with shoulder length saffron hair and wearing a yellow T-shirt emblazoned WRAPPED WALK WAYS on the back, was assigned to a Constant Cleanup Crew. Preceding the nailing crews, Constant Cleanup swept the walks and picked up twigs, debris, and "doggie messes." Eventually, pooper-scoopers were flown in from New York. A seamstress made large trash bags from the fabric for each cleanup team. Smithson said, "Jeanne-Claude was a driving force in the project. She directed workers with a handheld bullhorn. There was no goldbricking unless you put some park between yourself and Jeanne-Claude. [As for Christo,] he moved quickly from crew to crew, and you never knew when he might surface to suggest a better way to do something. He even stopped to examine stitches."[25]

On Monday afternoon, the sky darkened. So did the fabric. Work continued throughout an extended downpour. Smithson said, "Rush-hour traffic was treated to the scene of Catherine Mathews, professional seamstress, with

Kansas City, Missouri, 1978: Christo and Jeanne-Claude during the *Wrapped Walk Ways*. (Photo: Wolfgang Volz)

her sewing machine and a small army of gold-shirted assistants with needles and thread, hammers and spikes, working on great folds of shimmering fabric in the rain."

Amateur and professional photographers and videographers, as well as TV and print journalists, documented every move. At exactly 5:00 P.M. on Wednesday, October 4, the sewing, nailing, and tucking ended, just in time for a scheduled celebratory feast. Jim Fuller and Mitko Zagoroff beamed, impressed by the clockwork operation. Tom Golden and Ted Dougherty joined the festivities at the northern edge of the park. Workers occupied long tables, joyously toasting Christo and Jeanne-Claude. Jeanne-Claude's parents marveled at the smooth, handsome, oh-so-American event. Précilda de Guillebon cut fabric samples for visitors and helped with the sewing. With his gentle smile, General de Guillebon quietly admired the flawless campaign.

Busloads of schoolchildren mingled with joggers, sight-seers, workers, neighborhood residents, dogs on and off leashes, and an international cast of supporters. John and Naomi Kaldor came from Australia. Project photographer Wolfgang Volz, with his sister Bettina helping him, Carl Flach, Serge De Bloe, and Willi Bongard were among the Europeans on hand. Scott Hodes, *Running Fence* ranchers, Barbara Pozzi and Rosie Ielmorini, David Bourdon, Leo Steinberg, Dorothy and Herbert Vogel, David and Helen Johnson, Harrison Rivera-Terreaux, Alanna Heiss, Tom Garver, and Dick Bellamy joined the ever-swelling throng. Cyril Christo spent one day in Kansas City to see the golden pathways and his grandparents.

Two and a half miles of fabric delineated with baroque folds flowed like molten metal in the sunlight. Every Frisbee, soccer ball, or soaring kite, each small sailboat in the duck pond—in fact, all moving objects—were chartered in relation to the shimmering cloth. It became the momentary center of the universe for crawling babies and picnicking families. In changing light and weather, cars stopped while drivers and passengers paid homage, enjoying a brief tactile interlude, fondling the sensual fabric. Joggers reported feeling energized by the inviting golden river of cloth. Christo said, "It was a very simple work. We slipped folded, soft fabric between people's feet and the cement, gravel, and asphalt walkways. It made you conscious of walking. If you didn't pay attention, you could break your neck."

Smithson would write, "Children took one look and immediately removed their shoes and socks and skipped barefoot. A woman jogger stopped to say, 'Wonderful. It's like running on a yellow brick road.'" Christo recalled a group of blind people arriving by bus. "They walked the paths barefoot. Later, one man, holding his shoes, said, 'We saw your project with our feet. It is beautiful.'"

The two-week life span of *Wrapped Walk Ways* passed quickly. In the meantime, the overall budget had soared. Newspapers reported total expenditures in excess of $130,000. During the project's duration, twenty young monitors patrolled and cleaned pathways while twenty-four off-duty police maintained security. On October 10, Kansas City Mayor Charles Wheeler presented Christo with a key to the city. On October 17, the golden walkways returned to everyday gray. Jeanne-Claude sighed when she said, "It went so fast, Christo likes to say, 'If *Running Fence* was a concerto, *Wrapped Walk Ways* was chamber music.' I think that's a lovely analysis. It was an exquisite project that we loved dearly. The only reason it didn't make the front page of every newspaper in the world is that there was almost no opposition." She smiled. "How strange, everything went so smoothly."

14

Nomads for Art

Christo and Jeanne-Claude appear indefatigably mobile and ceaselessly active. New ideas, places, and situations stimulate the cores of their beings; more than that, these stimuli are the lifeblood of their existence. In a time when Western societies are characterized by drawn curtains, antiseptic comfort, anonymous housing, and sedentary lifestyles, these restless wanderers revel in the gritty reality of rugged journeys.

After periods of intense work at Howard Street, Christo and Jeanne-Claude emerge like nomads with an irresistible compulsion to explore. They embark on novel, spirited migrations with a shared vision. Their wanderlust is its own reward. "Travel must be adventurous," wrote Robert Louis Stevenson in *Travels with a Donkey*, "to feel the needs and hitches of life more nearly; to come down off this feather bed of civilization, and find the globe granite underfoot, and strewn with cutting flints."[1]

These wayfaring artists are guided by their unique imagination. Seemingly irrational, subversive themes featuring cloth, steel barrels, and other low-tech materials recur like vivid dreams foretelling a destined event. Their efforts *appear* simple, nontechnological, fleeting, and in concert with nature. Each realized work, however unusual, offers a joyful, hallucinatory experience, along with justification and motivation to continue on another rewarding path.

As the 1970s drew to a close, these artists' dreams included wrapping the Reichstag; wrapping the Pont Neuf in Paris; wrapping the Christopher Columbus monument in Barcelona; erecting fifteen thousand gates in New York City's Central Park; and *The Mastaba of Abu Dhabi, Project for the United Arab Emirates*. These ambitious projects, sixteen solo exhibitions, and numerous group shows led them to Vienna, Barcelona, Paris, Abu Dhabi, Greenville (South Carolina), Kansas City, Cleveland, London, Boston, Freiburg, Basel, Milan, Nice, Saint Louis, Dayton, Chattanooga, Austin, San Diego, Minneapolis, Zurich, Washington D.C., Cologne, Düsseldorf, Innsbruch, Munich, Berlin, Frankfurt, Rio de Janiero, and other cities.

Most of the travel involved realization of the projects; everything revolved around them—exhibitions, lectures, reading, openings, postopening gatherings, dinners, and conversations. Of course, there were exceptions—escapist binges at the movies, the occasional TV event, or time spent with family and friends. While those interludes were infrequent, inactivity was virtually unknown. Jeanne-Claude guarded their time like a jealous lover protecting an irreplaceable beauty.

In providing protection and freedom for her loved one, Jeanne-Claude's fierce regulation of time and calculated or spontaneous fits of short temper struck some as unnecessarily cruel. Jeanne-Claude defended herself, saying, "This is my best quality. It has protected Christo all these years. I think every artist needs a monster." Friends and family understood Jeanne-Claude's strict regulation of access to Christo, or tried to. The urgent demands of each work dictated the time and priority of most other activities.

Asked if he ever felt neglected, their son Cyril once said, "The projects are my brothers and sisters. What can I say? Despite everything you have, you realize how singular you are." Cyril quoted Rainer Maria Rilke, "'Don't think that destiny is more than what is packed into childhood.'" Looking back, he tried to grasp his parents' unbending commitment to the projects. "I understand the human drive and passion," he said. "Christo still says things a boy of twenty-three would say to a girl he had just met if he were madly in love, the same wonderful things, the same drive he puts into the work, the same love he gives his wife—there are things I find in him, qualities of a superman, which I don't fully understand. I am still in awe because he is absolutely, totally unique. He's got a will of tungsten and a passion that is mind-boggling."[2]

In 1979, exhibitions were mounted at institutions both small and lofty, ranging from the fledgling Housatonic Museum of Art in Bridgeport, Connecticut, to the venerable Corcoran Gallery in Washington, D.C. One event that might have been memorable never took place. In February, Whitney Museum curator Paul Cummings approached Christo with an idea for a comprehensive drawing show. Its focus, unlike each project's documentation exhibit, would be an overview of the artist's visionary drawings. The overture from a museum of American art was particularly gratifying, given repeated references in print to Christo as Bulgarian, Greek, or any nationality but American. But, Jeanne-Claude said, "Christo has always been against any type of national museum of *American* art. What kind of art is that? Art is art."

Jeanne-Claude recalled the Whitney misadventure: "Paul Cummings came here twice, asking to do a drawing exhibition. Each time, Christo refused. 'I'm doing a project now and don't have time,' he said. On the third request, Christo agreed. We supplied four hundred names and addresses, listing what each collector had, with a cross next to specific pieces Christo wanted included. Then the Whitney wrote letters asking to borrow the work. Meanwhile, Christo and I went to Abrams. We thought it would be good to have a book for people who knew about the projects but had rarely, if ever, seen the preparatory drawings. Abrams agreed. The publication would be used as the exhibition catalog, and of course, as always, it would be edited and laid out by Christo."

Christo, Jeanne-Claude, Cummings, and Whitney Museum director Thomas Armstrong decided to meet to discuss the exhibition. "There were immediate problems," Jeanne-Claude recalled. "They didn't want to work with Abrams. Armstrong said, 'We've had bad relations in the past.'"

Christo pointed out that he would be paying Abrams, saving the museum money. "I don't want a miserable catalog, but the same kind you usually do, even better." Then he raised another issue. "Many artists have guest curators," he said. "I want to chose a guest curator."

Without hesitation, Armstrong replied, "No. Cummings is doing the show."

Christo asked, "How can he? He's never seen one of my projects." A heated discussion ensued about the relationship of the drawings to the projects. Christo proclaimed loudly that the drawings are not just aesthetic exercises but are relevant to the projects. "They are not isolated things!" he screamed. "Those drawings have only one aim. They are about the project."

Other disagreements surfaced. Christo and Jeanne-Claude wanted the show to travel, particularly to the Kröller-Müller Museum in Holland. The Whitney only favored one venue. Armstrong and Cummings envisioned a retrospective of the drawings. The artists preferred a show that would include large color photomurals of the projects with preparatory drawings—"a selection, not a retrospective." Things became further entangled when Christo remarked, "Your walls are horrible. It's like a tomb inside. Let me do the museum a favor and ask my dear friend Gaetana Aulenti to redesign the space for this show. She is the best in Europe and probably the best in the world at doing that." In 1973, Aulenti had redesigned a Baroque chapel in Milan to accommodate the *Valley Curtain* documentation exhibition. Her recent accomplishments included redesigned interiors for the Centre Pompidou and the new Musée d'Orsay in Paris.

Armstrong indicated he might work with Abrams, and might even consider a guest curator, but not a designer. He said that was impossible, as it would cost too much.

Christo responded, "We'll find somebody to pay for that. It won't cost the Whitney one cent."

Armstrong said, "You're asking too much, Christo. We can't do that."

Christo stood up. "Fine. Then I can't do the show." Jeanne-Claude thanked

Armstrong and Cummings for the flattering invitation and said, "Perhaps we'll try again sometime in the future."

"They didn't believe us," Jeanne-Claude said. "A week later they called. There was a curatorial meeting scheduled, and they wanted us attend. I remember wearing my big black Issey Miyake cape. We and the curators sat down facing Armstrong. He sat behind his desk, pretending that Christo had never canceled the show. He tapped a pencil on the paper in front of him and said, 'Point one: Four hundred letters sent, and almost everybody has responded. Fine. Point two: Paul Cummings will be the curator—"

"What are we doing here? Christo blurted out. "I have already canceled the exhibition."

Taking her cue, Jeanne-Claude slipped into her cape and got up in one sweeping motion. She said, "Thank you very much, ladies and gentlemen." She and Christo marched out of the office. "It's a long corridor between Tom's office and the elevator. We walked very fast. They were all running after us. When the show was canceled, they really screwed us, because the four hundred letters that went out never said who had canceled the show. Later, we heard from friends that Armstrong was comparing Christo to Clyfford Still, which means: difficult. In a few weeks, we saw [Armstong] at an opening. He said, 'You don't love me anymore.' I smiled and said, 'Tom, I love you, but I love Christo much more.'"

Christo and Jeanne-Claude made five trips to Paris in 1979. On February 15, her father took them to a City Hall meeting he had set up with Deputy Mayor Raymond Dohet, who had served under him in World War II. Sitting beneath a large photo of Charles de Gaulle, the engaging couple explained the Pont-Neuf project and asked for help in obtaining permission to wrap the nearly four-hundred-year-old bridge.

Carole Weisweiller also helped; she happened to be a good friend of Mrs. Georges Pompidou, widow of the former French president. "Carole arranged for us to have dinner at Madame Pompidou's residence on our way to Abu Dhabi in April," Christo recalled. On July 2, at Mrs. Pompidou's suggestion, the unflagging artists visited Michel Boutinard-Rouelle, director of cultural affairs for the city of Paris. The young administrator quickly became an ardent supporter of the project. By their second meeting in October, he and the artists had developed a solid rapport and consensus regarding strategy. Carole Weisweiller arranged a second dinner at Madame Pompidou's for the Christos and Jeanne-Claude. This time, the guests included Boutinand-Rouelle, Paris mayor Jacques Chirac, future premier Edouard Balladur, Pontus Hulten, the Director of the Centre Pompidou, and Niki de Saint-Phalle. "I'm not sure if

Jean Tinguely was there," Christo said. "At the last minute, Madame Pompidou told Carole that Jacques Chirac would be more at ease talking about the Pont-Neuf proposal if Jeanne-Claude and I were not present. So we were not there, even though we had flown to Paris for that dinner. Later, we heard that Balladur, who was very close to Chirac at that time, said that it would be a political disaster to let the project happen."

On December 21, Christo, Jeanne-Claude, and Jacques de Guillebon prepared for an important meeting with Michel Debré, the Fifth Republic's first prime minister. Known for his elegant clothes and short temper, Debré was often described as more Gaullist than de Gaulle. Jacques called him "the ayatollah of the party." Filmmakers Albert and David Maysles followed Christo, Jeanne-Claude, and her father into Debré's office. Christo wore a jacket, open shirt, and jeans; Jeanne-Claude had chosen a floral-patterned silk dress and high maroon boots; Jacques had on a dark business suit and tie. A *Pont Neuf* collage drawing was placed on the floor facing Debré. Jeanne-Claude recalled, "We hardly spoke. Father did most of the talking. Debré said that he would be seeing Chirac in a few days at a Gaullist party congress in southern France. Then we read in the newspapers that they had a giant political fight that ended with them swearing not to talk to each other again. There went our hope."

Christo and Jeanne-Claude plunged into the new decade, tenaciously pursuing four major projects on three continents: *Wrapped Reichstag, The Pont Neuf Wrapped, The Mastaba of Abu Dhabi,* and *The Gates* (for New York's Central Park). At the end of 1979, the couple, at the urging of Scott Hodes, had tried to take their first and only vacation. It had been a disaster of boredom, and they returned home early in order to get back to work.

In early 1980, Christo and Jeanne-Claude drafted their project statement for *The Gates.* It projected a utopian vision of Central Park, which would be transformed for two weeks into "a true Public Work of Art" meant to be experienced equally by the city's "rich variety of people." The plan envisioned fifteen thousand steel portals hung with saffron-colored fabric; these would snake through New York City's 843-acre oasis. The rectangular shape of the steel gates would reflect the geometry of the street grid surrounding Central Park, while the capriciously moring panels of fabric would be in harmony with the curving pattern of the walkways within the park. Each fifteen-foot-high gate would vary in width from nine to twenty-eight feet, depending on the width of the walkways. In the absence of wind, free-flowing fabric attached to the horizontal crosspiece atop each steel gate would drape down to five feet six inches above the ground. "*The Gates* will be spaced at 9 foot intervals, allowing the synthetic woven panels to wave horizontally towards the next gate." The

New York, June 1980: Henry Geldzahler (second from left), Commissioner of Cultural Affairs of the City of New York, and his assistant Randall Bourscheidt discuss *The Gates Project* with Christo and Jeanne-Claude. (Photo: Wolfgang Volz)

wind, Christo said, would create "a golden ceiling" for pedestrians; apartment dwellers around the park would see a twenty-seven-mile-long "golden river appearing and disappearing through the branches."

In 1980, Christo and Jeanne-Claude made forty-one formal presentations of *The Gates* project to city officials, museum administrators, civic leaders, and community boards. The target date for *The Gates* was October 1983. The estimated $5,221,000 cost would again be financed entirely through the sale of Christo's art. Naturally, the project generated opposition. Christo said, "City politicians are afraid we'll set a dangerous precedent—next, someone will want to paint the rocks pink. Harlem blacks come to the meetings, and they say, 'We need jobs, not golden banners.' I tell them that the construction of *The Gates* will create jobs. And I tell them it will be like a walk through a marvelous golden corridor with the fabric playing above your head, inviting you to watch the open space. The banners will move at the slightest breeze, creating a continuous golden chain."[3]

The *New York Times* quoted the artist as saying, " 'Henry Geldzahler, the city's Commissioner of Cultural Affairs . . . told me to watch out. "Two things in this city are sacred. One is motherhood and the other is Central Park." ' " The *Times* also identified some initial backers. " 'As of now,' " said Borough President Andrew J. Stein, " 'I support the project. It's unique and it's innovative. We are that kind of city and we should support innovations.' "[4] Philippe de Montebello, director of the Metropolitan Museum of Art, also embraced the proposal.

The idea seemed absurdly alien to some protectors of the park. One called *The Gates* "an example of cultural imperialism." Another resident described it as "a mustache on the Mona Lisa." An agitated Fred Beckhardt, chairman of Community Board Five, saw "another example of how Christo dwells on death, like the way he mummifies buildings."[5] Christo listened intently, even smiled at criticism. "You know, people used to say I'm not an artist. Now they at least admit I am an artist. But they ask me to do the project somewhere else."[6]

Years later, Christo reported on a Human Impact study by sociologist Kenneth Clark. Clark's study, based on interviews with 660 New Yorkers and discussions with various groups, found that a majority favored the installation. Three out of four blacks and four out of five Hispanics responded favorably; a smaller percentage, but still a majority, of whites also supported the project. The report concluded that realization would be a unifying artistic event that would bring diverse groups of people together. Christo said, "The darker the skin, the poorer the people, the more they liked the project. The whiter the skin, the richer the people, the more they disliked it."

During a lecture at the Pratt Institute, a man in his sixties introduced himself as an official who had opposed *The Gates* proposal. "The project would have upset a fabulous urban amenity," he said. "I think Prospect Park in Brooklyn was offered as an alternative. If it were taken to an outer borough, it would bring excitement and probably fulfill your end somewhere else. Do you want to discuss alternative sites?" Without missing a beat, Jeanne-Claude jumped to her feet and said, "Before Christo answers intelligently, I want to ask the gentleman a silly question. Did you marry the lady you wanted or did you marry an alternative woman?"[7] The audience exploded with applause and laughter.

Christo and Jeanne-Claude continued to thrive on adversity. Christo often talked about "working on the edge of the impossible." *The Mastaba of Abu Dhabi, Project for the United Arab Emirates* easily fit that description. Its concept, cost, logistics, and authorization process all spelled trouble. Even those familiar with the artists' accomplishments could only smile, shrug, or try to detect a spark of rationality in the plan to construct forty-nine-story-high oil-barrel structure in the desert. The concept contained several departures: First, unlike past ephemeral projects, this undertaking would be "permanent"—meaning that it might take centuries, rather than weeks, to reveal the work's impermanence. "Nothing is forever," Jeanne-Claude explained. "The pyramids are disappearing. Ted Dougherty thought the mastaba could last five or six thousand years if properly maintained." After demonstrating their independence from patronage,[8] the artists hoped, for the first time, to enlist a sponsor—in this case, Sheikh Zayed, ruler of Abu Dhabi and president of the United Arab Emirates, and his advisers—to underwrite an estimated $400 to $500 million budget. They saw their role as that of "architects" to Sheikh Zayed. Jeanne-Claude said, "I could never sell enough drawings to pay for it."

Envisioning the mastaba (the word *mastabah* means "stone bench") was one thing; trying to bring it to life simply defied logic. *The Mastaba of Abu Dhabi* would measure 492 feet high by 984 feet wide by 738 feet deep, enough volume to encompass a sizable number of skyscrapers. Brightly colored custom-made fifty-five-gallon stainless-steel oil barrels—390,500 of them—would be positioned horizontally around a massive core of sand and concrete. The roof surface would measure 416 by 738 feet. Jeanne-Claude said, "The core would consist of a mountain of sand restrained by a twenty-one-foot-thick shell of concrete on solid concrete footings. Then two layers of multicolored barrels would provide a veneer." In 1972, the artists wrote, "There will be no ingress except for a passageway to the elevators to take visitors to the top. From there they will enjoy superb views, being able to see approximately 50 kilometers across the countryside." They painted an inviting picture: "Nothing comparable has ever existed in any other country. Hundreds of bright colors, as enchanting as the Islamic mosaics, will give a constantly changing visual experience according to the time of day and the quality of light. The grandeur and vastness of the land will be reflected in the majesty of the Mastaba."[9] However improbable this apparition seemed to some, Christo and Jeanne-Claude had no doubt that their desert dream could be realized. While Christo's name had long been associated with fabric and the gesture of wrapping, he also had a history of stacking oil barrels. In addition to *Dockside Packages* (1961), *Iron Curtain* (1962), and *1,240 Oil Barrels Mastaba* (1968), there were two unrealized projects in this vein: *Ten Million Oil Barrels Wall, Project for the Suez Canal* (1967) and *Houston Mastaba, Texas* (1969).

Christo and Jeanne-Claude faced a herculean, if not hopeless, task: convincing the conservative Sheikh Zayed to endorse an extravagantly expensive, clearly controversial, seemingly preposterous plan that could expose the royal family to ridicule or worse. On April 8, 1980, Jeanne-Claude and Wolfgang Volz left New York for Abu Dhabi. Later that day, Christo and Ted Dougherty followed. Jeanne-Claude said, "We had great difficulty getting admitted into the country. We never went as artists because the category doesn't exist. We were architects. The Architectural League in New York had made up cards for us."

The artists' initial trips to Abu Dhabi consisted of a series of meetings with government officials and businessmen, dinners to introduce them to influential people, and drives through the region to select a site for the mastaba. "We drove for thousands of miles in that little country," Jeanne-Claude said. "All over the place. Every road. It was very, very, very hot. We were always red and perspiring. Whenever a car broke down, the driver abandoned it by the road. On one trip, we laughed hysterically because someone had abandoned an airplane by the road."

French Ambassador Jean-Claude Guisset arranged four consecutive dinners to introduce the couple to prospective supporters. Among his guests were Bernard de Lamotte, head of the French oil company Total, and his wife, Roseline. Christo had painted portraits of her and of their children in Geneva in 1957 and 1958. The artists met a diverse group of people. Jeanne-Claude recalled, "You know, on one trip a young sheikh tried to buy Wolfgang Volz for money. Wolfi covered the back of his pants and begged, 'No, no, Christo, please don't do it.'"

Christo, Jeanne-Claude, Cyril, and Wolfgang Volz returned to the United Arab Emirates in late May to install an exhibition at the French Cultural Alliance, one of eleven solo shows in 1980. Despite a Christo interview on the radio, there was little headway made in obtaining an audience with Sheikh Zayed. Even after the artists chalked up six more trips to the region, made countless phone calls, and sent an enormous amount of correspondence, they still had not met Sheikh Zayed or members of the royal family. But nearly two decades later, Jeanne-Claude still refused to admit defeat, saying, "No, the Abu Dhabi project is not dead. You might say it's on hold. It's sleeping."

Christo recalled, "During the Carter administration, many Bulgarians in the West received a form letter saying that if they returned by December 31, 1980, they would be given amnesty. However, we needed to repent, to admit our guilt! About that time, the Bulgarian ambassador called us and said he was with a journalist from an important Bulgarian magazine who wanted to do an article. At the time, the Museum of Modern Art was showing the *Running Fence* film, so we met there for lunch. The 'writer' was a young man, a typical KGB type. After a long discussion, we realized that he really didn't want to write anything. He had come to invite me to do a project in Bulgaria celebrating the anniversary of the nation's founding. I told him we don't do commissions and that we were busy with Central Park, Paris, Berlin, and Abu Dhabi. We gave him photographs and posters for an exhibition of books and magazines organized by a Bulgarian library and the USIA. Later, the American embassy showed the *Valley Curtain* and *Running Fence* films, but only by invitation to upper-class Communists. They were not shown publicly. Nobody from my family was invited—not even Anani. There was no reason he should not have been invited. At the last minute, his wife, Didi, heard about it and managed to get herself invited."

Christo's mother, Tzveta, and his father, Vladimir, were finally granted their second travel visa to the West in 1980. At age seventy-four, Tzveta required specialized medical treatment following the multiple surgeries on her knees and the removal of her cataracts in 1977. Joan Mondale had again en-

New York, summer 1980: Christo and Jeanne-Claude with Christo's parents, Vladimir and Tzveta, in Central Park. (Photo: Wolfgang Volz)

listed American officials to help persuade the appropriate Bulgarian bureaucrats to issue the visa. On July 11, 1980, an elated Christo and Jeanne-Claude met the senior Yavachevs at New York's Kennedy Airport. It was Tzveta's first trip to the United States and Vladimir's second. A waiting limousine whisked the foursome to Manhattan's Plaza Hotel. The next day, Christo and Jeanne-Claude took fresh fruit to the Plaza and proposed possible activities for a memorable five weeks in New York. There were museum visits, movies, dinners, and ample relaxation. One afternoon, Tzveta and Vladimir visited the office of Albert and David Maysles to see the *Valley Curtain* and *Running Fence* films for the first time.

On August 6, Christo and Jeanne-Claude accompanied his parents to the Whitney Museum. Later, they shared a hansom ride through Central Park, where they talked about their vision for *The Gates.* Nine days later, a limo took Christo's parents from the Plaza to JFK. It was the last time he saw his mother and father.

On August 30, 1980, longtime supporter Jan van der Marck first telephoned to propose that Christo participate in Miami's 1982 New World Festival of the Arts; the answer was a firm no. The demands of projects in progress in Paris, Berlin, Barcelona, New York, and Abu Dhabi were more than enough. Van der Marck, who had become the founding director of Miami's Center for the Fine Arts, followed several additional calls with a November 19 visit to

Manhattan, New Year's Eve, 1981: Daniela Yavacheva, Jeanne-Claude, Christo, and Anani Yavachev celebrate at L'Odéon restaurant. (Photo: Archive XTO+J-C)

Howard Street. After considerable arm twisting, Christo and Jeanne-Claude finally agreed to visit Miami after Christmas and see if an exciting, feasible idea would emerge. This trip to Miami prevented them from attending the wedding of Jeanne-Claude's brother Jean-Marie d'Essertaux to Béatrice Mahé on December 20.

In Miami, they were guests at van der Marck's home. One afternoon, *Miami Herald* architecture critic Beth Dunlop drove them around the city and provided a running commentary on landmarks. The thought of wrapping another structure failed to excite the artists. During the tour, they noticed numerous man-made islands as they crossed the causeways spanning Biscayne Bay. These "spoil islands" were formed from dredged material evacuated during the construction in the 1920s of the Intracoastal Waterway, which runs north-south along the bay.

The Christos enjoyed sight-seeing but remained noncommittal. Jeanne-Claude called to mind a private moment with Christo on one of the causeways: "I remember the two of us standing there, looking out at those little green islands in the middle of the bay. I said, 'Wouldn't it be beautiful to surround them with pink floating fabric? What do you think?' It was my idea, but if I'd waited ten seconds, he might have opened his mouth to say the same thing. I was thinking two or three islands. In the end, he chose eleven. The choice of islands was entirely his." Christo later spoke of the "incredible flatness of Miami landscape that is not only horizontal but completely flat and a very fluid situation between earth and water."[10]

Jeanne-Claude envisioned pink. "I chose pink," she said, "because I knew Miami. It's obvious. The color wasn't very subtle for Christo. It's kitschy and very feminine, but he loved it."

In early 1981, there were strong warning signs that *The Gates* proposal for Central Park would be rejected. On January 6, Christo and Jeanne-Claude's lawyer, Theodore W. Kheel,[11] went to Parks Commissioner Gordon J. Davis's office to withdraw the project application. A postponement seemed wise, given reliable information that an elaborately detailed document was being prepared that would justify denial of the controversial application. Undeterred by what some regarded as a potential deathblow, Christo welcomed opposition. "It gives energy and enriches the process," he noted. "The park is not going anywhere. I'm healthy, and I intend to do this project."

On January 8, Christo and Jeanne-Claude presented *The Gates* concept to City Council President Carol Bellamy at City Hall. The next day, a former parks commissioner, August Heckscher, arrived at Howard Street to see preparatory drawings and discuss the proposal. Three days later, Christo and Jeanne-Claude were drumming up support from members of the Municipal Art Society. Then, on January 19, standing before his drawing, Christo tendered a lively vision of *The Gates* to a packed lecture hall at New York University; a contentious panel discussion followed his remarks.

The *New York Times* reported comments by five panelists. Paula Deitz, *Hudson Review* editor and writer, felt the project would spawn "a vast golden river created by the wind" and engender "new awe and respect for the park." Alexander W. Allport, executive director of the National Association of Olmsted Parks, objected to the planned boring of 22,000 holes in the ground and the "pre-emption of space" from park devotees. Joe Bresnan, director of New York's Historic Parks, remained neutral, explaining the Parks Department method for selecting and placing artwork. *Amsterdam News* art editor Mel Tapley spoke enthusiastically about "aesthetic freedom" and potential jobs for the black community. Fred Beckhardt, chairman of Community Board Five, also thought *The Gates* would limit usage of the park, especially in terms of the elderly: "Really, what he's trying to do is bury us and bury the park." Some in the audience also expressed concern. What if a fabric panel caught fire? Would that set off a twenty-five-mile fuse? Would trees be damaged? One member of the New York Audubon Society feared disruption of bird migration and called the work "an act of cultural dictatorship." Anna Levin of the Central Park Community Fund ridiculed the scheme, saying that "the monotony of all the green trees and rocks in Central Park" could be remedied by introducing graffiti artists. The *Times* quoted an upbeat Christo, "It's marvelous that this crowd has come. That's part of my work; the physical product is only the end of the project. The fact that people are passionately involved with us is a significant demonstration of how important this work of art is for New York City."[12]

Kheel recalled, "We also had dozens of meetings with community boards, civil leaders, and the art community. All kinds of questions were raised. Would the fabric's color distract and confuse migratory birds? Would they think it was the wrong season and fly in the wrong direction? Christo remained clam and patient. We did a study on whether the color would have any impact on birds. Others thought putting pipes in to the ground would interfere with worms! Concerns about adverse environmental impact meant we had to do another study. Suppose someone got hurt? We agreed to have liability-insurance policies. Yes, we'd post a bond. Then someone raised the question of exploitation rights. Any revenues from T-shirts, movie productions, et cetera, would go to the city, with Christo paying all of the expenses of the project."

Kheel explained, "Central Park is rectangular. The southern part is Community Board Five, the western part is Community Board Seven. The community board in the north is mostly black, and the southeast community board is rather elitist. Sally Goodgold, a lovely woman who headed Community Board Seven, told me that she liked the project because it would be seen from all sides of the park. She saw *The Gates* as a unifying force that could bring together blacks, Hispanics, and whites, liberals and conservatives."[13]

Community Board Seven endorsed the idea. Community Board Five, however, resisted Christo's pitch on February 11; twenty-one of thirty-five members agreed that the plan endangered Central Park. Then, on February 25, Parks Commissioner Davis issued a 251-page report denying permission to build *The Gates*. Kheel said, "It was the longest written decision in the history of parks, worldwide, on an application to use park space. The report said all these wonderful things about Christo. Immediately, you knew the answer was no. He gave Christo the words, not the decision. He said, 'If we allowed Christo to do this, we would have to do the same for everyone. That would make a shambles of the park.'"[14]

Davis wrote, "The project is, after all, in the wrong place, at the wrong time, and in the wrong scale." A *New York Times* editorial agreed. It credited Davis with reaching "the right decision for all the right reasons": the risk of widespread damage to the fragile, man-made landscape; the cost of services from understaffed city departments; interference with normal park usage; and the setting of a dangerous precedent. The editorial complained that a projected $5 million cost (which Christo alone would bear) is "one million more than the park's annual maintenance budget. . . . There is also the inescapable question about exploiting public land for private gain; the project would be financed out of the highly profitable sale of related drawings." Variations on these arguments seemed to surface with each project. The *Time*'s editorial joined the Parks Department in citing Christo's disregard for the law when he completed the *Running Fence*'s ocean portion without the required permit.[15]

Davis also noted "substantial unknown risks." He said, "The defects of the physical project mirror the defects in the artist's grasp and understanding of Central Park." Although the report found the work "visually seductive and of great charm," Davis maintained, "the Gates simply cannot and should not be forced to fit into New York's greatest public space." He suggested alternative city-owned sites: property in the Rockaways, the Coney Island boardwalk, an East River pedestrian walk, or the Park Avenue or Lenox Avenue malls. The artists rejected any alternative site.

In January, in the midst of the crisis over *The Gates*, Christo and Jeanne-Claude agreed to undertake *Surrounded Islands, Project for Biscayne Bay, Greater Miami, Florida* for the 1982 New World Festival of the Arts. Christo had already completed a number of sketches. On February 27, he flew to Miami for his opening at the Hokin Gallery. He showed Jan van der Marck the initial drawings and explained the novel concept. The first studies depicted a light pink fabric floating around a still-undetermined number of dark green spoil islands.

Van der Marck observed, "Fabric is to Christo what steel had been to an earlier generation of modernist sculptors. He likes the dual meaning of woven fiber and fabric in the metaphorical way—that which holds our society together. In explaining his work, he often refers to human interaction, legal fencing, environmental posturing, and technical problem solving as what he calls 'the real fabric' of his work."[16]

In March, Christo and Jeanne-Claude began assembling their team. Mitko Zagoroff and Ted Dougherty each spent a few days at Howard Street to begin preliminary engineering on the project. On April 3, Christo, Jeanne-Claude, and Wolfgang Volz returned to Miami; to demonstrate an earlier success, they installed the *Running Fence Documentation Exhibition* at the Metropolitan Museum in Coral Gables. Then on April 6, Christo and Jeanne-Claude made a one-day trip to Tallahassee and retained a respected environmental attorney, Joseph W. Landers, Jr.

The next few weeks were fraught with problems: The first fabric test revealed flaws; discussions with local, state, and federal agencies grew increasingly complex; and an attempt to regroup in New York with a second application for *The Gates* hit a stone wall with Parks Commissioner Davis. Then, in late May 1981, *Rolling Stone*'s lastest issue hit the newsstands. It contained the aptly named article "Whither Christo," by Carol Caldwell. She wrote about "body-bagging" the Pont-Neuf and about *The Gates* project, "turned down here in the heart of Anything Goes New York." Caldwell noted, "He's got to want to do what he does real bad to go through what he does to get there." Writing about one setback, she observed:

> He's badly out of sync in Harlem tonight. He should've introduced himself as Christo from Planet Nylon and wrapped himself. . . . He needs more showbiz and swash. This evening, at Community Board Eleven, New York City, the citizens of Harlem aren't up for art talk. Christo's being weird, gesticulating and jawing fast, but he's not weird enough. Right now, all he is, is white. White, and he don't talk right.[17]

Worse were the photographs accompanying the article. Christo recalled meeting with photographer Annie Leibovitz: "I went to her studio on East Twenty-first Street. She took very nice portraits there. Later, they said she would like to take photographs in the park." Christo met Leibovitz at Central Parks' Tavern on the Green. Somehow, she convinced him to be wrapped in red-and-white cloth for a picture.

Later, Christo whispered sheepishly, "I didn't like that photograph."

Jeanne-Claude heard the comment and snapped, "That's all you have to say about it?"

"I hated it!" he admitted.

Pressing the point, Jeanne-Claude asked, "Did I like it?"

He said, "No. You didn't like it at all."

"It was my fault," Jeanne-Claude said. "If I had gone, I would never have let her wrap him. Never! We almost divorced over that photo. I was so furious he didn't have the balls to say no."

Despite intense efforts in Berlin, Barcelona, and Paris, progress on various projects seemed glacial, particularly in Abu Dhabi. When filmmaker David Maysles gently suggested, "There are too many projects," Christo mechanically repeated, "Too many projects. In a way, we are caught in a vicious cycle," he mused. "In the sad and frustrating moments when we have problems, the drawings are sometimes the only hope that the project will be done." Christo projected determination but understood the odds: "I have fear. I have doubts. I take risks. . . . [The] projects have a dimension of being nearly impossible that makes them almost suicidal. Failure is very public. When we have a failure, it's like a cold shower over your ego."[18]

Case in point: On October 1 in Paris, despite a full schedule of meetings, Christo, assisted by Harrison Rivera-Terreaux, wrapped a large *Pont Neuf* scale model that was to be installed in a display window at La Samartaine, the giant department store situated on the Right Bank, by the bridge. Christo and

Jeanne-Claude arrived shortly after 6:30 P.M. for the unveiling of the window display. A large crowd greeted them with applause. As the Maysles brothers filmed the action at the busy intersection, a journalist called out, "The mayor [Chirac] just said he's against it on television."

The triumphant moment shattered, Christo screamed, "This is crazy. I'm not going to get upset."

Jeanne-Claude instantly assumed a motherly role, insisting, "You're going to take a pill now. Put a pill in your mouth now. Do what I tell you!" She was afraid that this upset would affect his heart. They had expected more time and more discussion before Chirac took a public stand. They were both shaken, although not about to abandon the project.

Prospects for wrapping the Reichstag were no less dismal. Back in New York on October 4, when Willy Brandt was to visit Howard Street, Christo and Jeanne-Claude had to scramble to borrow several *Reichstag* drawings. "We called a New Jersey collector," Christo said. "At the moment, we felt very low. Bundestag president Richard Stücklen had turned down the project, and we were very depressed. We were not even discussing the Reichstag project. It was over! I didn't even have drawings in the studio. They were all in storage."

Brandt was joined by his chief of staff, Klaus-Henning Rosen, as well as by Berlin's former mayor Dietrich Strobbe, a *Der Spiegel* reporter, Cyril, Wolfgang Volz, and the Maysles brothers. Christo said later, "Brandt came here to ask us not to give up the project. I asked if he could help us change Mr. Stücklen's position. He said, 'No, Stücklen is quite an independent member of his party's right wing.' He suggested other people who might help, and he gave us the impression that Stücklen would not stay in power long. It was absolutely true. Stücklen was gone a few months later, replaced by another conservative."

Against a backdrop of decrepit, peeling studio walls, Brandt looked aristocratically elegant striding slowly across the narrow, battered floor. He listened as attentively to Christo's comments about the work as he might to a royal discourse on palace paintings. Christo used the occasion to give an honest appraisal of the project's status. He said, "I tried to tell him what we did, what mistakes we made, whom we saw, who said no, who said yes, all the information. What he felt about the project—that 'it's great'—was not something that would help us. We could read that in the newspaper. We asked him to help solve our problems. This is why I tried to pinpoint whom we saw, the rumors we heard, where the project was going."

Klaus-Henning Rosen said, "This is a very controversial project in Germany. It is a difficult building erroneously connected with Nazism. For the Social Democrats, who lost many of their deputies in Nazi concentration camps, it is a building with special historic connections. I would like to see this experiment happen. I think the man in the street will accept it. It doesn't harm the

Paris City Hall, February 1982: Christo, Johannes Schaub, Françoise de Panafieu, Jacques Chirac, and Jeanne-Claude discussing the permit for the wrapping of the Pont-Neuf. (Photo: Wolfgang Volz)

building, and it could attract people and teach them what the Reichstag means to us. The problem with Germans is we take things too seriously."[19]

Back in Paris, Christo and Jeanne-Claude finally had a chance to present their case to Jacques Chirac on February 22, 1982. The meeting took place in the mayor's posh office. Also present were Johannes Schaub; Françoise de Panafieu, a deputy mayor in charge of cultural affairs; Michel Boutinard; Gabriel Pallez, a banker; Professor André Lichnérowicz; and Henriette Joël, president of the Societé des Amis du Musée d'Art Moderne de la Ville de Paris. Albert and David Maysles documented the proceedings. Christo and Chirac sat on opposite sides of an ornate coffee table, a few feet from a sumptuously decorated fireplace. The large *Running Fence* book sat on the table, and a *Pont Neuf* drawing rested next to Christo's leg. Postcards depicting other projects were used to illustrate points of discussion. The face-off between artist and politician offered a study in contrasts. Both men were about the same age, and both wore horn-rimmed glasses, but the similarity ended there. Christo's shoulder-length mop of hair ran counter to Chirac's thinning, slicked-down hair; the artist wore a white safari jacket, an open orange shirt, and blue jeans, while the mayor was dressed in a three-piece suit, white shirt, and tie. One man sought to change the status quo and briefly energize everyday Parisian life; the other sought damage control and, above all, reelection.

Christo, looking at Chirac, who stared intently back at him, said, "Artists have great passions. This project has been close to my heart."

"I'm not sure it will be that exciting for Parisians, or well received for cultural reasons, and also because they think it will be very expensive," replied Chirac.

"People are used to going to museums to see completed works," parried Christo. "My projects involve a lot of preparatory activity, so there are emotional expectations. People fantasize and anticipate the completed work, so there's a more dynamic public."

His eyes fixed on Christo, Chirac asked, "What will it cost Paris?"

Gesturing with his hands, Christo responded firmly, "Monsieur le Maire, not a centime. The money will come from the sale of my drawings and collages. Absolutely no money from the state or taxpayers, nor from industry. No donations."

Jeanne-Claude puffed on a cigarette as the mayor raised his eyebrows, looked quizzically, and said, "You can't imagine how many letters I've received telling me it's too expensive—better build a daycare center." Then, unexpectedly, and despite some advisers' advice to the contrary, Chirac said, "I'm for it personally, but we can't say the decision has been made. This affair must not be turned into a political battlefield. But after the elections, and if I stay in power, as I expect, we will be entering a six-year period of calm and serenity. Then we can take the initiative without being attacked, except on cultural grounds, which will be of no importance then. So we'll meet again after the '83 election, in a year." The surprising statement of support and the request to delay the project in effect ended the meeting.

Much had happened that could have changed Chirac's decision in the five months since he had originally announced his opposition to *The Pont Neuf Wrapped*. The scale model of the bridge in the display window at La Samaritaine had stimulated public dialogue. Bus and metro stations at the busy intersection ensured maximum exposure. Chirac had stopped by to see the display. In addition, with the consent of the store's CEO, Maurice Renand, the artists spent three days speaking to individuals and groups of workers during their lunch breaks, trying to build support among the store's eighteen hundred employees.

Johannes Schaub, a Swiss-born management consultant based in Paris, had become the project director for *The Pont Neuf Wrapped* in mid-1981. He convinced the artists to mount an American-style political campaign in the surrounding neighborhood. The hope was to build popular support by talking to residents, shopkeepers, and office workers; an aroused constituency, including influential business leaders, would, Schaub felt, inevitably lead to political backing. It was Schaub who had introduced Christo and Jeanne-Claude to Renand and who planned the door-to-door lobbying campaign. He also organized a small group of attractive young women with missionary zeal to canvas the area, distribute postcards, and drum up support for the project. Schaub arranged a 1981 Christo lecture series that included some of France's best universities. Supporters of the project sponsored dinners and other events to promote it. The artists engaged Paris lawyer François Sage to represent the project. By 1982, he had organized the Pont Neuf Corporation, a subsidiary of the C.V.J. Corporation, U.S.A.

On the afternoon of April 27, 1982, Jeanne-Claude routinely answered the telephone. As an operator read, then spelled out, a telegram from Bulgaria, she transcribed the text into the family agenda: "Mama Potchina, 27 April—23 h." It came from Christo's father. "There were no faxes then, and it was hard to telephone," Jeanne-Claude said. "I had no idea what it was about, so I went up to the studio and asked, 'What does Mama Potchina mean?' Christo burst out crying, and I understood. He cried like a little boy." Tzveta Yavachev had died at 11:00 P.M. Plovdiv time.

The next day, a perplexed Jeanne-Claude called her father in Paris. "'Papa,' I said, 'I've never seen him cry like this before. I don't know what's happening. He cries nonstop, pauses, then cries again. I realize his mother passed away, but it doesn't seem natural. His reaction is too strong.' Father said, 'Sweetheart, you have to understand that he's not crying for that wrinkled old lady, but for the beautiful young woman he knew as a child.' Then I understood. He had been crying just like a four-year-old." Christo could not face the thought of returning to Bulgaria for the funeral. Technically, he remained a defector, a deserter who had renounced his citizenship. As such, he would have been subject to criminal charges. It was agreed that Jeanne-Claude would apply for her visa and make arrangements to visit Christo's family.

On June 13, 1982, Christo and Jeanne-Claude both turned forty-seven years old. He splurged and bought her a small star. A very fancy document issued by the International Star Registry listed the celestial body, RD 9H 39 MDJ5FD 25° 30', located in the Leo constellation, as now bearing Jeanne-Claude's name. Jeanne-Claude loved the gift. "Now, Christo and I know where to meet later," she said.

On July 10, Jeanne-Claude flew to Sofia to comfort Christo's father. Anani met Jeanne-Claude at the airport; the famous actor whisked her past security guards, workers, and Communist officials with a tip of his hat and a warm smile. As a national celebrity, he usually encountered quiet admiration and a respectful restraint unknown to American movie stars and their public. This was Jeanne-Claude's initial contact with much of Christo's family and a closed Communist society. The first morning in Sofia, she was joined at her hotel for breakfast by Christo's father, his brother Anani, Didi, and their son,

Vladimir, Christo's brother Stefan, his wife, Elka, their son, Atanas, and their daughter, Tzveta.

The contrast between Bulgaria and the West was startling. The atmosphere in downtown Sofia had no Western counterpart. As in one of Edvard Munch's street-scene paintings, people walked as if in a daze on damaged sidewalks, past stores lined with empty shelves. Jeanne-Claude had heard about endemic shortages, but she needed convincing. She said, "While we were walking around the city, the family complained there was nothing in the stores. But I could see that some stores looked filled. One day, I said, 'I'm going to see for myself.' They laughed and said, 'Okay, let's go in.' Every shelf was full, but with something that nobody wanted. Every can was the same. There really was nothing in the stores."

Vladimir took Jeanne-Claude to his wife's grave site outside Plovdiv. Jeanne-Claude said, "The way Father lived was absolutely horrible. To take a shower, that poor old man had to fill a pail of water and then sit on a little wooden bench less than a foot high and pour water over himself. It was in a bathroom shared with another tenant in the same apartment. At that time, the law said that if you had two or more rooms, you had to share your apartment with someone the government designated. Christo's parents' only home was that single room. Father showed me a suitcase full of Christo's drawings. He knew that I didn't have a wedding ring because we were so poor when we married, so he put Tzveta's wedding ring on my finger." After her four-day whirlwind tour of Sofia, Plovdiv, Gabrovo, and the Balkan countryside, Jeanne-Claude returned to New York.

Soon afterward, Anani again applied for permission to travel in the West. He recalled, "I hadn't seen Christo for twenty-six years. After he defected, it was impossible for me to leave." He viewed the Bulgaria of the early 1980s as far more benign than it had been in previous decades. So why had Christo refused to return? "He isn't sensible about this," Anani said. "Saul Steinberg once told him, 'If you return, you'll destroy your childhood memories.' Christo feels strongly about not coming back. He's stubborn. He's convinced that the authorities would never allow him to leave. I told him that wasn't true, but he's afraid. Jeanne-Claude and her mother are also afraid for him."[20]

Over the years, colleagues and government bureaucrats increasingly heard about their expatriate artist, Christo Javacheff. Anani said, "People didn't know what to make of him. He's too avant-garde. Artists kept asking me about him, asking me to explain what he is doing, what he will do next. I don't feel competent to explain. For instance, a chair is a practical thing. You can see it, use it. It's there. But when he wraps it, that's another thing. With every great painting, there is a moment, a very special moment like when the sun sets and dusk comes. That is the moment of art. Like when the *Running Fence* moved into the water. It's a brief moment. That's art. It's hard to explain. You hear that Christo is going to do something, but you don't really know what's going to happen. When you see it, it's suddenly very comprehensible and a moving experience. It's like the sunset. Even though you know it will occur every day, you don't know how it's going to look. The moment it happens, you understand the whole thing. All you have to do is see it."

Epilogue: Working with Christo and Jeanne-Claude*

WOLFGANG VOLZ

SURROUNDED ISLANDS

In May 1983, Christo and Jeanne-Claude completed the *Surrounded Islands* in Miami's Biscayne Bay. Eleven islands were surrounded with 6.5 million square feet of floating pink fabric. Preparations for the project had begun in 1980, and part of these preparations involving testing the fabric under real-life conditions in Florida. In June 1982, the artists had invited a number of collaborators for a weeklong Think Tank Session in Key Largo, at the home of art collectors Joan and Roger Sonnabend, in order to solicit their advice on dealing with the various new challenges *Surrounding Islands* presented. Many of these people had helped them in the past, and, as always, Christo and Jeanne-Claude derived enormous pleasure from gathering together a large and diverse group to help get a project launched.

Tests on preselected fabrics proved disheartening. Some tests showed that the pink color disappeared after only two days, fading away quickly in the Florida sun. And when the fabrics were immersed in water, they became saturated and sank. Jeanne-Claude in particular was disappointed by the results—the idea for the project had been hers—and discussions about how to make improvements went on for days.

By July 1982, the state of Florida, Dade County, and the cities of Miami and Miami Shores had all granted their approval for the project to proceed, though not before there had been heated public discussion and last-minute maneuvering. It took a second vote for the Dade County board to grant its permit, for example, and even then Christo and Jeanne-Claude first had to

---

*Burt Chernow died suddenly in June 1997, leaving this biography of Christo and Jeanne-Claude unfinished. This epilogue, written by Wolfgang Volz, a close friend of the artists, as well as the exclusive photographer of their projects, continues their story from 1982 to the present. It was translated from the German by Andrea Heyde.

consent to donate to the Biscayne Bay Preservation Fund signed posters worth $100,000.

Moreover, it had been clear from the beginning that *Surrounded Islands* would trigger problems similar to those encountered with *Running Fence*. A group of opponents had organized itself, this time led by Jack Kassewitz, Jr., of the National Wildlife Rescue Team. Its goal was supposedly to protect the Biscayne Bay islands, which had been created in the 1930s during dredging for the Intracoastal Waterway. In addition to forty tons of garbage (which would eventually be removed by the project team), the islands contained the nests of ospreys. Kassewitz and others worried that the project would disturb the birds. In the end, the case had to be decided in federal court. Final authorization for *Surrounded Islands* arrived just shortly before the project's actual completion, and only after endless and nerve-racking negotiations. Christo and Jeanne-Claude had chosen to proceed with the hope that, as in the past, all matters would eventually be resolved.

Still in search of a suitable fabric, I remembered their German friend, Dieter Rosenkranz, a collector of Christo's art, who had helped them find fabrics in the 1960s. He owned a company that produced weaving machines; nobody knew fabric producers better than he did. He recommended that we contact the J. F. Adolff Company in Backnang, a town near Stuttgart. Indeed, Adolff turned out to be the only fabric manufacturer who agreed to develop a fabric specifically for *Surrounded Islands*. American companies declared that 6.5 million square feet was too small an order for them to develop a new fabric. During laboratory tests that took months, Adolff developed a yarn made of polypropylene that would float and retain its pink color for longer than two weeks. A special color pigment and microscopic air bubbles injected into the yarn produced the desired result. Tests with buckets of Biscayne Bay water kept on the roof of the Miami Library for fourteen days provided the necessary proof.

The U.S. Army Corps of Engineers, which regulates and protects American coastal waters and therefore has the authority to issue permits governing any activity in Biscayne Bay, asked Christo and Jeanne-Claude to ensure that their project wouldn't disturb the manatees. Therefore in September 1982, an experiment involving five manatees was conducted by Dr. Daniel K. Odell in Orlando's Seaquarium. Half of a pool filled with seawater was covered with the type of fabric that would be used for *Surrounded Islands;* the other half was left uncovered. Dr. Odell reported that the manatees not only preferred to linger under the fabric but also used its shade "to engage in mating procedures."

In October 1982, Jeanne-Claude asked me to order 6.5 million square feet of pink polypropylene, the largest quantity of fabric every required for one of their projects—enough to cover ninety football fields. The Corps of Engineers issued their official permission at the end of the month.

Although other pending projects—namely *The Pont Neuf Wrapped* and

Wrapped Reichstag—also demanded their attention, Christo and Jeanne-Claude devoted themselves to *Surrounded Islands*. Ted Doughtery, the leader of the team, moved to Miami in September 1982 and attempted to find a company that would be capable of sewing all of the fabric that would be used in the project. Unfortunately, however, he couldn't find one, so Christo and Jeanne-Claude bought five industrial sewing machines, rented a space in Hialeah, in northern Dade County, and hired forty-five seamstresses to sew the seventy-two sections of fabric needed to surround all eleven islands. They hired Herman Becker of Technical Textiles in Miami to oversee the work. The Hialeah space proved too small. The only space large enough to spread out and, later, to fold the fabric needed to surround one entire island turned out to be a former zeppelin hangar in Opa Locka. The hangar was soon awash in an ocean of pink.

While one team was working in the zeppelin hangar, another, led by Jon Becker and Brian Dougherty, installed anchors designed to hold the fabric in place—610 underwater, and 900 on the island beaches. In February 1983, the National Wildlife Rescue Team filed suit in federal court to stop the project. In March, after three days of hearings, an agreement was reached before the federal judge, James Lawrence King. The court granted the National Wildlife Rescue Team the right to monitor the project; Christo and Jeanne-Claude were instructed to pay for the rental of a boat the NWRT would use to do this.

In the early spring, Christo went back to his studio to create more preparatory drawings. It was his last chance to do this before the actual completion of *Surrounded Islands*, as he never does drawings or collages after a project has been realized. On April 18, Christo and Jeanne-Claude moved to Miami to oversee the launching of *Surrounded Islands*. It was the end of what they call the "software period" and the beginning of the "hardware period."

As the project's official photographer, I logged endless hours in a helicopter, piloted by a Vietnam veteran; I felt as if it had become a second home.

On April 27, five hundred prospective workers streamed through the gate of Pelican Harbor, the project's headquarters. They were given their *Surrounded Islands* T-shirts and hats, designed by the artists' friend Willy Smith. In the days that followed, the teams were also given instructions in first aid and fire prevention. Then Christo and Jeanne-Claude introduced them to the project and organized teams for each island. Both were so busy taking care of various last-minute details that even the sad news of Christo's father's death in Plovdiv was attenuated by the immensity of the work.

Finally, by the early morning of May 2, everything was ready: The seventy-two fabric sections were bundled up in preparation for their launch into the water at Interrama. Some of the sections were more than 330 feet long. Everybody helped carry the fabric bundles into the water. Using megaphones, Christo, Jeanne-Claude, and Ted Dougherty coordinated the carriers teams; it was critical to synchronize everyone's activities. As soon as all the sections for

Biscayne Bay, Miami, Florida, 1983: Christo, Jeanne-Claude, and Ted Dougherty at the training site for *Surrounded Islands.* (Photo: Wolfgang Volz)

one island were secured together, they were floated to their designated island. Jeanne-Claude broke a rib while carrying one of the bundles. The launching marathon was finished after midnight, and only after many delays. Additional workers, mostly Haitians, had been hurriedly hired from a temp agency.

By the evening of May 3, every one of the eleven islands had been surrounded by bundles of pink fabric 220 feet from shore. The next morning, the teams tried to open the bundles simultaneously, but because of heavy winds, only the smallest island blossomed into pink by evening. On another island, a breeze created a giant bubble that could only be deflated by people literally throwing themselves onto the fabric.

While Jeanne-Claude oversaw the entire installation process from a helicopter, Christo shouted his orders from a boat—holding a megaphone but not, despite repeated urging from others, using it—moving from island to island, his hair windblown and his clothes soaked, urging on the workers. He did everything he could to convince everyone that pulling on the ropes to unfold the pink fabric was the most important job in the world. In the process, he began to lose his voice. But by May 6, Biscayne Bay was an orgy of pink.

Seen from the air, the islands resembled inverted water lilies, with the pink outside and the green inside. "These are my Monet water lilies," an-

Biscayne Bay, Miami, Florida, 1983: Cyril working at *Surrounded Islands*. (Photo: Wolfgang Volz)

nounced Christo. *Surrounded Islands* was, to date, their most aesthetically striking project, and Christo and Jeanne-Claude reveled in it in different ways. Sidney Chaplin, one of Charlie Chaplin's grandsons, drove Christo around the islands in a small motorboat, giving him a chance to observe and reflect upon the project. Jeanne-Claude surveyed the islands from a helicopter. She watched over the monitors, who in turn watched over the islands around the clock by circling them in rubber dinghies.

Albert and David Maysles urged Christo to view *Surrounded Islands* from the air. During previous projects, Jeanne-Claude had always insisted Christo never go up in a helicopter. This time, however, she nearly forced him onto one. It was, she realized, the only way he would see the project the way she had. He cheerfully gave in. And what he saw nearly overwhelmed him with excitement. Over and over, he shouted, "Look! Look! It's wonderful! Incredible! Beautiful!" When he returned, Jeanne-Claude asked, tongue in cheek, "So, did we do a good job for you, Mr. Christo?" "Much beautiful job," replied the still-dazzled Christo.

"We were constantly wet during *Surrounded Islands,*" Christo remembered later. "Whether we took sandwiches out to the young people on the islands or fixed something, our clothes were always soaked up to our hips." The project had one curious outcome: Nine months after it was completed, a number of babies were born to workers, monitors, and collaborators. Perhaps more than any other project, *Surrounded Islands* required intensive human interaction. Bathing suits were the workers' most common attire.

On May 17, the process to remove everything—except for the underwa-

Miami, Florida, May 1983: The mayor of Miami congratulating the artists. From left, Attorney of the Surrounded Islands Project, Joseph Fleming, Mayor Maurice Ferre, Ted Dougherty, Jeanne-Claude, Christo, and art historian Jonathan Fineberg. (Photo: Wolfgang Volz)

ter anchors—began. But the process was not a sad one. Everybody felt enriched. Even the ospreys had benefited from the project; the work of art had prevented visitors from coming to their island and afforded them some peace.

In July, after attending a wedding in Paris—that of Jeanne-Claude's sister Alexandra to Daniel Gérard—Christo, Jeanne-Claude and I set out for Arles. Slides of *Surrounded Islands* were to be shown at the Recontres Internationales de la Photographie. We were still exhausted by the project, and therefore decided to treat ourselves to something special. We bought a Michelin guide at a gas station and agreed that we would eat only at two- and three-star restaurants on our way to Arles. When we finally reached Arles, Christo and I had upset stomachs and no longer wanted to eat any kind of food. Nevertheless, Arles was a complete success. Everyone enjoyed my slides of *Surrounded Islands,* which were shown in the Roman amphitheater. Robert Rauschenberg was in the enthusiastic audience, and he warmly congratulated all of us.

THE PONT NEUF WRAPPED

The year 1984 started off with the hope that the Berlin Reichstag project, which Christo and Jeanne-Claude had been pursuing since 1971, might indeed become a reality. Harald Seidel, bureau chief of West German president Rainer Barzel, visited the artists at their home on Howard Street. Seidel led them to believe that permission to wrap the venerable German building might be issued as early as the following fall.

Unfortunately, an official meeting with President Barzel couldn't take place; too many people in Bonn—after catching wind of the project—had become nervous about the idea of the Reichstag being wrapped. Instead, a dinner for friends of the artists and supporters of *Wrapped Reichstag* was held at the home of Winnie and Otto Wolff von Amerongen on February 21, 1984. In addition to Barzel, among the distinguished guests were Dr. Arend Oetker, Count and Countess Peter and Marie-Christine von Wolff Metternich, Hugo Borger—director of Cologne's museums—Michael Cullen, and Karl Ruhrberg. Also present were members of the Committee for Wrapped Reichstag, which had been founded in 1978, including Dr. Ernst Houswedell, Dr. Gerd Bucerius, Professor Reimar Lüst, Dr. Wieland Schmied, and Professor Carl Vogel.

In the meantime, there were plenty of other things keeping Christo and Jeanne-Claude busy.

They received permission from the mayor of Barcelona, Pascual Maragall, to wrap the monument to Christopher Columbus in Barcelona's harbor. They had made their original request in 1975. Christo and Jeanne-Claude decided to decline the offer. It had come nine years too late; they simply had lost interest.

In March 1984, Jeanne-Claude became an American citizen—eleven years after Christo had. She decided, however, to keep her French passport, as well. Also in March, Christo, Jeanne-Claude, and I—along with Tom Golden, Harrison Rivera-Terreaux, and Josy Kraft—prepared an exhibition documenting *Surrounded Islands* for the Berlin National Gallery; it opened in July. Berlin's mayor, Eberhard Diepgen, gave a speech praising *Surrounded Islands,* but he carefully avoided any comment on the pending permission for *Wrapped Reichstag.*

The day after the couple celebrated their forty-ninth birthday on June 13, 1984, the Architectural Museum in Basel opened its doors. Inside was an installation by Christo and Jeanne-Claude. The small museum's four floors and the stairways were covered with drop cloths. The windows were covered with brown wrapping paper, bathing everything in a honey-colored light.

In August 1984, after nine years of negotiating, Jacques Chirac gave Christo and Jeanne-Claude permission to wrap the famous Pont-Neuf. At that point, neither the artists nor their team were as thrilled by this news as they might have been; they were concerned that the project would interfere with the Reichstag project, permission for which we were expecting at any moment.

But in October 1984, Rainer Barzel had left his post as president of Germany's Bundestag (and speaker of the House), and the prospects for the project seemed to be dimming. Nonetheless, during their Berlin visit in the summer of 1984, with the help of Annemarie Renger, Christo, Jeanne-Claude, and I were allowed to visit the Reichstag in order to examine and analyze it from every angle, including the roof. I took lots of photos.

With the Reichstag project being held in abeyance, Christo and Jeanne-Claude began serious preparations for *The Pont Neuf Wrapped*. They had devised a method for using climbers for *Wrapped Coast*, which would prove useful not only for the Pont-Neuf project but also for future projects, including the Reichstag. They also built a detailed scale model of the wrapped bridge.

In search for the right fabric, I once again turned to Adolff, the company that had recently produced the fabric for *Surrounded Islands*. Sadly, Jeanne-Claude's father, Jacques de Guillebon died in February 1985. He had been a strong supporter of *The Pont Neuf Wrapped* and had tried to help convince Jacques Chirac of its artistic merits.

While the *Surrounded Islands* exhibition was being installed in Hamburg that February, Christo and Jeanne-Claude revealed to the closest members of their team that they had a new idea in the works—*The Umbrellas, Joint Project for Japan and USA.*

Later that month in France, the artists and their team gathered at a bridge in Grez-sur-Loing, a town near Paris. The team included the engineers for the project, Mitko Zagoroff, John Thomson, Vahé Aprahamian, and Ted Dougherty, as well as Antonio Pagnotta, Susan Astwood, Tom Golden, Harrison Rivera-Terreaux, and their son Cyril. The weather was bitterly cold and Jeanne-Claude wore a goose-down coat as they watched workers and climbers, led by project director Johannes Schaub, test-wrap this small bridge, a trial run for the wrapping of the Pont-Neuf. Like the Pont-Neuf, Grez-sur-Loin's bridge is a historical monument and therefore had to be fully protected. There would be no drilling into the stone. Wooden boards and rubber-buffered steel scaffolding served as protection for the bridge, as well as a support for the fabric.

During this and a second test, performed in March, the artists tried out a number of methods until they found the one most appropriate for wrapping the Pont-Neuf. During that second test, they also decided on which fabric to use. It would be made of polyamide, and its color would closely resemble the shade of sandstone of the Pont-Neuf. The color and the fabric's ability to reflect light subtly would make the bridge take on different tones—gold, straw, or champagne—depending on the time of day.

Mayor Chirac, concerned that allowing the project would somehow damage him politically, unexpectedly announced his intention to withdraw his permission. Christo and Jeanne-Claude decided to continue with their plans anyway. They started thinking about the color and thickness of the ropes, and asked me to order 454,178 square feet of nonflammable polyamide fabric from the Adolff Company. To prepare for the sewing of the pattern, they ordered new measurements of the bridge. None of the old technical drawings of the Pont-Neuf were nearly precise enough to establish what pattern should be used for the bridge's twelve arches, each of which had a different curve and size.

Meanwhile, the search for a suitable site in Japan for *The Umbrellas* had begun in earnest. In April 1985, Christo, Jeanne-Claude, *New York Times* bureau chief Henry Scott-Stokes and Torsten Lilja went on a tour of Japan to explore the landscape near Kyushu, Fukuoka, Kyoto, Shiga, Toyama, Niigata, Karuisawa, and in the Fukushima and Kobe provinces.

On June 13, Christo and Jeanne-Claude celebrated their combined age of one hundred.

Though still waiting for permission from Chirac's office to proceed with the Pont-Neuf project, Christo and Jeanne-Claude's workers began actual construction on August 25. Steel cables, building blocks, and chains were fixed around the bridge's piers below the waterline. By September, all the protective gear and every component for securing the fabric had been installed on the bridge. Not a single nail or screw had been used—everything was fastened with rubber bearings. Wearing life vests, Christo and Jeanne-Claude oversaw every detail of the installation. With enormous enthusiasm, Parisians greeted the arrival of the climbers and workers who were to wrap the silky fabric around the bridge. The work, however, was exhausting. The crew worked three straight shifts. "One can sleep once it's over" was the general consensus. Johannes Schaub and Simon Chaput hired 660 monitors, whose job was to explain the project to visitors, and to watch the bridge continuously.

When later they were asked which of their projects they had found most difficult, Christo and Jeanne-Claude invariably replied that it was the *Pont Neuf Wrapped.* "In July of 1985, we were still waiting for permission but had already spent a vast amount of money," Jeanne-Claude recalled. Christo added, "I had flown to Paris before Jeanne-Claude and went immediately to a briefing with the police. There, when I heard everybody talk seriously about the project, I knew that it started to become real."

The official letter granting them permission arrived on September 16, 1985. By then, the first arch had already been wrapped. In a press release about the project, the artists stated the following:

> Begun under Henri III, the Pont-Neuf was completed in July 1606, during the reign of Henry IV. No other bridge in Paris offers such topographical and visual variety, today as in the past. From 1578 to 1890, the Pont Neuf underwent continual changes and additions of the most extravagant sort, such as the construction of shops on the bridge under Soufflot, the building, demo-

Paris, 1985: Jeanne-Claude and Christo in front of *The Pont Neuf Wrapped,* 1975–1985. (Photo: Wolfgang Volz)

lition, rebuilding and once again demolition of the massive rococo structure, which housed the Samaritaine's, water pump. Wrapping the Pont-Neuf continues this tradition of successive metamorphoses by a new sculptural dimension and transforms it, for fourteen days, into a work of art.

After 42,900 feet of rope had been secured, Christo himself wrapped the bridge's forty-four streetlights, helped by Rivera-Terreaux, Golden, and Chaput. The project was completed on September 22, 1985. Christo and Jeanne-Claude walked with Mayor Chirac across the bridge. In addition to relishing the chance to be photographed by journalists from around the world, Chirac claimed that he had never really understood why some on his staff had been so vehemently against this project.

For the entire two-week period that the bridge was wrapped, the traffic over the Pont-Neuf as well as on the river ran its usual course. The Pont-Neuf was now both a sculpture and a fully functioning bridge. Parisians celebrated by having picnics; romance flourished, as did lively debate and the occasional dancing; the clochards continued their lives below it. Dozens of artists sketched, painted, and drew their impressions. All told, three million visitors came to see *The Pont Neuf Wrapped.*

Christo and Jeanne-Claude received visitors from all over the world at La Cantine, the project's restaurant, located on a barge anchored near the bridge. They took their more distinguished guests for a viewing from a small tugboat, affording some privacy.

"We didn't expect that the fabric's color would take on so many nuances,"

Jeanne-Claude said later. "The colors were incredible. In the morning, the fabric looked like straw, and by late afternoon it had turned into a rich golden tone." Christo agreed with this assessment. "The color was a complete surprise," he said, "and then there were also the glowing seams in the arches. We had tried to fill those with energy, and we got those beams of light along the seams—fantastic."

Among their prominent guests were officials from Germany. This proved useful in reviving interest in the Reichstag project. The success of *The Pont Neuf Wrapped* reignited discussion in Germany, though not all of it was supportive. Nonetheless, the artists met a Berlin businessman named Roland Specker, who had founded Berliners for the Reichstag, an organization that would eventually collect over 70,000 signatures from people in favor of the wrapping of the Reichstag.

THE UMBRELLAS

Since 1971, Christo and Jeanne-Claude have tried only twice to take a vacation. As Jeanne-Claude put it, "We don't need vacations; our work is our life." But in January of 1986, Jeanne-Claude made an attempt to take a break. Still exhausted from working on *The Pont Neuf Wrapped,* she told Christo that she needed two months off to work for a "good cause." She volunteered her services to charitable organizations, offering to do anything, but none was willing to take on a volunteer for so short a period of time. Instead, in exchange for one of Christo's collages, she spent two weeks at a health spa in Bermuda. Christo visited her on weekends.

One day, while waiting for Christo at the airport, Jeanne-Claude saw a lipstick that she liked in one of the boutiques. "This is a great color," she said to the salesperson, who replied, "Yes, for redheads. You don't have red hair." When Christo arrived, she asked him how he would like her with red hair. Jeanne-Claude had been plucking her gray hairs for a while, but she decided that she couldn't go on doing that forever. "Red?" Christo replied. "Yes, this is a great idea, but I'd like to pick the shade." Since then, her hair has remained red. Christo's hair had also turned gray—premature grayness is a family trait. Jeanne-Claude asked him whether he wanted to dye his hair, too. He declined, indignant.

In the spring of 1986, Christo and Jeanne-Claude traveled with Henry Scott-Stokes to Japan to look for a valley for their umbrellas project. They started their 2,300-mile tour in Tokyo, having stocked up on every topographical map they could get their hands on. During the trip, Jeanne-Claude fell in love with Jinba, a small village in the Ibaraki province that she called her private Shangri-la. The color for the umbrellas had already been determined: blue for Japan and yellow for California. The blue represented the omnipresence of water in Japan; yellow signified the dryness of the California hills.

In July 1986, driven by Thomas Golden, Christo and Jeanne-Claude traveled around California for nine days, covering over three thousand miles as they searched for the American site for their project. Tom Golden did the driving. Christo and Jeanne-Claude sat in the backseat of the car, Christo poring over the topographic maps and Jeanne-Claude looking out the window. Christo tried guessing at the landscape's character by reading the maps. After reaching a location that had at first seemed promising, judging from the maps, they often found the view disappointing. If a site seemed promising, Jeanne-Claude took photos. There was, of course, ceaseless debate about the merits of each possible site. In the end, Christo and Jeanne-Claude agreed upon a valley sixty miles north of Los Angeles along Interstate 5 and the Tejon Pass, between the towns of Gorman and Grapevine.

Having decided upon the California site for the project, the artists returned to New York for a quiet end of summer. There is a routine to life on Howard Street in August: working all day, and then in the evenings going to the movies, dragging along anyone around. They prefer comedies. Jeanne-Claude is known for laughing so loudly that friends have sometimes been known to keep their distance. Both Christo and Jeanne-Claude love to laugh, firmly believing that it is good for one's health.

Later that month, they appeared on a popular German TV talk show, promoting the wrapping of the Reichstag. The project was constantly on their minds. In September, Berlin's newly elected mayor, Eberhard Diepgen, visited Christo and Jeanne-Claude at Howard Street. Although interested in their project, he was noncommittal. Christo made it clear that unless they were given an unambiguous sign that things would move ahead, he and Jeanne-Claude would concentrate exclusively on *The Umbrellas*.

After the opening of their *Wrapped Reichstag* exhibition at the Satani Gallery in Tokyo, the artists and I went on another trip through Japan, still in search of a site for *The Umbrellas*. The team had grown considerably—Golden, Masa Yanagi, Harriet Irgang, Chaput, Sylvie and I were now also involved. For nine days, we visited preselected locations, as well as some new ones. As they walked across harvested rice fields, they carried long bamboo sticks, which helped them visualize how the umbrellas would fit into the landscape. I took photos which Christo would later use as a basis for his collages and drawings. Finally, they settled upon an area between Hitachiota and Ota, in the province of Ibaraki—mostly because of the little village called Jinba, the very place Jeanne-Claude had liked immediately during their first visit.

Then they returned once again to Berlin, where they presented their new large-scale model for the *Wrapped Reichstag* at the New National Gallery. Despite the fact that Berliners for the Reichstag, under Roland Specker's leadership, had collected even more signatures in favor of the project, Mayor Diepgen and Philipp Jenninger, president of the German Bundestag, were still opposed to it.

The first scale model of *Wrapped Reichstag* had been sold to the Teheran Museum in Iran. After its arrival, however, the museum's workers accidentally unwrapped it, realizing too late that they had destroyed the work. Due to political turmoil surrounding Khomeini's arrival, the scale model was thought to be lost, but later restored. This was not the only time such a mistake had been made. When the scale model of the *Wrapped Teatro Nuovo, Project for Spoleto,* was sent to Stockholm's Aronowitsch Gallery, for example, Swedish customs officers removed the wrapping to inspect the inside. The scale model is in Christo's studio, but not yet repaired. In another case, Künstlerhaus, an art museum in Munich, intended to exhibit *Package on a Luggage Rack.* When Christo arrived for the opening of the exhibition, workers had already unwrapped the baby carriage and the mattress and had carefully laid out everything on the floor. "Now you can start your work," they told him. Then, as Christo and Jeanne-Claude learned long after the fact, someone at the Richard Feigen Gallery in Chicago unwrapped *Wrapped Fire Hydrant;* it was exhibited bare nonetheless as a "Christo sculpture."

In January 1987 came the sad news that David Maysles had died. Together with his brother Albert, David had been one of Christo and Jeanne-Claude's closest friends since 1971, having filmed every important project. David's death confirmed for them the value of good health. Both now go regularly to the Mayo Clinic for checkups.

Given that the Reichstag project seemed stalled (knowing that President Jenninger was firmly against it, Christo had canceled a meeting with him), preparations for *The Umbrellas* continued. The process of getting all the requisite permissions in Japan began with a meeting with the governor of the Ibaraki province in July 1987. Before that, however, the entire team made a pilgrimage to a shrine in Tokyo to receive the blessings of a tenth-century Japanese warrior hero named Masakado. Masakado is said to curse those who don't show him proper respect.

The Japanese governor looked at drawings and collages of *The Umbrellas* project, as well as at books about completed projects, and listened calmly to Christo, who was visibly nervous because of the importance of the meeting. Fortunately, the lengthy translations gave him time to relax. As it turned out, the governor was interested, immediately instructing members of his staff to support Christo and Jeanne-Claude and to accompany them while they did the preparatory work. Subsequent meetings with Japanese officials—Sakon Tonooka, the president of the Farmers' Association, as well as mayors of those cities that would be involved in the project—were equally successful. Everyone treated the project with great respect and seriousness, delighted that something like this would be taking place in their region. Christo and Jeanne-Claude walked through Jinba, happily envisioning what the charming Japanese village would look like with their umbrellas.

During the same trip, the team installed an exhibition of Christo's work from the collection of the Rothschild Bank in Zurich at the Takanawa (Seibu) Museum of Art in Karuisawa. One evening, while at a hot-spring bath, Christo slipped and dislocated his right shoulder. He was rushed by ambulance to a hospital. Communicating what had happened in Japanese was difficult. Told the next day whom he had treated, the attending doctor asked Christo for an autograph—though he himself had ordered Christo not to use his right hand.

His arm and shoulder bandaged, Christo returned to New York. Unable to do any drawings, he worked on the layouts of the book on *The Pont Neuf Wrapped,* using his left hand.

In September 1987, work on the Californian side of *The Umbrellas* continued, thanks to Tom Golden. He had organized meetings with Willie Brown, Jr., speaker of the Lower House, and Senators Diane Watson and Barry Keene. The California legislature issued a resolution thanking Christo and Jeanne-Claude for having chosen California as their site for the project. The California team, too, had grown considerably, and included Masa and his wife Harriet, Simon Chaput, Ted's wife Phyllis, Sylvie Schmidt, and myself. In October, the artists presented the project to officials from Kern and Los Angeles counties. They contacted local landowners and described their idea. Later, they walked through the area they had chosen, locating positions for the yellow umbrellas by holding up eighteen-foot poles. Once again, I took photographs. The area was spacious, sparse, and parched. Cows grazed on the golden-brown hills. Most of the land was owned by a public company called the Tejon Ranch. Tom Golden immediately bought shares in the company for the artists. The first encounter with the ranch's chief executive officer was strained, but over time, communications improved markedly.

Returning to Japan, the team hiked through the Ibaraki valley to mark the Japan locations. Through a translator, Christo and Jeanne-Claude talked with almost everybody they came across on the streets, in the rice fields, and in restaurants. Most of the rice farmers they encountered seemed to enjoy listening to these two strangers—one with flaming red hair (red hair is a particular novelty in that corner of the world), and the other who underscored his speech with wild gestures. The farmers had no problem grasping the concept that umbrellas in their rice fields could be a form of art. To the Japanese, art is not limited to exhibitions in museums; flower arrangements (*ikebana*) and rock gardens are also works of art. They felt honored that two *gaijin* (non-Japanese) artists had traveled so far to transform their valley into a work of art. The team drank thousands (six thousand, in all) cups of green tea and learned all about the cultivation of rice.

During evening meetings with the team, heads of family clans and village elders sat together and discussed the lease agreement, as well as the dates and chronology of the installation. The mood of these meetings was both relaxed and serious. Everyone took notes. I took photos. Albert Maysles and his new partner, Henry Cora filmed.

Preparations for *The Umbrellas* continued in May 1988, when Christo and Jeanne-Claude invited a number of international umbrella manufacturers to Cheyenne, Wyoming, to demonstrate their products. Cheyenne is one of the windiest places in the United States, and on the day before the umbrellas competition, a heavy snowstorm rampaged through the area. The winds were so strong, snowflakes flew horizontally. The next morning, however, as if by magic, the weather calmed. The competition took place in a field Ted Dougherty had rented outside town. The goal was to find a model that was approximately nineteen feet tall and twenty-eight feet in diameter and yet light enough to be carried and opened by ten people. Each manufacturer was asked to assemble that company's umbrella and to quote a price. A wide variety of designs was on display. One of them, a steel model built in Japan, was so heavy that it could be manipulated only by means of a crane. No model was declared a winner.

The process of contacting landowners in both Japan and California continued. There was a far greater number of landowners in Japan, where plots of land can be minuscule. The situation was less complicated in California, and a provisionary permit to gain access to the land was obtained by project director Tom Golden. On September 5, another expedition was made to identify potential umbrellas positions in Los Angeles and Kern counties. Christo and Jeanne-Claude walked ahead of the team, carrying surveyor's stakes, each of which had a luminescent red ribbon attached to its tip, so that the stakes would be visible from a distance. Christo registered the possible positions on his map. Now and then, Christo and Jeanne-Claude entered into a heated debate. From time to time, they also reevaluated a number of umbrella positions from a distance. Once they signaled their approval, Simon Chaput and Vahé Aprahamians hammered shorter and sturdier poles into the ground next to the tall wooden sticks to make them, hopefully, cow-resistant. In addition, a small magnet was embedded next to each pole, so that the team would later be able to locate it with a magnetic device. Vahé noted and numbered each position. Because of the distances that separated them, team members often communicated via radio. I, of course, photographed the proceedings.

The sun-parched Californian hills are covered with sharp-edged grasses, and members of the crew protected themselves by wrapping duct tape around their trousers and shoes to keep grass seeds from getting into their socks. The seeds are spiked and can make walking painful and later impossible. Jeanne-

Los Angeles County, September, 1988: Christo and Jeanne-Claude during the survey of the land for *The Umbrellas* project. (Photo: Wolfgang Volz)

Claude protected her head and hands with a Japanese farmer's hat and white gloves. For three weeks, she and the others—a somewhat odd-looking band—wandered up and down the Southern California hills. They covered over 150 miles. A team of professional surveyors followed behind them, recording the precise geodesic coordinates of each umbrella position.

On September 27, 1988, my girlfriend, Sylvie Schmidt, and I were married under an old oak on the land where *The Umbrellas* would be standing. Jeanne-Claude had ordered a blue-and-yellow wedding cake. Tom Golden had obtained the legal authority to perform the ceremony. Christo and Jeanne-Claude served as witnesses, and Christo poured champagne.

Finally, after 1,760 umbrella positions had been established, the team began to relax. They looked around at the landscape, which was dotted with wooden stakes, each one playfully positioned to reflect the character of the land, and began to imagine what the finished project might look like.

That October, almost the same team traveled to Japan. But there, the procedure was completely different. The project's dual character naturally invited comparisons between the two cultures. Two days were spent explaining the necessary preparations for *The Umbrellas* to local officials. At one point Christo became so enraged by these seemingly futile discussions that it was decided it would be better if he stayed on the bus and didn't attend the meeting that day. Everything, even the small magnets used for marking umbrella positions, triggered lengthy discussions. Finally the team was given permission to negotiate minor details with the village elders themselves.

In the middle of October, they went to the village of Satonomiya, the first

Ibaraki, Japan, 1988: Christo and Jeanne-Claude during the staking for *The Umbrellas, Japan-USA.* (Photo: Wolfgang Volz)

stop, to meet the local guides. These guides, most of them over seventy years old, would be instrumental in sorting out property issues involving each potential umbrella position. In Japan, there are no land-registration offices; to make things more confusing, these guides are usually familiar with only a small area. Unfortunately, the first umbrella position, which Christo and Jeanne-Claude had chosen, turned out not to be possible. Christo was so incensed by this that he loudly declared that the entire project was cancelled. Henry Scott-Stokes, the project director, tried to mediate, but the Japanese were scandalized that a Westerner would lose his temper right at the beginning. The authorities finally gave in. During the next two weeks, similar incidents occurred almost daily: Christo and Jeanne-Claude would mark a position, and immediately a discussion about whether it was too close to something else would start. Land ownership became an issue for almost every umbrella position. Usually, the guide would go to the nearest house to make inquiries; he also accompanied the surveyors on their rounds. Everybody the team met offered advice. When, after some reflection, Christo and Jeanne-Claude selected a new position, the procedure started all over again. A difference of merely six feet between proposed positions meant asking permission from a different property owner.

Heat and dryness had proved problematic in California. In Japan, however, frequent drenching rains were the problem. From time to time, the team sank up to the knees into the muddy rice fields, and there was constant danger from poisonous snakes. The other rice farmers, meanwhile, rarely interrupted their work to watch what was going on. Before long, ninety positions for umbrellas had been established in the Sato River. From dawn to dusk, the members of the team were busy in the fields; in the evenings, they met with property owners to negotiate the terms of the leasing contracts. In the end, 1,340 umbrella positions were established and 459 separate leases signed.

During *The Umbrellas* project, a new era of communications technology began for the artists: they finally got a fax machine, which helped coordinate activities on two continents. Later, after some resistance, Jeanne-Claude even consented to buying a computer, though her assistants Susan Astwood and Calixte Stamp would be the ones to use it at first; years later, Jeanne-Claude learned to make friends with it.

In February 1989, Christo and Jeanne-Claude enjoyed a small moment of satisfaction when former New York City Parks Commissioner Gordon Davis, an opponent of *The Gates* project, visited Howard Street with the intention to buy an original work about the project. But he found the prices too steep. Christo and Jeanne-Claude made him a present of twenty signed posters. That somebody so strongly opposed to *The Gates* was interested in acquiring art connected with the project encouraged them not to give up hope that someday it might be realized.

In March, Christo and Jeanne-Claude's friends and collaborators—Golden, the Doughertys, August ("Augie") L. Huber III, the Thomsons, Vahé and Donna Aprahamian, Jim and Josephine Fuller, Mitko Zagoroff, Masa and Harriet Yanagi, Chikara Iwamoto, Ted Green, Simon Chaput, and I met at Howard Street for another brainstorming session about *The Umbrellas*. Because the umbrellas contest in Cheyenne hadn't resulted in the choice of a suitable model for the project, the artists and their friends had tried to design their own. At first, this didn't seem too difficult, but it was soon apparent that the requirements complicated matters. The umbrella needed to be both lightweight and able to withstand winds whose strength had not yet been determined. It also had to be recyclable, not overly expensive, and easy to open. Moreover, the pole needed to be adjustable, so that the umbrella could stand vertically on uneven (and sometimes steep) terrain. Christo and Jeanne-Claude had faced challenges such as these with their projects. At first, things always seem easy—a running fence, surrounded islands, a wrapped bridge—but each project inevitably reveals its complexities the moment concrete planning begins.

During such brainstorming sessions, Jeanne-Claude had gradually developed the habit of constantly asking the engineers questions, saying that she didn't understand how things work. This, of course, drove the engineers nuts, but it does force them to reevaluate the technical details. In this case, thanks to her ceaseless questions, the team decided that the umbrella's poles would be made out of aluminum, which is lighter and easier to recycle than other metals.

In June 1989, at a public hearing in Kern County, Golden and Augie Huber presented *The Umbrellas* project. Golden had suggested that the artists not be present. He wished to avoid attracting media attention, which might trigger local resistance. This turned out to be a wise decision. Following the hearing, Christo, Jeanne-Claude, attorney Scott Hodes, and representatives of the Tejon Ranch met for dinner and worked out most of the details regarding the leases.

In Knokke-Zoute, Belgium, a large exhibition of original preparatory works for *The Umbrellas* opened on June 18. The catalog of the Guy Dieters Gallery was the first extensive publication on the project.

During another think-tank session at Howard Street at the end of August, experts from North Sails, a well-known sail manufacturer in Connecticut, helped the artists determine how the fabric for the octagonal umbrellas should be sewn. In the meantime, lobbying activities for other projects continued. Rita Süssmuth had by this point become the new president of the German Bundestag. During a September meeting with Roland Specker, representing Berliners for the Reichstag, she expressed her interest in *Wrapped Reichstag*.

In October, prolonged negotiations were resumed in Ibaraki, Japan, to resolve a number of legal issues involving the project's possible interference with the upcoming rice harvest, its effects on fishing in the Sato River and on traffic management, as well as the potential for contact between the umbrellas and telephone and electrical wires. There were also questions regarding airspace and water rights. Despite all the negotiating, Christo and Jeanne-Claude found time to think more about the project and to reshuffle some of the designated umbrella positions.

On November 9, something happened that nobody could have predicted: the fall of the Berlin Wall. The Berlin Wall had, of course, inspired the Rue Visconti project in Paris almost three decades earlier. It now regained importance for the artists. Jeanne-Claude learned the news in New York and immediately called Christo, who was giving a lecture about *Wrapped Reichstag*, in Cleveland. He interrupted his lecture to share the news with his audience.

In January 1990, a new challenge regarding *The Umbrellas* presented itself. Project engineers were asked to meet at Tokyo's Building Center, an institution that reports to the Japanese Ministry of the Building Trade. Aluminum, they were informed, was not permitted as a building material in Japan. Only this high-ranking institution could issue a special permit for its use.

Officials from the Building Center also asked the engineers to test one of the umbrella prototypes in a wind tunnel. At the time, there were four wind tunnels in the West large enough to test a nearly twenty-foot-tall umbrella. Three were owned by NASA and had been booked for years in advance. Luckily, the engineers managed to secure an appointment at the Aerodynamic Laboratory of the National Research Council in Ottawa, which operated the

New York, 1989: Christo installing some preparatory collages for *The Umbrellas* in the D.O. (Downstairs Office) reception area. (Photo: Sanjiro Minamikawa)

world's second-largest wind tunnel. The California-based company Rain for Rent, Inc., located in Bakersfield, produced two prototypes to be tested in Ottawa. The tests were to determine whether the umbrellas could endure wind gusts up to sixty-five miles per hour when opened and one hundred miles per hour when closed. The winds would come from various angles. Christo and Jeanne-Claude watched and commented on the highly scientific procedure, supervised the video documentation, and offered advice to everybody. It was a tense moment; the future of the project depended not only on the results but on their scrupulous documentation.

Christo and Jeanne-Claude decided to resolve all remaining aesthetic questions regarding *The Umbrellas*—such as choosing the final hue and pattern for the fabric—on-site. They determined that the umbrellas should have a pointed top, yet meeting this seemingly simple requirement proved enormously challenging. North Sails had sewn the prototypes umbrellas' fabric from the various yellow and blue samples I had found in Germany. The first life-size test took place in secret in California in February 1990. This test was of critical importance not only for the umbrellas but also for the companies providing their services, as it would establish whether or not they would be able to collaborate on the project.

This test was held on the Tejon Ranch property. Ten members of the team carried the two prototypes up and down the California hills. The same group also installed at various locations umbrellas of varying hues of yellow. Jeanne-Claude tried to crank open an umbrella. She managed to do it within forty-five seconds, the time designated for this in their specifications. "This should be easy," she announced. "Even I can handle it."

Christo and Jeanne-Claude rushed up distant hilltops to view the different hues of yellow from all angles and to make their decision. Finally, they agreed on a color called "golden yellow," which of course made Tom Golden ecstatic. Augie Huber had brought Vince and Jonita Davenport, who would turn out to be invaluable members of the team.

The same procedure took place in Ibaraki two weeks later, led by Akira Kato of the Muto Construction company, but because of a lack of space the tests could not be done in secret. The artists chose to have them take place in Jinba. Two prototypes, with fabric of four different hues of blue, had been flown over from California. The difference between the two cultures once again became obvious. Workers from the Japanese firm involved in the project arrived wearing uniforms and helmets. Their boss, Kato-san, issued his orders; everything was perfectly organized. Because rain was expected during the time of the installation of the project, Christo and Jeanne-Claude asked to have the fabric doused with water from the Sato River to gauge what effect rain would have on the color.

Satomi's mayor was accorded the honor of opening the first blue umbrella. The artists tried to solicit the team's input regarding the blue hues. First, Christo and Jeanne-Claude loudly and vehemently debated the pros and cons of each color variation, then asked team members to give their opinion. Everyone quickly learned that the best way to voice an opinion was to do so in such a manner that did not inspire Christo and Jeanne-Claude to start the whole decision process all over again. Otherwise, the process would have gone on for weeks.

The tests also proved useful in establishing a procedure to open all 3,100 umbrellas. Everything, down to the smallest detail, needed to be written in both English and Japanese, requiring a huge amount of translation work.

The project's permit application, which contained all the test results and weighed almost twenty-two pounds, was submitted to the engineers of the Construction Ministry at the Tokyo Building Center in early June. Officials were already evaluating it by the middle of the month. As each umbrella was roughly equal to the size of a two-story house, the ministry issued permits to construct 1,340 houses.

The J. F. Adolff Company was chosen once again to manufacture the fabric; I purchased from them 2.6 million square feet of yellow and 2 million square feet of blue fabric. We tend to be loyal customers; part of our decision to choose Adolff was based on how well the company had performed with regard to *Surrounded Islands* and *The Pont Neuf Wrapped*. Adolff also helped to find a company to dye the fabric. The umbrellas for both Japan and California were to be assembled by Rain for Rent. To fill the order, Rain for Rent had to set up an extra factory floor. The white fabric was woven in Germany by Adolff, then sent to the town of Bayreuth to be dyed. From there, it was shipped to San Diego, where North Sails sewed the fabric. Each umbrella consisted of eight fabric triangles.

That September, Christo, accompanied by myself, Sylvie, Josy Kraft, and Simon Chaput wrapped the floor of the vestibule of the Art Gallery of New South Wales in Sydney, Australia. The gallery's statues and columns were also covered with an off-white cotton drop cloth generally used by professional housepainters to protect floors and furniture. This indoor installation was part of a large Christo exhibition at the museum. On our way back from Australia, we met Jeanne-Claude in Japan, where, after yet another round of meetings with different local authorities, including the police, we switched the positions of a few more umbrellas.

In the meantime, the production of steel bases and leveling devices for the California umbrellas had begun in Kansas. The aluminum poles, ribs, and struts were made in Virginia and California, the steel connecting elements in Iowa. Everything was to be shipped to Bakersfield, for final assembly. The sheer numbers were daunting: 24,800 struts and 24,800 ribs mounted on 3,100 bases, with a winch for opening the fabric attached to each pole. Then the aluminum parts of 1,340 umbrellas had to be painted blue, 1,760 yellow. As a last step, the fabric had to be fitted to the aluminum structure.

The plan was to open the umbrellas in Japan and California simultaneously in October 1991. The exact timing would depend on Japan's rice harvest, which needed to be finished before the installation could start. By the early fall of 1990, it had become more and more apparent that most of the steel bases for the umbrellas would have to be installed before the rice-planting season started, because afterward the fields would be submerged. In November, Christo and Jeanne-Claude invited all landowners to an evening meeting to discuss ways they could compensate the farmers for the loss of rice caused by the steel bases. The majority of farmers had nothing against the bases being installed as early as December of 1990.

However, these bases proved far too heavy to ship from the United States to Japan. Therefore, the 1,250 bases for the Japanese umbrellas were ordered in Ibaraki. For those ninety umbrellas that would be positioned in the Sato riverbed, ninety special bases had to be manufactured. These were equipped with an additional steel plate, increasing the weight of a single base to nearly 6,500 pounds.

Despite being busy with *The Umbrellas,* Christo and Jeanne-Claude were paying close attention to what was happening in Germany. On October 3, 1990, the reunification was celebrated in front of the Reichstag. It was becoming clear that Berlin would eventually again become Germany's capital and, should the government move from Bonn, that the German parliament would take up residence in the Reichstag. The artists watched those developments with both enthusiasm and anxiety—they worried that they might not have an opportunity to realize *Wrapped Reichstag.* They knew it wouldn't be possible to wrap a parliamentary building once it was in full use.

On Christmas Eve of 1990, the first preassembled bases—each one measuring six and a half feet by six and a half feet, and consisting of two steel crossed bars and a center receiving sleeve—were installed by Kato and his team in the rice fields. The soil was frozen; manually inserting the anchors that would hold the bases into the ground was grueling work. The bases were deposited at the side of the road near a designated location, then carried by hand to the exact spot. Whole families of Japanese rice farmers—who knew their land best—were enlisted to be part of the work teams. For some reason, the tiny magnets that had been installed in the fall of 1988 to help relocate umbrella positions couldn't be found.

Under Vince Davenport's supervision, installation of the California umbrella bases began in January 1990, when the hills were covered with snow. The anchors were screwed into the ground by hydraulic drills. As in Japan, each anchor had to resist a pull of 3,300 pounds. The teams in both Japan and California reported by fax their daily progress to Howard Street.

In early February 1989, a small crisis erupted when the Adolff Company filed for bankruptcy; creditors confiscated the fabric produced for *The Umbrellas.* I immediately went to Adolff and the dyers. After six hours of intense negotiation, I managed to convince the two factories to continue the dying of the fabric. I had to agree to a higher price for the finished dyed product; Adolff had underestimated the costs involved, and the firms realized they had the upper hand. After four weeks of talks with Adolff's creditors, the crisis was finally under control. The artists managed to negotiate a $5 million line of credit with the Bank of Liechtenstein. Christo's original artworks served as collateral. The project's cost continued to rise, eventually amounting to $26 million.

In Japan, rice farmers started planting rice around the steel bases. In California, poppies began to blossom on the hills, which looked as if someone had emptied buckets of red paint over the grass. Some of the bases were transported to their positions by helicopter, to avoid road traffic as much as possible. By July 1990, 1,454 bases had been installed. The process had started a little earlier in Japan, where 1,057 steel bases were in place by the end of March. In Bakersfield, the blue umbrellas for the Japanese part of the project were placed in containers—a total of eighty-eight, divided into ten different shipments from Long Beach Harbor, California to Hitachi Harbor in Ibaraki, Japan. Jeanne-Claude had requested that the umbrellas' transportation be done in multiple shippings to minimize potential loss.

Installation activities proceeded simultaneously; the teams in California and Japan were in constant contact with the Howard Street headquarters. The time difference meant that Jeanne-Claude didn't get much sleep. Christo worked feverishly in his studio. October 8 was the date set for opening the umbrellas—or the "blooming," as we all called it.

The rice plants were already waist-high while the installation of the bases continued. The receiving sleeves at the center of each base were wrapped in plastic to prevent animals, snakes especially, from nesting inside them. Every detail of the project's daily progress was carefully documented by me.

The blue umbrellas were stored at Hitachi Harbor. When one container was opened for customs inspection, water was discovered inside. To everyone's relief, none of the umbrellas showed any signs of water damage, but my wife Sylvie discovered that one yellow umbrella, inside a blue bag, had accidentally been shipped to Japan. We were all horrified. It was, luckily, the only mistake, and it was shipped back to California.

The California Highway Patrol and the Department of Transportation started preparing for a rush of visitors. Two hundred and twenty road signs, paid for by Christo and Jeanne-Claude, were posted along the roads and highways. In Japan, too, there was careful preparation for dealing with the traffic flow during the time of *The Umbrellas*. Meanwhile, divers installed the ninety bases in the Sato River by a crane.

In September, the closed umbrellas in their bags were carried to their positions. In Japan, some of this was done using vans, carts, and tractors, but most of the carrying was done by hand. Teams of ten to twelve Japanese men and women hauled the umbrellas through harvested fields, holding the handles sewn on the bag. In California, most of the umbrellas were carried to their positions by helicopters, which picked them up from temporary storage locations. Given the occasionally steep position of some umbrellas, helicopters offered the only possible way of getting them into place. Other locations could be reached by foot.

"Only 12 days to go" reads the notation on Jeanne-Claude's agenda for September 26. She flew to California; Christo flew to Japan. They had decided that it would be best to share supervisory duties for each side of the project; therefore, their paths crossed many times over the Pacific.

Teams on both sides of the ocean had calculated exactly how many people would be needed to implement the artists' request that all the umbrellas be opened on the same day. On October 3, over two thousand additional workers—mostly artists, teachers, and students from nearby universities and art schools in Japan and California—were hired. Some had worked with Christo and Jeanne-Claude before. Everybody was given a short training course in carrying, installing, and opening the umbrellas. They also received T-shirts that read THE UMBRELLAS in yellow and in blue, in Japanese on one side and in English on the other.

By the evening of October 7, the crowd of workers, divided into teams, had carried each umbrella to its position and secured it to its base. Everything was prepared for "blossom day." Christo's brothers, Stefan and Anani came from Bulgaria, along with their wives, Elke and Didi, and Anani's son Vladimir.

Then came a bombshell: the news that a typhoon was approaching Japan. Christo announced during a press conference that because of the rain, the umbrellas, including those in California, would be opened a day later. At that point, the weather in California was perfect, and his announcement was greeted with bewilderment. Visitors who had traveled a long distance for the grand event were deeply disappointed about the change in plans.

On October 9, at 5:30 A.M., umbrella number 809 was opened in the artists' presence in Jinba. For the next few hours, they watched blue umbrellas sprouting everywhere as they were driven from one viewpoint to another to get as many perspectives as possible. I worked my camera feverishly. By 11:30 A.M., all the umbrellas were open. While Sylvie continued to take photos under Jeanne-Claude's direction, Christo, Masa Yanagi, and I raced to the airport to catch a flight to California. Flying over the international date line and into Los Angeles, we arrived on the same day at 8:00 A.M. We had landed in California before we had left Japan.

A helicopter immediately took us to the project site, where the unfurling of the yellow umbrellas had already begun. Watching the yellow dots spreading across the open landscape was an amazing spectacle. By 1:30 P.M., all the umbrellas were open. Christo was overwhelmed by the speed with which it happened. Everything looked exactly the way he and Jeanne-Claude had envisioned it; if anything, the sight was even more splendid than they had imagined. This is the most dramatic moment of a project—when they learn whether the reality matches the expectations, whether everything that has been planned for

California, 1991: Christo and Jeanne-Claude with their yellow umbrellas in California. (Photo: Wolfgang Volz)

years turns out the way it is supposed to. "In the end," said Jeanne-Claude, "the projects turn out to be much better than the drawings, more beautiful than our wildest dreams."

There was little time for contemplation. The next day, the typhoon that had forced us to postpone the project for twenty-four hours changed course again, heading back toward Japan. The local workers had already gone home, but Jeanne-Claude managed to organize enough help to close every umbrella. They were reopened on October 15, though only for three hours. Still, what a three hours! The sunlight reflected the umbrellas' blue color in the waters of the rice fields, and the result was magical—a fairy-tale landscape.

In California, the yellow umbrellas looked like precious stones capriciously strewn around the valley. Visitors drove by in pickup trucks, RVs, cars, buses, motorcycles, and bicycles. On the nearby highway, traffic slowed. People sat under the umbrellas and ate picnics; a wedding ceremony took place in the shade of one of them. Some enjoyed sunbathing on the bases. Cowboys, policemen, children—everyone wanted to be photographed under the umbrellas. All kinds of kitschy souvenirs were being hawked along the road, much to Christo's and Jeanne-Claude's disapproval.

In Japan, there were frequent traffic jams on the narrow main roads during the weekends. Policemen were positioned near the umbrellas, directing traffic and distributing official information sheets about the project. To the Japanese, the umbrellas seemed like houses without walls; to the artists' delighted surprise, they removed their shoes before stepping on the bases. As in California, picnics were common. Rice farmers ate their lunch in the umbrellas' shade, for despite all the hoopla, work went on the fields. Farmers sold visitors fresh vegetables they had grown or grilled trout they had caught.

On October 20, many of the umbrellas on the California side were closed because of a storm warning. The storm never materialized, and the umbrellas were reopened a day later. Jeanne-Claude learned from one of the monitors that President Ronald Reagan had stopped by to see *The Umbrellas.*

Up to this point, Christo and Jeanne-Claude had looked at their creation separately, each on a different continent. It was obviously important that they enjoy *The Umbrellas* together. They met in Japan on October 24 and visited some of the spots that weren't accessible to the public. "I was excited to see my umbrellas from those hidden places," recalled Christo. "I loved going back to those locations, because I remembered what they'd looked like without the umbrellas."

While in Japan, Christo and Jeanne-Claude received tragic news from California: During a prethunderstorm gust of wind, an umbrella had killed a visitor. Upon hearing this news, Christo burst into tears, and for a time he was unable to stop sobbing. Jeanne-Claude ordered all umbrellas to be closed at both sites. Together with their team, they closed the umbrellas nearest the project's headquarters and flew immediately to California.

In California, they learned more about the deadly accident from site manager Vince Davenport: "It was a nice beautiful day with a southerly breeze. Within fifteen minutes' time the wind had shifted and somebody said, 'Look at the canyon, here's this massive white thing working its way up the canyon.' It came, it went from a white puffy, rolling thing until all the sudden it was black. High winds and rain pelted the Tejon Pass late this afternoon. One gust ripping an umbrella from its foundation. The strong wind not only uprooted the umbrella itself but it also uprooted the base and then it went across the street and threw the woman into this hill. She was running, she had contact lenses supposedly and shielding her eyes from the dust, her husband trying to pull her, all kinds of things, we don't know."

In a public statement, Christo and Jeanne-Claude offered their sympathy to the family of Lori Rae Keevil-Matthews. They visited her husband and attended the funeral service.

During the storm, winds of ninety miles an hour knocked over power lines. Parts of Bakersfield, forty miles away, were without electricity for an entire day.

Four days later, Christo and Jeanne-Claude returned to Japan, where another sad duty awaited them: offering condolences to the family of Masaaki Nakamura, a worker on one of the teams who had been killed when an electric charge jumped from a power line to his crane; the crane itself had never touched the wires.

Three million people on two continents had visited and been moved by *The Umbrellas*. The two who had died would always be remembered. The book about the project is dedicated to them. Most of the materials used in the project were recycled and the landscape was returned to its original condition.

WRAPPED REICHSTAG

During a press conference in California, a journalist asked how Christo and Jeanne-Claude planned to proceed with their Reichstag project. Christo replied, "if the Germans want us to wrap the Reichstag, they should write to us."

In December 1991, the artists received an important letter of support from Rita Süssmuth, president of the Bundestag. She wrote that she wanted "to help realize your dream of wrapping the Reichstag." The letter went on to say, "Although I cannot promise anything, I am hopeful that we can achieve it together." Süssmuth invited Christo and Jeanne-Claude to meet with her in early February 1992. The letter put them in high spirits. A lunch meeting with Süssmuth was set for February 9, 1992, in Bonn.

Christo and Jeanne-Claude arrived in Düsseldorf a day before the meeting, and the next day, along with Roland Specker, Michael Cullen, and Sylvie, I drove them to Süssmuth's residence in Bonn. Jeanne-Claude had insisted on leaving ahead of time in case we got lost. We arrived almost an hour early and spent the remaining time sitting in the car, talking strategy.

Rita Süssmuth, a member of the Christian Democratic party, had invited Peter Conradi, a member of the Social Democratic party, to the lunch meeting. She came straight to the point. "Are you still interested in wrapping the Reichstag?" she asked Christo and Jeanne-Claude point-blank. Both nodded. "Good. Then we should talk about how we want to go about it."

Mrs. Süssmuth explained that her support for the project wouldn't be enough by itself. She would need to consult with leaders of the various parties represented in the parliament, as well as with the Ältestenrat, the Bundestag's senior advisory committee. She suggested that, in the meantime, mounting an exhibition of Christo's works in Bonn might win more public support. The artists emphasized that they would need eighteen months to prepare the project, and that wrapping the Reichstag after its restoration would not be an option. The lunch concluded with the feeling that some kind of agreement could be hammered out.

The next day, Christo, Jeanne-Claude, and I went to Berlin and looked at the Reichstag with new eyes. We were again given access to the roof. Once more, I took photographs of the building from every conceivable angle. These photos would become the basis for new collages and drawings; Christo had done no artwork related to the project between 1989 and 1991.

The jury assigned with judging the architecture competition for the restoration of the building was in favor of the wrapping. A scale model of *Wrapped Reichstag* was exhibited in Bonn as well as in the Reichstag itself, along with architectural models of the proposed restoration.

Convincing the members of the Bundestag turned out to be incredibly time-consuming. After a lobbying marathon that had lasted over two years, the team had, according to my calculations, spoken directly with some three hundred members of the German parliament.

Finally, on February 25, 1994, the Bundestag debated the wrapping project for seventy minutes. Opponents were afraid that it would be a mockery of Germany's democratic traditions. Supporters, most of them from the left, viewed the wrapping as an opportunity for the public to reflect upon the Reichstag's, and Germany's, troubled history, as well as an opportunity to exhibit new openness and tolerance. The project's most prominent opponent was Chancellor Helmut Kohl. There was a roll-call vote: 292 members voted yes; 223 voted no. The Reichstag would be wrapped.

After the vote, Süssmuth invited the entire team to her office. There were hugs all around. She confessed that the evening before she had bet five bottles of champagne that the project would be turned down. To her great delight, she had lost her bet.

I called Jeanne-Claude and gave her the good news. She had had to return to New York because of a visit from an important collector. She immediately sent out faxes to friends and supporters. As Christo summarized it during the press conference, "The software period just ended, and the hardware period begins."

The next morning, news of the vote was plastered on the front page of every German newspaper. Roland Specker and I became, respectively, financial and technical project directors. Christo was delighted to be able to return to his studio. He and Jeanne-Claude had spent six of the previous twelve months in Germany, and he had done very few drawings, and it was the drawings that would pay for the project.

But in other ways, they were ahead of the game. I had found the fabric for the wrapping, for example. Stephan Schilgen, the owner of a German factory specializing in industrial fabrics, had written a letter to Christo and Jeanne-Claude, offering to produce the material for them. Sylvie and I visited him at his factory in Emsdetten, near Münster, then sent a few samples to New York. In October 1992, Christo and Jeanne-Claude wrote us a letter. "Dear Mr. and Mrs. Fabric," it began, "we love the samples. . . ."

The hardware preparations for the *Wrapped Reichstag* started on March 10. I had to have the building measured and then locate rope manufacturers, stress analysts, and steel builders, as well as a sewing company. Perhaps most importantly, a contract between Christo and Jeanne-Claude's corporation (CVJ) and the German Bundestag needed to be drawn up. On May 6, 1994, the Verhüll-ter Reichstag GmbH—Wrapped Reichstag, Ltd., was incorporated. Roland Specker and I were appointed its executive directors. The company's sole purpose was organizing the wrapping of the Reichstag, and the funds, of course, were provided by the CVJ Corporation USA.

An initial secret test was carried out the following July with IPL, a German engineering company the artists had hired. The goal was to try out a variety of sizes of folds in the fabric. In New York, Jeanne-Claude had sewn a small scale model, showing the type, width, and spacing of the folds that would be used in the test. In the town of Constance, IPL had constructed scaffolding on the roof of a modern building the same height as the Reichstag. This allowed us to experiment with various ways of installing the fabric on the roof and unfurling it over the facade. The test also helped us to estimate the quantity of fabric we would need, as well as the thickness and color of the rope. A lengthy process of testing all the materials that would be used for the wrapping had already begun at the Federal Administration for Material Research and Testing in Berlin. German authorities needed to be assured of the fabric's nonflammability. The Berlin fire department even ran an open-air test using Molotov cocktails. The fabric steadfastly resisted igniting.

In August 1994, 119,600 square yards of polypropylene fabric were woven and then coated with aluminum. Roland Specker and I began to search for a space large enough to handle large sections of fabric. We considered only spacious, well-protected hangars. We negotiated for permits from various German authorities, in particular the police and fire departments, throughout the summer.

Christo and Jeanne-Claude gave a number of lectures about *Wrapped Reichstag* throughout Germany. Most of these had been scheduled long before the project's final approval, at the request of various Bundestag members. The Wrapped Reichstag, Ltd., set up headquarters in Berlin at 27 Ebertstrasse, located directly behind the Reichstag. In addition to office space, there was a conference room large enough to exhibit artwork related to the project.

In October, after seven and a half months of negotiations, the "contract regarding the short-term use of the Reichstag by Christo and Jeanne-Claude," as the official language put it, was signed in Bonn by Rita Süssmuth, Roland Specker, and myself. The time frame for the wrapping was established: June 17 to July 6, 1995.

On November 10, 1994, Rita Süssmuth was reelected president of the German Bundestag. The next day, the forty-five-pound application for wrapping the Reichstag was filed at the district office of Berlin's Tiergarten. On November 29, a long-prepared press conference took place, with Christo, Jeanne-Claude, and Rita Süssmuth discussing the realization of the project. The press conference went smoothly. Together, they announced the date for the wrapping (until then, a closely guarded secret). In the end, President Süssmuth thought that it would be a good idea to hold more frequent joint press conferences.

In the beginning of December, two factories, one located near Leipzig and the other near Cottbus, were selected to sew the gigantic fabric sections. Later, a third company had to be hired because of time pressure. Given that this company was located in northern Italy, coordination proved difficult.

The entire surface of the Reichstag, including its inner courts, had been surveyed to determine how much fabric would be needed. The 119,600 square yards I had estimated included an additional 50 percent to allow for the folds in the fabric, as requested by the artists. The fabric was divided into seventy sections, each sewn according to the patterns. Every section was designed to fit exactly in a predetermined position. When finished, sections were first measured, then rolled up inside the hangar, the location of which was kept a secret because of fear of sabotage. (Ever since the incidents that took place during preparations for *Running Fence*, Christo and Jeanne-Claude have paid close attention to security.) The hangar was located at Berlin, at a former Soviet airport. Even with its interior space of 33,000 square feet, the hangar was barely large enough to accommodate the folding of the sections, some of which were 22,200 square feet. There was always the fear, of course, that a fabric panel would turn out to be too short. Therefore, the team measured the sections over and over, comparing the results with the numbers obtained from the survey. The sewing companies had a tough job; some of the fabric sections weighed as much as 2,645 pounds.

In January 1995, Christo and Jeanne-Claude went to the Würth Museum in Künzelsau, Germany. Reinhold Würth himself had asked them to create an indoor installation at the museum during an exhibition of their work. Josy Kraft and his assistants, Simon Chaput, Vladimir Yavachev, Sylvie and I helped Christo wrap floors, staircases, some of the museum's furniture, and even some of the administrative offices. The skylights were covered with brown wrapping paper. So many people came to the museum on the day the exhibition opened that it was actually difficult to see any of the *Wrapped Floor*. Three days later, at the World Economic forum in Davos, Switzerland, Christo and Jeanne-Claude received the Crystal Award. They lectured about their work—particularly about *Wrapped Reichstag*.

After sending out a 450-page document asking for bids to build the steel substructures for the Reichstag project, I received a number of offers. The special framework the artists wanted needed both to accentuate the outline of the building and to hold the fabric in place. The contract, worth $2.8 million, was eventually awarded to a firm located in one of the newly formed German states. The company began work immediately. Meanwhile, in Bremen, the 51,200 feet of polypropylene rope I had ordered—its thickness one and a quarter inches—was rigged, tagged, and assigned a precise location on the building.

Christo and Jeanne-Claude continued to prepare the world for their project. They gave a lecture at the Royal Academy in London and had dinner afterward with Sir Norman Foster, the architect who in 1995 had been awarded the contract to restore the Reichstag. Sir Norman had already visited the artists at Howard Street. In London, he offered to do whatever he could to help with their project. His Berlin office was located one floor above the Wrapped Reichstag, Ltd., office.

From the very beginning, Christo and Jeanne-Claude were determined not to use heavy equipment or scaffolding for the wrapping; it would, they had decided, be done entirely by hand, as was the case with their previous projects. One reason for this was practical: At the time, there was little heavy equipment in the former East Germany; there were, as a consequence, plenty of climbers used to working with ropes, which was the most common method for restoration work and construction. Some companies had already contacted me, offering their services. Regulations required that all workers take a course taught by a certified expert before being allowed on the Reichstag. Two of the climbers on the team—Frank ("Selle") Seltenheim and Robert ("Robbie") Jatkowski—had helped to assemble a group of ninety professional climbers, each of whom had first to earn a special certificate to work on the project. Vince and Jonita Davenport flew to Berlin to supervise the work and help at the office.

In April 1995, the first shipment of steel structures, out of the total 204 tons, arrived at the Reichstag and was installed on the building's supporting structure. The German landmarks commission ordered that the whole process be filmed, at the artists' expense. The entire roof was covered with platforms in order to allow workers to move around freely. Other shipments of the steel framework began to arrive daily. Rectangular steel blocks, weighing one ton per square yard and designed to anchor the fabric to the ground, were placed at the foot of the building's walls. Drilling into the sidewalks or into the stone of any part of the facade was out of the question. Decorative urns and statuary were protected by specially designed steel cages, then covered temporarily with fabric.

During the spring of 1995, Christo and Jeanne-Claude crossed the Atlantic ten times. (Jeanne-Claude later calculated that she and Christo had flown to Germany a total of fifty-four times in connection with the Reichstag project.) By June 13, their birthday, Jeanne-Claude had moved to Germany, where she would stay until the project's completion. Christo remained in his studio, finishing up the last drawings. Everyone in the Berlin office took time off to wish happy birthday by phone to the lonely Christo in New York.

Christo arrived from New York the following day. The final phase had started, beginning with signing up twelve hundred project monitors. After re-

Berlin, 1985: The two Project Directors of the *Wrapped Reichstag*. Wolfgang Volz and Roland Specker. (Photo: Sylvia Volz)

ceiving the customary T-shirts (designed by my wife Sylvie, following the artists' specifications), the monitors were given a crash course in all aspects of the wrapping. As with other projects, these monitors would serve as the artists' ambassadors to the public. It was their job to prevent damage to the wrapping and to give out small fabric samples (1,200,000 in all) to visitors, as well as to distribute flyers and answer questions.

At 2:00 A.M. on June 16, escorted by police, seven trucks were loaded with the first of the seventy rolls of fabric panels, left the hangar; they arrived at the Reichstag three hours later. Under my direction, each truck was parked at a specially designated location so that cranes would be able to lift the panel bundles to their assigned positions on the roof. I knew that precision was critical; moving these bundles by hand would be impossible, each weighing between one thousand and five thousand pounds. To avoid mistakes, each tagged bundle was checked and then double-checked by several teams. By the evening of June 16, all the bundles were in place on the roof.

Visitors and journalists from around the world began gathering behind a chain-link construction fence that had been set up around the periphery of the Reichstag. The wrapping began on the building's inner courts, the idea being to keep potential problems from public view. Everything went smoothly, and on the morning of Sunday, June 18, the wrapping of the outer facades began. The crowd outside the fence began to cheer with excitement. However, at 8:00 A.M., the weather service issued a storm warning. Safety regulations permitted the wrapping to take place only if winds were below a certain velocity; the storm was predicted to bring winds exceeding that. Work was therefore postponed and the climbers sent home. I announced the news to onlookers by megaphone from the roof. But the storm never materialized; the winds turned out to be gentle. Christo was irritated, and he asked me to call the climbers back. It was too late, however. The interruption disrupted the entire schedule. Only the press seemed to take some pleasure from the delay; it had added drama to the whole proceeding.

The next day, the unfurling process resumed. Christo and Jeanne-Claude constantly circled the Reichstag's roof, offering advice and instructions or summoning me or Frank Seltenheim, the chief climber, whenever a problem arose. Relaying instructions often involved a series of simultaneous translations—from Christo's Franco-Bulgarian English into German and then sometimes into Saxonian or some Bavarian dialect, depending on which climbing crew was working at the time. The *New York Times* later published a photo of Christo and Jeanne-Claude, with the caption "Christo and Jeanne-Claude directing the wrapping of the Reichstag." The photo shows them both with outstretched arms, pointing in opposite directions.

The number of spectators began to grow; they applauded loudly when a panel was unfurled down the side of the building. The weather turned mild, bringing out even more spectators. Radio Free Europe set up a broadcast booth next to the Reichstag, where they conducted nonstop interviews with Christo and Jeanne-Claude, Roland Specker, and myself.

Once all the fabric was unfurled—and the worry that some panels might turn out to be too short had dissipated—the climbers began attaching the blue ropes. These ropes performed a practical as well as an aesthetic function. They ensured that the fabric would not get blown off by the wind. On the other hand, it was equally critical that the fabric not be too tightly bound, so that it could breathe, turning the building into a dynamic sculpture. As it turned out, however, some of the ropes were not tight enough; Christo and Jeanne-Claude asked Mitko Zagoroff and John Thomson to tighten them from the anchor points inside the building.

As the artists moved around the building, the media noted that they were frequently accompanied by unidentified persons of the same sex. Jeanne-Claude, for example, was often observed walking hand in hand with a woman; and everywhere Christo went, a young man shadowed him. Some speculated they were lovers. They were, in fact, bodyguards. Friends had urged the artists to hire protection—and with good reason. It had become nearly impossible for Christo and Jeanne-Claude to walk around Berlin without being besieged for autographs. The bodyguards enabled them to walk unencumbered between the Reichstag and their office. Later, after the chain-link fence had been taken down, even this became impossible, and they almost always had to cover the short distance by car.

One moment of true drama occurred when the fabric panels got stuck on the statues on the building's four gigantic towers. Everyone offered advice about what to do. In the end, the climbing crews came up with a solution, suggesting that the space between the statues be bridged with girths. It worked, to loud applause from the spectators, who were mesmerized by the climbers' acrobatic maneuvers. The climbers were the true heroes of the wrapping, which ended on June 24.

The fence was taken down in the middle of the night, because the crowds had grown so vast and so impatient. There was some worry that when the fence was gone, there might be rioting and the fabric could be damaged. Vandalism had been threatened—an anonymous group had called for a graffiti contest. (I had prepared for any damage to the fabric by stocking up on cans of silver-colored paint.) Moreover, on June 19, some lunatic, a would-be Robin Hood, had shot a flaming arrow at the fabric. But the nonflammable surface kept it from catching fire, and the only effect from the attack was a small hole. Naturally, the press covered this incident—the only one of its kind—extensively.

Despite all the worries, nothing serious happened once the fence was removed. The visitors stormed toward the building, but all they really wanted was to touch the fabric and the ropes. Indeed, during the two weeks of the artwork's existence, the most common sight was that of visitors approaching the wrapping and stroking it with almost reverential gentleness. In a few places, small pieces of fabric were cut out, but the holes were easily repaired. (My silver paint was never needed.) The lack of vandalism didn't surprise Christo and Jeanne-Claude, who knew from past experience that visitors themselves often make sure that no damage is done to the work of art.

Five million visitors, at all hours of day and night, came to see *Wrapped Reichstag* (or, as some newspapers termed it, "the UFO"). They watched as the shimmering silvery fabric fluttered and changed color. At sunrise, that color shifted gradually from pink to orange; around noon, it took on a deep blue hue; and in the evening, it turned golden and pink. On cloudy days, the fabric reflected the grayness of the sky. In sunny weather, it sparkled with silver and gold. The variations were endlessly delightful. The wind played with the fabric and brought it to life, exactly as Christo and Jeanne-Claude had hoped. "The wind is our best friend and, at the same time, our worst enemy," Jeanne-Claude said later.

The artists gleefully took special guests and friends to the roof, which could be reached only via a staircase located on the south side of one inner court. Once they got there, everyone agreed that it had been worth the climb. The roof was a fairy-tale landscape, completely transformed by the fabric. Peo-

Berlin, 1995: Christo and Jeanne-Claude on the roof of the *Wrapped Reichstag,*
1971–1995. (Photo: Sylvia Volz)

ple felt as if they were walking through a winter wonderland or exploring the
North Pole. Only Christo, Jeanne-Claude, Roland Specker and I had unlimited
access to the roof; everyone else needed to be issued a special permit by Wrapped
Reichstag, Ltd. One day, the Reichstag's director, half-infuriated and half-
amused, came to me for a permit; even he had needed permission to get into
his building.

Before long, the Reichstag was a nonstop happening. People camped out
in sleeping bags on the front lawn; there were thousands of parties and picnics,
constant music and dancing. The bushes were alive with activity. One evening,

when a naked woman stepped in front of the spotlights, her outline was projected onto the facade. This discovery inspired a number of individual performances, which occasionally turned into stripteases.

Christo and Jeanne-Claude wrote in their press release:

> Throughout the history of art, the use of fabric has been a fascination for artists. From the most ancient times to the present, fabric, forming folds, pleats and draperies, is a significant part of paintings, frescoes, reliefs and sculptures made of wood, stone and bronze. In the Judeo-Christian civilization, as in weddings and other ritual celebrations, veiling has a sacred and joyful message. The use of fabric on the Reichstag follows this classical tradition.
>
> For a period of two weeks, the richness of the silvery fabric, shaped by the blue ropes, creates a sumptuous flow of vertical folds highlighting the features and proportions of the imposing structure, revealing the essence of the Reichstag.
>
> Fabric, like clothing or skin, is fragile; the *Wrapped Reichstag* will have the unique quality of impermanence. The physical reality of art will be a dramatic experience of great visual beauty.

To thank Berliners for all their support and enthusiasm, Christo and Jeanne-Claude agreed to sign a special edition of the newspaper *Der Tagesspiegel.* The signing started at 5:00 A.M. on June 28, at a table in front of the west gate. The line of people seeking autographs wound around the entire building and then half of it again. When they stopped six hours later, the artists had signed seventeen thousand newspapers.

Politicians visited the Reichstag to bask in the project's success. Some of the original opponents in the Bundestag became converts. Only Helmut Kohl, then Germany's chancellor, maintained his disapproval. He told journalists that he would rather drink coffee at a café than see the *Wrapped Reichstag.* It was later learned that he viewed it from his helicopter.

The beginning of the removal of the wrapping was scheduled for July 7. The evening before, the police estimated the crowd near the Reichstag to number approximately half a million people. Moving around was almost impossible. Christo and Jeanne-Claude appeared one last time before the public in front of the wrapping. Every time they got up and waved, the crowd went wild, frantically chanting their names.

The removal took only a few days—as usual, most of the materials were recycled—and Wrapped Reichstag, Ltd., returned the building, undamaged and swept clean, to the German people. Christo and Jeanne-Claude went home (on separate flights, of course; they still refuse to fly on the same plane), though they later returned to my home in Düsseldorf for a few days to select the final photographs of the work of art. At the airport in Frankfurt, Jeanne-

Claude couldn't walk five feet without being asked for an autograph. "I'm glad that I don't have red hair," said Christo with a smile. "People don't recognize me so easily."

OVER THE RIVER, WRAPPED TREES, AND THE WALL

Beginning in the early 1990s, Christo and Jeanne-Claude had been thinking about a project involving a river. *Over the River, Project for the Arkansas River, Colorado,* is, at the time of this book's publication, still a work in progress.

Between 1992 and 1994, with Simon Chaput, the artists inspected eighty-nine possible river sites in the Rocky Mountains. By the end of 1994, they had narrowed their list to six possible rivers, all of which seemed to satisfy both aesthetic and practical considerations. The riverbanks needed to be high enough so that the fabric panels and cables they imagined spanning the river wouldn't interfere with rafting. Moreover, it was important that whichever river chosen be accessible to the public and, if possible, located near an international airport. In the summer of 1996, Christo, Jeanne-Claude, and some members of their team—Sylvia, Golden, Vladimir Yavachev, Chaput, Davenport, Rivera-Terreaux, and I—decided to revisit all six final candidates: the Arkansas and Cache La Poudre rivers in Colorado, the Payette and Salmon rivers in Idaho, the Wind River in Wyoming, and the Rio Grande in New Mexico.

At locations on each of these rivers, we performed the same ritual: taking photographs and stretching three yellow ropes across the river. The ropes simulated the steel cables that would eventually hold the large fabric panels. We carefully measured and documented the distance between the ropes and the surface of the water.

Jeanne-Claude, wearing her Japanese farmer's hat and gloves, and carrying an umbrella for protection from the sun, observed the activities from a distance and, with her binoculars, scanned the area for wild animals. She loves nature and wilderness. But she also covers herself—and everyone on the team—with insect spray from head to toe whenever we leave the car. Christo scrutinized the landscape with his eyes, already creating collages and drawings in his mind.

By the fall of 1996, it had become more and more apparent that they had made up their minds: the stretch of the Arkansas River between the towns of Salida and Cañon City, Colorado. Again and again, the river had come up in discussions; after a point, all the other rivers were being compared to it. The choice seemed to have made itself.

In November 1996, Christo and Jeanne-Claude took the first steps toward obtaining permission for *Over the River.* Their first visit to the Bureau of Land Management (BLM) left them with the impression that things might not be

Colorado, 1996: Taking a rest along the Arkansas River during work on *Over the River Project*. From left, Jeanne-Claude, Harrison Rivera-Terreaux, Christo, and Wolfgang Volz. (Photo: Sylvia Volz)

too complicated. The Department of the Interior owns the entire stretch of river between Parkdale Siding and Salida.

Over the River will consist of a succession of fabric panels seven miles long over a forty-mile stretch of the river. The fabric will therefore not be continuous, but interrupted in places where there are natural obstacles, such as trees, rocks, or bridges; where the riverbank isn't high enough to support the cables; where the road does not run along the river; and for aesthetic reasons. The panels will be high enough to allow rafting underneath them; this part of the Arkansas is especially popular because of its gentle white-water rapids. The project will also be viewed by walking or driving along the river's banks.

Throughout 1996 and early 1997 Christo and Jeanne-Claude contacted fishermen and rafters, as well as officials from Fremont and Chaffee counties, conservation organizations, the Department of Transportation, the Colorado State Patrol, the Arkansas Headwaters Recreation Area and the Parks Department. Everyone listened patiently, and initially there was every sign that an agreement would be possible. But it gradually became clear that the permission process would not be as simple as they had first hoped.

In April 1997, meetings were held in Salida and Cañon City, where Christo and Jeanne-Claude presented their ideas to the public. What became immediately evident was that the two communities are markedly different. In the 1960s and 1970s, Salida was something of a counterculture center. Cañon City, on the other hand, has more prisons than any other town in the entire

Colorado, 1996: The *Over the River Project* team taking measurements. From left, Project Director Tom Golden, Jeanne-Claude, Christo, Construction Manager Vince Davenport, Adriana Quelroz, Alexander Fils, and Harrison Rivera-Terreaux. (Photo: Wolfgang Volz)

United States. In Salida almost everyone was enthusiastic about the project. In Cañon City, on the other hand, the reception was distinctly cooler.

At the end of April, the artists gathered friends at Howard Street to start planning *Over the River*. John Thomson explained that no scientific studies on fabric stretched horizontally existed, and that, from a physical and engineering point of view, the situation was very different from what would be the case for, say, sails and flags. It would therefore probably be necessary to commission some tests. While some basic questions could be addressed using experiments with bed sheets, other problems could only be resolved by on-site testing.

Christo and Jeanne-Claude agreed, but they wanted the tests to be done in secret. It was decided to perform them in a canyon near the Colorado town of Grand Junction, on the western slope of the Rocky Mountains, where the topography closely resembles that along the Arkansas River. Ground anchors, steel cables, and other necessary hardware were ordered by Vince Davenport. I ordered a variety of panels made of different fabrics, colors, and patterns.

Only the artists and close associates were allowed to witness the test. Those present had to help stretch the five 32-by-118-foot fabric panels across the canyon. Although only a small brook runs through this area, the dimensions were right. "We learned about four hundred different things not to do," said Jeanne-Claude, "therefore, the test was a big success." One thing confirmed beyond a doubt was that the fabric was water-permeable. A water truck had drenched it with ten thousand gallons of water. This was an extremely important thing to learn—some had worried that the overhanging panels probably wouldn't survive a summer rainstorm.

In September 1997, the team returned to Grand Junction to experiment with new kinds of fabrics. By this point, Christo and Jeanne-Claude had chosen the hooks that would connect the fabric to the steel cables. It had also become increasingly clear what the final choice of color would be: silver. The clouds, sky, and mountains will be visible when seen from underneath. Because the fabric would be given an aluminum coating, the water and the surrounding sky and mountains would reflect off of it.

At about this same time, Christo, Jeanne-Claude, and I were conducting tests for a project called *Wrapped Trees,* which they had wanted to do since 1966. Somewhat earlier, they had been invited by Ernst Beyeler, a well-known Swiss gallery owner, to Riehen, a town near Basel, where Beyeler was building a museum to house his collection. For this new museum, which was to be designed by the architect Renzo Piano, Beyeler planned an exhibition that would highlight the importance of trees in the arts. When they went to Riehen, Christo and Jeanne-Claude were shown a group of trees in the park near the museum; they immediately decided to wrap those trees—whose height varied between six and eighty-two feet—for the opening of the exhibition, choosing a fabric that is commonly used in Japan to protect trees from snow and frost. Right after they had finished tests on the fabrics they intended to use for *Over the River,* Christo and Jeanne-Claude had me wrap a magnolia located in the garden of their German fabric manufacturer, using a fabric modeled on the Japanese fabric. I experimented with varying sizes, styles, and patterns of fabric panels, trying to establish how best to wrap and tie up a tree using as little heavy machinery as possible. The artists were fairly satisfied with the results; other details would be taken care of during a second set of tests.

In December 1997, the artists again met with the public in Colorado, this time in Cañon City and in Cotopaxi, a small town located in the center of the forty-mile stretch of the Arkansas River. Mostly hunters and fishermen attended the meeting, and it was soon clear that many felt little sympathy for *Over the River.* Their greatest concern, they said, was protecting their valley; they worried that it would be endangered by masses of visitors—though it remains unclear how many could reasonably be expected, as the area in question is fairly remote.

This was Christo and Jeanne-Claude's first meeting with the project's opponents. Some of the more vocal critics seemed slightly taken aback by the artists' presentation; everyone read the information sheets that were made available. Experience has taught Christo and Jeanne-Claude that it would be a miracle if everything were to proceed smoothly. Success in one part of the world is not necessarily indicative of what will happen in another area; it can work against you, as well. The number of people who visited *Wrapped Reichstag* would probably not descend upon Colorado, though the opponents to *Over the River* used the five million visitors to the Reichstag as an argument against the project.

In February 1998, another fabric test was conducted, under my direction, in Germany and a suitable material was found for *Wrapped Trees*. A zippered cover would be designed for each tree—thus avoiding the use of heavy machinery. The artists also decided on the color and thickness of the rope. I was given the green light, and production began.

Over the River, however, proceeded more slowly. In April 1998, Christo and Jeanne-Claude went to Guelph, a town near Toronto, to observe wind-tunnel tests on three miniature fabric panels. Miniature steel cables the thickness of threads were equipped with measuring devices to record stress levels on the anchors, cables, hooks, and fabric panels. The tests continued for four weeks; when they were completed, the results provided precise indications of what would happen under actual conditions.

During the negotiations and testing for *Over the River,* another endeavor presented itself. The Emscher Industrial Park Organization asked me whether the artists would be interested in doing something at the Gasometer, one of the largest gas-tank structures in the world, located in Oberhausen, Germany, in the industrial Ruhr valley. Christo and Jeanne-Claude had once visited the Gasometer, built in 1928 to store the by-products of iron-ore processing. They had been impressed with the enormity of the space. They had agreed to show *Wrapped Reichstag* and *The Umbrellas* documentation exhibitions there. However, the organizations' director, Karl Ganser, had something more ambitious and monumental in mind. I suggested building a wall of oil barrels in the upper portion of the cathedrallike structure, which was 361 feet high. We had in mind something reminiscent of the 1962 Rue Visconti project and the indoor barrels installations in Philadelphia and Cologne—only far, far larger. Christo and Jeanne-Claude's eyes lighted up when I spoke to them about the possibility. Work began immediately.

In the meantime, the 56,000 square feet of fabric needed for *Wrapped Trees* was being manufactured in Germany. A special treatment helped stabilize the weave. The number of trees to be wrapped had increased to 178—and some of the trees had grown since they were first measured the year before—so I ordered additional fabric. I also took a crash course in developing sewing patterns on the computer, and spent three months designing individualized tree covers. Every tree was given a number and assigned a separate pattern. At the factory, every cover, including its zipper, was double- and triple-checked, then rolled into a compact bundle. Thankfully, the material was lightweight.

In August 1998, Christo and Jeanne-Claude introduced the idea of po *Wrapped Trees* to the local community in Riehen. At the same time, the permission process with German building authorities had begun with the Gasometer oil barrels wall. Everybody loved the idea of erecting an eighty-five-foot-high wall of oil barrels, and I quickly got in touch with some manufacturers of oil barrels. One of them assured me that he once had piled up oil barrels as high as fifty feet without the barrels at the bottom of the pile getting crushed. It was obvious that some kind of solid support system would be needed.

Earlier, in June, new tests for *Over the River* had been conducted. This area was chosen because its weather and topographical conditions were similar to those in the Arkansas River valley. The team decided to set up camp right at the testing ground because during previous tests their cars had gotten stuck in the mud on their way there. The tests were invaluable; the team was able to resolve a number of issues, such as how much extra fabric would be needed for the folds in the panels and how best to attach the fabric to the cables.

The Christo family expanded because of two weddings. One was their son Cyril's marriage to Marie Wilkinson. The other was the marriage of Jeanne-Claude's niece and goddaughter, Julia Henery, to Darren Maum. There was also sad news. On September 24, 1998, Jeanne-Claude's mother died in Paris after a long illness.

The realization of *Wrapped Trees* began on November 13, 1998—a bitterly cold day. The fabric had arrived, as had a group of Berlin-based climbers who had worked on *Wrapped Reichstag*. They were joined by a team of Swiss tree pruners. Selle Seltenheim and I chose tree number 130 to demonstrate the artists' concept to the entire team. The folded fabric was lifted over the top of the tree; then two workers unfolded it from underneath and below and wrapped the tree, paying careful attention to wind direction. The fabric was then zipped from top to bottom. Each tree would be wrapped following this procedure. The next step, sculpting the covered trees with fourteen miles of rope, took a great deal of time. "Only two of our projects truly required our presence—*Wrapped Coast* in Australia and the *Wrapped Trees* in Riehen," Jeanne-Claude said. "For all other projects, we had precisely planned engineering designs. For the trees, as in Australia, we had to decide at the site where the ropes should go. We listened to the trees, and their branches told us where the ropes belonged."

The reality was somewhat more complicated. The tips of the branches literally seemed to grab at the fabric; again and again, the climbers had to unsnag it. For some of the taller tress near the north end of the park, the cherry-pickers were not tall enough and a big truck-mounted crane was necessary. The trees were so close to one another that the climbers had to thread the somewhat-fragile fabric carefully through the branches. Whenever there was a breeze, things got even more complicated. There were four teams of four climbers each, and three teams of three people on ladders for the smaller trees. Various

Riehan, Switzerland, 1998: Jeanne-Claude and Christo in front of some of the 178 *Wrapped Trees*. (Photo: Wolfgang Volz)

stages of wrapping were going on simultaneously. Christo and Jeanne-Claude ran from one team to the next, giving instructions on where to place the ropes. From time to time, Jeanne-Claude sat on a chair positioned in the middle of the meadow, some distance away from the trees, and communicated via radio. Finally, however, the wrapping started to proceed smoothly. The process was fairly enjoyable, despite icy weather, occasional rain, snow, and wind. The biggest worry was whether the fabric covers would fit each tree properly. In the end, only four small trees were underwrapped—they had grown higher than had been expected—and additional fabric was sewn on.

The choice of fabric turned out to be perfect. It glistened with colors in sunshine, taking on varying hues at different times of day. It also allowed the light to shine through every branch. Each tree was a separate sculpture. At midday, the fabric seemed almost transparent; at sunset, the wrapped trees turned into gigantic glowing pink lanterns. Twice, it snowed; on each occasion, the snow gave the work of art a haunting fairy-tale quality.

Three hundred thousand people came to see the 178 tree sculptures. The artists themselves were amazed by the outcome. "*Wrapped Trees* was a complete surprise for us," remembered Christo. "From our tests, we got the image of a somewhat banal-looking tree, and we were afraid that in Riehen, things would look a bit boring." *Wrapped Trees* was anything but boring. Christo and Jeanne-Claude strolled through the park, hand in hand, enjoying their work at different times of the day. Awed by the work, they also knew that, as with all their projects, they should not deny its temporary quality. They agreed immediately with Ernst Beyeler that the trees be unwrapped earlier than scheduled.

For Beyeler, too, it had become obvious that the shorter the duration of the project, the more intense its effects. Originally, he had requested that the wrappings remain until spring. Christo and Jeanne-Claude decided that December 13 would be the artwork's final day, and they issued an explanation:

> The temporary character of a work of art creates a feeling of fragility, vulnerability, and an urgency to be seen, as well as a presence of the missing, because we know it will be gone tomorrow.
>
> The quality of love and tenderness that human beings have towards what will not last, for instance the love and tenderness we have for childhood and our lives, is a quality we want to give to our work as an additional aesthetic quality.

Even while everyone was still enjoying *Wrapped Trees,* the pressure to advance the work on the Gasometer barrels in Oberhausen increased. A special eighty-five-foot-high scaffolding was needed to support the entire construction. I found a company that could provide the scaffolding on schedule. Christo and Jeanne-Claude had chosen the colors of the barrels even before the completion of *Wrapped Trees.* In January 1999, I made a reduced-scale drawing that depicted a wall of all thirteen thousand barrels as a cluster of colored circles. The drawing was used as a kind of construction manual. Forty-five percent of the barrels would be bright yellow; 30 percent would be orange; the remaining barrels would be ultramarine, azure, gray, ivory, and lime green. The support construction as well as the wall of barrels rose to the designed height of eighty-five feet between February and April 1999. When it was eventually finished, *The Wall,* 85 feet high, 223 feet in length, and 23 feet deep, bisected the cavernous Gasometer.

Christo had created original preparatory drawings for *The Wall;* they were exhibited at Oberhausen castle at the time of the installation. Christo and Jeanne-Claude went to Oberhausen to install *The Umbrellas* and *Wrapped Reichstag* documentation exhibitions. Christo himself had designed the exhibition space, measuring 3,280 square feet, in the Gasometer's ground floor, a space large enough to accommodate nearly a thousand original artworks, photos, documents, and material samples. It was perhaps the largest temporary museum of art ever created. The mosaic of colored oil barrels, overwhelming in dimension and brightness, glowed in the gigantic gas tank. Nearly 400,000 came to see the indoor installation and the two documentation exhibitions during the four months they were open.

Meanwhile, preparations for *Over the River* were still proceeding slowly. Christo and Jeanne-Claude had decided not to place their faith in the wind-tunnel tests. They organized a fourth and final life-size test in Grand Junction. With the newly installed panels of silver fabric in place, actual wind forces were studied. Canadian scientists from Guelph had set up all devices for running the tests. Various members of the extended Christo family watched the test over a period of six weeks. This turned into a kind of working vacation. From time to time, Christo and Jeanne-Claude explored the wilderness in an off-road vehicle called a Grizzly. Even Christo, who has never driven in his life and doesn't have a driver's license, felt confident enough to take the wheel occasionally.

Besides *Over the River,* the other great project still in progress is *The Gates, Project for Central Park, New York City,* started in 1979, which had been rejected by Parks Commissioner Gordon J. Davis in 1981. Christo and Jeanne-Claude haven't stopped thinking and talking about, and working on, *The Gates,* a project that has remained close to their hearts since 1979. The main argument against the project has always been that Central Park is the Mona Lisa of urban landscape architecture. Why should anyone be allowed to use it to please his or her ego? In 1981, the *New York Times* published an editorial making that argument. On the other hand, after the completion of *Wrapped Reichstag,* Stephen Wiseman wrote in a *New York Times* editorial, "Now is the time to realize *The Gates.*"

When Rudolph W. Giuliani was reelected mayor of New York in 1998, he handed the administration of Central Park over to the Central Park Conservancy. Its thirty-two members give enormous amounts of money to the park and decide every detail concerning it. The artists are now trying to form a core group of supporters for *The Gates* among the members of the conservancy.

The works being created in the Howard Street studio at the moment focus on *The Gates* and *Over the River.* The year 2004 is the earliest that either of the two projects might be realized. As always, Christo and Jeanne-Claude know that perseverance, persuasiveness, luck, and hard work will be needed.

LIFE ON HOWARD STREET

Christo and Jeanne-Claude continue to live in their loft on Howard Street, whose interior hasn't changed much since they moved in 38 years ago. In addition to works by Christo, there are many works by other artists, and an original, signed chair by Rietveld. The walls are fairly bare, except for a drawing of *Running Fence* and a piece by Saul Steinberg. The office, however, is covered from floor to ceiling with photos. Christo and Jeanne-Claude now own the entire building. The ground floor is leased to a stationery store. A reception area where potential buyers can look at drawings and collages is located on the second floor; it is a plain, well-lighted space.

Life at Howard Street follows the same routine. Christo gets up shortly before 7:00 A.M., shaves, drinks coffee, and eats fruit for breakfast. He works at his studio until the mail arrives, usually around eleven o'clock. Then he reads the *New York Times* and opens the daily stack of mail. Every other day, Christo walks down to an art-supply store on Canal Street to buy paper, charcoal, pencils, wax crayons, and glue. He then remains in his studio until the afternoon.

Working and living on the fourth and fifth floor of the building keeps Christo and Jeanne-Claude in shape; they don't want to install an elevator, though it sometimes comes up in conversation. They would rather spend the money on their art projects.

At around 11:00 A.M., Jeanne-Claude's assistant arrives. Lunch consists only of water and vitamin C pills. Answering every fax and piece of mail as quickly as possible has always been one of Jeanne-Claude's abiding principles. The archive needs attention, and the phones ring constantly—calls from team members working on a project, collectors, gallery owners, museum curators, and fans. Christo and Jeanne-Claude often receive guests in the afternoon: friends and journalists, and sometimes an entire college class or a group from a guided museum tour. Three times a week, Christo and Jeanne-Claude get shiatsu massages to keep them in good shape.

They listen exclusively to music by Mozart. It has become an unwritten law that wherever Christo and Jeanne-Claude appear, any music other than works by Mozart should be turned off. "It's very easy," says Jeanne-Claude. "We like only the best." Mozart is played all day at Howard Street at a fairly low volume. It has been suggested that listening to Mozart temporarily increases one's IQ by 30 percent.

In the evening, if they go out or have guests, Christo shaves a second time and changes his clothes. At 7:30 P.M., there are often guests in the downstairs floor; Christo serves drinks. For a number of years now, dinners have taken place at a nearby restaurant. Because there are always collectors, engineers, specialists, or other collaborators among the guests, most conversations center on the latest project. Every now and then, Christo and Jeanne-Claude eat their meals at home. They often have the doggy bags from the previous evening's dinner. Jeanne-Claude hates to throw away food, as she dislikes wasting anything. After dinner, Christo and Jeanne-Claude work for another hour or two.

Christo's studio is the only place where he creates his drawings and collages. The studio hasn't been painted since the sixties because he does not want to spend his time on this. He doesn't have an assistant, preferring to do everything himself; he even does his own framing. He has two main workplaces: a small table for collages and a wall where he does his large drawings. He always works standing. Because the glue on the collages needs to dry, he works on several works simultaneously, such as a collage for *The Gates* and a drawing for *Over the River*.

When a work is finished, Christo sprays it with fixative and frames it in

Plexiglas. André Grossmann photographs the original before it is taken to the downstairs floor. The revenue from the sale of these preparatory works, and those works done in the 1950s and 1960s, entirely finances the big projects. They have never accepted sponsors, nor ever will, whether private or public. Christo and Jeanne-Claude would regard it as a limitation on what they prize most deeply—their artistic freedom.

Notes

1. BEHIND THE IRON CURTAIN

1. Anani Yavachev, interviews with the author, in Sofia, Gabrovo, and Katchoree, Bulgaria, October 11–14, 1986; and in Ota, Japan, Lebec, California, and New York City, 1991, 1994. Translations from the French in Bulgaria and New York City by Ann Chernow.
2. Ibid.
3. Ibid.
4. Ibid.
5. From Vladimir Mayakovski's "Order to the Army of Art" ("Prikaz armil iskusstva"), quoted in Camilla Gray, *The Russian Experiment in Art, 1863–1922* (London: Thames and Hudson, 1976), p. 224.
6. Letter from Christo to Anani, December 24, 1956, Prague, translated by Maria Radicheva.
7. Ibid.
8. Ibid.

2. THE GENERAL'S DAUGHTER

1. Précilda de Guillebon, interviews with the author in Paris, September 23, 1985; in New York City, April 16, 1987; and later in Lebec, California, and New York City. This and subsequent quotes are from these interviews.
2. Yolande Karsenti Medina, interview with the author in New York City, August 28, 1990.
3. Ibid.
4. Ibid.
5. Nicole Manuello, "Jacques de Guillebon," *Jours de France: Histoires vécues.* 1588 (June 6–14, 1985): 20.
6. *De Gaulle's War Memoirs, 1942–1944,* trans. Joyce Murchie and Hamish Erskine (New York: Simon and Schuster, 1959), pp. 404–405.

3. IN TRANSIT: VIENNA AND GENEVA

1. Andersen was the professor who twice flunked Adolf Hitler at the Vienna Art Academy, decisively affecting the course of history.
2. Letter from Christo to Anani, March 23, 1957, Vienna; translated by Maria Radicheva.
3. Letter from Christo to Anani, May 1957, Vienna; translated by Maria Radicheva. On this trip, Christo met his first lover, a woman named Isabella.

4. Ibid.
5. Saul Steinberg, interview with the author in New York City, March 27, 1987.
6. Dr. Alexandre Todorov, telephone interview with the author, July 23, 1989.
7. Ibid., August 6, 1989.
8. Ibid., September 12, 1989.

4. PARIS: LIKE BROTHER AND SISTER

1. Letter from Lourdes Castro to the author, October 12, 1988.
2. Janet Flanner, *Paris Journal, 1956–1964* (New York: Harcourt Brace Jovanovich, 1970), p. 69.
3. Dieter Rosenkranz, telephone interview with the author, March 27, 1990.
4. Pamela Wye, "Splendor in the Glass: Mary Bauermeister's Boxes and Gardens," *Arts,* November 1989, p. 78.
5. Ibid., p. 75.
6. John Vinton, ed., *Dictionary of Contemporary Music* (New York: E. P. Dutton, 1974), p. 118.
7. Pierre Restany, interviews with the author in Paris, September 23, 1985; in New York City, April 16, 1987; and subsequently in Lebec, California, and New York City.
8. Précilda de Guillebon, interview with the author.
9. Ibid.
10. Ibid.
11. Ibid.
12. Letter from Christo to Anani, November 21, 1958, Paris.
13. Letter from Christo to Anani, June 8, 1958, Paris.
14. This remained true until Christo and Jeanne-Claude heard of a study that claimed that listening to Mozart stimulates thought; since then, Sonatas 23 and 27 have filled their living and work spaces for hour after hour.
15. Also Pellegrini, *New Tendencies in Art* (New York: Crown Publishers, 1966), pp. 257–259.
16. Joyce May Henery, interviews with the author in Yonkers, New York, August 26 and November 6, 1989, and subsequently in New York City and Connecticut. This and subsequent quotes are from these interviews.
17. Carole Weisweiller, interview with the author in Paris, January 4, 1991.
18. Quoted from the divorce agreement prepared for Philippe Planchon, March 1, 1960.
19. Ibid.
20. Précilda de Guillebon, interview with the author.
21. Carole Weisweiller, interview with the author.

5. TURNING POINT

1. Joyce May Henery, interview with the author.
2. Quoted from the divorce agreement prepared for Philippe Planchon, March 1, 1960.
3. Joyce May Henery, interview with the author.
4. Précilda de Guillebon, interview with the author.
5. Ibid. When discussing Jacques's comments on the appointment of Pierre Messmer, Précilda de Guillebon cited the historians Merry and Serge Bromberger.
6. Letter from Christo to Anani, February 26, 1960, Paris.
7. Camilla Gray, *The Russian Experiment in Art, 1863–1922* (London: Thames and Hudson, 1976), p. 220.
8. David Bourdon, *Christo* (New York: Harry N. Abrams, 1970), p. 9.
9. Rob Morse, article on Christo, *Florida Magazine,* April 17, 1983.

10. Stephen Prokopoff, *Monuments and Projects* (Philadelphia: Institute of Contemporary Art, University of Pennsylvania, 1968).
11. Morse, article on Christo.
12. Jean-Louis Ferrier, ed., *Art of Our Century* (New York: Prentice-Hall, 1988), p. 559.
13. Michéle Cone, "The Late Fifties in Europe: A Conversation with Pierre Restany," *Arts,* January 1990, pp. 67, 69.
14. Calvin Tomkins, *The Bride and the Bachelors: Five Masters of the Avant-Garde* (New York: Penguin, 1965), pp. 166–169.
15. Ibid., pp. 167–169.
16. Ibid., pp. 169–171.
17. Ibid., pp. 173–182.
18. Ibid., p. 186.
19. Jan Voss, interview with the author in Paris, January 2, 1991.
20. Letter from Lourdes Castro to the author, October 12, 1988.
21. Jan Voss, interview with the author.
22. Ibid.
23. Ibid.
24. Niki de Saint-Phalle, interview with the author in New York City, October 8, 1990.
25. Pierre Restany, "The New Realism," *Art in America,* February 1963, p. 103.
26. Jan Voss, interview with the author.
27. Carole Weisweiller, interview with the author.
28. Précilda de Guillebon, interview with the author.
29. Ibid.
30. Letter from Christo to Anani, April 23, 1961, Paris.
31. Ferrier, ed., *Art of Our Century,* p. 579.
32. David Bourdon, *Christo* (Milan: Edizioni Apollinaire, 1966).
33. Mary Bauermeister, interviews with the author in New York City and Connecticut, April 6 and 13, 1992.
34. A few days after his opening, Paik arrived with the police and a court order that allowed him to recover his pianos. In the future, he would admit to bad judgment in unwrapping them.
35. Siegfried Bonk, "Abgenütztes verhüllt sein zweites Gesicht," *Kölner Stadt-Anzeiger,* July 31, 1961; translated by Mary Bauermesiter.

6. BORDERS AND BARRIERS

1. By mid-1961, Shunk and Kender had begun working with Christo, after having been introduced to him at Galerie J.
2. Quoted in *Christo: Early Works, 1958–1964* (Tokyo: Satani Gallery, 1991), pp. 14, 16.
3. Arman, interview with the author in New York City, September 3, 1987.
4. Pierre Restany, *Yves Klein* (New York: Harry N. Abrams, 1982), p. 234.
5. Larry Rivers, with Arnold Weinstein, *What Did I Do?* (New York: HarperCollins, 1992), p. 383.
6. Letter from Maurice Papon to Gen. Jacques de Guillebon, June 25, 1962.
7. Pierre Restany, interview with the author.
8. *Iron Curtain* consisted of eighty barrels stacked in three rows horizontally.
9. Pierre Restany, interview with the author.
10. Letter from René Bertholo to the author, October 16, 1991.
11. Jan Voss, interview with the author.
12. Richard Tuttle, quoted in *Time,* February 7, 1969, p. 60.
13. Leo Castelli, interview with the author in New York City, March 7, 1986.
14. Pierre Restany, interview with the author.

15. Carole Weisweiller, interview with the author.
16. Arman, interview with the author.
17. Pierre Restany, interview with the author.
18. Ibid.
19. Albert Maysles, interviews with the author in Paris, September 20, 1985; in Hitachiota, Japan, October 7, 1991; and subsequently.
20. Sidney Janis, *New Realists: On the Theme of the Exhibition* (New York: Sidney Janis Gallery, 1962).
21. John Ashbery, "The New Realism," in Janis, *New Realists.*
22. Sidney Tillim, "In the Galleries: The New Realists," *Arts,* December 1962, p. 44.
23. Lucy Lippard, *Pop Art* (New York: Frederick A. Praeger, 1966), pp. 174–175.
24. Jan van der Marck, *Arman* (New York: Abbeville Press, 1984), p. 33.
25. Jan van der Marck, "Arman: The Paris Avant-Garde in New York," *Art in America,* (November–December 1973, p. 89.
26. Pierre Restany, interview with the author.
27. Ileana and Michael Sonnabend, interview with the author in New York City, May 14, 1991.
28. Pierre Restany, interview with the author.
29. Ibid.
30. Ibid.
31. Jean-Louis Ferrier, ed., *Art of Our Century* (New York: Prentice-Hall, 1988), p. 590.
32. Pierre Restany, interview with the author.
33. Quoted from an unidentified magazine clipping.
34. Christo was referring to Ernst Scheidegger's photograph of clay sculptures covered with wet cloth in Giacometti's studio.
35. Jan van der Marck, *George Segal* (New York: Harry N. Abrams, 1975), p. 81.
36. George Segal, telephone interview with the author, October 1, 1991.
37. Giovanni Camuffo, interview with the author in New York City, November 13, 1989. This and subsequent quotes are from this interview.
38. Leo Castelli, interview with the author.

7. IN TRANSIT AGAIN

1. Larry Rivers, with Arnold Weinstein, *What Did I Do?* (New York: HarperCollins, 1992), pp. 406–407.
2. Ray Johnson, telephone interview with the author, April 14, 1990, and subsequent telephone conversations.
3. Jesse Kornbluth, "La Vie de Bohème" *Savvy,* December 1983, p. 78.
4. Dominique G. Laporte, *Christo,* trans. Abby Pollak (New York: Pantheon Books, 1986), p. 58.
5. Brian O'Doherty, "Season's End," *New York Times,* May 31, 1964.
6. Jean-Louis Ferrier, ed., *Art of Our Century* (New York: Prentice-Hall, 1988), p. 608.
7. Hilton Kramer, interview with the author, May 31, 1991.
8. Serge Guilbaut, ed., *Reconstructing Modernism* (Cambridge, Massachusetts: MIT Press, 1990), p. 408.
9. Ibid., p. 416.
10. Ileana Sonnabend quoted in Allen Rosenbaum, *Selections from the Ileana and Michael Sonnabend Collection* (Princeton: Princeton University Art Museum, 1985), p. 10.
11. Quoted in *Christo: Early Works, 1958–1964* (Tokyo: Satani Gallery, 1991), pp. 30, 32.
12. David Bourdon, *Christo,* (New York: Harry N. Abrams, 1970), p. 28.
13. Giovanni Camuffo, interview with the author.
14. In 1964, the pieces at issue ranged in price from one hundred to six hundred dollars. The total retail value was $2,200.

15. Harry Shunk, interviews with the author in New York City, November 7, 1990, and subsequently.
16. Pierre Restany, interview with the author.
17. Ileana and Michael Sonnabend, interview with the author.
18. Claes Oldenburg, telephone interview with the author, October 18, 1988.
19. Carole Weisweiller, interview with the author.
20. Quoted in David Molnar, "Portrait: Christo," trans. Mary Bavermeister, *Lufthansa
Bordbuch,* September–October 1993, p. 22.

8. NEW YORK

1. Cyril Christo, interviews with the author in Miami, May 1983, and in Paris, September
18, 1985.
2. Ivan Karp, interviews with the author in New York City, February 28, 1986, and April
27, 1994.
3. Marvin Elkoff, "Left Bank of the Atlantic," *Show,* April 1965, p. 61.
4. Ibid., pp. 62, 67.
5. Ibid., p. 67.
6. Ibid., p. 60.
7. The *London Observer* piece was quoted in Michel Ragon, "In Paris It's All Crisis, Crisis,
Crisis," *New York Times,* January 3, 1965.
8. Calvin Tomkins, *The Bride and the Bachelors: Five Masters of the Avant-Garde* (New
York: Penguin, 1965), p. 66.
9. John Canaday, "The Bandwagon Toboggan," *New York Times,* March 7, 1965.
10. David Bourdon, interviews with the author in New York City, September 26, 1985, and
April 14, 1994. This and subsequent quotes are from these interviews.
11. They repaid their debt to the Chelsea within a year. The construction used as collateral
was eventually donated to the Israel Museum in Jerusalem by both Stanley Bard and
Jeanne-Claude.
12. Ivan Karp, interview with the author.
13. David Bourdon, interview with the author.
14. Holly Solomon, interview with the author in New York City, April 1, 1986.
15. Calvin Tomkins, *Post- to Neo-* (New York: Henry Holt, 1988), pp. 34–35.
16. Ivan Karp, interview with the author.
17. Ibid.
18. Barbara Moore, notes concerning preparations for the Artists' Key Club event, March
12, 1965.
19. Allan Kaprow, telephone interview with the author, July 25, 1993.
20. Barbara Moore, notes concerning preparations for the Artists' Key Club event, March
12, 1965.
21. Allan Kaprow, telephone interview with the author.
22. Bruce D. Kurtz, *Contemporary Art, 1965–1990* (Englewood Cliffs, New Jersey: Prentice-
Hall, 1992), p. 16.
23. Elkoff, "Left Bank of the Atlantic," p. 58.
24. Harrison Rivera-Terreaux, interview with the author in Paris, September 26, 1985.
25. David Bourdon, interview with the author.
26. Canaday and Kramer quoted in Judith Goldman, *James Rosenquist* (New York: Viking
Penguin, 1985), p. 44.
27. Holly Solomon, interview with the author.
28. Ivan Karp, interview with the author. This and subsequent quote from this interview.
29. David Bourdon, interview with the author.
30. Ibid.
31. Ray Johnson, telephone interview with the author.

32. David Bourdon, interview with the author.
33. Holly Solomon, interview with the author.
34. Allan Kaprow, telephone interview with the author.
35. Allan Kaprow, "Calling," *Tulane Drama Review* 10 (Winter 1965): 203.
36. Allan Kaprow, telehpone interview with the author.
37. Kaprow, "Calling," p. 203.
38. George Segal, telephone interview with the author.
39. Allan Kaprow, telephone interview with the author.
40. Kaprow, "Calling," pp. 203–204.
41. Allan Kaprow, telephone interview with the author.
42. The 1966 group shows were: the Institute of Contemporary Art, Philadelphia; "Salon de Mai," the Musée d'Art Moderne de la Ville de Paris; Staatliche Kunsthalle, Baden-Baden; Louisiana Museum, Denmark; Goldovsky Gallery, New York City; "Sixty-eighth American Exhibition" at the Chicago Art Institute; "Eight Sculptors" at the Walker Art Center, Minneapolis; and the American Federation of the Arts, New York City.
43. Letter from Précilda de Guillebon to Jeanne-Claude, May 5, 1965.
44. Lawrence Alloway, Catalog for Christo's show at the Stedelijk van Abbemuseum, Eindhoven, the Netherlands, May 6–June 5, 1966.
45. Lawrence Alloway, interview with the author, March 7, 1986.
46. Tomkins, *Post- to Neo-*, p. 43.
47. Ibid., pp. 43–44.
48. Martin Friedman, in *Eight Sculptors: The Ambiguous Image* (Minneapolis: Walker Art Center, 1966).
49. Jan van der Marck, in *Eight Sculptors*.
50. Arnold Herstand, interview with the author, January 21, 1987.
51. Ibid.
52. David Johnson, interview with the author in Paris, September 27, 1985.
53. Arnold Herstand, interview with the author.

9. AT WORK AROUND THE WORLD: 1967–1969

1. Calvin Tomkins, *The Bride and the Bachelors: Five Masters of the Avant-Garde* (New York: Penguin, 1962), p. 67.
2. Quoted in *Christo: The Early Works, 1958–1964* (Tokyo: Satani Gallery, 1991), p. 16.
3. Ivan Karp, interview with the author.
4. Leo Castelli, interview with the author.
5. William Rubin, in *Christo Wraps the Museum . . . a Non-Event* (New York: Museum of Modern Art, 1968).
6. John Gruen, "Christo Wraps the Museum," *New York,* June 24, 1968.
7. John Gibson, quoted in *The Art Dealers* (New York: Clarkson Potter, 1984), pp. 204–205.
8. David Bourdon, "Crisis of Christo's Balloon," *Life,* September 6, 1968, pp. 76–90.
9. Dimiter Zagoroff, interview with the author in Boxton, June 14, 1988.
10. David Bourdon, *Christo* (New York: Harry N. Abrams, 1970), p. 34.
11. Dimiter Zagoroff, interview with the author.
12. David Juda, interview with the author in Paris, September 23, 1985.
13. Dimiter Zagoroff, interview with the author.
14. Grace Glueck, remarks at the National Arts Club dinner honoring Christo as "Artist of the Year," January 22, 1992.
15. Bourdon, *Christo*, p. 40.
16. Ian Ball, "Christo the Wrapper," *Daily Telegraph Magazine,* March 27, 1970, pp. 18–23.
17. Dimiter Zagoroff, interview with the author.

18. Ibid.
19. Ibid.
20. Ibid.
21. Lawrence Alloway, *Christo* (New York: Harry N. Abrams, 1969), p. x.
22. Joyce May Henery, interview with the author.
23. Christoph Kuhn, "Christo in New York," *Du*, August 1968.
24. From a project description, October 1968, in the "Allied Chemical" file of Harry Torczyner.
25. Stephen Prokopoff, *Monuments and Projects* (Philadelphia: Institute of Contemporary Art, University of Pennsylvania, 1968).
26. Suzanne Delehanty, interview with the author in Purchase, New York, March 10, 1987. This and subsequent quotes are from this interview.
27. Maurice Tuchman, *Art & Technology* (Los Angeles: Los Angeles County Museum, 1971), p. 78.
28. John Gibson, quoted in *The Art Dealers*, pp. 204–205.
29. John Gibson, telephone interview with the author, January 10, 1995.
30. Bourdon, *Christo*, p. 41.
31. Calvin Tomkins, "Onward and Upward with Arts," *The New Yorker*, March 28, 1977, p. 50.
32. Sherman Lee, *Art News*, April 1969, p. 27.
33. "All Package," *Time*, February 7, 1969, p. 60.
34. "Under Wraps," *Newsweek*, February 10, 1969, p. 77.
35. John Kaldor, interview with the author in Paris, September 23, 1985.
36. Ibid.
37. The letters and telegram transcribed in this section appear in *Christo—Wrapped Coast, One Million Square Feet, Little Bay* (Minneapolis: Contemporary Art Lithographers, 1969).
38. Quoted in Nicholas Baume, "Christo," *Art in Australia* 27 (Spring 1989): 82, 86.
39. Kaldor quoted in Nam June Paik, *Du Cheval à Christo et Autres Ecrits*.
40. Imants Tillers, interview with the author in New York City, May 22, 1989.
41. Quoted in Baume, "Christo."
42. Ibid.
43. Harry Shunk, telephone interview with the author.
44. Kaldor quoted in Paik, *Du Cheval à Christo et Autres Ecrits*.
45. Daniel Thomas, "Australia, Bulgaria, Christo," in *Christo* (Sydney: Art Gallery of New South Wales, 1990), p. 26.
46. Quoted in Baume, "Christo," p. 85.
47. Kaldor quoted in Paik, *Du Cheval à Christo et Autres Ecrits*.
48. Thomas, "Australia, Bulgaria, Christo," p. 27.
49. Edmund Capon, in ibid., p. 9.

10. *VALLEY CURTAIN:* AN EAGLE WITH TWO HEADS

1. Carole Weisweiller, interview with the author.
2. Quoted in Jerry Tallmer, "With $7 Million and Some Silver Fabric, SoHo's Christos Plan Reichstag Sweep," *New York Observer*, April 3, 1995.
3. Albert Elsen, "The Freedom to Be Christo," in *Christo* (Sydney: Art Gallery of New South Wales, 1990), p. 15.
4. Rosa Esman, interview with the author in New York, May 26, 1987.
5. Elsen, "The Freedom to Be Christo," p. 15.
6. Lawrence Alloway, interview with the author.
7. Arman, interview with the author.
8. Barbara Rose, telephone interview with the author, September 28, 1994.
9. Rosa Esman, interview with the author.

10. Joyce May Henery, interview with the author.
11. Quoted in Jesse Kornbluth, "La Vie de Behème," *Savvy,* December 1983, p. 79.
12. Emily Genauer, "Unclear Visions of an Antiwar Theme," *Newsday,* July 18, 1970.
13. Scott Hodes, interview with the author in Paris, September 21, 1985.
14. Pierre Restany, interview with the author.
15. Ibid.
16. Jan van der Marck, "The Valley Curtain," *Art in America,* May–June 1972, p. 55.
17. Jan van der Marck notes, January 13, 1971, quoted in *Christo: Valley Curtain* (New York: Harry N. Abrams, 1973), p. 44.
18. Anthony Ripley, "Art for Rockies' Sake: Mountain Gap to Get Big Orange Curtain," *New York Times,* July 14, 1971.
19. Calvin Tomkins, "Maybe a Quantum Leap," *The New Yorker,* February 5, 1972, pp. 57–67; reprinted in Calvin Tomkins, *The Scene* (New York: Viking Press, 1976), p. 150.
20. Ibid.
21. Weber quoted in ibid.
22. Van der Marck, "The Valley Curtain," p. 56.
23. Van der Marck notes, April 7–9, 1971, quoted in *Christo: Valley Curtain,* p. 45.
24. Van der Marck notes, February 18–21, 1971, quoted in ibid.
25. Ibid.
26. Ingeborg van der Marck notes, May 6, 1971, quoted in *Christo: Valley Curtain,* p. 52.
27. Letter from Charles E. Shumate, May 28, 1971, in *Christo: Valley Curtain,* p. 66.
28. Van der Marck.
29. *Christo: Valley Curtain,* p. 84.
30. Van der Marck, "The Valley Curtain," p. 60.
31. Ibid., p. 62.
32. Michael Sonnabend, interview with the author.
33. Van der Marck, "The Valley Curtain," p. 62.
34. Tomkins, *The Scene,* p. 158.
35. Dimiter Zagoroff, interview with the author.
36. Van der Marck, "The Valley Curtain," pp. 63–64.
37. Pierre Restany, interview with the author.
38. Alexandra de Guillebon, interview with the author in New York City, February 24, 1995.
39. Van der Marck, "The Valley Curtain," p. 64.
40. Tomkins, *The Scene,* p. 160.
41. Michael Cullen, interview with the author.
42. John Thomson, interviews with the author in Paris, November 23, 1991; in Westport, Connecticut, November 23, 1991; and in Berlin, June 23, 1995.
43. Ibid.
44. Ted Dougherty, interviews with the author in Miami, May 1983, and in Paris, September 2, 1985; interview with Ann Chernow in Lebec, California, October 11, 1991.
45. Norbert de Guillebon, interview with the author in New York City, April 3, 1989.
46. Grace Glueck, "The Gap That Wouldn't Stay Closed," *New York Times,* August 20, 1972.
47. Thomas Garver, interview with Ann Chernow in Lebec, California, October 8, 1991.
48. Tomkins, "Maybe a Quantum Leap."
49. Jan van der Marck, "The *Valley Curtain* Is Up! But . . ." Art in America, January–February 1973, pp. 75–76.
50. Priscilla Morgan, interview with the author in New York City, November 6, 1996.
51. Torczyner, a brilliant international lawyer fluent in six languages, represented a number of well-known painters and had assembled an impressive art collection of his own. He had also written several books on René Magritte.
52. Harry Shunk, interview with the author.

1. Mary Fuller McChesney, "What's in the Package? Is Christo Javacheff All Wrapped Up?" *Current,* April–May 1975.
2. Calvin Tomkins, "Running Fence," *The New Yorker,* March 28, 1997, p. 61.
3. Lynn Hershman, interview with the author in San Francisco, February 14, 1987.
4. Peter Selz, interview with the author in New York City, January 24, 1989.
5. One writer described the meeting lightheartedly: "It, uh, may be curtains for Sonoma County. . . . 'It's only an art project,' Bulgarian-born Christo Javacheff, 38, told a gathering of about 150 bemused dairymen and ranchers. . . . He's serious folks. . . . 'It only has to stay up one day and I'll be happy,' he said in a confusing French-Bulgarian accent. . . . But before the first pole is driven into the Sonoma County earth, Christo and his rapidly expanding local organization face bureaucratic hurdles which would give a major land developer fainting spells." Robert Hollis, "He'd Artfully Curtain Off Sonoma Hills," *San Francisco Examiner,* January 27, 1974.
6. Dominique Laporte, *Christo,* trans. Abby Pollak (New York: Pantheon, 1986), p. 21.
7. Harry Shunk, interview with the author.
8. Howard Nemerovski, telephone interview with the author, October 11, 1995. Nemerovski recalled finally asking a secretary to prepare an invoice for the artists. "Jeanne-Claude wrote me a check on the spot. She said, 'We pay our own way.' I asked if she remembered my offer when we first met in Christo's studio. 'Of course,' she said, 'but that's not the way we do business.'"
9. Edwin Anderson, telephone interview with the author, October 15, 1995.
10. Peter Selz, interview with the author.
11. Ray Johnson, "Abandoned Chickens," *Art in America,* November–December 1974, pp. 107–111.
12. Lynn Hershman, interview with the author.
13. Tomkins, "Running Fence," p. 59.
14. Edwin Anderson, telephone interview with the author. This and subsequent quotes are from this interview.
15. David Bourdon, in *Christo: Running Fence* (New York: Abrams, 1978), pp. 112, 120.
16. Temko quoted in McChesney, "What's in the Package?"
17. Tomkins, in *Christo: Running Fence,* p. 34.
18. Don Stanley, "Running Fence, Inc.," January 23–29, 1975.
19. Andrew H. Malcolm, "Artists' Plan on Fence Hits Stone Wall," *New York Times,* January 22, 1975.
20. Ibid.
21. McChesney, "What's in the Package?"
22. Jeanne-Claude quoted in Mary Crawford, "The Uncertain Future of Running Fence," *San Francisco Examiner and Chronicle,* February 2, 1975.
23. Edwin Anderson, telephone interview with the author.
24. Edwin Anderson, telephone interview with the author.
25. The combative article contained enough inaccuracies that Christo and Jeanne-Claude contemplated a libel suit. Howard Nemerovski wrote a warning letter to *Current* magazine, but the affair never escalated into litigation. McChesney called the threatened suit "totally frivolous," saying her statement that the artists owned a Mercedes-Benz was only "a takeoff on a Janis Joplin song. They didn't get the joke. They have absolutely no sense of humor. None!" Mary Fuller McChesney, telephone interview with the author, January 2, 1996.
26. McChesney, "What's in the Package?"
27. Tomkins, "Running Fence," p. 62.
28. Christo quoted in David Bourdon and Calvin Tompkins (New York: Harry N. Abrams, Inc. 1978) *Christo: Running Fence,* p. 152.
29. Edwin Anderson, telephone interview with the author.

30. Howard Nemerovski, telephone interview with the author.
31. Alfred Frankenstein, "Christo Waits for Go-Ahead," *San Francisco Chronicle*, August 17, 1975. Another journalist wrote about "staff resentment at being inundated with letters supporting Christo (including recommendations from Lady Bird Johnson, Jacques Cousteau, Jonas Salk, George Plimpton [and] . . . Nelson Rockefeller); see Tim Findley, "The Battle of Running Fence," p. 32.
32. Edwin Anderson, telephone interview with the author, October 15, 1995.
33. Lynn Hershman, interview with the author.
34. Environmental Science Associates, "Environmental Impact Report, *Running Fence*," 1975.

12. *RUNNING FENCE:* PART TWO

1. Joyce May Henery, interview with the author.
2. On December 20, 1975, Peter Selz had written the artists: "As you know (I think I've told you), I'll be leaving for Israel at the end of March to teach at the University of Jerusalem in the Spring semester. I don't believe that much needs to be done as far as I am concerned between now and then—but let me know if there is. If you want me to come back from the Near East and Europe in mid-summer to resume my work as Project Director, please let me know soon so that I can make plans. Naturally, I would have to be compensated again for my time."
3. Ted Dougherty, interview with the author.
4. Ibid.
5. Ibid.
6. Douglas David, "Esthetic Terrorism," *Newsweek,* August 9, 1976, p. 78.
7. Jeanne-Claude quoted by Calvin Tomkins, in *Christo: Running Fence* (New York: Abrams, 1978), p. 29.
8. Ted Dougherty, interview with the author. This and subsequent quotes in this section are from this interview.
9. John Thomson, interview with the author.
10. Ted Dougherty, interview with the author.
11. Edwin Anderson, telephone interview with the author.
12. Ted Dougherty, interview with the author.
13. Other visitors included Jan and Ingeborg van der Marck, Harald Szeeman, Otto Hahn, Peter Selz, Willi Bongard, David Bourdon, Scott Hodes, Dieter Rosenkranz, Alana Heiss, James Rosenquist, Dorothy and Herbert Vogel, Werner Spies, Pontus Hulten, and Serge De Bloe.
14. Ted Dougherty, interview with the author.
15. Ibid.
16. Tomkins, in *Christo,* p. 30.
17. Lynn Hershman, interview with the author.
18. Jeanne-Claude quoted by Tomkins, in *Christo,* p. 31.
19. Elizabeth Whitney, "Christo's Running Fence," *Tomales Bay Times,* September 10, 1976.
20. Ibid.
21. Paul Kayfetz, telephone interview with the author, January 13, 1996.
22 Christo quoted by Tomkins, in *Christo,* p. 19.
23. Whitney, "Christo's Running Fence."
24. Kevin Wallace, "The Running Fence's Illegal Leap," *San Francisco Chronicle,* September 8, 1976.
25. Edwin Anderson, telephone interview with the author.
26. Paul Kayfetz, telephone interview with the author.
27. Whitney, "Christo's Running Fence."
28. Tomkins, in *Christo,* p. 33.

29. Edwin Anderson, telephone interview with the author.
30. Mary Fuller McChesney, telephone interview with the author.
31. "Christo: Plain and Fency," *Time,* September 20, 1976, p. 74.
32. Whitney, "Christo's Running Fence."
33. Ibid.
34. Ibid.
35. Charlotte Zwerin quoted in Carolyn Lumsden, "Christo: 'I Am a Political Artist,'" *Soho Weekly News,* April 6, 1978.
36. Christo quoted in Jane Katz, *Artists in Exile* (New York: Stein and Day, 1983), p. 151.
37. Dorothy Vogel, interview with the author in New York City, October 4, 1990.
38. John Walker quoted in promotional material for Albert Maysles, David Maysles, and Charlotte Swerin, *Running Fence.*
39. David Bourdon, interview with the author.
40. Edwin Anderson quoted by Tomkins, in *Christo,* p. 33.
41. Edwin Anderson, telephone interview with the author.
42. Werner Spies, *The Running Fence Project: Christo* (New York: Abrams, 1977), p. 1.
43. Lady Marina Vaizey, "A Wall That Lets You In," *The New Republic,* October 23, 1976, pp. 22–24.
44. Ted Dougherty, interview with the author.
45. Tom Golden, telephone interview with the author, April 28, 1996.
46. Ibid.
47. Lynn Hershman, interview with the author.
48. J. Hoberman, "Nylon Sheets and Vinyl Freaks," *The Village Voice,* April 17, 1978.
49. Michael Florescu, "The Maysles' Film of Christo's Running Fence," *Art in America.*

13. TEAM CHRISTO

1. Harold Rosenberg quoted in Henry M. Sayre, *The Object of Performance: The American Avant-Garde Since 1970* (Chicago: University of Chicago Press, 1989), p. 233.
2. Christo, "Masterpiece of the Month," *Scholastic,* April/May 1985, p. 8.
3. "Christo: Plain and Fency," *Time,* September 20, 1976, p. 94.
4. Ted Dougherty, interview with the author.
5. Carl Flach, interview with the author in Paris, September 25, 1985.
6. Torsten Lilja, interview with the author in Paris, September 24, 1985, and in Berlin, June 20, 1995.
7. Torsten Lilja, *Christo and Jeanne-Claude Projects: Works from the Lilja Collection* (Azimuth Editions, 1995), pp. 7–11.
8. A scale model of *Wrapped Reichstag* was included in these shows.
9. Ellen Goheen, telephone interview with the author, April 15, 1996.
10. James Fuller quoted in Donna Furlong, "Wrapping up the World," *Daily Evening Item* (Lynn, Massachusetts), May 10, 1979.
11. Ellen Goheen, telephone interview with the author.
12. Dr. Jivka Langvad, interview with the author, Hornback, Denmark, June 13, 1995, and at the Louisiana Museum.
13. Ellen Goheen, telephone interview with the author.
14. Ileana Ingraham quoted in John A. Dvorak, "Park Pathway Art Tripped Up," *Kansas City Times,* February 22, 1978.
15. James Fuller quoted in Furlong, "Wrapping up the World."
16. All quotes in this paragraph in John A. Dvorak, "Christo to Test Park 'Carpet,'" *Kansas City Times,* March 15, 1978.
17. "Christo Experiments, Councilman Agitates," *Kansas City Star,* April 12, 1978.
18. Robert L. Carroll, "Christo Raps on Wrap Art," *Kansas City Times,* April 12, 1978.
19. Robert L. Carroll, "Christo the Star," *Kansas City Times,* April 13, 1978.

20. Pat Loving, "Staying Loose in the Park with Christo," *Kansas City Star Magazine,* August 13, 1978.
21. Lee Goodman and Douglas Stone, letter to the editor, *Kansas City Star,* April 5, 1978.
22. C. O. Wigham, Jr., quoted in Jeanne Meyer, "Workers Prepare Way for Artist," *Kansas City Times,* September 30, 1978.
23. Suzanne Richards, in "Narratives by Project Workers," Kansas City Artists Coalition Forum, November 1978.
24. Susan Lawrence, in ibid.
25. Rosemary Smithson, "What Was It Like Turning Walks into Rivers of Gold?" *Kansas City Star,* October 6, 1978. This and subsequent Smithson quotes are from this article.

14. NOMADS FOR ART

1. Robert Louis Stevenson, *Travels with a Donkey,* quoted in Bruce Chatwin, *Anatomy of Restlessness: Selected Writings, 1969–1989* (New York: Viking, 1996), p. 102.
2. Cyril Christo, interview with the author.
3. Christo quoted in Jane Katz, *Artists in Exile* (New York: Stein and Day, 1981), p. 161.
4. John Russell, "Artist Hoping to Transform Central Park," *New York Times,* October 6, 1980.
5. Quoted in Gerald Marzorati, "Artful Dodge," *Soho News,* January 21, 1981.
6. Christo quoted in Katz, *Artists in Exile,* p. 162.
7. Discussion at a slide lecture at the Pratt Institute, March 14, 1995.
8. The artists' files bulge with hundreds of project suggestions from around the world. These serious, unsolicited proposals often promised to eliminate bureaucratic barriers and deliver enormous amounts of money. Each has been politely refused.
9. Christo.
10. Christo, interview with Jonathan Fineberg at the College Art Association's annual meeting, New York City, February 27, 1982.
11. Kheel was referred to the artists by collectors John and Kimiko Powers.
12. Quotes appeared in Grace Glueck, "Christo's Plan for Project in Park Starts Fireworks," *New York Times,* January 22, 1981.
13. Theodore Kheel, interview with Ann Chernow in Lebec, California, October 10, 1991.
14. Ibid.
15. "Closing Christo's Gates," *New York Times,* May 5, 1981.
16. Jan van der Marck.
17. Carol Caldwell, "Whither Christo," *Rolling Stone,* May 1981.
18. Christo.
19. Klaus-Henning Rosen.
20. Anani Yavachev, interview with the author. This and subsequent quote are from this interview.

Bibliography

BOOKS (BY YEAR OF PUBLICATION)

Christo. Texts by David Bourdon, Otto Hahn and Pierre Restany. Designed by Christo.Milano, Italy: Edizioni Apollinaire, 1965.

Christo: 5,600 Cubic Meter Package. Photographs by Klaus Baum. Designed by Christo. Bauerbrunn, Germany: Verlag Wort und Bild, 1968.

Christo. Text by Lawrence Alloway. Designed by Christo. New York: Harry N. Abrams Publications, 1969. Verlag Gerd Hatje, Stuttgart, Germany. Thames and Hudson, London, England.

Christo: Wrapped Coast, One Million Square Feet. Photographs by Shunk-Kender. Designed by Christo. Minneapolis, Minnesota: Contemporary Art Lithographers, 1969.

Christo. Text by David Bourdon. Designed by Christo. New York: Harry N. Abrams Publications, 1970.

Christo: Projekt Monschau. By Willi Bongard. Köln, Germany: Verlag Art Actuell, 1971.

Christo: Valley Curtain. Photographs by Harry Shunk. Designed by Christo. New York: Harry N. Abrams Publications, 1973. Pierre Horay, Paris, France. Gianpaola Prearo, Milano, Italy.

Christo: Ocean Front. Text by Sally Yard and Sam Hunter. Photographs by Gianfranco Gorgoni. Edited by Christo. Princeton, New Jersey: Princeton University Press, 1975.

Environmental Impact Report: Running Fence. Prepared by Paul E. Zigman and Richard Cole, Environmental Science Associates Inc. Foster City, California, 1975.

Christo: The Running Fence. Text by Werner Spies. Photographs and editing by Wolfgang Volz. New York: Harry N. Abrams, Inc., 1977. Édition du Chêne, Paris, France.

Christo: Running Fence. Chronicle by Calvin Tomkins. Narrative text by David Bourdon. Photographs by Gianfranco Gorgoni. Designed by Christo. New York: Harry N. Abrams, Inc., 1978.

Christo: Wrapped Walk Ways. Essay by Ellen Goheen. Photographs by Wolfgang Volz. Designed by Christo. New York: Harry N. Abrams, Inc., 1978.

Christo: Complete Editions, 1964–82. Catalogue Raisonné. Introduction by Per Hovdenakk. New York: New York University Press, 1982. Verlag Schellmann and Kluser, München, Germany.

Christo: Works 1958–83. Text by Yusuke Nakahara. Tokyo, Japan: Publication Sogetsu Shuppan, Inc., 1984.

Christo: Surrounded Islands, Biscayne Bay, Greater Miami, Florida, 1980–83. Text by Werner Spies, photographs and editing by Wolfgang Volz. New York: Harry N. Abrams, Inc., 1985. Dumont Buchverlag, Köln, Germany, 1984. Fondation Maeght, Saint-Paul de Vence, France, 1985. Ediciones Poligrafa, Barcelona, Spain, 1986.

Christo-Der Reichstag. Compiled by Michael Cullen and Wolfgang Volz. Photographs by Wolfgang Volz. Suhrkamp Verlag, Frankfurt, Germany, 1984.

Christo. Text by Dominique Laporte. New York: Pantheon Books, 1986. Art Press/Flammarion, Paris, France.

Christo: Surrounded Islands, Biscayne Bay, Greater Miami, Florida, 1980–83. Photographs by Wolfgang Volz. Introduction and Picture Commentary by David Bourdon. Essay by Jonathan Fineberg. Report by Janet Mulholland. Designed by Christo. New York: Harry N. Abrams, Inc., 1986.

Le Pont-Neuf de Christo, Ouvrage d'Art, Oeuvre d'Art, ou Comment Se Faire une Opinion. By Nathalie Heinich. Photographs by Wolfgang Volz. A.D.R.E.S.S.E. Publication, 1987.

Helt Fel I Paris. By Pelle Hunger and Joakim Stromholm. Photographs by J. Stromholm. Butler and Tanner Ltd. The Selwood Printing Works, Fromme, England, 1987.

Christo: Prints and Objects, 1963–1987. Catalogue Raisonné edited by Jörg Schellmann and Josephine Benecke. Introduction by Werner Spies. New York: Abbeville Press, 1988. Editions Schellmann, München, Germany.

Christo: The Pont Neuf Wrapped, Paris, 1975–85. Photographs by Wolfgang Volz. Texts by David Bourdon and Bernard de Montgolfier. Designed by Christo. New York: Harry N. Abrams, Inc., 1990. Adam Biro, Paris, France. Dumont Buchverlag, Köln, Germany.

Christo. By Yusuke Nakahara, Shinchosha Co., Ltd., Tokyo, Japan, 1990.

Christo. By Marina Vaizey. New York: Rizzoli, 1990. Albin Michel, Paris, France. Meulenhoff/Landshoff, Amsterdam, Holland. Verlag Aurel Bongers, Recklinghausen, Germany. Bijutsu Shupan-Sha, Tokyo, Japan.

Christo: The Accordion-Fold Book for The Umbrellas, Joint Project for Japan and U.S.A. Photographs by Wolfgang Volz. Foreword and interview by Masahiko Yanagi. Designed by Christo. San Francisco: Chronicle Books, 1991.

Christo: The Reichstag and Urban Projects. Edited by Jacob Baal-Teshuva. Photographs by Wolfgang Volz. Contributions by Tilmann Buddensieg, Michael S. Cullen, Rita Süssmuth and Masahiko Yanagi. New York: Prestel Publications, 1993. In German for the exhibitions at the Kunsthaus Wien, Austria—the Villa Stück, Munich—and the Ludwig Museum, Aachen. Prestel Publications, München, Germany.

Christo and Jeanne-Claude: Der Reichstag und Urbane Projekte. Edited by Jacob Baal-Teshuva. Contributions by Tilmann Buddensieg and Wieland Schmied. Interview by Masahiko Yanagi. Chronology by Michael S. Cullen. Photographs by Wolfgang Volz. Prestel Verlag, München, Germany, 1994.

Christo and Jeanne-Claude. By Jacob Baal-Teshuva. Photographs by Wolfgang Volz. Designed by Christo. Edited by Simone Philippi and Charles Brace. Taschen Verlag, Germany, 1995.

Christo, Jeanne-Claude, Der Reichstag dem Deutschen Volke. By Michael S. Cullen and Wolfgang Volz. Photographs by Wolfgang Volz. Bastei-Lübbe, Gustav Lübbe Verlag GmbH, Bergisch-Gladbach, Germany, 1995.

Christo and Jeanne-Claude, Prints and Objects 1963–95. Catalogue Raisonné. Edited by Jörg Schellmann and Joséphine Benecke. Editions Schellmann, München-New York. Schirmer Mosel Verlag, München, Germany, 1995.

Christo and Jeanne-Claude Poster Book. Photographs by Wolfgang Volz. Text by Thomas Berg. Taschen Verlag, Germany, 1995.

Christo and Jeanne-Claude: Wrapped Reichstag, Berlin, 1971–95. The Project Book. Photographs by Wolfgang Volz. Taschen Verlag, Germany, 1995.

Christo and Jeanne-Claude, Wrapped Reichstag, Berlin 1971–1995. Photographs by Wolfgang Volz. Picture Notes by David Bourdon. Edited by Simone Philippi. Designed by Christo. Taschen Verlag, Germany, 1996.

Christo and Jeanne-Claude Projects: Selected from the Lilja Collection. Photographs by Wolfgang Volz. Preface by Torsten Lilja. Text by Per Hovdenakk. London, England: Azimuth Editions, 1996.

Christo and Jeanne-Claude, The Umbrellas, Japan-USA, 1984–1991. Photographs by Wolfgang Volz, Picture notes by Jeanne-Claude and Masa Yanagi. Designed by Christo. Edited by Simone Philippi. Taschen Verlag, Germany, 1998.

Christo and Jeanne-Claude, Wrapped Trees, 1997–1998. Photographs and Picture Notes by Wolfgang and Sylvia Volz. Introduction by Ernst Beyeler. Edited by Simone Philippi. Taschen Verlag, Germany, 1998.

Erreurs les plus Fréquentes. Edited by Jeanne-Claude. In French. Editions Jannink, Paris, 1998. In 2000 in English and French.

XTO + J-C. Christo und Jeanne-Claude, Eine Biografie von Burt Chernow, Epilog von Wolfgang Volz. In German. 496 pages, 55 illustrations, plus 28 in color (in German). Verlag Kiepenheuer & Witsch, Köln, Germany, 2000.

XTO + J-C. Christo e Jeanne-Claude, Una Biografia di Burt Chernow, Epiliogo di Wolfgang Volz. (in Italian) 366 pages, 99 illustrations, plus 28 in color. Publication Fondazione Ambrosetti Arte Contemporanea / Skira, Italy, 2001.

Christo & Jeanne-Claude. By Jacob Baal-Teshuva. Photographs by Wolfgang Volz. Designed by Christo. Edited by Simone Philippi. 96 pages. 120 illustrations. Taschen Verlag, Germany, 2001.

Christo and Jeanne-Claude: Early Works 1958–69: Texts by Lawrence Alloway, David Bourdon, Jan van der Marck, photographs by Ferdinand Boesch, Thomas Cugini, André Grossmann Eeva-Inkeri, Jean-Dominique Lajoux, Harry Shunk, Wolfgang Volz, Stefan Wewerka, and many others, 2001.

"Christo and Jeanne-Claude in the Vogel Collection." National Gallery of Art, Washington, D.C. Introduction by Earl A. Powell, III; Text and interview by Molly Donovan, photographs by Wolfgang Volz. New York: Harry N. Abrams, Inc., 2002.

CATALOGUES: PERSONAL EXHIBITIONS (PARTIAL LISTING)

1968 "Christo Wraps the Museum." Museum of Modern Art, New York, USA. Text by William Rubin.

1968 "Christo." I.C.A. University of Pennsylvania, Philadelphia. Text by Stephen Prokopoff.

1969 "Christo: Woolworks." National Gallery of Victoria, Melbourne, Australia. Text by Jan van der Marck.

1970
–72 "Christo." Documentation Exhibition. Text by Maurice Besset.

1977 "Wrapped Reichstag, Project for Berlin." Annely Juda Fine Art, London, England. Photographs by Wolfgang Volz. Texts by Wieland Schmied and Tilmann Buddensieg.

1979 "Urban Projects." I.C.A., Boston—Laguna Gloria Art Museum, Austin, Texas—Corcoran Gallery of Art, Washington, D.C., Introduction by Stephen Prokopoff. Text by Pamela Allara and Stephen Prokopoff.

1981 "Surrounded Islands, Project for Florida." Juda-Rowan Gallery, London, England. Photographs by Wolfgang Volz. Text by Anitra Thorhaug.

1981 "Collection on Loan from the Rothschild Bank AG, Zürich." La Jolla Museum of Contemporary Art, La Jolla, California. Introduction by Robert McDonald. Text by Jan van der Marck.

1984 "Objects, Collages and Drawings, 1958–84." Juda-Rowan Gallery, London, England.

1988 "*The Umbrellas,* Joint Project for Japan and USA." Annely Juda Fine Art, London, England. Photographs by Wolfgang Volz. Interview and text by Masahiko Yanagi.

1990 "Works from 1958–1990." The Art Gallery of New South Wales, Sydney, Australia. Foreword by John Kaldor. Texts by Albert Elsen, Toni Bond, Daniel Thomas, and Nicholas Baume. Photographs by Wolfgang Volz.

1991 "Projects Not Realized and Works in Progress." Annely Juda Fine Art, London, England. Foreword by Annely Juda and David Juda.

1995 "Christo and Jeanne-Claude, *Three Works in Progress.*" Annely Juda Fine Art, London, England. Foreword by Annely Juda and David Juda. Photographs by Wolfgang Volz.

1997 "Christo & Jeanne-Claude Sculpture and Projects 1961–1996." Yorkshire Sculpture Park, U.K. Preface by Peter Murray. Designed and produced by Claire Glossop.

2000 "Christo and Jeanne-Claude, Black and White." Annely Juda Fine Art, London, England.

2001 "Christo and Jeanne-Claude: The Art of Gentle Disturbance." Macy Gallery, Teachers College, Columbia University, New York, USA. (Brochure: photographs by Wolfgang Volz, Jean-Dominique Lajoux, and Harry Shunk.)

2001 "Christo and Jeanne-Claude. Two Works in Progress: Over the River, Project for the Arkansas River, Colorado, and The Gates, Project for Central Park, New York." State University Art Gallery, Kennesaw, Georgia. (Brochure: photographs by Wolfgang Volz.)

2001 Christo and Jeanne-Claude: Early Works 1958–69: Texts by Lawrence Alloway, David Bourdon, Jan van der Marck, photographs by Ferdinand Boesch, Thomas Cugini, André Grossmann Eeva-Inkeri, Jean-Dominique Lajoux, Harry Shunk, Wolfgang Volz, Stefan Wewerka, and many others.

2001 "Wrapped Reichstag," pictures commentary by David Bourdon, Michael S. Cullen, Christo and Jeanne-Claude, photographs by Wolfgang Volz.

2002 "Christo and Jeanne-Claude in the Vogel Collection." National Gallery of Art, Washington, D.C. Introduction by Earl A. Powell, III; Text and interview by Molly Donovan, photographs by Wolfgang Volz. New York: Harry N. Abrams, Inc.

FILMS (AND VIDEOS)

1969 *Wrapped Coast.* Blackwood Productions. 30 minutes.

1970 *Works in Progress.* Blackwood Productions. 30 minutes.

1972 *Christo's Valley Curtain.* Maysles Brothers and Ellen Giffard. 28 minutes. The film was nominated for the Academy Award in 1973.

1977 *Running Fence.* Maysles Brothers / Charlotte Zwerin. 58 minutes.

1978 *Wrapped Walk Ways.* Blackwood Productions. 25 minutes.

1985 *Surrounded Islands.* Maysles Brothers / Charlotte Zwerin. 57 minutes.

1990 *Christo in Paris.* (*The Pont Neuf Wrapped, 1975–85*). David and Albert Maysles, Deborah Dickson, Susan Froemke. 58 minutes.

1995 *Christo and Jeanne-Claude, an overview of the oeuvre 1959–1995.* Blackwood Productions. 58 minutes.

1996 *Umbrellas. Albert Maysles, Henry Corra and Graham Weinbren.* 81 minutes. The film won the Grand Prize and the People's Choice Award at the 1996 Montréal Film Festival.

1996 Christo and Jeanne–Claude, "Dem Deutsche Volke," Verhüllter Reichstag, 1971–1995. (*Wrapped Reichstag*). Wolfram and Jörg Daniel Hissen, EstWest. 98 minutes.

1998 *Christo and Jeanne-Claude.* Wrapped Trees Gebrüder Hissen, EstWest. 26 minutes.

A Note from Christo and Jeanne-Claude

Many years ago our friend Burt Chernow told us that he wanted to write our biography. At first we didn't take his idea seriously, because we had known Burt as a collector and professor of art history. Our work is visual and should be experienced with one's senses. We couldn't imagine that words could capture its physicality. We were also afraid that we would have to spend too much time talking about our lives. Nonetheless we agreed to his idea.

Burt was present wherever we were: at lectures, exhibitions, meetings, and project sites. We soon realized how determined he was. Once, Burt and his wife, Ann, came back from Europe and gave us news of all our old friends. We were amazed that the Chernows would spend their vacation talking to our friends. Later they announced that they were leaving for Bulgaria and asked for family addresses. We provided the addresses, feeling that at least they should know someone behind what was then still the Iron Curtain in case they needed help. They returned with accounts of Christo's childhood that even Christo himself did not remember—and that Jeanne-Claude would otherwise never have known about. We took Burt very seriously from then on.

He was extremely discreet when trying to make an appointment. He knew how precious time is to us. Little by little, as he brought us chapter after chapter, we became amazed by his thoughtfulness and determination. Through his research, we discovered so many forgotten details about our lives, sometimes laughing when we read what people who knew us—or said they knew us—had to say about us.

Gradually, this biography, which had seemed an impossible undertaking, started taking shape. Reading Burt's work enabled us to remember our past, not foggy or out of focus but precise and carefully documented.

When Ann called us in June 1997 to tell us that Burt had suddenly died of a heart attack, we were devastated. We had lost a wonderful friend. We had also lost a wonderful biographer. Burt had written and polished every chapter, starting from before the birth of our grandparents, through the Balkan War,

World War I, World War II, our childhood, our teenage years, and our lives from 1958 to 1982.

But our lives did not stop in 1982.

The German publisher Kiepenheuer & Witsch contacted Wolfgang Volz and asked if he would complete Burt's book. Wolfi has been working closely with us since 1971, first as a photographer and then as our exclusive photographer. For decades he has worked with us on every aspect of our projects—legal, technical, aesthetic, and diplomatic. His wife, Sylvie, and we sometimes wonder when he has the time to take all those photographs that fill the books about our projects. After we received permission to wrap the Reichstag in Berlin, we turned to him. "Wolfi," we said, "*you* wrap the Reichstag." Together with our friend Roland Specter he was in charge of the whole project.

Because he is so much a part of our working family, it seems fitting that Wolfi complete Burt's book. We are grateful to Ann for lending him Burt's notes and interviews. They helped him enormously in talking about the experiences he has lived with us during the last seventeen years.

We are delighted that this biography will now be published in the United States.

Christo and Jeanne-Claude
New York, September 2001

Acknowledgments

Burt Chernow wrote this biography over a fifteen-year period, from 1982 until his untimely death in 1997. During this period he also wrote monographs, catalogues, and art reviews for national publications, as well as collections of poems and short stories. He chaired the art department and was an instructor at Housatonic Community College in Bridgeport, Connecticut. He developed an important collection of contemporary and ethnic art, which evolved into the Housatonic Museum of Art; he founded and chaired the Westport Arts Advisory Council, and organized the Westport Arts Awards ceremonies; and, when possible, he made art. He was also a loving husband, father, and grandfather. No one who knew him can quite understand how Burt could have accomplished so much in what was too short a lifetime.

Burt thoroughly enjoyed writing this book. He felt that the Christos were the most remarkable artistic team of the twentieth century, and was honored to be writing their biography. We all wish he could have seen it through to completion, but are grateful that he was able to write as much as he did. He left copious notes and interviews, dealing with those years of Christo and Jeanne-Claude's lives he was not able to address.

My deepest thanks go to Christo and Jeanne-Claude, for their friendship, and for giving Burt so much of their time; to Ron Chernow, a dear cousin and friend, whose advice and encouragement made the publication of this book a reality; to Cynthia Cannell, agent extraordinaire, who championed Burt's manuscript and held my hand throughout the process of finding a publisher; to Tim Mennell, whose initial editing was crucial to the presentation of the manuscript; to Wolfgang Volz, for his epilogue; to Anani and Didi Yavachev, for their friendship, and for their hospitality during our stay in Bulgaria; to Maria Radicheva, Wanda Ramsey, and Iris Nemni, who assisted Burt in translating Bulgarian and French research material; to Virginia and Herbert Lust; to all the members of "Team Christo"—everyone who worked with Burt on Christo and Jeanne-Claude's projects and who patiently gave sometimes lengthy interviews to Burt; to Martin West, whose empathy, humor, and love have carried me through the last few years; and last, but most definitely not least, to our editor at St. Martin's Press, Tim Bent, whose complete professionalism and insight made the whole thing possible.

Ann Chernow
Westport, Connecticut

Index